GILBERT

AF884766

Securities Regulation

NIELS B. SCHAUMANN

California Western School of Law

WENDY G. COUTURE

University of Idaho College of Law

Eighth Edition

GILBERT

860 Blue Gentian Road, Suite 350
Eagan, MN 55121
1-877-888-1330

Printed in the United States of America

ISBN: 978-1-68561-093-7

Summary of Contents

CAPSULE SUMMARY V

GILBERT EXAM STRATEGIES LI

Chapter One. Introduction to Federal Securities Regulation 1
Key Exam Issues 2
A. Why Regulate Securities 2
B. How to Regulate Securities 4
C. The Securities Industry Generally 4
D. The Securities and Exchange Commission 9
E. Securities Acts Administered by the S.E.C.—an Overview 10
F. Jurisdiction and Interstate Commerce 14
G. Self-Regulatory Organizations 15

Chapter Two. Regulating the Original Distribution of Securities—the Securities Act of 1933 17
Key Exam Issues 19
A. Introduction 20
B. 1933 Act Section 5—Offers and Sales 23
C. Persons Covered by the 1933 Act 38
D. Property Interests Covered by the 1933 Act 45
E. The Registration Statement 52
F. Exemptions from Registration Requirements 64
G. Liabilities Under the 1933 Act 90

Chapter Three. Regulation of Securities Trading—the Securities Exchange Act of 1934 105
Key Exam Issues 107
A. Overview of the 1934 Act 107
B. Civil Liability Under Rule 10b–5 of the 1934 Act 115
C. The Private Securities Litigation Reform Act of 1995 140
D. Insider Liability for Short-Swing Profits 144
E. Tender Offers and Repurchases of Stock 152
F. Regulation of Proxy Solicitations 157
G. Liability of Attorneys in Securities Transactions 174
H. Criminal Prosecution 178

Chapter Four. Regulation of the Securities Markets 183
Key Exam Issues 184
A. Regulation of the National Securities Exchanges 184
B. Regulation of the Over-the-Counter Market 189
C. Regulation of Market Manipulation and Stabilization 192
D. Regulation of Securities Analysts 199
E. Regulation of Broker-Dealers 200

Chapter Five. Application of Federal Securities Laws to Multinational Transactions 203
Key Exam Issues 204
A. Registration Under the 1933 Act 204
B. Application of the 1934 Act 206

Chapter Six. Regulation of Securities Transactions by the States 209
Key Exam Issues 210
A. Uniform Securities Act 210

B. Preemption of State Securities Laws 210
C. Secondary Distribution of Securities 212

REVIEW QUESTIONS AND ANSWERS 213
Review Questions 214
Answers to Review Questions 225

EXAM QUESTIONS AND ANSWERS 237

TABLE OF CASES 243

TABLE OF SECURITIES ACT OF 1933 245

TABLE OF SECURITIES EXCHANGE ACT OF 1934 247

TABLE OF SECURITIES ACT RULES 249

TABLE OF SECURITIES EXCHANGE ACT RULES 251

INDEX 253

Capsule Summary

I. INTRODUCTION TO FEDERAL SECURITIES REGULATION

A. WHY REGULATE SECURITIES?

Various grounds (and criticisms) have been advanced regarding regulation of the securities markets.

1. Investor's Need for Information

Because the value of securities is not readily verifiable, government regulation may be the most efficient means of disclosure for investors.

2. Consumer Protection

Protection against fraud establishes consumer confidence and protects the health of the national economy.

3. Economic Efficiency

Broad disclosure rules foster accuracy with respect to prices. *Criticisms* of this ground include the argument that, because trading is speculative, extensive regulation merely adds to the cost of investing. Other critics feel that disclosure violates enterprises' interest in confidentiality, while still others endorse the idea of efficiency but consider consumer protection goals unsubstantiated.

4. Disclosure to Reduce Costs

Others contend that disclosure should focus on reducing agency costs, *i.e.*, shareholders should have greater control over an enterprise's managers.

5. Alternatives to Securities Markets

Other means of providing access to capital, *e.g.*, loans from banks, may be superior to a market-based system.

B. THE SECURITIES INDUSTRY GENERALLY

1. Private Investment and the Venture Capital Market

Before publicly selling its securities, a company will seek investment from private sources such as wealthy individuals, other companies interested in the start-up product (strategic investors), or investment funds (mutual funds or hedge funds).

2. Securities Markets

a. Primary Markets

These are the facilities where the securities are *first* issued or distributed to the public.

b. Secondary Markets

These exist for ongoing trading of securities *after* original distribution and include the following:

(1) Stock Exchanges

These are organized facilities that have trading floors on which listed stocks are bought and sold, *e.g.*, New York Stock Exchange ("NYSE").

(2) **Over-the-Counter Trading**

Securities not listed on an exchange are said to be traded over-the-counter (or "OTC") by broker-dealers.

(3) **Other Securities Markets**

These include the "third market" wherein securities listed on national exchanges are traded over-the-counter, and the "fourth market" wherein persons owning securities trade them without the assistance of an intermediary.

3. **Securities Firms—Brokers and Dealers**

The securities laws regulate not only the securities markets but also the firms engaged in trading securities. Note the following general functional definitions.

a. **"Brokers"**

These are persons who buy and sell securities as agents for their customers on a commission basis.

b. **"Dealers"**

These persons act as principals—buying securities for their *own account* and subsequently reselling them to their customers at a marked-up price.

c. **Dual Functions Common**

The same person can be a broker in one transaction and a dealer in another transaction. Note that many firms operate both in the exchange markets and in the over-the-counter market.

4. **Changing Role of Banks**

In 1999, the Gramm-Leach-Bliley Act effectively repealed statutes prohibiting banks from underwriting securities. Deregulation has resulted in the growth of financial holding companies, which can now legally offer many financial services, including banking, brokerage, and insurance.

5. **Other Financial Markets**

The U.S. securities market is increasingly affected by other financial markets, both *foreign and domestic*. The rapidly expanding domestic market includes products such as the money market, government and municipal securities markets, and derivative products markets (*e.g.*, options, futures, swaps (typically interest rates or currencies), and portfolio insurance (hedging)).

6. **Levels of Regulation**

Securities markets are regulated at three levels: S.E.C. regulation, self-regulatory organizations, and state blue sky regulation subject to federal preemption.

7. **Regulatory Issues**

The proliferation of new financial instruments has resulted in conflict between agencies as to which has jurisdiction over an instrument, *e.g.*, whether it is a security, a futures contract, or an option.

C. THE SECURITIES AND EXCHANGE COMMISSION

1. **S.E.C. Functions**

These include (i) adopting *substantive rules,* (ii) *interpreting* securities laws and S.E.C. rules, generally by issuing *"releases"* or giving parties *"no action" letters,* (iii) *investigating* possible violations of the laws and rules, and (iv) *initiating formal proceedings* against wrongdoers.

a. Private Actions

Private plaintiffs may seek remedies when they have been injured by a violation of a securities law if the law provides for an express or implied cause of action.

2. S.E.C. Administrative Procedures

S.E.C. proceedings are conducted in accordance with the federal Administrative Procedure Act, which requires a *hearing* before an administrative law judge, followed by *review* by the full Commission on request of any party, and *appeal* to a U.S. court of appeals.

D. SECURITIES ACTS ADMINISTERED BY THE S.E.C.—AN OVERVIEW

1. Securities Act of 1933

This Act primarily regulates the *original issuance* of securities. The Act's two main purposes are to compel *disclosure of material facts* in public offerings and to *prevent fraud and misrepresentation* in distributions of securities.

2. Securities Exchange Act of 1934

This Act primarily governs trading of securities that are already issued.

a. Registration and Reporting

The 1934 Act requires a company to register its securities with the S.E.C. and thereafter file periodic reports on its financial condition if the company's securities are (i) *traded on a national securities exchange* or (ii) traded over-the-counter and the company has more than *$10 million* in assets and a sufficient number of shareholders (either 2,000 or 500 non-accredited shareholders) of a class of equity securities; such companies are called *"reporting companies."*

b. Other Functions

Proxy solicitation, tender offer solicitations, insider trading, and margin trading are also regulated by the S.E.C. The S.E.C. additionally conducts market surveillance of certain trading practices that are based on fraud or market manipulation.

c. Registration of Securities Exchanges and Broker-Dealers

National securities exchanges and broker-dealers who conduct an interstate over-the-counter securities business must register with and make periodic reports to the S.E.C.

d. Antifraud Provisions

The 1934 Act contains a number of provisions, including Rule 10b–5, that impose liability for fraud in the purchase or sale of securities.

3. Sarbanes-Oxley Act ("SOXA")

In response to corporate scandals, in 2002, Congress amended the 1934 Act by passing SOXA. Its objectives are to (i) *improve the reliability of issuers' disclosures*, *e.g.*, by regulation of accountants, lawyers, and securities analysts; (ii) *broaden aiding and abetting prohibitions*; and (iii) *improve the quantity and quality of enhanced corporate disclosures*.

4. Integrated Disclosure

The 1933 Act and the 1934 Act originally established two distinct disclosure systems. The S.E.C. has lightened the disclosure burden by integrating the reporting requirements of the two Acts. Regulation S–K prescribes a single standard set of instructions for filing forms under the two Acts, and in some cases 1933 Act registration forms can incorporate by reference 1934 Act reports.

E. JURISDICTION AND INTERSTATE COMMERCE

1. Interstate Commerce

a. Definition Under 1933 Act

The S.E.C. and the courts have adopted a broad interpretation of what constitutes "interstate commerce" under the 1933 Act. Any transaction involving more than one state or using any means of interstate commerce, such as *intrastate* use of the telephone or the mails, constitutes interstate commerce.

b. Definition Under 1934 Act

Under the 1934 Act, "interstate commerce" includes trade, commerce, transportation, or communication among several states plus *intrastate* use of any facility or instrumentality of interstate commerce.

F. SELF-REGULATORY ORGANIZATIONS

The 1934 Act also permits self-regulatory organizations ("S.R.O.s") to regulate the securities industry in order to aid in prevention of fraud and manipulative practices. However, the S.E.C. retains power to overrule an S.R.O. if necessary, and to change an S.R.O.'s operating rules. The three most important S.R.O.s are as follows:

1. Stock Exchanges

The SEA requires that, upon meeting certain requirements, all national securities exchanges must be registered.

2. FINRA

The Financial Industry Regulatory Authority ("FINRA") is the only association registered with the S.E.C. under the SEA.

3. Public Company Accounting Oversight Board

All accounting firms that audit public companies must register with this board.

II. REGULATING THE ORIGINAL DISTRIBUTION OF SECURITIES—THE SECURITIES ACT OF 1933

A. INTRODUCTION

1. Distribution Process

Typically, the original distribution of securities involves an underwriting—*i.e.,* the passing of securities from the issuer through a syndicate of underwriters, dealers, and, ultimately, into the hands of purchasers who intend to hold the securities for investment.

a. Pattern of Distribution

The sequence of events in a typical underwriting is as follows:

(1) The issuer *decides to issue* the securities;

(2) The issuer agrees with a securities firm to have the firm *underwrite the issue* (*i.e.*, buy the securities, arrange for a syndicate to buy them, or otherwise take responsibility for their sale);

(3) The underwriter(s) agrees with other securities firms (*i.e.*, *"dealers"*) to have them buy the securities for resale to their customers; and

(4) The dealers sell the securities to *retail customers*.

b. Initial Investors

In a typical distribution, the initial retail investors intend to hold the securities for only a short time. The distribution continues until the securities come to rest with investors who intend to hold them for a *substantial* period of time.

c. Types of Underwriting Agreements

(1) "Stand-By" Underwriting

Here, the underwriter provides advice and agrees to buy whatever the issuer cannot sell.

(2) "Firm Commitment" Underwriting

Here, the issuer sells the securities outright to the underwriter, which then resells to dealers or the public.

(3) "Best-Efforts" Underwriting

Here, the underwriter acts as a sales agent for the issuer on a commission basis.

(4) Direct Offering

A company might not use an underwriter at all, such as when the company is either very well-established or when the company is not selling securities to the public.

2. Objectives of 1933 Act

a. Full Disclosure to Potential Investors

One of the primary objectives of the 1933 Act is to provide investors with *material investment information* relating to an original issuance of securities (*i.e.,* full disclosure). This is accomplished through the filing of a *"registration statement"* with the S.E.C. prior to an issuance of securities and distributing a *"prospectus"* (which contains the most important information in the registration statement) to investors prior to or simultaneously with delivery of the issuer's securities.

b. Prevention of Fraud and Misrepresentation

Another objective of the 1933 Act is to prevent fraud and misrepresentation. This objective is accomplished through several liability provisions affording defrauded purchasers certain advantages compared with liability at common law.

3. Scope of 1933 Act

The 1933 Act applies only to offers and sales in interstate commerce by issuers, underwriters, and dealers of securities. Failure to comply with the registration requirement may result in civil, and possibly criminal, liability.

B. 1933 ACT SECTION 5—OFFERS AND SALES

1. The Challenges of Section 5

Because Section 5 is probably the most difficult, but fundamental, provision of the 1934 Act, application of the regulations here is organized by class of issuer and time period.

2. Classes of Issuers

Some issuers will qualify for exceptions under Section 5, dependent on how they are categorized.

a. **Nonreporting Issuers**

Because these issuers are not required to file periodic reports under the 1933 Act, the rules are strictly applied.

b. **Unseasoned Issuers**

Issuers who must file periodic reports but who are not eligible to use Form S-3 to register offerings are in this category.

c. **Seasoned Issuers**

This category is comprised of investors who have timely filed reports for the past 12 months, have not failed to pay any dividend or required payment on preferred stock, and have not committed a material default in the current fiscal year, thus qualifying to use Form S-3.

d. **WKSIs—Well-Known Seasoned Issuers**

These issuers have met the most stringent reporting requirements and, thus, receive the largest number of exceptions from Section 5 regulation.

e. **Emerging Growth Companies**

This new classification of issuers was added by the Jumpstart our Business Startups Act of 2012. Various restrictions are eased for EGCs, with the goal of easing access to the public markets.

3. **Time Period Regulation**

a. **Regulation During the Pre-Filing Period**

Before a registration statement is filed with the S.E.C., it is unlawful for issuers, underwriters, and/or dealers *to buy, or to offer to buy, or sell, or offer to sell*, the issuer's securities by any means of interstate commerce.

(1) **Exemption for Agreements Between Issuer and Underwriter**

Negotiations and agreements between the issuer and the underwriter are exempted from the prohibition against offers and sales.

(2) **Meaning of "Offers" and "Sales"**

The terms "offer" and "sale" are broader under the securities laws than at common law; *e.g.*, a contract to sell is a sale under the 1933 Act. Care must be taken to avoid contract formation until the post-effective period.

(a) **No Conditioning of Market**

"Offer" includes the dissemination of any material that might heighten market interest in the issuer before the actual offer of securities (*e.g.*, *press releases* can be offers in violation of Section 5). However, a press release in the *normal course of business* is not prohibited.

(b) **Permitted Dissemination of Information by Issuers**

Communications *by issuers made more than 30 days before filing* may fall within a safe harbor if they are made by or on behalf of an issuer, they contain no reference to the securities offering, and reasonable steps are taken to prevent further dissemination during the 30 days. Exceptions also exist for some communications not qualifying under the safe harbor. Communications *by persons other than the issuer, or by the issuer and made 30 or fewer days before filing* may use a safe harbor if certain requirements are met. Even if no safe harbor exists, other provisions of the 1933 Act may permit communications by the following persons:

1) *WKSIs*. They are given the greatest latitude under the rules.
2) *Seasoned and unseasoned reporting issuers* may communicate *factual business information and forward-looking information*.
3) *Nonreporting issuers* may include regularly released *factual business information*, but *not* forward-looking information.
4) *Any issuer* has a limited opportunity to notify the public about its intention to make an offering in the future under *SA Rule 135*.

(c) Permitted Dissemination of Information by Underwriters and Dealers

Underwriters and dealers generally are permitted to conduct their normal business operations, such as publishing and distributing information, recommendations, and opinions regarding an issuer's securities *if no compensation* is paid for the report. *Participating broker-dealers* are subject to certain conditions regarding a report's contents.

b. Regulation During the Waiting Period

After a registration statement has been filed and before the S.E.C. declares it effective, actual sales are still prohibited, but underwriters may arrange with brokers and dealers for assistance in selling to retail customers. Underwriters and dealers may also *solicit offers to purchase* using certain types of information. However, the use of any prospectus in interstate commerce is prohibited, unless it meets the requirements of SA Section 10.

(1) "Prospectus" Defined

A prospectus includes any *written* communication, or one communicated by radio or television, that *offers any security for sale or confirms a sale*. Note that oral offers are still permitted.

(2) Permitted Offer During the Waiting Period

Oral offers and *written offers* in Section 10 prospectuses are permissible. The S.E.C. has authorized the following types of prospectuses under Section 10.

(a) Preliminary ("Red Herring") Prospectus

This is similar to a final (Section 10(a)) prospectus, but lacks some important information that is not yet available, *e.g.*, price of securities.

(b) Summary Prospectus Prepared by Issuer

This prospectus has become outmoded and is seldom, if ever, used.

(c) Free Writing Prospectus

Most issuers can use this prospectus during the waiting period, and WKSIs can use one at any time. A free writing prospectus (*i.e.*, written offer) is one that is neither a preliminary Section 10(b) prospectus nor a final Section 10(a) prospectus, does not pertain to certain kinds of asset-backed securities, and is not exempted by the SA definition of prospectus. "Writing" includes writing, printing, and graphic (*e.g.*, radio, TV, Internet) communication. Live communications to an audience are excluded.

1) **Timing of Use**

WKSIs can use a free writing prospectus *at any time* while *seasoned issuers* may use it only *after the registration statement is filed. Unseasoned and nonreporting issuers* are limited to use only *after* the registration statement is filed, and it must be accompanied by the *preliminary prospectus*.

2) **Contents and Filing Requirements**

The S.E.C. requires certain contents (*e.g.,* a specific legend) and allows optional information that does not conflict with information in the registration statement. A free writing prospectus *must* be filed before or on the date of its first use.

(d) **Written Offers That Are Not Prospectuses**

Written statements used after the registration statement becomes effective, if accompanied or preceded by a final prospectus and written offers that only identify the security, its price, and by whom orders will be executed are not considered prospectuses.

1) **Tombstone Ads**

Tombstone ads that may also be published during the waiting period are proposed offers that must contain certain information such as the issuer's name, the kind and price of security, from whom a prospectus may be obtained, and a statement that no offer to purchase may yet be accepted and that this is not a solicitation.

(3) **Required Distribution of Preliminary Prospectus**

Although distribution of a preliminary prospectus is not required by the 1933 Act itself, as a practical matter the S.E.C. forces distribution of a preliminary prospectus by refusing to *accelerate* the effective date of registration statements unless a preliminary prospectus has been distributed (absent an acceleration order, the issuer must wait until the completion of a 20-day waiting period before sales can be made, and market conditions can change during this time).

c. **Regulation During the Post-Effective Period**

Once the registration statement is declared effective by the S.E.C., sales may begin.

(1) **Objective of Regulation**

The objective now is to see that all purchasers receive complete disclosure, whether by actual receipt of a written prospectus, or merely by electronic access to the prospectus.

(2) **Distribution of Statutory Prospectus**

After the registration statement is effective, the 1933 Act *permits* written offers in any form (free writing). However, it is important to *distinguish* a free writing prospectus from post-effective free writing. In the latter situation, if any *offering participants* want to use free writing, they will *have to ensure that the free writing is accompanied or preceded by a final prospectus*.

(a) **Rule 172—Access to Final Prospectus Equivalent to Delivery**

Under 1933 Act Rule 172, a confirmation of sale or a delivery of securities may be sent without being accompanied by a final prospectus, contrary to the previous rule, *if* the requirements of Rule 172 are met, *e.g.*, a registration statement is in effect and a final prospectus has been filed with the S.E.C. The delivery rule has been eased since the financial world has many means to access a final prospectus (*e.g.*, S.E.C.'s web site). Note that Rule 172 does *not permit post-effective free writing without delivery of a final prospectus*.

(b) Notice of Registration Statement

Even if a final prospectus is not sent with a confirmation of sale or transfer of a security, the seller must generally, within two days after the sale, provide the buyer with a final prospectus or a notice that a registration statement is in effect.

(3) Duration of Post-Effective Regulation Under Section 5

Section 5 continues to regulate parties to a public offering, mainly by requiring delivery of, or access to, a final prospectus. *Issuers* must comply with Section 5 as long as they are offering securities to the public. *Underwriters* are subject to Section 5 for as long as they continue to sell their allotted shares.

(a) Dealers and 1933 Act Section 4(3)

A dealer is a person who acts, directly or indirectly, as an agent, broker, or principal in the offering, buying, selling, or other trading of securities issued by another person. All dealers must comply with Section 5 until their *entire allotment* is sold. Even after the allotment is sold, if the offering is an initial public offering ("IPO"), dealers are subject to Section 5 *90 days* from the effective date of the registration statement or commencement of the IPO, whichever is later. If the offering is *not an IPO*, this period is shortened to *40 days*. If, as of the offering date, the securities are listed on an exchange, the period is further shortened to 25 days. Finally, if the issuer is a reporting company on the offering date, the subjection period is eliminated altogether.

(4) Loophole in the 1933 Act

Sales may often be consummated in person or by telephone during the post-effective period without giving the buyer a statutory prospectus, as long as the preliminary prospectus is widely distributed and a final prospectus is filed.

(5) Updating the Prospectus

Generally, the prospectus *must be updated* if it is used for more than nine months and *should be updated any time* new material facts develop.

C. PERSONS COVERED BY THE 1933 ACT

1. In General

Although Section 5 of the Act provides that a distribution of securities by *any person* must be registered with the S.E.C., Section 4(a)(1) of the Act *exempts* persons who are *not issuers, underwriters, or dealers*.

2. Issuers

An "issuer" is any person who *issues or proposes to issue* any security. An issuer is subject to the 1933 Act whenever it makes a distribution of its securities to the public.

3. Underwriters

An underwriter is any person who: (i) *purchases securities* from the issuer *with a view toward public distribution* (*e.g.*, an offering to a substantial number of unsophisticated investors); (ii) *offers or sells securities for an issuer* in connection with a distribution; or (iii) *participates in a distribution*.

a. Participants in a Distribution

The test for whether one is a participant in a distribution is whether the person took part *in some significant way* in the underwriting, whether or not monetarily compensated.

(1) Presumptive Underwriter Doctrine

Any person who purchases a significant percentage of the securities offered in a registered public offering and then resells the securities without registering them generally is considered an underwriter.

(2) Exceptions

(a) Purchasers of Unsold Securities

Persons unaffiliated with the issuer or any principal underwriter who enter into an agreement with one of the **principal *underwriters* (but *not*** with the issuer) to purchase any portion of the securities unsold after a specified time are excluded from underwriter status if their purchase is for investment purposes (*i.e.*, they intend to hold the securities for a significant time).

(b) Dealers Selling for Normal Commission

Dealers who are part of the selling group in an underwriting who merely receive from the underwriter or another dealer a commission "not in excess of the *usual and customary* distributors' or sellers' commission" are excluded from the definition of underwriters. Note that *no* commission can be received *from the issuer*.

1) Distinguish—Dealers Performing Additional Functions

If a dealer is to *manage the distribution* of a substantial part of the issuance or performs other normal functions of an underwriter, she will be deemed an underwriter.

b. Underwriters for "Control Persons"

For the purpose of determining who is an underwriter, "control persons" (*i.e.*, persons having the power to direct the management and policies of the issuer) are deemed "issuers." Thus, the term "underwriter" includes a person who buys from, sells for, or participates in a distribution for a control person who makes a public distribution of her stock (a secondary distribution).

4. Dealers

Dealers are also subject to the registration and prospectus requirements of the 1933 Act.

D. PROPERTY INTERESTS COVERED BY THE 1933 ACT

1. Act Applies Only to "Securities"

To come within the Act's registration requirement, the property interest that is offered or sold must be a security.

2. Securities Subject to Registration

a. Interests or Instruments Specifically Mentioned in the Act

The Act provides that the following interests or instruments constitute securities unless "the context otherwise requires": (i) stocks; (ii) promissory notes; (iii) preorganization subscriptions for securities; (iv) fractional, undivided interests in oil, gas, or mineral rights; (v) collateral trust certificates; (vi) certain types of receipts for securities; and (vii) equipment trust certificates and certificates of interest in unincorporated investment trusts.

b. Investment Contracts

The broadest classification of securities is this catchall phrase, which includes a wide variety of financial schemes.

(1) Traditional *"Howey"* Test

The traditional test of whether a transaction constitutes an investment contract is whether the contract is a *profit-making scheme* whereby a person invests *his money in a common enterprise* and *expects to make a profit* solely from the *efforts of the promoter* or a third party who is responsible for management.

(2) Modern Trend

For many years cases have gone beyond *Howey* to reach situations where the investors *participated* to some extent in management and where the benefits received were something *other than cash.*

(a) Factors Determining "Investment Contract"

Under the modern trend, ask:

1) Does the investor have an expectation of profit?

2) Is there a *common enterprise* (*i.e.*, a number of investors who stand in a similar relationship to a business in which they invest in common)?

3) Does the success of the enterprise *depend mainly on persons other than the investors*?

4) Do the investors *need the protection* of the 1933 Act?

(b) Requirement of a Common Enterprise

Under the *"horizontal"* test, there must be a sharing or pooling of assets by several investors and profits derived from these combined funds. All courts find the "common enterprise" requirement to be satisfied by horizontal commonality.

1) Vertical Test

In addition, some courts will find a common enterprise if the investment manager participates in the profits made in the account (narrow version) or if the investment manager's efforts are essential (broad version).

(c) Efforts of Persons Other than Investors

The *Howey* test requires that profits come *"solely"* from the efforts of others. The modern application requires only that the success of the enterprise depend *mainly* on the efforts of persons other than the investors. The *timing* of the third party's efforts may make a difference as to a court's determination.

(3) The "Comparable Regulation" Limitation

The Supreme Court has held that if a detailed scheme of federal regulation applies to a particular instrument, the 1933 Act may not apply.

c. Catchall Provision

The 1933 Act also covers "in general, any interest or instrument commonly known as a 'security.' "

3. Application of Definitions

A property interest is a security if it is *specifically mentioned* in the 1933 Act, or it is an *investment contract*, or it is an interest *commonly classified as a security.*

E. THE REGISTRATION STATEMENT

1. In General

Part I of the registration statement is the prospectus; Part II contains supplemental information.

2. Preparing the Registration Statement

After an issuer decides to issue securities, the issuer and proposed underwriter *investigate* each other. Following investigation, the parties *negotiate* the terms of the underwriting and may then sign a *letter of intent*, after which the drafting process begins.

a. Registration Forms

The S.E.C. has adopted a set of registration forms.

(1) Form S-3

This contains the least amount of disclosure and incorporates by reference 1934 Act reports made by the issuer. Form S-3 may be used only by firms that have been filing under the 1934 Act, have *timely* filed all reports under the 1934 Act for the preceding 12 months, and can meet certain financial stability standards. Certain *transactional requirements* must also be met, *e.g.*, offerings of securities for cash, secondary offerings, automatic shelf registrations by WKSIs.

(2) Form S-1

This permits the least incorporation by reference and is the general form used by most companies unless another form is authorized or required.

(3) Other Registration Forms

Other particularized forms exist, including Form S-8, for stock option plans, and Forms SB-1 and SB-2, which are simplified forms for use by qualified small businesses.

b. Contents of the Registration Statement

The objective of the registration statement is to provide potential investors with information that a reasonable investor would consider important in deciding whether to buy the securities registered. To this end, each form prescribes certain disclosure items. A registration statement must also contain all *additional information* needed to make it *not misleading.*

(1) Financial Information

The issuer generally must include a balance sheet and profit and loss statements, adhering to the S.E.C.'s accounting regulations and certified by independent accountants who meet the requirements of the Public Company Accounting Oversight Board.

(2) **Other Material Facts Require Disclosure**

The registration statement should also include material facts, such as those affecting price or value of securities, risk, the issuer's status, conflicts of interest, and pending legal proceedings.

(3) **"Soft" Information**

This covers forward-looking statements concerning matters likely to affect the value of securities. *Safe harbor provisions* exist for these disclosures. Such disclosures must be made in *good faith* and with a *reasonable basis*. Issuers have a duty to update the statements.

(a) **The "Bespeaks Caution" Doctrine**

This court-developed doctrine provides that overly optimistic forward-looking statements are harmless if surrounded by cautionary statements outlining the possibilities of less favorable results. The doctrine is the basis of the safe harbor for forward-looking statements codified by the Private Securities Litigation Reform Act ("PSLRA").

(b) **Two Kinds of Protection**

Under the PSLRA, a plaintiff must prove that the forward-looking statement was made with *actual knowledge* of its falsity. A *defendant* may show *meaningful cautionary statements*.

(4) **Management Discussion and Analysis ("MD&A")**

Issuers *must* include an MD&A in registration statements and certain other filings. A certain amount of forward-looking disclosure is *required* to allow an investor to examine the company through the eyes of management.

3. **Organization of Material**

The S.E.C. closely regulates organization of the registration statement. Disclosures in the statement and prospectus must be in *"plain English,"* and the entire prospectus must be clear, concise, and understandable.

4. **Liability Based on Contents**

Section 11 of the 1933 Act imposes civil liability on preparers for misstatements or omissions in registration statements.

5. **Processing the Registration Statement**

a. **Effective Date of Statement**

The registration statement becomes effective on the *20th* day after its filing with the S.E.C. unless it is subject to a refusal or stop order (*infra*) or becomes effective sooner under an acceleration order. (The S.E.C. will declare a registration statement effective if it is satisfied with it, even if the 20-day period has not run.) Note that if the registration statement is amended, the waiting period starts running anew.

b. **Review of the Registration Statement**

Once filed, the S.E.C. begins reviewing the registration statement to ensure that the issuer has complied with all disclosure requirements.

c. **Formal Proceedings by the S.E.C.**

(1) **Formal Examination**

If a serious problem is indicated by the S.E.C.'s initial review or the issuer's responses to that review, and the issuer appears uncooperative, a formal examination may occur with grave consequences—the offering is essentially returned to the pre-filing period. If completion of the examination is unreasonably delayed, a court may order the S.E.C. to either terminate the examination or issue a stop order.

(2) **Refusal Orders**

If the S.E.C. finds that the issuer failed to comply with the Act's disclosure requirements, it may issue a refusal order (if the statement is clearly inadequate on its face) within 10 days after the statement is filed. Refusal orders are always issued *prior to* the registration statement's effective date.

(3) **Stop Orders**

A stop order either delays the effective date *or* stops the selling of securities if selling has begun so that the S.E.C. can conduct an investigation.

(4) **Use of Acceleration Power**

As a practical matter, issuers state on the statement that it will not be effective until approved; the S.E.C. then grants acceleration immediately upon approval, thus bypassing formal actions.

d. **Withdrawal of Registration Statement**

If there are problems with the issuing company or the registration statement after filing, the issuer may seek to withdraw. The S.E.C. allows withdrawal if it is consistent with the public interest. A withdrawal request is usually honored if filed *before* a stop order proceeding.

e. **Underwriter Refuses to Proceed**

If an underwriter's investigation reveals *material misstatements* by the issuer, it may refuse to proceed despite its contractual obligation.

f. **Blue Sky Qualification**

In some cases, issuers must be qualified under the securities law of each state in which the securities are intended to be offered, absent a state exemption.

g. **FINRA Clearance**

The issuer must also receive clearance from FINRA that the underwriting commissions being paid are "fair."

6. **Post-Effective Amendments to Registration Statement**

a. **Errors Existing at Time of Effectiveness**

If the registration statement contains an error at the time it is declared effective, and the error is discovered after the effective date, the appropriate way to update the prospectus is to file a "post-effective" amendment with the S.E.C.

b. **Errors Caused by Subsequent Developments**

If developments after the effective date make information in the registration statement or prospectus misleading or false, a correction may be made by placing a sticker on the cover of the prospectus and supplying the correct information in the prospectus.

c. **Updating Requirement**

The 1933 Act requires a prospectus to be updated if it is still in use nine months after its effective date, whether or not any errors are discovered.

d. "Blank Check" Offerings

A blank check company is defined by the 1933 Act as a development stage company issuing penny stock that either has no business plan or purpose or plans to merge with an unidentified company. To prevent misuse of the funds, the Act imposes additional requirements on such companies. The sale proceeds must be placed in *escrow* until after the issuer files a *post-effective amendment* to the registration statement, describing its acquisition of business assets, after which investors then have a right to *rescind* their purchases.

7. Shelf Registration

A shelf registration occurs when an issuer files one statement covering securities it may offer at various times in the future. Shelf registrations are generally prohibited (because of inadequate disclosure), with some exceptions, *e.g.*, *traditional shelf registrations*, some *mergers*, and *registration Form S-3 companies*.

a. Automatic Shelf Registration for WKSIs

In addition to the traditional shelf registration exceptions, the 2005 SOR provides for automatic shelf registration for WKSIs. All shelf registrations for WKSIs are *effective immediately* upon filing and can be amended to add additional securities. Shelf registrations are *effective for three years* and a new statement may be filed, thus offering the same securities on a continuing basis.

b. Disclosure

A shelf registration issuer files a "base prospectus" as part of the registration statement. Information regarding future offerings is disseminated by distribution of the additional information or by a supplemental prospectus, or by incorporating information from 1934 Act filings, or by a post-effective amendment to the shelf registration statement.

F. EXEMPTIONS FROM REGISTRATION REQUIREMENTS

1. Exempt Securities

Certain types of securities are exempt from registration under Section 5 of the 1933 Act, including:

a. *Bank and government* securities;

b. *Short-term notes* and other debt instruments;

c. Securities issued by *charitable organizations*;

d. Securities issued by *savings and loan institutions*;

e. Securities issued by *common carriers* to finance acquisitions of rolling stock;

f. Securities issued by *receivers or trustees in bankruptcy* with the approval of the court; and

g. *Insurance, endowment, or annuity policies* issued by companies supervised by state agencies.

2. Exempt Transactions

The exempt securities above can be sold and resold without ever being subject to the Section 5 registration requirements. There are also transaction exemptions that cover only one sale; resales of the same securities might be subject to registration unless the resale is also exempt. Note that an "exempt" transaction is exempt only from the registration and prospectus delivery requirements, and not from the anti-fraud provisions of the 1933 Act.

3. Issuer Transactional Exemptions

The key considerations for each issuer transactional exemption are the following:

a. What is the policy rationale for the exemption from registration?

b. Is there a limit on the amount of money an issuer can raise or that a single investor can invest in the exempt offering?

c. Is there a limit on the number of offerees or purchasers?

d. Are the offerees or purchasers required to be of a certain type?

e. Is certain information required to be disclosed to offerees or purchasers in order to satisfy the exemption?

f. Are there manner or place of sale restrictions?

g. Is there a limit on the number of offerees or purchasers?

g. Does the issuer have to satisfy certain qualifications?

h. Is an S.E.C. filing required?

i. Are the securities "restricted," such that resale by initial investors is prohibited?

j. Are state registration requirements preempted?

k. How clear is the exemption, and is there grace for noncompliance?

4. Resales and "Statutory Underwriters"

Because most exempt *transactions* do not involve exempt *securities*, and because nonexempt securities that were sold in an exempt transaction cannot be sold without another exemption, a resale of securities can easily violate Section 5. Furthermore, under the 1933 Act, anyone who purchases from a control person and resells to the public risks becoming an underwriter, even if not in the "business" of being an underwriter *e.g.*, a broker. Such persons are called "statutory underwriters."

a. Buyer's Intent Important

Underwriter status often depends on intent. If a buyer purchases from the issuer (or a control person) intending to distribute the securities, and a distribution occurs, the buyer has become an underwriter.

(1) Traditional Factors Showing Investment Intent

Whether an original purchaser bought for investment or distribution is a *question of fact*. The following factors are usually considered:

(a) Whether the original purchasers gave the issuer a *letter indicating that it is buying for investment purposes* rather than resale;

(b) The *length of time* the original purchaser holds the securities; and

(c) Whether the securities certificate includes a *legend* that the certificates cannot be transferred without the issuer's permission.

b. Rule 144 Safe Harbor

Rule 144 provides a safe harbor to permit resale without qualifying as an underwriter. The applicable rules depend on the following two attributes:

(1) "Restricted Securities"

Rule 144 defines "restricted securities" to include (i) *privately offered securities* acquired from an issuer or control person; (ii) securities *issued pursuant to Rules 505 or 506*, or to Rule 701(c) (employee benefit plans); (iii) securities *sold under Rule 144A* (*infra*); and (iv) other securities *not previously offered to the public*.

(2) Sales by Control Persons

Rule 144 states when and how many securities a control person may sell without making those who purchase and resell "underwriters." The rule applies to ***both restricted and nonrestricted*** securities held by control persons.

c. Alternatives to Rule 144

(1) "Section 4(1½)"—Private Sales of Restricted Securities

While there is no express exemption for private sales of restricted securities, the S.E.C. informally recognizes one. The standards partly resemble the standards under SA Section 4(a)(2) (private placements) and partly resemble the standards under SA Section 4(a)(1) (transactions not involving an issuer, underwriter, or dealer), and so these have come to be called "Section 4(1½) offerings."

(2) Rule 144A—Resales to "Qualified Institutional Buyers" of Privately Placed Securities

Rule 144A is designed to make restricted securities easier to sell in certain cases.

G. LIABILITIES UNDER THE 1933 ACT

1. Introduction

a. Conduct Resulting in Liability

(1) Liability for Improper Disclosure or Violation of Section 5 Registration Provisions

Liability can arise under Section 11 for misrepresentation or material omission in a registration statement. Liability can arise under Section 12(a)(1) as the result of an improper offer in the pre-filing period, failure to deliver a required prospectus in the post-effective period, or other violations of Section 5.

(2) Liability for Fraud or Misrepresentation in a Public Offering

This can arise under Section 12(a)(2).

(3) Liability for Fraud or Misrepresentation in General

This can arise under Section 17.

b. Remedies for 1933 Act Violations

(1) Private Lawsuits

A plaintiff entitled to damages under Section 11 receives the amount lost, subject to certain limitations. Sections 12(a)(1) and (2) permit a plaintiff to rescind the sale, receiving back her purchase price.

(2) **S.E.C. Lawsuits**

(a) **Cease-and-Desist Orders**

These resemble injunctions in that they direct the respondent not to violate the Act further, but a cease-and-desist order can be *issued by the S.E.C.* (an injunction must be issued by the courts), and violation of the order may result in a *civil penalty* under the Act (while violation of an injunction results in a contempt citation). Cease-and-desist orders can be temporary or permanent. In the case of a permanent order, the S.E.C. may order a respondent to furnish an accounting and to disgorge any monies received in violation of the Act.

(b) **Injunction**

Section 20(b) of the 1933 Act gives the S.E.C. power to seek injunctive relief (and civil fines) from the courts whenever it appears that the Act or the rules have been, or are about to be, violated.

(c) **Criminal Sanctions**

Section 24 of the 1933 Act imposes criminal penalties for *willful violations* of any provision of the Act.

2. **Express Civil Liabilities**

a. **Section 11—Liability for Misstatements or Omissions in Registration Statement or Prospectus**

Section 11 imposes liability on designated persons for materially false or misleading statements or omissions in an effective registration statement or prospectus. Section 11 does *not apply to a free writing prospectus* because it is not part of the registration statement.

(1) **Persons Subject to Liability**

(a) *Every person who signs the registration statement* (issuer, principal executive officers, principal financial officer, controller or principal accounting officer, and a majority of the board of directors must sign the statement);

(b) *Every director of the issuer*;

(c) *Every person about to become a director,* who consents to being named in the registration statement;

(d) *Every "expert"* who consents to being named as having prepared or certified part of the registration statement;

(e) *Every underwriter* involved in the distribution; and

(f) *Control persons* of the issuer, unless they are without knowledge of the facts on which liability is based.

(2) **Elements of Plaintiff's Cause of Action**

(a) **Material Misstatements or Omissions**

Material facts are those to which there is a substantial likelihood that a reasonable investor would attach importance in deciding whether to purchase the security. If liability is premised on an omission, there must have been a duty to disclose.

(b) **Limited Reliance Requirement**

There is *no* reliance requirement *unless* the issuer sends out an earnings statement covering the period of one year *after* the effective date of the registration statement (a person thereafter acquiring some of the registered securities must prove reliance on the misrepresentation or omission to recover).

(c) **Secondary Market Purchasers**

There is a split of authority as to whether secondary market purchasers can recover under Section 11. However, most courts hold that such persons can recover if they can prove that the purchased securities were issued pursuant to the defective registration statement ("tracing"). Privity of contract is *not* required.

(d) **Causation and Damages**

Plaintiff need *not* prove that the loss was caused by defendant's misrepresentation. (But *defendant* can prove that all or some portion of the damages is due to some cause other than the misrepresentation.)

(3) **Defenses**

(a) **General Affirmative Defenses**

Any defendant, *including* the issuer, may plead the following defenses.

1) *Plaintiff knew* of the misrepresentations and invested anyway; and

2) *The statute of limitations* has run.

(b) **Due Diligence Defenses**

All defendants, *except* the issuer, have a due diligence defense.

1) **Statements Made by Experts**

Experts may avoid liability as to the portions of the registration statement they certified if they can show that they *actually believed that the statements made were true,* and that their belief was *reasonable* (*i.e.*, they made a *reasonable investigation* of the supporting facts).

2) **Statements Made by Nonexperts**

Nonexperts are held to the same standard as experts. A reasonable investigation for a nonexpert must be the kind of investigation that a *prudent person* in the same position, with the same responsibilities, skill, and background would have made (*e.g.*, a nonexpert director-attorney drafting part of the registration statement must conduct an independent investigation to verify the material facts stated in the registration statement).

3) **Nonexperts for Statements Made by Experts**

Here the standard of care is lower. *No investigation* need normally be made by the nonexpert, because nonexperts are entitled to rely to a greater extent on the statements of experts. The reviewing nonexpert need only show that she did not believe and had no reasonable ground to believe the statements made by the expert to be false. However, an investigation is *required* if facts suggest that the registration statement contains misstatements.

(4) **Measure of Damages**

(a) **If the Stock Is Sold Prior to Filing Suit**

Plaintiff may recover the difference between the price paid for the stock (but not exceeding the price at which the security was offered to the public) and the price at which it was sold prior to suit.

(b) **If the Stock Has Not Been Sold Prior to Suit**

Plaintiff may recover *either* the *difference* between the price paid (not exceeding the offering price) and the value of the security *at the time suit is filed, or* the *price* at which the stock was sold *after suit was instituted*, but before judgment, if such damages are less than those that result from using value at the time of suit.

(c) **Plaintiff Not Required to Mitigate Damages**

The plaintiff need not sell if the market price rises.

(d) **Loss Causation Defense**

A defendant is not liable for damages resulting from factors other than the misstatement.

(e) **Joint and Several Liability**

All persons (except outside directors) who are liable under Section 11 are jointly and severally liable and may recover contribution.

1) **Exception**

In actions under Section 11, *outside directors* of the issuer are *jointly and severally* liable for *knowing* violations, and *proportionately liable* to their respective degrees of fault for all other violations.

b. **Section 12(a)(1)—Liability for Offers or Sales in Violation of Section 5**

Under Section 12(a)(1), any person who offers or sells a security in violation of any of the provisions of Section 5 of the Act is liable to the purchaser for (i) the *consideration paid* (with interest) less the amount of any income received on the securities (*i.e.*, a suit for *rescission*); or (ii) for *damages* if the purchaser no longer owns the security.

(1) **Any Violation of Section 5**

Liability attaches for any violation of any provision of Section 5 (*i.e.*, a sale of unregistered securities, failure to deliver the required prospectus, etc.).

(a) **"Control Persons"**

Persons who control a person liable under Section 12(a)(1) may be jointly and severally liable with the controlled person.

(b) **Participant Liability**

"Sellers" (or offerors) liable under Section 12(a)(1) include the person who *actually passes title* to the security and persons who *solicit the purchase* from the purchaser, but *not* persons whose sole motivation in acting is to benefit the buyer.

(2) **Defenses to a Section 12(a)(1) Cause of Action**

The most common defense to a Section 12(a)(1) action is that the *privity* requirement has not been met; *i.e.,* direct privity of contract between plaintiff-purchaser and the seller-defendant is necessary. *Lack of any violation* and running of the *statute of limitations* are also defenses.

c. **Section 12(a)(2)—General Civil Liability Under the Act**

Section 12(a)(2) of the 1933 Act prohibits fraud in the interstate offer or sale of securities. It provides that any person (i) who offers for sale a security by the use of any means of interstate commerce, (ii) by means of a prospectus or oral communication that contains an untrue statement or omission of material fact, and (iii) who cannot sustain the burden of proof that he did not know and in the exercise of reasonable care could not have known of such untruth, is liable to the purchaser of such security.

(1) **Plaintiff's Cause of Action**

Plaintiff may sue for *rescission or damages*, but in any case must show the following:

(i) *Sale* of a *security;*

(ii) Use of some means of *interstate commerce;*

(iii) Sale by means of an *oral communication or prospectus* (Section 12(a)(2) is applicable only to public offerings); and

(iv) An *untrue statement or omission* of material fact.

Plaintiff must also *plead* that *defendant knew* or, in the exercise of reasonable care, *should have known* of the untrue statement or omission of material fact. However, defendant carries the burden of proof on this issue. Note that plaintiff need *not* prove *reliance* on the misrepresentation.

(2) **Defenses**

Defendant may raise the following defenses:

(a) *Lack of knowledge*. Defendant may show that she did not know, and was not negligent in not knowing, of the untrue statement or omission.

(b) *Waiver or estoppel* (*i.e.*, plaintiff has shown acceptance of defendant's conduct).

(c) *Plaintiff knew of the untrue statement.*

(d) *No privity of contract.*

(e) *No participation*. Most lower courts require the defendant to have been a "participant," as under Section 12(a)(1), *supra*.

(f) *Statute of limitations.*

(g) *Loss causation* (*i.e.*, defendant is not liable for losses caused by something other than defendant's misstatements and/or omissions).

3. **Section 17—S.E.C. Antifraud Enforcement**

Section 17 is a general antifraud provision aimed at protecting purchasers of securities. Section 17 makes it unlawful for any person in the *offer or sale* of securities by use of any means or instrumentalities in interstate commerce, or of the mails, directly or indirectly, to (i) employ any device to defraud; or (ii) obtain money or property by means of misstatements or omissions of material fact; or (iii) engage in any transaction that operates as a fraud or deceit upon the purchaser. Section 17 is generally used by the government in civil and criminal fraud cases.

a. **Implied Civil Liability**

Courts are divided as to whether an implied cause of action for damages may be brought under Section 17(a). The *trend is clearly away* from an implied remedy.

b. **Culpable Conduct**

In *S.E.C. injunction* actions, Section 17(a)(1) requires scienter, while only negligence need be shown under the remaining subsections.

4. **Indemnification**

a. **Officers, Directors, and Control Persons**

State laws differ as to whether such persons may be indemnified by the issuer against liability arising in connection with the 1933 Act, and there is no direct authority from the federal courts. The S.E.C. policy is to *require waiver* of such indemnification to get acceleration of effectiveness of a registration statement.

b. **Underwriters**

The S.E.C. has no such policy with respect to underwriters. But the courts have held that where the underwriter has *actual knowledge* of materially misleading statements, it cannot rely on an indemnification agreement with the issuer to escape liability.

5. **Contribution**

Most courts and the S.E.C. permit persons who are liable under the 1933 Act to seek contribution from others who are liable.

6. **Liability Insurance**

The S.E.C. permits insurance against liability under the 1933 Act.

7. **Stipulations Contrary to Liability Provisions Void**

Provisions waiving a seller's compliance with any provision of the 1933 Act are void.

III. REGULATION OF SECURITIES TRADING—THE SECURITIES EXCHANGE ACT OF 1934

A. OVERVIEW OF THE 1934 ACT

The Securities Exchange Act of 1934 ("SEA" or "1934 Act") regulates the trading of securities subsequent to their original distribution.

1. **Purpose of the Act**

The purpose of the SEA is to protect interstate commerce and the national credit, and to ensure a fair and honest market for the trading of securities.

2. **Registration and Reporting Requirements—Section 12**

a. **Companies Required to Register Their Securities**

Companies whose securities are traded on a stock exchange (*listed* companies), *or* companies having assets of more than *$10 million and* a class of equity security *held by either 2,000 investors or 500 non-accredited investors* (*over-the-counter* companies) *must* register that class of equity securities with the S.E.C. Such companies are known as *"reporting"* companies.

b. **Information Required with Registration**

The required information is similar to that in a registration statement under the 1933 Act.

c. **Exemptions from Registration Requirements**

There are many exemptions, including securities of investment companies, savings and loans, and charitable, religious, or educational organizations. In addition, the *S.E.C. has power to exempt* securities.

d. **Reporting Requirements of Registered Companies**

All companies registered with the S.E.C. pursuant to Section 12 must make periodic public reports to the S.E.C. to keep the markets apprised of the registrant's financial condition. Issuers of securities registered under the 1933 Act must also file periodic reports with the S.E.C.

e. **Integration of the Disclosure Requirements**

The S.E.C. relies on continuous reports under the 1934 Act to keep disclosure about issuers current. Therefore, the disclosure requirements of the 1933 and 1934 Acts have largely been integrated.

(1) **Integrity of Accounting**

Under the Foreign Corrupt Practices Act and portions of the Sarbanes-Oxley Act of 2002 ("SOXA"), the S.E.C. has broad authority to regulate the accounting of publicly held companies. Regulations include requirements to keep accurate books and records, use reasonable internal accounting controls, and provide specific signatures and certifications.

3. **Additional Registration Requirements Under the 1934 Act**

a. Registration of national securities exchanges;

b. Registration of brokers and dealers transacting a securities business in interstate commerce;

c. Registration of information processors; and

d. Registration of transfer agents and clearing houses.

4. **Additional Reporting Requirements Under the 1934 Act**

a. Reports by purchasers of 5% of a class of equity security registered under Section 12 of the 1934 Act;

b. Reports by officers, directors, and owners of more than 10% of a class of security registered under Section 12 of the 1934 Act;

c. Reports by national securities exchanges and associations; and

d. Reports by institutional investors.

5. **Regulation of Practices Relating to Stock Ownership**

Proxy solicitation and tender offers are also regulated under the 1934 Act.

6. **Regulation of Accounting Records and Internal Controls**

The 1934 Act requires reporting companies to keep books and records that reflect the financial transactions of the issuer.

7. **A National Securities Market**

The 1934 Act also establishes a goal of a "national market system" and directs the creation of a National Market Advisory Board to move the securities markets in that direction.

8. **Role of the S.E.C. in Administering the 1934 Act**

The S.E.C. has broad power, including powers to investigate, make and enforce rules, and impose penalties.

9. **Sarbanes-Oxley Act**

In addition to detailed regulation of auditors and accountants of reporting companies, SOXA also regulates lawyers and securities analysts. The Act also changed disclosure rules and enhanced fines and penalties for financial crimes.

10. **Liability Provisions of the 1934 Act**

There are several *express* remedy provisions providing private civil causes of action under the 1934 Act. In addition, the courts have sometimes permitted *implied* causes of action for violation of various provisions of the 1934 Act. However, the trend is away from implying private causes of action.

a. **Exception—Rule 10b–5**

Even if an express remedy is provided, courts will imply a remedy under *Section 10(b) and Rule 10b–5* of the 1934 Act.

11. **Role of the Courts**

Federal district courts have *exclusive* original jurisdiction over violations of the 1934 Act.

B. CIVIL LIABILITY UNDER RULE 10b–5 OF THE 1934 ACT

Rule 10b–5 is the most significant securities antifraud remedies provision.

1. **Statement of Rule 10b–5**

Under Rule 10b–5, it is unlawful, in connection with the *purchase or sale of any security*, for any person, directly or indirectly, by the use of *any means or instrumentality of interstate commerce*, or of the mails, or of any facility of any national securities exchange, to: (i) employ any device, scheme, or artifice *to defraud*; (ii) make any *untrue statement of material fact* (*or to omit a material fact*); or (iii) *engage in any act*, practice, or course of business which *operates as a fraud or deceit* upon any person.

2. **Securities and Transactions Covered**

For Rule 10b–5 to apply, a "security" must be involved. All securities transactions are covered, no matter where they occur (exchange, over-the-counter, etc.), although the trend appears to be to narrow the interpretation of what is a security. Rule 10b–5 *applies to both purchases and sales*.

a. **Interstate Commerce Requirement**

Some means of interstate commerce must be used in connection with the purchase or sale of securities.

3. **Jurisdiction, Venue, and Service of Process**

a. **Jurisdiction**

The federal courts have exclusive jurisdiction over all Rule 10b–5 civil actions.

b. **Venue**

Suit may be brought in any district court in the district where any act or transaction in violation of the rule occurred, or in any district where the defendant is found, resides, or transacts business.

c. **Service of Process**

Process may be served anywhere in the world.

4. Elements of Cause of Action

The elements depend on whether the government or a private plaintiff is seeking to establish liability.

a. Actions by Private Plaintiffs

In a private civil action, a plaintiff must prove the following elements:

(1) the plaintiff has standing to assert the claim;

(2) the defendant is a primary violator;

(3) the defendant engaged in manipulation or deception;

(4) with respect to a material fact;

(5) in connection with the purchase of sale of a security;

(6) scienter;

(7) reliance;

(8) loss causation; and

(9) damages.

Note: As a practical matter, most private Rule 10b–5 actions are asserted as class actions. Accordingly, there are additional procedural requirements imposed by the Federal Rules of Civil Procedure and the securities laws. Most important are the requirements imposed by the Private Securities Litigation Reform Act of 1995. Some of those procedural requirements interact with the substantive elements and are thus important to note alongside the elements of the claim.

b. Actions by the Government

In a government action under Rule 10b–5, the government must prove the above-listed elements with some exceptions. In particular, the government is ***not*** required to prove the following elements:

(1) the plaintiff has standing to assert the claim (the government has standing!);

(2) the defendant is a primary violator (the government *may* pursue secondary violators);

(3) reliance;

(4) loss causation; and

(5) damages.

The remaining elements are the same.

5. Insider Trading and the Duty to Disclose

Rule 10b–5 has been found to prohibit some cases of trading on the basis of "inside" information.

a. Elements of a Rule 10b–5 Insider Trading Case

The elements for an insider trading case are the same as in other Rule 10b–5 cases, but analysis revolves around whether the activity was fraudulent. The standard today is that a purchase or sale of a security on the basis of material nonpublic information, *in breach of a duty* owed to the issuer or shareholders, or to any person who is the source of the information, violates Rule 10b–5.

(1) **Insiders**

An insider is an officer, director, controlling shareholder, or corporate employee of an issuer. *Constructive insiders* are persons in a confidential relationship with the issuer, *e.g.*, accountants, lawyers, bankers.

(2) **Tippees**

A tippee is a person who receives a tip from an insider and subsequently trades securities related to the information.

(3) **Misappropriators**

Persons who misappropriate material, nonpublic information in breach of a duty to the source of the information may also be liable for insider trading.

(4) **Breach of Duty**

A defendant must have *breached some* ***identifiable duty not to use*** *the information for* ***personal benefit***.

(5) **"On the Basis of" Material Nonpublic Information**

The problem of whether a person violates Rule 10b–5 when in possession of information without actually using it to trade was resolved by adoption of *Rule 10b5–1*: A person will be deemed to have purchased or sold a security on the basis of material nonpublic information if she was *aware of it* when purchasing or selling.

b. **"Selective Disclosure" and Regulation FD**

Regulation FD ("Fair Disclosure") was promulgated to control the *selective disclosure* by insiders of material nonpublic information to securities analysts (*i.e.*, disclosure by a regulated person to a regulated person).

(1) **Timing of Public Disclosure**

In the case of an intentional regulated disclosure, there is an obligation to *simultaneously* make the information public; in the case of an *inadvertent* disclosure, the public must be *promptly* informed.

c. **Specific Insider Trading Legislation**

(1) **Insider Trading Sanctions Act**

This Act allows the S.E.C. to seek civil penalties of up to ***three times*** the ill-gotten profits.

(2) **Insider Trading and Securities Fraud Enforcement Act of 1988**

This Act provides a cause of action for persons who sold or purchased a security in the market at the time defendant sold or purchased a security of the same class in violation of the 1934 Act. However, damages are limited to defendant's *profit gained or loss avoided.*

6. **Remedies**

a. **Rescission**

Although most 10b–5 actions seek damages, there is some authority permitting rescission, *i.e.*, plaintiff recovers the money or securities she parted with.

b. **Restitution**

Most courts grant the plaintiff *damages* based on restitution (what she has lost).

(1) **Defendant's Profits**

As an alternative measure of damages, some courts are requiring that defendant disgorge any profits made in the securities transaction that violated Rule 10b–5.

(2) **Benefit of the Bargain**

Sometimes the plaintiff may recover the benefits she expected to make in the bargain.

(3) **Insider Trading Cases**

Insider trading in an impersonal market could subject the insider to potentially huge damages that far exceed the profits realized or loss avoided (*e.g.*, class actions). Thus, courts tend to limit damages in such cases.

c. **Punitive Damages**

Punitive damages are ***not*** available under Rule 10b–5.

d. **Liability of Multiple Defendants**

In *private actions*, persons who knowingly commit securities fraud are jointly and severally liable; all others are liable in proportion to their respective fault. A right of *contribution* exists.

e. **S.E.C. Actions**

When the S.E.C. brings a Rule 10b–5 action, it may seek remedies different from those sought by private plaintiffs, *e.g.*, injunction, criminal penalties.

7. **Defenses**

a. **Failure to Plead with Particularity**

Under the Private Securities Litigation Reform Act of 1995 ("PSLRA"), actions based on fraud and *filed under the 1934 Act by a private party* must meet heightened standards of specificity at the complaint stage. The plaintiff must: (i) identify each misleading statement; (ii) state the reasons why they are misleading; (iii) specify the facts forming this belief; and (iv) specify the facts giving rise to a strong inference that the defendant acted with scienter.

b. **Other Defenses**

Other defenses include the *statute of limitations* (two years after discovery and no more than five years after the alleged violation occurred), certain *common law defenses* (*e.g.*, in pari delicto), and *lack of due diligence* by the plaintiff.

8. **Section 17(a) of the 1933 Act and Rule 10b–5**

Sometimes both Section 17(a) and Rule 10b–5 may apply in an action. Although the language of the two provisions is almost identical, the scope and burdens of proof may differ.

9. **Class Actions Under Rule 10b–5**

Rule 10b–5 actions are frequently brought as class actions and are governed by the Federal Rules of Civil Procedure regarding class actions.

10. **Private Securities Litigation Reform Act of 1995**

The Act's procedural provisions make it considerably more difficult for private plaintiffs to bring securities class actions.

C. TENDER OFFERS AND REPURCHASES OF STOCK

A "tender offer" is an offer by a person (the "bidder") to purchase the securities of a corporation (the "target"), which is made directly to the shareholders of the target.

1. Federal Regulation of Tender Offers

In 1968, the Williams Act was added to the 1934 Act specifically to regulate tender offers in areas of *reporting, disclosure*, and *antifraud.* Although the 1934 Act does not contain *remedies* for violation of tender offer rules, courts have *implied* remedies. The most recent trend, however, is to limit implied remedies for private rights of action.

2. Preliminary Reporting Requirement—Section 13(d)

a. Ownership Criteria

Any person (or group of persons, such as a partnership) who within 12 months acquires beneficial ownership in excess of 5% of a class of equity security registered under Section 12 of the 1934 Act, must, within 10 days after the acquisition, file an information statement with the S.E.C., sending copies to the issuer of the security and to any exchanges on which the security is traded.

b. Information Required

The information statement must disclose information about the *purchasers,* the *consideration* paid, the *purpose* of the purchases, the percentage of *ownership,* and the *contracts* or other arrangements the purchaser has made regarding the issuer and its securities.

c. Implied Private Rights of Action

The *target* has an implied right of action against the bidder for a violation of Section 13(d), and the *shareholders of the target* also have standing.

3. Basic Tender Offer Rules—Section 14(d)

Section 14(d) contains the basic regulatory provisions concerning a tender offer.

a. Definition of a "Tender Offer"

There is no explicit statutory definition of the term "tender offer," but it is generally thought to be an offer to purchase that is made "publicly" and not in normal exchange or over-the-counter market transactions. The courts look at the facts of each case and define the term broadly to effectuate the purposes of the 1934 Act.

b. Requirements of Section 14(d)

Under Section 14(d) it is unlawful to use the means of interstate commerce to make a tender offer if, at consummation, the bidder will be the beneficial owner of more than 5% of the class of securities tendered, *unless* the following requirements are met:

(1) Disclosure of Information

(a) Schedule TO

At or before the commencement of the tender offer, the bidder must file a Schedule TO, which is similar to Schedule 13D, but contains additional information (*e.g.*, past contacts with the subject company, persons who will be retained or employed in connection with the offer, financial statements of the bidder (if material), etc.).

(b) **Disclosure and Publication of Tender Offer Documents**

The bidder must either publish a summary of the Schedule TO information in a newspaper or publish a short advertisement stating the offer's essential terms and where complete offer materials may be obtained.

4. **Actions for Misstatements or Insufficient Disclosure—Section 14(e)**

Under Section 14(e), it is unlawful for any person to make untrue statements or to omit to state material facts, or to engage in any fraud or deception in connection with any tender offer or in opposition thereto.

a. **Private Remedies**

Section 14(e) may be enforced by private persons or by the S.E.C. Private persons may seek *damages or an injunction.*

b. **Private Action for Damages**

A private plaintiff seeking damages must prove standing, misstatements, nondisclosure or other fraud, materiality, and *maybe* reliance (transaction causation), loss causation, and scienter.

c. **Private Action for Injunction**

As an alternative to damages, a plaintiff may also bring an action for a temporary or permanent injunction to remedy violations of the tender rules.

d. **Enforcement by the S.E.C.**

Tender offer rules may be enforced by injunctions, criminal prosecutions, cease-and-desist proceedings, or orders for compliance.

D. REGULATION OF PROXY SOLICITATIONS

1. **"Proxy" Defined**

A proxy is a power of attorney to vote shares owned by someone else and is usually revocable at any time. Solicitation of proxies is regulated by both state and federal law. The federal courts have *exclusive jurisdiction* over the application of the *federal proxy rules*. A proxy solicitation is any communication to the shareholders reasonably calculated to result in granting, withholding, or revoking of a proxy.

2. **Federal Proxy Rules**

Pursuant to SEA Section 14(a), the S.E.C. has adopted rules regulating proxy solicitation for reporting companies. These rules are designed to accomplish three objectives:

(i) *To encourage full disclosure;*

(ii) *To prevent fraud;*

(iii) *To allow shareholder proposals* to be included in the proxy solicitations made by management.

a. **Scope of Coverage of Proxy Rules**

The rules apply to *all companies with securities registered* under SEA Section 12 and to *all securities registered* under Section 12. Thus, whenever a corporation has a matter that calls for the vote of a shareholder owning a registered security, it is subject to the proxy rules.

3. Proxy Disclosure Requirements

a. The Proxy Statement

The proxy statement must include all material facts regarding matters to be voted on by the security holders and identification of the participants in the solicitation.

b. The Annual Report

If directors are to be elected at the meeting for which proxies are sought, the registrant must provide the shareholders with an annual report before the meeting.

c. Antifraud Provisions

The proxy rules include antifraud provisions that apply to all proxy solicitations, whether or not the solicitation is exempt from other rule requirements.

4. Proxy Statement Delivery Requirements

Solicitation is generally *prohibited without delivery* of the proxy statement and, if directors are to be elected, an annual report.

a. Exceptions

Delivery requirements do not apply to *public solicitations* (*e.g.*, by advertisement), if the soliciting person (other than an issuer) is *not seeking proxy authority*, or during *proxy contests* before a proxy statement is filed.

5. Proxy Statement Filing Requirements

All written materials used in a solicitation must be filed with the S.E.C. Generally, both the proxy statement and the form of proxy (*i.e.*, the actual form on which shareholders grant authority to vote their shares) must be filed with the S.E.C. *at least 10 days before* definitive versions are sent to the shareholders. Preliminary copies need not be filed for meetings where only routine matters are scheduled, *e.g.*, election of directors.

6. Proxy Statement

The proxy statement must include details about the solicitation and about director election, specific matters (*e.g.*, mergers), executive compensation, and some general matters (*e.g.*, significant changes in control).

7. Proxy Contests

Proxy contests usually result from a fight between management and other shareholders (insurgents) for control of the company. To gain control, insurgents may solicit proxies to elect a majority of directors. To keep control, management may solicit proxies to support a merger with another company.

a. Exception to Filing Requirements

Because proxy contests often require quick action, the general exception is used before actually filing a proxy statement.

b. Shareholder Lists

State law normally governs the question of when a corporation must make a shareholder list available to a shareholder. The *federal* proxy rules do not require management to provide a list *except* when management is itself soliciting proxies (then it must either give the requesting shareholder complete access to the registrant's shareholder list *or* mail the shareholder's proxy solicitation material to the other shareholders).

8. Shareholder Proposals

An alternative to independent proxy solicitation allows a shareholder to serve notice on management of an intention to propose action at the shareholders' meeting. In such a case, management may be compelled to include the proposal in its proxy statement.

a. Requirements

The proponent must meet certain share ownership requirements and procedural requirements.

b. Management's Omission of Shareholder Proposals

If management opposes the proposal and wishes to omit it from the proxy statement, it must file the proposal and the reasons for opposing it with the S.E.C. The S.E.C. will review the proposal and state its position. Management may properly omit a shareholder proposal in the following situations:

(1) The proposal is *not a "proper subject"* for action by shareholders.

(2) The proposal is *illegal.*

(3) The proposal is *contrary to S.E.C. rules or regulations.*

(4) The proposal relates to *redress of a personal claim.*

(5) The proposal *relates to insignificant operations of the registrant* (*i.e.*, accounts for less than 5% of the registrant's total assets and net earnings and is not significant to the corporation in any other way).

(6) The proposal deals with a *matter beyond the registrant's power to effectuate.*

(7) The proposal deals with the *ordinary business operations* of the registrant and (possibly) does not involve any substantial public policy or other considerations.

(8) The proposal relates to an *election to office.*

(9) The proposal is *counter to a proposal to be submitted by the registrant* at the meeting.

(10) The proposal has been rendered *moot.*

(11) The proposal is *duplicative* of an earlier submitted proposal.

(12) The proposal or a substantially similar proposal was *rejected* within the preceding five years and received less than a specified percentage of votes.

(13) The proposal relates to *specific amounts of cash or stock dividends.*

9. Exemptions from Proxy Rules

The following are exempt from some or all the federal proxy rules:

a. Solicitations of 10 or fewer persons;

b. Solicitations by the beneficial owners of securities from the ***registered*** owners;

c. Tombstone ads;

d. Broker-dealers' impartial transmission of solicitation materials to beneficial owners;

e. Statements of intended vote, *i.e.,* written communications from a security holder stating how the holder intends to vote and the reasons therefor;

f. Solicitations by persons not seeking proxy authority;

g. Solicitations by public broadcast, speech, advertisement, etc.; and

h. Proxy voting advice (under certain circumstances).

10. Enforcement Provisions

There is a *private right of action* for violation of proxy rules.

a. Antifraud Provisions

Actions claiming a violation of the proxy rules may be brought under the antifraud provisions of the 1934 Act relating to the solicitation of proxies. [*See* SEA Rule 14a–9] To establish a cause of action for fraud, the following elements must be proved:

(1) Misrepresentations or omissions of fact

(2) Materiality

(3) Standard of culpability

(4) Causation

b. Remedies for Violation of the Proxy Rules

(1) Actions by the S.E.C.

The S.E.C. may bring actions for *injunctions* (to prevent proxy solicitation or to require resolicitation, etc.).

(2) Implied private actions

The courts will fashion whatever relief is appropriate to remedy the loss caused by the proxy violation (*e.g.*, damages or rescission of the transaction, etc.).

E. INSIDER LIABILITY FOR SHORT-SWING PROFITS

1. Introduction

SEA Section 16 is designed to prevent corporate insiders from using inside information about their companies to make short-swing profits by buying and selling or selling and buying securities of their corporation within six months. Section 16(a), which is strictly enforced, requires insiders to *file periodic reports* of their holdings and Section 16(b) requires insiders to *disgorge "profits"* from short-swing trading.

a. Short Sales by Insiders

Section 16(c) makes it *unlawful* for insiders to make short sales of their company's equity securities. A "short sale" is a sale of securities that the seller does not yet own but plans to purchase just in time to honor the sale.

b. Rule 10b–5 Distinguished

Rule 10b–5 governs insider trading based on a fraudulent misrepresentation or failure to disclose. Section 16 is based on the amount of time between a purchase and sale (or sale and purchase). Note that Rule 10b–5 and Section 16(b) *can* apply to the same transaction.

2. Nature of a Section 16 Cause of Action

Sections 16(a) and (c) are enforceable only by the S.E.C. Private plaintiffs can sue under Section 16(b), which provides that an issuer can recover an insider's profits from short-swing trading of any officer, director, or owner of more than 10% of any class of a *registered* equity security who realizes any profit from the prohibited trading.

3. **All Equity Security Transactions Regulated**

Once a person qualifies as an insider by being an officer, director, or more than 10% owner, purchases and sales of *any equity security* of the issuer may result in liability.

4. **Beneficial Ownership**

Beneficial ownership, not record ownership, is the relevant standard under Section 16. Two tests are used in determining beneficial ownership:

a. **More than 10% Holder**

In determining whether a person is a more than 10% holder of a class of registered equity securities, all securities of the class beneficially owned by him are counted. *For this purpose only*, beneficial ownership means having *voting power* over the securities.

b. **All Other Section 16 Purposes**

For all other purposes (*e.g.*, calculating profits) beneficial ownership means having a direct or indirect *pecuniary interest in the shares*. Officers and directors are *presumed* to have a pecuniary interest in all securities *owned by family members* (*i.e.*, virtually *all relatives who share a household* with the insider).

5. **"Insiders" Defined**

a. **Officers and Directors**

Officers and directors of *subsidiaries* may be deemed officers of the issuer if they perform policy-making functions for the issuer.

b. **More than 10% Shareholder**

Every person who directly or indirectly is the beneficial owner of more than 10% of any class of registered securities is subject to Section 16. Remember that having or sharing the *power to vote* more than 10% of any class results in insider status.

6. **Equity Security Defined**

The 1934 Act defines "equity security" as including any stock or similar security, or any convertible security, and certain acquisition rights to securities.

7. **Purchase and Sale Requirement**

Section 16(b) requires a purchase and sale or sale and purchase. Generally, a "purchase" occurs when a purchaser undertakes an irrevocable obligation to take and pay for the stock, and a "sale" occurs when the seller incurs an irrevocable liability to deliver and accept payment for the stock.

8. **Within a Period of Less than Six Months**

Under Section 16, a *fractional day counts as a full day*. Thus, the statutory period of "less than six months" begins at any time on day 1 and ends at midnight on the day that is *two days before* the date that is six months later, so that the period comprises *less* than six months. If it ended on the day before the six month anniversary, the period would be exactly six months, not "less than" six months.

9. **"Profit" Under Section 16(b)**

The profit under Section 16(b) is calculated by matching the highest and lowest prices of stock transactions of *any* purchase or sale during any six-month period. Any *loss* transactions are ignored.

10. Other Elements of Damages

A Section 16 plaintiff can recover defendant's profits. Additionally, the court has discretion to award interest on the profit made. Dividends declared on the actual shares sold while the insider held them may also be part of the profit. Attorneys' fees are usually recoverable too.

11. Strict Liability

The general rule is that there are no defenses to a Section 16(b) action *except* for *unorthodox transactions*.

12. Procedural Aspects of Actions Under Section 16

a. Jurisdiction

Jurisdiction is exclusively in the federal courts.

b. Service

Service of process is nationwide.

c. Venue

Venue lies where any act or transaction constituting the violation occurred or where the defendant can be found or transacts business.

d. Statute of Limitations

Actions must be brought within *two years* after the profit is realized, but if the insider has not filed reports under Section 16(a), the period is tolled until the profits should have been discovered.

e. Proper Plaintiff

The corporation may sue, but if it declines, *any* security holder may bring a *derivative action* on behalf of the corporation. The S.E.C. may *not* bring an action for violation of Section 16(b).

F. LIABILITY OF COLLATERAL PARTICIPANTS IN SECURITIES TRANSACTIONS

This section discusses the potential liability of persons who aid, abet, participate in, or render advice in connection with a transaction violating the securities acts.

1. Liability of Collateral Participants

Collateral participants are persons involved in the securities transaction in some way, but not directly responsible for it.

a. Liability Under 1933 Act

(1) Section 11

Only parties named in the statute are potentially liable. Importantly, underwriters are named.

(2) Section 12(a)(1)

Section 12(a)(1) provides a rescission remedy to purchasers of securities that were required to be registered but were not. The remedy is applicable against the *"seller,"* which includes *persons who solicit the purchase*, but *not* persons whose sole motivation in acting is for the benefit of the buyer.

(3) **Section 12(a)(2)**

Section 12(a)(2) provides a rescission remedy to purchasers of securities that were sold by means of a prospectus or oral communication that contained a materially misleading statement or omission. The action may be brought only against the seller, which probably will be defined as under Section 12(a)(1).

(4) **Section 17**

It is highly unlikely that a private civil cause of action is available under Section 17.

b. **Liability Under Rule 10b–5 of the 1934 Act**

For many years, the courts and the S.E.C. upheld aider and abettor liability under Rule 10b–5, but the Supreme Court has since ruled that there is *no implied private right of action* against one who aids or abets a Rule 10b–5 violation.

(1) **S.E.C. Civil Actions**

In 1995, Congress enacted a provision clearly granting the S.E.C. power to bring civil actions against those who aid and abet any violators of the 1934 Act or rules thereunder.

(2) **SOXA and the Scandals of 2001–2002**

It appears that Congress and courts are both willing to impose secondary liability. A SOXA provision directs the S.E.C. to study data from 1998 through 2001 to determine, in part, how many secondary persons (*e.g.*, accountants, lawyers, etc.) aided and abetted securities laws violations but were not sanctioned.

2. **Liability of Controlling Persons**

Both the 1933 Act and the 1934 Act make "controlling persons" liable for the securities law violations of persons they control.

a. **Liability Under 1933 Act**

Any person who controls a person found liable under Sections 11 or 12 is jointly and severally liable along with the liable party, *unless* the controlling person had no knowledge of, nor reasonable grounds to know of, the facts underlying the controlled person's liability. [SA § 15]

b. **Liability Under 1934 Act**

Controlling persons are liable for the securities violations of persons they control, unless they acted in "good faith" and did not directly or indirectly induce the acts underlying the controlled person's liability. [SEA § 20(a)]

c. **"Controlling Person"**

Whether a person is controlling depends on the degree of power and influence the person has. In general, persons have control over their *agents*, but not necessarily over independent contractors.

d. **Defenses Compared**

Ignorance is a clear defense under Section 15 of the 1933 Act, whereas Section 20(a) of the 1934 Act requires a controlling person to prove that it did not induce the offense *and* that it acted in *good faith*. Proving good faith might require more than proving ignorance; generally the defendant must prove that it had some reasonable procedure for supervising the primary wrongdoer.

3. Liability of "Outside" Directors

a. Under 1933 Act

An outside director may be held liable under Section 11 or as a controlling person under Section 15.

b. Under 1934 Act

(1) Liability as an Aider or Abettor

Outside directors might be held liable as aiders or abettors if they knowingly assist others in violations of the securities laws.

(2) Liability of a Controlling Person

Outside directors might be held liable as "controlling persons" under Section 20(a).

4. Liability of Underwriters

a. Liability Under 1933 Act

Section 11 makes underwriters specifically liable for material misstatements or omissions in the registration statement (subject to the "due diligence" defense).

b. Liability Under 1934 Act

Underwriters may be held liable under the liability provisions of the 1934 Act either as *"principals"* or as *"controlling persons."* They could possibly also be liable as aiders and abettors in actions by the S.E.C.

5. Liability of Accountants

a. Liability Under 1933 Act

The accountants that certify the financial statements in a registration statement are subject to liability under Section 11 if they fail to establish their due diligence defense with respect to either the audit or accounting functions.

b. Liability Under 1934 Act

These cases usually involve Rule 10b–5 actions. In private actions, they must qualify as primary violators. In S.E.C. actions, however, they can been held liable for aiding and abetting securities fraud.

(1) Standard of Culpability

It is important to remember that in actions under Rule 10b–5, the plaintiff must prove *scienter* (*i.e.*, fraud, deceit, or recklessness).

(2) Liability for Material Omissions

In cases of omissions, not only must scienter be proved, but also a duty to speak.

6. Liability of Lawyers

There are two views on the lawyer's role. Traditionally, lawyers are responsible chiefly to their clients. The S.E.C., however, maintains that lawyers owe a duty to the public and should inform the government if a client decides not to follow the lawyer's advice. However, SOXA has greatly expanded regulation of securities lawyers.

a. Liability to Clients

Lawyers may be held liable to their clients for intentional or negligent failure to perform properly. *Third parties* may also have a cause of action.

b. Liability as Principals

In addition, a lawyer may become so involved in a client's transaction that she becomes liable as a principal.

c. Liability to Those Affected by Securities Transactions

Determine whether the claim results from the lawyer's involvement as a principal or as an aider and abettor.

(1) Liability as a Participant

If lawyers go beyond merely counseling their client (*e.g.*, where the lawyer is a *director* of the issuer, participates as an *expert*, or qualifies as a *"seller"*), liability can arise from these additional roles.

(2) Aiding and Abetting Liability

(a) Under 1933 Act

Most of the 1933 Act's remedial provisions state specifically who may be liable and do not include aiders and/or abettors. The government, however, may claim that a lawyer aided and abetted a client's violation under Section 17(a) (general fraud provision).

(b) Under 1934 Act

After *Central Bank*, *private* actions are *not* permitted against an aider and abettor, although the *S.E.C. can* proceed against such persons.

d. Injunctions

The S.E.C. has traditionally punished lawyers with injunctions. For Rule 10b–5 actions, the S.E.C. must show that a lawyer *knowingly* violated securities laws; under many other provisions, only negligence need be shown.

e. Professional Responsibility Under SOXA

SOXA mandates "*up-the-ladder*" reporting of a *material violation* of securities law, *breach of fiduciary duty*, or similar violations by an issuer or its agents. Thus, a lawyer is required to report violations to the issuer's chief legal officer. If that person does not *appropriately respond*, then the lawyer must report "higher up" to the audit committee or other committee. Lawyers may, in the future, be subject to a noisy withdrawal requirement. SOXA provides explicit authority for S.E.C. discipline of attorneys practicing before it.

G. THE PRIVATE SECURITIES LITIGATION REFORM ACT OF 1995

In addition to its safe harbor for forward-looking statements, the PSLRA made several other important changes to the securities laws, mainly regarding the conduct of litigation by private parties:

1. Stay of Discovery

A stay of discovery is entered when the defendant files a motion to dismiss, thus eliminating unnecessary costs that often forced issuers to settle. However, discovery will not be stayed when the plaintiff would suffer undue prejudice from the stay or when loss of evidence may result.

2. Damages Capped

Damages in 1934 Act actions are limited to the difference between the price paid (or in a sale, the price received) and the average trading price of the security during the 90-day period beginning on the day corrective information is disseminated to the public.

3. Contribution and Proportionate Liability

To reduce "deepest pocket" lawsuits, joint and several liability has been sharply limited.

4. Settlement Terms

Plaintiff's counsel must provide extensive disclosure of settlement terms, and her fees are limited.

5. Mandatory Sanctions

Federal Rule of Civil Procedure 11 sanctions are mandatory.

6. The Securities Litigation Uniform Standards Act of 1998

Because of the more difficult federal requirements, the 1995 Act resulted in the movement of class actions to state courts. In response, Congress passed this 1998 Act, which preempts state law class actions that allege misrepresentation or omission of a material fact, or the use of a manipulative or deceptive device, in connection with the purchase or sale of a security. In effect, *blue sky fraud litigation is preempted* if it is a class action or involves consolidated actions of more than 50 plaintiffs.

I. CRIMINAL ENFORCEMENT AND RICO

In addition to fraud and insider trading, criminal prosecutions include *willful violations of any provision* of the 1933 and 1934 Acts, with the possibility of imprisonment. Criminal enforcement is authorized under mail and wire fraud statutes, RICO, and SOXA, the latter of which created several new crimes and enhanced penalties.

1. Commencing a Criminal Action

The S.E.C. cannot commence a criminal action, but it can recommend prosecution to the Justice Department. The S.E.C. frequently cooperates in Justice Department proceedings.

2. Standard of Culpability

a. Under 1933 Act

Willful violations of the 1933 Act are criminal. "Willful" means having the intent to do the act charged together with knowledge that the act is wrongful. In a fraud case, scienter is required and "willfulness" includes the intent to deceive, but not necessarily the intent to violate the securities laws.

b. Under 1934 Act

The 1934 Act includes two culpability standards: "willfulness," as defined above, and for false statements made in filings, "willful and knowing."

(1) "Lack of Knowledge" Defense

The 1934 Act provides that a defendant who proves that he did not know of the rule or regulation violated cannot be sentenced to prison.

c. SOXA-Defined Crimes

Crimes defined by SOXA have varying standards of culpability. The meaning of the words "knowing" and "willful" are unclear under SOXA, but it is unlikely they mean the same things as in the 1933 and 1934 Acts.

(1) Crimes Committed "Knowingly"

Such offenses include *tampering* with or *destruction of documents* and *defrauding shareholders of public companies*.

(2) **Crimes Committed "Knowingly and Willfully"**

Knowingly and willfully failing to maintain records (for five years) and workpapers may result in a fine and imprisonment for up to 10 years. A *knowing false certification* of financial statements may result in a fine of up to $1 million and a 10-year prison term; the penalties for a *knowing and willful certification* are increased to up to a $5 million fine and a 20-year prison term.

(3) **Crimes Committed Corruptly**

SOXA broadens the "tampering" crime to include corrupt actual or attempted alteration, destruction, or concealment of a record (or other object) to impair its availability in an official proceeding, or other actual or attempted obstruction of, or influence on, an official proceeding. A fine and up to 20 years' imprisonment may be imposed.

d. **Statute of Limitations**

The statute of limitations for S.E.C. actions is five years.

3. **Mail Fraud and Wire Fraud**

A criminal case for mail fraud or wire fraud requires proof of a *scheme to defraud, specific intent to defraud,* and *the mailing* of a letter or sending of a wire in furtherance of the scheme. SOXA increased prison sentences for such frauds from five years to 20 years.

IV. REGULATION OF THE SECURITIES MARKETS

A. REGULATION OF THE NATIONAL SECURITIES EXCHANGES

1. Introduction

In regulating the interstate trading of securities subsequent to their original distribution, the SEA also regulates the national securities exchanges.

a. **Listing Securities for Trading**

To trade its securities on a national exchange, the issuer must "list" the security with the exchange. Once listed, the security must also be *registered* with the S.E.C. under SEA Section 12.

b. **Exchange Membership**

Each national exchange sells memberships to securities firms and/or individuals in the securities business. Members have the privilege of executing transactions over the exchange.

c. **Dissemination of Price Information**

Each exchange has an information system for disseminating price information to market participants. This information is sold and is an important source of revenue for the exchanges.

d. **Exchange Functions**

Exchange rules establish various *broker and dealer functions* to make exchanges effective marketplaces for the purchase and sale of securities.

2. Competition of Markets for Trading of Securities

a. **Competing Markets**

Many markets compete for the trading of securities:

(i) National and regional exchanges;

(ii) Over-the-counter markets; and

(iii) Institutional trading.

b. National Market System

With the development of sophisticated communications technology, a national securities market (combining all of the above markets) is now possible. Congress has directed the S.E.C. to use its authority to develop such a system.

3. Self-Regulation of Exchanges v. S.E.C. Supervision

a. Registration with the S.E.C.

Absent an exemption, a broker-dealer is prohibited from trading on an exchange not registered with the S.E.C.

b. Self-Regulation with S.E.C. Supervision

The exchanges may adopt rules for their own regulation, but the S.E.C. has power to review such rules and to propose others. The SEA also gives the S.E.C. extensive power to impose sanctions on exchanges, their members, and associates for violations of the federal securities laws.

B. REGULATION OF THE OVER-THE-COUNTER MARKET

1. In General

Securities traded outside the exchanges are traded "over-the-counter" ("OTC") and are subject to regulation under the SEA.

2. Role of Securities Firms

Securities firms act as brokers (*i.e.*, as agents for the buyer and/or seller) in the OTC market, and as dealers (*i.e.*, as principals owning the security and acting as either a buyer or seller in the transaction).

3. Regulation of Broker-Dealers

The SEA requires all broker-dealers who transact a securities business in interstate commerce to register with the S.E.C. (This includes virtually all broker-dealers.) In addition, broker-dealers must be members of FINRA.

a. Dealer Markups

FINRA regulates the profit dealers can make on transactions involving OTC securities. Excessive profit subjects a dealer to FINRA sanctions, S.E.C. sanctions, and private actions based on Rule 10b–5.

4. Regulation of the "Penny Stock" Market

The Securities Enforcement Remedies and Penny Stock Reform Act gives the S.E.C. power to regulate "penny stock" (*i.e.,* stocks worth less than $5 per share) transactions.

C. REGULATION OF MARKET MANIPULATION AND STABILIZATION

1. Regulation of Short Sales

The S.E.C. has authority to forbid short sales. A short sale is a sale of securities that a seller does not own or any sale consummated by the delivery of a security borrowed by or for the seller. Such sales are advantageous when an investor thinks the price of a security will drop.

a. Dangers of Short Sales

Short sales increase the volatility of market prices because it can be cheap to sell short a large quantity of an issuer's shares which can trigger other sales due to rumors. They also expose the seller to uncertain risk in that every time the price of the security goes up, it will cost the short seller more to cover the contract.

b. Short Sales Must be Identified

The S.E.C. requires all sales of exchange-traded securities to be identified as "short" or "long."

c. Short Sales Prohibited After a Circuit Breaker Triggered

Short sales are not permitted to be made if a circuit breaker has been triggered.

2. Prohibition of Market Manipulation

Market manipulation is an attempt to set stock prices or other important criteria of stock market performance by entering into transactions for the specific purpose of such manipulation.

a. Manipulation of Listed Securities

Section 9 of the 1934 Act *prohibits* use of the means of interstate commerce or of any national exchange to engage in specified manipulative activities regarding securities listed on a national exchange.

(1) Per Se Violations

Violations listed in Section 9 include attempting to create a misleading appearance of active trading and disseminating misleading information with respect to a security.

(2) Violation of S.E.C. Rules

The S.E.C. may also adopt rules pursuant to Section 9 for regulation of market manipulation.

(3) Limited Use of Section 9

Section 9 is used infrequently because it applies *only to listed securities* and because a cause of action must be based on defendant's *intentionally* fraudulent conduct if brought by the S.E.C. and *"willfulness"* if brought by a private plaintiff.

b. General Prohibition—Rule 10b–5

Rule 10b–5 may also be applied to prevent market manipulation. The courts have held that all of the specific prohibitions of Section 9 are incorporated under Rule 10b–5.

c. Liability Provisions Applicable to Broker-Dealers—Section 15(c)

Section 15(c) of the 1934 Act is a general fraud provision, specifically applicable to transactions involving broker-dealers in the over-the-counter market.

(1) S.E.C. Application

The S.E.C. has adopted rules pursuant to Section 15(c) prohibiting certain manipulative and deceptive practices. The S.E.C. may bring disciplinary actions for violations of these rules. Note that Section 15(c) contains *no* willfulness element, as does Section 9.

3. Regulation of Market Stabilization

Market stabilization is a particular form of market manipulation.

a. **"Stabilization" Defined**

"Stabilization" is an attempt to set a fixed minimum price for a security in the market by purchasing all the shares that are offered at a lower price than that desired.

b. **Regulation of Stabilizations in Public Distributions**

The SEA prohibits transactions aimed at pegging or stabilizing the price of a security *only* when such transactions violate rules and regulations adopted by the S.E.C. Rule 104 of Regulation M is used by the S.E.C. to regulate stabilization and, unlike most of Regulation M, *Rule 104 is a safe harbor* provision.

4. **The "Hot Issue" Problem**

a. **"Hot issue" Defined**

A "hot issue" is a security offered through a public distribution for which there is tremendous demand. There will usually be more offers to purchase than there are available shares.

b. **Hot Issue Problems**

Normally, a hot issue will immediately rise to a premium price over the initial offering price, and underwriters and dealers may attempt to profit from this to the detriment of the public (*e.g.*, by holding back a portion of the initial issue to be sold later, at a higher price).

c. **Violation of the Securities Acts**

Any such manipulative practices are a violation of the securities acts.

D. **REGULATION OF SECURITIES ANALYSTS**

1. **Analysts and Regulation AC**

In reaction to the analyst scandal of 2001–2002 (*e.g.*, analysts were recommending securities to the public even though they privately believed the securities were not a good investment), SOXA authorizes either the S.E.C. or the S.R.O.s to adopt rules for regulating analysts and research reports. In response, the S.E.C. adopted Regulation AC ("Analyst Certification") which, among other things, requires the following.

a. *Certification of written statements that accurately reflect the analyst's personal views;*

b. *A statement attesting that the analyst's compensation is not related to specific recommendations or views in the research report and other related disclosures; and*

c. *Certifications regarding public appearances.*

2. **Additional SOXA Requirements**

Because Regulation AC does not completely fulfill the rules for regulation required in Section 501 of SOXA, more rulemaking is likely.

E. **REGULATION OF BROKER-DEALER TRADING ACTIVITIES**

1. **Registration of Broker-Dealers with the S.E.C.**

Under the 1934 Act, all brokers and dealers who engage in securities transactions in interstate commerce *must register* with the S.E.C. They are regulated by both the S.E.C. and FINRA. If members of a national exchange, they are subject to the exchange's rules.

2. **Regulation Under General Antifraud Provisions**

General antifraud provisions in the SEA and SA may be used to regulate activities of broker-dealers. [SEA Rules 10b–5, 15c1–2; SA § 17(a)]

a. **Requirement of Intent**

Plaintiff generally must show that defendant broker-dealer acted with scienter.

3. **Regulating Conflicts of Interest**

a. **Dealer Markups**

Broker-dealers are limited as to the markup of prices.

(1) **FINRA Policy**

Dealer markups in price must be reasonably related to the *current market price* of the security. A 5% markup is probably not a violation of FINRA rules, but all of the facts are looked at in determining what is reasonable. Commissions must also be reasonable.

(2) **S.E.C. Policy**

The S.E.C. has no specific rules as to markups and commissions, but it has regulated markups via the general antifraud provisions of the 1934 Act. The S.E.C. considers a markup of *more than 10% to be fraud per se*.

4. **Regulation Best Interest**

Regulation Best Interest imposes enhanced obligations that apply when a broker-dealer makes recommendations to retail customers. The broker-dealer must made recommendations in the best interest of the retail investor and must take specific steps to prevent conflicts of interest.

V. APPLICATION OF THE FEDERAL SECURITIES LAWS TO MULTINATIONAL TRANSACTIONS

A. REGISTRATION UNDER THE 1933 ACT

The 1933 Act applies whenever United States facilities of interstate commerce are used to effect a securities transaction, and under the 1933 Act, "interstate commerce" includes commerce between any foreign country and the United States.

1. **Territoriality as Basis for Application of 1933 Act**

Offerings taking place within the United States must comply with the 1933 Act. Offerings outside the United States need not comply.

B. APPLICATION OF THE 1934 ACT

The 1934 Act also defines "interstate commerce" to include commerce between any foreign country and the United States.

1. **Regulation Under the 1934 Act**

The registration requirements of the 1934 Act do not distinguish between foreign and domestic registrants. Thus, a foreign issuer must register if it has securities on a U.S. exchange or trades over-the-counter and has more than $10 million in assets and a sufficient number of shareholders (2,000 or 500 non-accredited).

2. **International Securities Fraud**

Under *Morrison*, Rule 10b–5 prohibits securities fraud "only in connection with the purchase or sale of security listed on an American stock exchange, and the purchase or sale of any other security in the United States. The Dodd-Frank Act amended the 1934 Act jurisdictional section to grant federal courts jurisdiction to hear securities fraud cases, brought by the S.E.C. or the D.O.J., based on a more lenient "significant steps" or "substantial effect" test.

VI. REGULATION OF SECURITIES TRANSACTIONS BY THE STATES

A. UNIFORM SECURITIES ACT

1. Structure of Act

The Commissioners on Uniform State Laws have adopted a Uniform Securities Act, divided into sections on (i) fraud, (ii) broker-dealer registration, (iii) registration for new securities offerings, and (iv) remedy provisions. However, (ii) and (iii) have been largely preempted by the National Securities Markets Improvement Act ("1996 Act"), and (i) has been partially preempted by the Securities Litigation Uniform Standards Act (the "1998 Act").

2. Adoption by the States

In drafting their own securities laws, most states have adopted some part of the Uniform Securities Act, as well as some provisions of their own choosing and some parts of the federal acts. In cases not preempted by federal law, nearly all states regulate the original distribution of securities and the subsequent trading thereof (including the registration of broker-dealers).

B. PREEMPTION OF STATE SECURITIES LAWS

1. Introduction

Section 18 of the 1933 Act effectively preempts most state securities laws (so-called blue sky laws). The 1998 Act preempts state-law securities fraud class actions.

2. Structure

Section 18 covers four broad classes of securities, prohibiting states from requiring registration or qualification of any of the covered securities. States are also barred from imposing any conditions on the use of offering documents prepared by the issuer, or on disclosure documents, that must be filed with the S.E.C.

3. Four Classes of Covered Securities

The four classes exempted from blue sky regulation are:

a. *Securities of issuers registered under the Investment Company Act of 1940*;

b. *Listed securities*;

c. *Offers or sales to "qualified purchasers"*; and

d. *Certain offers and sales exempt under the 1933 Act* (*e.g.*, brokers' transactions and transactions by any person other than an issuer, underwriter, or dealer when the issuer is a 1934 Act reporting company).

4. Left to the States

States still have authority to:

a. *Regulate penny stocks*;

b. *Regulate many small, intrastate, and other offerings* exempt from federal regulation under the 1933 Act;

c. *Bring actions against brokers for fraud* and other illegal conduct; and

d. *Require notice filings* and payment of fees therefor.

5. State-Law Class Actions

The Securities Litigation Uniform Standards Act ("SLUSA") *preempts* any class action based on state law if the action alleges misrepresentation or omission of a material fact, or the use of a manipulative or deceptive device, in connection with the purchase or sale of a security, *i.e.*, state law fraud litigation is preempted if it is a class action or involves a *consolidated action of more than 50 plaintiffs. Individual lawsuits and derivative actions* are *not* preempted.

a. Applies Only to Covered Securities

The 1998 Act applies only to lawsuits alleging fraud with respect to a covered security as defined in Section 18 of the 1933 Act.

C. SECONDARY DISTRIBUTION OF SECURITIES

Many states have statutory provisions regulating the trading of securities subsequent to their original distribution.

1. *General fraud provisions* have been adopted in nearly every state;
2. *Registration of broker-dealers* is required in many states;
3. *Other regulatory provisions,* such as provisions regulating *tender offers* made for companies domiciled within their borders, have also been adopted in many states. These tender offer rules may be held to be unconstitutional under the Commerce Clause (if they impose an *undue burden on interstate commerce*), or if they conflict with the Supremacy Clause.

Gilbert Exam Strategies

Law school courses in Securities Regulation generally focus on two federal statutes: the Securities Act of 1933 and the Securities Exchange Act of 1934. These laws regulate: (i) the original issuance and subsequent trading of securities; (ii) the markets in which securities are traded; and (iii) the parties that do the trading.

You should use the following general approach to identify the relevant issues in exam questions. (Refer also to the Key Exam Issues at the beginning of each chapter.)

A. THE SECURITIES ACT OF 1933

1. Coverage of the Act

The 1933 Act applies to the original distribution and, in limited circumstances, the secondary distribution of securities. Thus, the first question when a fact situation involves the distribution of securities is whether there is a "*distribution of securities*" covered by the 1933 Act.

a. Original Distributions

An "original distribution" is an offering by the issuer to the public of securities that have never been sold before.

b. Secondary Distributions

A "secondary distribution" has two important aspects:

(1) Offering by Shareholder(s)

A secondary distribution is an offering to the public of the issuer's securities, but by one or more *shareholders* of the issuer, rather than by the issuer itself.

(2) Shareholders Standing in for Issuer

In a secondary distribution, shareholders are standing in for the issuer; they are not merely persons who purchased the securities as a routine investment, but rather are either:

(i) "Control persons" of the issuer (*i.e.,* those who can influence the issuer); and/or

(ii) Persons who purchased the securities in a nonpublic transaction or series of transactions.

Note: A single group of selling shareholders in a secondary distribution may include persons within one or the other, or both, of the above categories.

c. Definition of "Security"

The 1933 Act applies only to the distribution of securities, but the universe of possible investments is much larger. In other words, not every investment offered to the public is a security. In general, therefore, it is a good idea to verify that the exam question involves a security; if it does not, the Act does not apply.

2. Factors to Consider in Covered Distributions

If a fact situation involves an original or secondary distribution, consider the following:

a. Jurisdiction

Are the facilities or means of interstate commerce involved in the offering?

b. Exemptions from Registration

If at all possible, the offeror (issuer or selling shareholder) will try to avoid by some exemption the time and expense of registering with the S.E.C.:

c. Registration

If the offering is *not* exempt, it must be registered, and the following issues may arise:

(1) Timing Requirements

Have the issuer and the other parties involved in the registered offering complied with the requirements of:

(a) The pre-filing period?

(b) The waiting period?

(c) The post-effective period?

(2) Disclosure

Did the registration statement disclose all required material facts concerning the issuer and its business?

(3) Processing Issues

Are there issues regarding the processing of the registration statement with the S.E.C.?

d. Liability Under the 1933 Act

Finally, there may be issues involving the liability provisions of the 1933 Act that apply to failure to register a nonexempt offering, and to misstatements or omissions of material facts in a covered securities offering.

B. THE SECURITIES EXCHANGE ACT OF 1934

1. Coverage of the Act

The 1934 Act generally covers the *trading of securities* in the market after the original or secondary distribution.

2. Registered Securities

The 1934 Act requires issuers to register securities meeting certain criteria.

a. Listed Securities

Are the securities (equity or debt) traded on a national securities exchange? If so, they must be registered under the 1934 Act.

b. OTC Securities

Does the issuer have more than $10 million in assets? If so, the issuer must register under the 1934 Act each class of equity security that is held of record by either 2,000 persons or 500 non-accredited investors.

3. Reporting Companies

All issuers with securities registered under the 1934 Act must file periodic reports with the S.E.C. Such issuers are often referred to as "reporting companies." The filed reports are public, and may be inspected and copied at the S.E.C.'s offices in Washington, D.C. These reports are of several kinds:

a. Annual reports on Form 10-K (or Form 10-KSB, for small business issuers);

b. Quarterly reports on Form 10-Q (or Form 10-QSB, for small business issuers);

c. Current reports on Form 8-K (triggered by the occurrence of significant events);

d. Proxy statements (which must be sent directly to shareholders as well as filed with the S.E.C.), prior to each shareholders' meeting at which directors are to be elected; and

e. Annual reports to shareholders, which must accompany or precede each proxy statement.

4. Jurisdiction

Because most provisions of the 1934 Act apply only if *interstate commerce* is involved, has this jurisdictional requirement been met?

5. Regulation of Broker-Dealers

Does the transaction involve a broker-dealer? If so, has there been a violation of the FINRA or S.E.C. rules relating to the conduct of broker-dealers?

6. Market Manipulation and Stabilization

Did any party attempt artificially to fix or determine the market price or volume of trading in a security? Or did any party unlawfully attempt to "stabilize" the market price for a security?

7. Tender Offers and Repurchases of Stock

Has there been an attempt to purchase shares of a company directly from the shareholders? If so, was this a "tender offer" subject to the 1934 Act? Were all of the rules applicable to tender offers met?

8. Short-Swing Trading

Has there been trading in an equity security by corporate "insiders" within a six-month period? If so, Section 16 may apply.

9. Proxy Solicitation

Have proxies been solicited from shareholders? If so, the rules and regulations applicable to proxy solicitations may apply.

10. Rule 10b–5

In *every* securities transaction, consider whether Rule 10b–5 is applicable. This general fraud provision is very broad and may apply whenever there is some nexus of fraud with a securities transaction.

C. LIABILITY OF "COLLATERAL PARTICIPANTS"

1. Who Is a "Collateral Participant"

Consider whether any "collateral participants" might be liable for a violation of the securities laws. "Collateral participants" are those who are involved in, but not directly responsible for, the transaction (*e.g.,* lawyers, accountants, underwriters, etc.).

2. Liability Under the 1933 Act

Although the "collateral participant" is not directly responsible for the securities transaction, has she "participated" to such a degree that she may be held liable? Could she be held liable as a "control person"?

3. Liability Under the 1934 Act

Could the person be held liable as a "control person" or co-conspirator under Rule 10b–5 or under one of the other general liability provisions of the 1934 Act?

D. STATE LAW

Finally, consider whether the *statutory or common law* of one or more states might apply to regulate either an original distribution or the subsequent trading of securities.

Securities Regulation

Eighth Edition

Chapter One

Introduction to Federal Securities Regulation

CONTENTS	PAGE

Key Exam Issues 2

A. Why Regulate Securities 2

B. How to Regulate Securities 4

C. The Securities Industry Generally 4

D. The Securities and Exchange Commission 9

E. Securities Acts Administered by the S.E.C.—an Overview 10

F. Jurisdiction and Interstate Commerce 14

G. Self-Regulatory Organizations 15

Key Exam Issues

The public has a strong interest in the regulation of securities and securities markets, both because securities are an important form of private property affecting the financial well-being of a large segment of the population, and because the condition of the securities markets has a major impact on the flow of capital to industry and therefore on the economy as a whole.

This chapter provides an introduction to Securities Regulation, giving you a broad overview of the securities industry, the federal securities acts, and the Securities and Exchange Commission. Although most of the information in this chapter is important only for a general understanding of this area of law, you may find a question on your exam asking you to determine whether interstate commerce is involved and thus whether the federal securities laws apply to the particular transaction.

A. Why Regulate Securities

1. Introduction

Although commentators are not all in agreement about why the securities markets should be regulated (or even whether they should be), a number of grounds for regulation are consistently advanced in academic writing on the subject. These are discussed below.

2. Investor Protection

Unlike commodities markets, which sell products that are classified and graded for quality and marketability, the securities markets (and especially the markets for ***equity*** securities, *i.e.*, stocks and the like) sell intangible interests in enterprises, the important aspects of which are not subject to ready verification by the great majority of investors. Earnings, competition, fixed and contingent liabilities—all are important to the price of a security, yet the typical investor has no means by which to determine them. Without this information, presented in a somewhat standardized form to facilitate comparison among enterprises, many investors would be unwilling to risk investing. Other investors, absent accurate information about the enterprise, might overpay for a security. Private entities (*e.g.*, securities markets) could impose information disclosure requirements without government regulation. Likewise, investors with sufficient bargaining power might demand certain disclosures before being willing to invest in an enterprise. However, the existence of numerous markets for securities would make consistent disclosure standards difficult to achieve, and many investors would lack the power to demand disclosures. Therefore, government regulation is arguably the most efficient way to specify the format and content of disclosure for investors.

3. Reduction of Systemic Risk

The public interest in an efficient, fraud-free securities marketplace includes not only an interest in protecting securities investors themselves from fraud, but also an interest in protecting the health of the national economy from the consequences of any flight from the securities markets by investors. It is no coincidence that the first federal securities regulation statutes were passed shortly after the great market crash of 1929, which not only impoverished many investors at the time, but also helped to cause the Great Depression of the 1930s. The lack of confidence in the markets prevailing in the years after 1929, in the view of many, also prolonged the Depression by making it extremely difficult for even worthy enterprises to raise capital.

4. Economic Efficiency

By ensuring broad disclosure of economically significant information about an enterprise, the securities laws foster economic efficiency in the markets. "Efficiency" in this context means, essentially, "accuracy" with respect to prices; an efficient market, in this sense, is one in which prices reflect all available information about the item traded. Price efficiency furthers allocative efficiency. In other words, if prices are accurate, capital will flow to the most lucrative projects.

Not everyone agrees that current regulation results in valuable efficiency, however. Some of the more common criticisms of this basis for regulation include:

a. Trading Is Speculative

Some argue that much, if not most, of the trading that takes place in the securities markets is speculative; *i.e.*, driven by the belief that someone else will pay more than one has just paid for a security, simply because the price is going up, rather than because of any consideration of intrinsic value. If this view is accurate, extensive regulation would contribute little of value to the markets, but rather would represent a substantial waste of money, with the cost of regulatory compliance adding to the transaction costs borne by investors.

b. Disclosure Violates Enterprise's Interest in Confidentiality

Others, while in principle tolerating efficiency as a legitimate goal of regulation, are concerned that in many cases disclosure of the kind required by the securities laws gives competitors of the disclosing enterprise information to which they are not entitled.

c. Efficiency v. Investor Protection

Finally, there are some who endorse the idea of efficiency, but resist the investor protection goals of regulation, at least insofar as such goals result in, for example, causes of action for securities fraud. From this perspective, giving investors such potent weapons to use against enterprises invariably results in the enterprises becoming less and less willing to provide information about themselves, ultimately reducing the efficiency of the regulated market.

5. Disclosure Should Focus on Reducing Agency Costs

Still others suggest that regulation, while important, should be principally concerned with permitting the owners of the enterprise (*i.e.*, the shareholders) to gain greater control over the enterprise's managers (*i.e.*, the officers and directors). These commentators, while endorsing the idea of regulation in a broad sense, suggest that a proper focus on reducing the shareholders' cost of monitoring managers would produce a regulatory regime significantly different from that prevalent today.

6. Alternatives to Securities Markets May Be Preferable

Finally, it is at least theoretically possible that some alternative means of providing access to capital is superior to a market-based system. For example, European industry tends to rely more on banks than does American industry. However, both cultural and economic factors make it unlikely that the United States capital markets will become bank-centered any time in the near future.

B. How to Regulate Securities

1. Merit Regulation v. Disclosure Regulation

A fundamental question is how to regulate securities. One option is merit regulation, whereby the regulator ensures that only meritorious (*e.g.*, fair, just, and equitable) securities are offered to investors. Another option is disclosure regulation, whereby the regulator mandates certain disclosures to investors, and—as long as those disclosures are complete and accurate—allows investors to decide whether to invest.

2. Federal and State Regulation

Federal securities regulation is premised on disclosure rather than merit. State securities regulation varies, with some states incorporating aspects of merit regulation.

C. The Securities Industry Generally

1. Private Investment and the Venture Capital Market

Before a company is ready to sell its securities to the public, it will seek investment from private sources, such as wealthy individuals ("angels"), other companies that might have an interest in the start-up company's products or services (strategic investors), or investment funds (regulated mutual funds or the largely unregulated "hedge funds") specifically set up to make such investments. The principal reason for this is that firms in their very early stages are untested and, therefore, are very difficult to value. Before selling securities to the public, more information about the company's value is usually needed. Private investors have more time to devote to assessing the value of such companies and, therefore, are in a better position to make such investments, generally with the hope that the company will become profitable and will eventually go public, with the early-stage investors cashing out and reaping a profit on their investment.

2. Securities Markets

Securities markets are the systems through which securities are bought and sold. The two basic types of securities markets are primary markets and secondary markets. Primary markets are the markets for the original distribution of securities; secondary markets are for the continuous trading of outstanding securities.

a. Primary Markets

Primary markets are the facilities through which the securities are ***first*** issued or distributed to the public. For example, if XYZ Corp. is formed and issues some of its common stock to the public, this issuance occurs in the primary market.

b. Secondary Markets

Secondary markets are markets that exist for the ongoing trading of securities ***after*** their original distribution. Securities already distributed may be bought and sold in one of two ways: through a stock exchange, or with the help of a securities firm in the "over-the-counter" ("OTC") market.

(1) Stock Exchanges

The securities of most large corporations are traded over stock exchanges (the most important of which are the New York Stock Exchange ["NYSE"] and the Nasdaq Stock Market ["Nasdaq"]).

(a) Stock Exchange "Listing"

To be traded on an exchange, securities must be "listed" (*i.e.*, registered and qualified) with that exchange.

(b) NYSE

The NYSE functions as an auction market, in which buyers' and sellers' orders "cross"—*i.e.*, orders to sell and orders to buy are matched. When there are more buy orders than sell orders, the price goes up, and vice versa. Market makers facilitate this matching.

(c) Nasdaq

Historically, Nasdaq functioned as an over-the-counter market. In 2006, however, the S.E.C. approved Nasdaq's application to be a registered national securities exchange.

(2) Over-the-Counter Trading

Securities traded outside the stock exchanges are said to be traded "over the counter." There is no physical location or exchange facility for the over-the-counter market. Instead, securities firms in many locations are linked through various communication systems (such as computer networks) used to match buyers and sellers.

(a) OTC Market Is a Dealer Market

In the OTC market, every transaction is with a dealer, and this market is therefore referred to as a "dealer market." That is, if an investor wants to buy a security, the investor contacts her dealer, who then seeks the lowest price from the dealers acting as principals for that security in the OTC market.

(b) "Spreads" in the Dealer Market

One drawback of dealer markets is the possibility of collusion among dealers to keep the difference between the prices at which they buy (the "bid" price) and those at which they sell (the "asked" price) artificially high. If all dealers were to collude to maintain a bid/asked "spread" of $1 per share, for example, the cost to customers of purchasing and selling shares would be high and dealers would pocket additional profits.

3. Securities Firms—Brokers and Dealers

Besides regulating securities markets, the federal securities laws also regulate the activities of firms engaged in trading securities. These firms function both as "brokers" and as "dealers." The definitions of "broker" and "dealer" given below are general, functional definitions. The securities acts also define the terms in several places where they are relevant to specific regulatory purposes. The definitions in the acts may or may not coincide with the general, functional definitions given here.

a. "Brokers"

Brokers are generally defined as agents who buy and sell securities for their customers on a commission basis. For example, assume A wishes to buy 100 shares of XYZ Corp. If B buys the shares for A at $10 per share and charges A a 5% commission, B has acted as a broker.

b. "Dealers"

Dealers, on the other hand, act as principals—buying the securities for their ***own account*** and subsequently reselling them to their customers at a marked-up price. Thus, in the above example, instead of charging A a 5% commission, B could have purchased the XYZ stock for $10 and resold it to A for $12 per share.

c. Dual Functions Common

Note that the same person or firm can be a "broker" in one transaction and a "dealer" in another transaction. Most firms in the securities business function in both capacities, and hence are referred to as "broker-dealers." Note that broker-dealers employ a variety of personnel, including salespeople, clerks, traders, and supervisory personnel.

d. Different Functions on Exchanges and in the Over-the-Counter Market

When a customer executes a purchase or sale order over an exchange, the firm through which he deals acts as a broker for the customer. The broker typically executes the order through a market maker on the floor of the exchange.

When a customer executes a purchase or sale order in the over-the-counter market, the firm through which the customer deals may act either as a broker (buying or selling for the customer on a commission basis) or as a dealer (buying or selling for its own account and charging the customer a markup). Note that many securities firms operate both in the exchange markets and in the over-the-counter market.

4. Changing Role of Banks

Since 1933, the Glass-Steagall Act prohibited commercial banks from underwriting corporate securities. Similarly, the Bank Holding Company Act prohibited companies that control banks from engaging in activities other than banking. However, beginning in the 1980s, federal banking regulators (including the Federal Reserve Board, the Federal Deposit Insurance Corporation, and the Comptroller of the Currency) have permitted banks to engage in more and more securities-related activities. Finally, in 1999, Congress passed a financial modernization statute known as the Gramm-Leach-Bliley Act, which effectively repeals most of the Glass-Steagall Act and the Bank Holding Company Act. The result has been the growth of financial holding companies, which are legally permitted to engage in a wide variety of financial services, including banking, brokerage, and insurance.

5. Other Financial Markets

Increasingly, the operation and regulation of the United States securities markets is affected by other financial markets, both foreign and domestic.

a. Foreign Markets

Growth in foreign markets has led the S.E.C. to seek to coordinate requirements among regulators from the United States and other countries. In particular, United States regulators are concerned that if the United States markets are seen as over-regulated,

United States issuers might flee to foreign markets to raise capital, and foreign issuers might avoid the United States markets.

b. Domestic Markets

There are a multitude of financial instruments trading in markets, including especially "derivative instruments," such as interest rate swaps, futures on financial indices, and options on other financial instruments. Not all of these instruments are securities. But they nevertheless form an important part of the context in which the securities industry functions.

(1) The Money Market

The money market involves primarily "commercial paper," *i.e.*, short-term debt instruments issued by corporations.

(2) The Government Securities Market

Government securities include direct obligations of the United States and obligations of agencies of the United States government.

(3) The Municipal Securities Market

The market for municipal securities resembles in many respects that for government securities, except that there is a much greater risk of default by a municipality than by the United States.

(4) Derivative Products Market

The derivative products market includes a variety of financial products, the most important of which are discussed below.

(a) Traded Options

Options are contracts giving the buyer of the option the right to buy or sell an asset at a price determined in advance. The holder of an option is ***not obligated*** to exercise it. Traded options are options written on standardized terms and issued by the Options Clearing Corporation, a corporation jointly owned by the exchanges on which options are traded.

(b) Futures

Futures contracts create an *obligation* to sell or to buy an asset at a future date, at a price determined in advance. Futures on stock market indices—for instance, the Standard & Poor's 500 index—give one of the parties the right to receive a sum of cash based on the price of the securities in the index. The party who gets paid depends on whether the index has risen or fallen since the parties entered into the futures contract. Futures are regulated by the Commodities Futures Trading Commission ("C.F.T.C.").

(i) 1987 Market Crash

Most commentators attribute the October 19, 1987, stock market crash at least partly to futures trading. On that day, many investors sold stock while simultaneously purchasing index futures. The resulting flood of stock onto the market contributed to the decline of stock prices.

(c) Swaps

Swaps are agreements whereby two parties agree to make periodic payments to each other. A typical ***interest rate swap*** involves one side paying interest at a fixed rate, while the other side pays a floating rate (*e.g.*, the prime rate in effect on each payment date). In a typical ***currency swap,*** one side agrees to pay a dollar amount to the other, and the other makes its payment in a foreign currency (*e.g.*, Swiss francs). Regulatory authority over swaps is divided between the C.F.T.C. and the S.E.C.

(i) 2008 Financial Crisis

Unregulated *credit default swaps*, which were purchased by investors to protect against the risk of default of mortgage-backed securities, are widely attributed with exacerbating the 2008 financial crisis. The Dodd-Frank Wall Street Reform and Consumer Protection Act, enacted in 2010, reformed the regulation of swaps, dividing regulatory authority between the C.F.T.C. and the S.E.C.

(d) "Portfolio Insurance"

Portfolio insurance is not really insurance at all. The term refers to a variety of complex hedging strategies, often employing one or more of the financial instruments described immediately above. The aim of these strategies is to hedge (*i.e.*, to reduce the risk of severe loss in) an investor's securities portfolio.

6. Levels of Regulation

The securities markets are regulated at three levels, each of which is discussed in this Summary:

a. The Securities and Exchange Commission

The Securities and Exchange Commission ("S.E.C.") is a federal administrative agency, and it is discussed below.

b. Self-Regulatory Organizations

The regulatory aspects of self-regulatory organizations ("S.R.O.s") are discussed below.

c. State "Blue Sky" Regulation and Federal Preemption

Every state regulates the original distribution of securities within its borders, typically by means of a requirement that distributions be registered with the state. In addition, each state offers some variety of antifraud sanction applicable to transactions in securities. However, Section 18 of the 1934 Act preempts state registration with respect to securities meeting certain criteria, including securities listed on the NYSE.

7. Regulatory Issues

The proliferation of new financial instruments has produced conflict between the S.E.C. and the C.F.T.C., as each agency tries to assert jurisdiction over a new instrument. Which agency succeeds in a given case depends on whether the instrument in question is a security, an option on a security, or a futures contract. Many new instruments, however, fit into more than one of these categories.

D. The Securities and Exchange Commission

1. S.E.C. Mission

The S.E.C. has a tripartite mission: to protect investors; maintain fair, orderly, and efficient markets; and facilitate capital formation. These goals are sometimes in tension. For example, the S.E.C. could mandate more disclosure by securities issuers with the goals of protecting investors and promoting market efficiency, but the costs of those disclosures might inhibit capital formation.

2. S.E.C. Functions

The S.E.C. is the agency responsible for administering and enforcing the federal securities laws. The basic functions of the S.E.C. are:

a. Rulemaking

The S.E.C. adopts substantive rules to implement the federal securities laws. The S.E.C. has the authority to adopt such rules pursuant to a congressional delegation of authority in the federal securities acts.

b. Interpreting

The S.E.C. interprets the securities laws and S.E.C. rules issued thereunder. The Commission does this in two principal ways:

(1) General Policy Statements

Periodically, the S.E.C. will issue "releases" to the general public which state the views of the S.E.C. on matters of current concern.

(2) No-Action Letters

In addition, private parties (such as lawyers for corporate clients) may inquire of the S.E.C. as to whether a specific transaction may be carried out in a specific manner without violating the securities laws. If the staff agrees that the action as described will not violate the securities laws, its response is called a "no-action" letter, since the S.E.C. staff indicates that it will not recommend enforcement action to the Commission if the transaction is carried out in the manner specified. No-action letters do not bind the S.E.C. with respect to anyone other than the party seeking the letter; however, as a practical matter, parties sometimes rely on no-action letters issued to others when seeking to structure transactions that comply with the securities laws.

c. Investigating

The S.E.C. also investigates possible violations of the securities laws and rules.

d. Initiating Formal Proceedings

The S.E.C. initiates formal proceedings against a wrongdoer—*i.e.*, seeks statutory remedies and sanctions for violation of the securities laws. *Examples:*

(i) *Civil injunctions and civil fines* may be sought in the federal district courts;

(ii) *Criminal prosecutions* may be brought by the United States Department of Justice (generally, upon referral from the S.E.C.); and

(iii) *Administrative remedies* (*e.g.*, suspension of a securities firm from trading, or issuance of a cease and desist order) may be pursued by the S.E.C. in administrative proceedings.

Note: Private actions may be brought by private (*i.e.*, nongovernmental) plaintiffs when they have been injured by a violation of the securities laws and when the law provides for either an express or implied cause of action.

3. S.E.C. Administrative Procedures

All administrative proceedings brought by the S.E.C. are conducted in accordance with rules conforming to the Administrative Procedure Act ("A.P.A."). These rules are designed to meet the requirements of constitutional due process—*i.e.*, proper notice, confrontation and cross-examination of witnesses, etc. (See Administrative Law Summary.) Briefly, the procedures are as follows:

a. Hearing Before Administrative Law Judge

The first step in S.E.C. proceedings is a hearing conducted by an administrative law judge appointed by the S.E.C. This judge makes the initial decision in the matter.

b. Commission Review

Following the hearing, either or both of the parties may seek review of the administrative law judge's decision by the full Commission. Alternatively, the S.E.C. may decide to review the decision on its own motion.

c. Appeal to the Courts

Finally, an aggrieved party may seek review of the S.E.C.'s decision by a United States Court of Appeals and, if *certiorari* is granted, by the United Stated Supreme Court.

E. Securities Acts Administered by the S.E.C.—an Overview

COMPARISON OF THE 1933 AND 1934 ACTS GILBERT

	1933 ACT	1934 ACT
MAIN PURPOSE	To regulate the ***original issuance*** of securities and to ***prevent fraud and misrepresentation*** in interstate offerings.	To regulate the ***trading*** of securities that are already issued and outstanding, to require issuers to make ***ongoing disclosure*** similar to that initially made under the 1933 Act, and to ***prevent fraud and misrepresentation*** in the offer and sale of securities.

MAIN METHOD	Compel ***disclosure*** of certain material information.	Require ***registration*** and regular ***reporting*** of financial information of issuers, securities exchanges, brokers, dealers, and securities associations; prohibit ***securities fraud*** (including insider trading); regulate trading of securities.

1. Securities Act of 1933

The Securities Act of 1933 ("SA" or "1933 Act"; discussed in detail, *infra*) primarily regulates the *original issuance* of securities—*e.g.*, where XYZ Corp. desires to issue 100,000 shares of its common stock to the public for $10 per share.

a. Purpose of the Act

The primary purpose of the 1933 Act is to *compel disclosure of certain material information* in securities offerings. [SA §§ 5, 12(a)(1)] A secondary purpose is to *prevent fraud and misrepresentation* in the offer or sale of securities. [SA §§ 11, 12(a)(2), 17]

2. Securities Exchange Act of 1934

The Securities Exchange Act of 1934 ("SEA" or "1934 Act"; also discussed at length, *infra*) governs trading in securities that are already issued and outstanding. The 1934 Act has a much broader scope than the 1933 Act, and in addition to regulating a wide variety of securities transactions, it requires ongoing disclosure by issuers. The 1934 Act regulates:

a. Registration and Reporting

The 1934 Act requires a company to register its securities with the S.E.C. and thereafter to file periodic financial reports with the S.E.C. if the company's securities are (i) traded on a regulated national securities exchange *or* (ii) the company has assets of more than $10 million and a sufficient number of shareholders (either 2,000 or 500 non-accredited). Corporations subject to the registration and filing requirements are called "registered companies" or "reporting companies." [SEA §§ 12, 13]

b. Proxy Solicitation

The SEA also regulates the solicitation of voting proxies from the shareholders of registered companies. [SEA § 14]

c. Tender Offer Solicitations

The 1934 Act also regulates situations in which one company seeks to acquire control of another by a direct offer to purchase stock from shareholders of the target company. [SEA §§ 13, 14]

d. Insider Trading

Provisions of the SEA restrict and penalize trading in a registered company's shares by company "insiders" (*i.e.*, company officers or directors, or owners of 10% of the outstanding shares of a registered class of equity securities). [SEA § 16]

e. Market Surveillance

The Act likewise authorizes the S.E.C. to regulate certain securities market trading practices that are based on fraud or market manipulation. [SEA § 9]

f. **Registration of Securities Exchanges, Broker-Dealers, and Securities Associations**

National securities exchanges (such as the NYSE) and broker-dealers who conduct an interstate over-the-counter securities business must register with, and make periodic reports to, the S.E.C. [SEA §§ 6—regulation of national exchanges, 15—regulation of broker-dealers]

(1) **S.E.C. Regulation**

The 1934 Act authorizes the S.E.C. to make rules and regulations governing the activities of broker-dealers and the national exchanges. [SEA §§ 19(b)–(c) & 15]

(2) **Self-Regulation**

The 1934 Act also permits the exchanges to make their own self-policing rules. In addition, self-policing associations of broker-dealers may organize and register with the S.E.C. [SEA §§ 15, 15A & 19]

g. **Antifraud Provisions**

The 1934 Act also contains a number of provisions that impose liability for fraud in the purchase or sale of securities—the most important of which is contained in Section 10(b) and Rule 10b–5 of the 1934 Act.

3. Sarbanes-Oxley Act ("SOXA")

In 2002, Congress reacted to a wave of corporate scandals (including those involving Enron and WorldCom) by passing a wide-ranging set of amendments to the 1934 Act, collectively called the Sarbanes-Oxley Act of 2002 ("SOXA"). SOXA had one key objective: to improve the reliability of issuers' disclosures. To accomplish this goal, SOXA:

a. Regulates *accountants*;

b. Regulates *lawyers*;

c. Regulates *securities analysts*;

d. Broadens the scope of *"aiding and abetting" prohibitions* under the securities laws;

e. Requires *additional and enhanced corporate disclosure*;

f. Reforms certain *corporate governance procedures,* notably those involving the audit committee; and

g. Enhances certain *fines and penalties* for securities violations.

4. Dodd-Frank Wall Street Reform and Consumer Protection Act ("Dodd-Frank Act")

Congress responded to the 2008 financial crisis by enacting the Dodd-Frank Wall Street Reform and Consumer Protection Act of 2010. The Dodd-Frank Act, which includes 1,506 sections, attempts to respond to the various underlying causes of the financial crisis in order to prevent future crises. Among various other reforms, the Act:

a. Provides whistleblower protections;

b. Disqualifies so-called "bad actors" from certain types of exempt offerings; and

c. Increases accountability for executive compensation.

5. Other Federal Acts Administered by the S.E.C.

The S.E.C. administers certain other federal securities acts not normally covered in a law school course in Securities Regulation. Briefly, these are:

a. Public Utility Holding Company Act of 1935

This Act is designed to prevent abuses in the financing and operation of public utility holding companies.

b. Trust Indenture Act of 1939

This Act regulates large issues of debt securities (*i.e.*, in excess of $10 million in total value). This Act contains provisions designed to protect security holders, such as a requirement that the trust indenture covering the securities (*i.e.*, the documents stating the terms under which the securities are issued) meet certain standards insuring the independence and responsibility of the indenture trustee.

c. Investment Company Act of 1940

This Act governs the activities of publicly owned companies that invest and trade in securities (*e.g.*, mutual funds). It regulates the composition of management, the capital structure of the company, its investment policies, etc.

d. Investment Advisers Act of 1940

This Act provides for registration and regulation of those in the business of advising others on securities investments.

6. Other Federal Statutes

Although they are not administered by the S.E.C., the following federal statutes are also helpful to an understanding of the S.E.C.'s function and of the securities industry in general:

a. Bankruptcy Code

The Bankruptcy Code authorizes the S.E.C. to serve as an adviser to United States district courts in federal bankruptcy proceedings—involving reorganization of debtor corporations—where there is a "substantial public interest." In this capacity, the S.E.C. may be asked to advise the court on the selection of the trustee, on the appropriateness of the reorganization plans for the debtor corporation, and Other related matters.

b. Securities Investor Protection Act of 1970

This Act creates a nonprofit membership corporation to which most broker-dealers must belong. It is funded by assessments. If a securities firm fails and cannot pay its customer accounts, then (up to certain maximum amounts) this corporation makes up the difference.

7. Integrated Disclosure

As the above material makes clear, there are many disclosure requirements under the securities laws. With respect to the two main acts (Securities Act of 1933 and Securities Exchange Act of 1934), originally there were two separate and distinct disclosure systems established. This dual system spawned separate sets of registration statements (at the time of initial issuance) and periodic reports (ongoing as securities were traded), each with its own set of instructions. Eventually, the S.E.C. lightened the burden of compliance by integrating the reporting requirements of the two Acts. Regulation S–K now prescribes a single standard set of instructions for filing forms under the two Acts, so that when the same type of information is required by the various forms under these Acts, a single set of instructions applies. Also, revisions to several rules and forms resulted in a uniform set of financial disclosure requirements for all documents required to be filed under the 1933 or 1934 Acts. Finally, the S.E.C. adopted forms for registration of offerings under the 1933 Act, which in some cases permit incorporation by reference of information in 1934 Act reports.

F. Jurisdiction and Interstate Commerce

1. In General

The provisions of the federal securities laws are based on Congress's power to regulate interstate commerce. Therefore, these acts generally apply only where the facilities or instrumentalities of interstate commerce are involved.

2. "Interstate Commerce"

a. Definition Under 1933 Act

Under the 1933 Act, "interstate commerce" is defined as "trade or commerce in securities or any transportation or communication relating thereto among the several states." [SA § 2(a)(7)]

(1) Expansive Interpretation

The S.E.C. and the courts have adopted a broad interpretation of what constitutes "interstate commerce."

(a) Use of Means of Interstate Commerce

Under modern interpretations of the Art, interstate commerce is involved not only whenever a transaction touches more than one state, but also when the "means" of interstate commerce (*e.g.*, the telephone, mails, etc.) are used in any part of a securities transaction.

Example: Thus, even *intrastate* telephone calls or mailings have been held to support federal jurisdiction under the 1933 Act, since the *means* of interstate commerce were used.

b. Definition Under 1934 Act

Under the 1934 Act, the term "interstate commerce" includes trade, commerce, transportation or communication among the several states—plus *intrastate* use of any facility or instrumentality of interstate commerce, such as a national securities exchange or a telephone. [SEA § 3(a)(17)]

c. Effect—Nearly All Transactions Covered

As a result of the expansive interpretation of these definitions, very few securities transactions are exempt from the 1933 or 1934 Acts on the grounds they do not involve "interstate commerce."

G. Self-Regulatory Organizations

1. In General

Under the 1934 Act, regulation of the securities industry is accomplished not only by the government, acting through the S.E.C., but also by the industry itself, acting through self-regulatory organizations ("S.R.O.s") charged with oversight responsibility. The S.E.C., however, retains the power to overrule the S.R.O.s, if necessary, and to change the rules under which the S.R.O.s operate. [*See* SEA § 19(c)] A discussion of the three most important S.R.O.s follows.

a. Stock Exchanges

Stock exchanges are probably the best-known examples of S.R.O.s. Under SEA Section 5, all stock exchanges must register as "national securities exchanges." And under SEA Section 6, the S.E.C. cannot register a stock exchange unless certain conditions are met, including that the rules of the exchange "are designed to prevent fraudulent and manipulative acts and practices, . . . and, in general, to protect investors and the public interest." [SEA § 6(b)(5)]

b. Financial Industry Regulatory Authority

SEA Section 15A permits the S.E.C. to register "an association of brokers and dealers" as a national securities association. The Financial Industry Regulatory Authority ("FINRA") is the only such association registered under Section 15A, and it is an S.R.O. much like the stock exchanges. The requirements for registration under Section 15A are similar to those under Section 6, discussed above, including similar requirements to protect the public and prevent fraud. [SEA § 15A(b)(6)]

(1) Broker-Dealers May Not Conduct Business Unless They Are FINRA Members

The 1934 Act requires broker-dealers to belong either to a national securities association (see above) or to conduct business solely on a national securities exchange of which the broker-dealer is a member. [SEA § 15(b)(8)] In practice, every broker-dealer is a FINRA member, because not to belong sharply limits the nature of the business in which the entity can engage.

c. Public Company Accounting Oversight Board

All accounting firms that audit public companies must register with the Public Company Accounting Oversight Board (the "PCAOB"). The PCAOB is also responsible for:

(i) *Maintaining quality control for public company audits,* including questions of ethics, independence, and other standards;

(ii) *Investigating and disciplining infractions* of its rules;

(iii) *Ensuring compliance with the securities laws and professional standards* regarding public company audits; and

(iv) *Conducting periodic inspections of the accounting firms* it registers:

i. Annually, in the case of accounting firms that regularly audit more than 100 public companies; and

ii. At least every three years for other accounting firms.

[SOXA §§ 103–105]

Chapter Two

Regulating the Original Distribution of Securities—the Securities Act of 1933

CONTENTS	PAGE

Key Exam Issues 19

A. Introduction 20

B. 1933 Act Section 5—Offers and Sales 23

C. Persons Covered by the 1933 Act 38

D. Property Interests Covered by the 1933 Act 45

E. The Registration Statement 52

F. Exemptions from Registration Requirements 64

G. Liabilities Under the 1933 Act 90

Key Exam Issues

This chapter covers the Securities Act of 1933 (the "Securities Act" or "1933 Act"). A lot of material is covered here, so to help you study, the most likely topics for exam questions are discussed below.

1. Transactions Covered by the 1933 Act

This part of the chapter contains very technical, detailed statutory and S.E.C. rule information. To master this material, you need to read carefully the S.E.C. rules and relevant sections of the 1933 Act. Read the rules and statute and the material in this chapter until you understand what exactly can be done to market securities that are being registered with the S.E.C. in the *pre-filing period,* the *waiting period* before the registration statement is effective, and the *post-effective period* (*i.e.*, after the registration is effective).

2. Persons Covered by the 1933 Act

The registration and prospectus requirements of the 1933 Act apply to the *"issuer," "control person," "underwriter,"* and *"dealer,"* unless they are otherwise exempted. Be sure you understand the definition of each category. Especially remember that the person or firm *helping the issuer distribute* securities to the public may be an "underwriter" (and must comply with the registration provisions of the 1933 Act). Also, if the person selling securities to the public is *able to influence the affairs* of the company whose securities are being sold (*i.e.*, is a control person), he is treated as an issuer. Finally, be aware that people who *sell for control persons* may be underwriters.

3. Property Interests Covered by the 1933 Act

Many Securities Regulation exams will have a question on whether some investment interest is a "security" and thus covered by the 1933 Act. Therefore, study this section carefully. The most likely issue would be whether an investment contract is involved. This analysis requires you to look at all of the facts of the situation and determine whether some investment interest should be treated as a security. To do this, consider four factors: (i) expectation of profit, (ii) common enterprise, (iii) risk capital test, and (iv) need for protection.

Another possible problem for an exam question would involve an investment interest that is one of the instruments *specifically named* as a security, but as to which the circumstances and economic realities of the situation make application of the 1933 Act questionable. Consider **Landreth Timber Co. v. Landreth** (*infra*) (stock and the "sale of business" doctrine), **United Housing Foundation, Inc. v. Forman** (*infra*) (stock in a housing cooperative), and **Reves v. Ernst & Young** (*infra*) (notes).

4. The Registration Statement

The main thing to note here is what type of information must be disclosed in a registration statement: financial information, information about the issuer's management, etc.

5. Exemptions from Registration Requirements

The importance of this topic cannot be overemphasized. Because registration is time-consuming and expensive, issuers generally try to avoid registering if possible. Thus, almost every exam will have at least one question asking whether one or more of the possible exemptions to registration apply to a given transaction. Some helpful hints:

a. Exempted security *transactions* are emphasized more than the exempted *securities.*

b. The *broker's exemption* is important to know because, when a security is sold outside the public offering itself, a broker is usually involved, and the broker may need to use this exemption.

c. The *private offering* exemption is a favorite test subject. Also likely are the *intrastate exemption* and the *Regulation D* exemptions.

d. The material on *restrictions on the resale* of securities that are first issued under a transaction exemption is very important for you to know (*e.g.*, if the issuer sells to X in a private offering, what happens if X then sells to Y?). Be sure you know the details of Rule 144.

6. Liabilities Under the Act

Be sure that you understand the various situations where the remedy provisions of the 1933 Act apply (*e.g.*, Section 11 of the 1933 Act applies only to misstatements in a registration statement, while Section 12(a)(2) applies more generally to securities sold by means of a fraudulent prospectus). Be sure that you understand the interrelation between the remedy provisions so that you know which might apply to a given situation and which may be preferable to sue for. Finally, integrate these remedies sections with the material on Rule 10b–5 (see below pp. 115 *et seq.*), a general liability section that applies to misstatements in connection with offers or sales of securities, either at the time of issuance or in later trading.

A. Introduction

1. Distribution Process

As noted above, the Securities Act of 1933 regulates the original distribution of securities by the issuer to the general public. The distribution of securities (called an "underwriting") is a process in which securities pass from the issuer through a syndicate of underwriters, including a "managing" or "lead" underwriter, to dealers, and ultimately into the hands of those purchasers who intend to hold the securities for investment (*i.e.*, for some substantial period of time).

e.g. **Example:** XYZ Corp. contracts to have Goldman Sachs (an investment bank) underwrite 100,000 shares of its capital stock. Goldman Sachs, as the managing underwriter, may organize a group of other underwriters (a "syndicate") to help it sell the issue of XYZ securities. Goldman Sachs and the other underwriters buy the stock from XYZ at $10 per share and then arrange for other dealer firms to purchase a portion of the shares at $11 per share. The dealers then sell the securities to retail customers at $12 per share. The managing underwriter, who negotiates the deal with XYZ and assembles the underwriting group, charges each of the other underwriters in the group a commission for its services.

a. Pattern of Distribution

Thus, the sequence of events in a typical underwriting is as follows:

(1) Decision to Issue

The issuer (XYZ Corp.) decides to sell 100,000 shares of its common stock to the public in order to raise capital.

(2) **Agreement with Underwriter**

XYZ goes to an investment bank (the managing, or maybe the only, underwriter) and enters into an agreement to have this firm "underwrite" the securities issue: The securities firm will either buy the securities from the issuer or take responsibility for their sale on some other basis.

(3) **Agreement with Dealers**

The underwriter then enters into agreements with a number of other securities firms ("dealers") to have them buy the securities for resale to their retail customers.

(4) **Sale to Retail Customers**

Finally, the dealers sell the XYZ securities to their retail customers.

b. **Initial Investors**

In a normal securities distribution, dealers often sell to retail customers who intend to hold for only a short time, hoping to make a quick profit by selling once the newly issued securities move up in price (which often occurs in the first hours or days of a new offering). A sale to such an investor does not mean the completion of a "distribution," this occurs only when the securities come to rest in the hands of those investors who intend to hold them for a *substantial* period of time.

e.g. **Example:** XYZ Corp. issues 100,000 shares of its common stock to the public through A, an underwriter. B, a dealer who has an allotment from A to sell 10,000 shares, sells 1,000 shares to C, a retail purchaser. C holds the XYZ stock for only one day (while the price goes up) and then resells the stock to D, who intends to hold it for a substantial period of time. The distribution is complete only when the stock is sold to D.

c. **Types of Underwriting Agreements**

Several types of underwriting agreements may be used between issuers and underwriters, and the 1933 Act applies in the same manner to each of these arrangements.

(1) **"Stand-By" Underwriting**

In this form of underwriting, the issuer itself advertises the issuance of the securities and sells directly to the public. In the event that the issuer does not sell all of its securities, the underwriter(s) agree (for a fee) to buy the unsold portion. Thus, the underwriter(s) act, in effect, as insurers of the success of the distribution. This structure is most common in offerings made only to existing shareholders of the issuer.

(2) **"Firm-Commitment" Underwriting**

Here, the issuer actually sells its securities outright to the underwriter(s), who then resell the securities to dealers and/or the general public. This is the kind of underwriting described in the examples above.

(3) **"Best-Efforts" Underwriting**

In this form of underwriting, the underwriter acts as a sales agent for the issuer on a commission basis. The underwriter agrees to use its best efforts to market the securities to the public but makes no guarantee that the issue will be completely sold. Best-efforts underwritings usually involve only a single underwriter, which acts as the issuer's agent.

(4) Direct Offering

In some situations, a company might not use an underwriter at all, even as an "insurer." Such situations generally occur when the company is well established (and does not need an underwriter) or when the company is not selling securities to the public.

2. Objectives of 1933 Act

Congressional inquiries into the stock market crash of 1929 determined that securities were often initially distributed to investors without any disclosure of facts relevant to the buyer's investment decision, and that the remedies provided by state law for fraudulent practices in these transactions were inadequate. Enactment of the 1933 Act therefore had as its objectives: (i) *full disclosure* of all material facts in public offerings; and (ii) *prevention of fraud and misrepresentation* in the interstate offer or sale of securities.

a. Full Disclosure to Potential Investors

The primary objective of the 1933 Act is to provide investors with all material investment information relating to the original issuance of securities.

(1) Registration Statement

To accomplish this goal, the Act requires the issuer to file a "registration statement" with the S.E.C. prior to issuing its securities. This statement must disclose extensive information about the issuer and the issuer's securities. [SA § 5]

(2) Prospectus

Part I of the registration statement is the "prospectus." It is the most important part of the registration statement, and it must be distributed to investors prior to (or at least simultaneously with) delivery of the issuer's securities. [SA § 5(b)(2)]

b. Prevention of Fraud and Misrepresentation in Interstate Sale of Securities

The second objective of the 1933 Act is to prevent fraud and misrepresentation in the interstate sale of securities. To accomplish this, the Act includes several liability provisions, potentially affording defrauded purchasers more liberal remedies than those available at common law. (See detailed discussion below pp. 90 *et seq.*)

3. Scope of the 1933 Act

The provisions of the 1933 Act apply only to certain *transactions* (offers and sales in interstate commerce) by certain *parties* (issuers, underwriters, and dealers) involving certain *property interests* (securities). The following sections of this chapter discuss the coverage of the 1933 Act in terms of these categories.

4. 1933 Act Pattern of Regulation

Under the 1933 Act, regulation is accomplished primarily by requiring disclosure by all regulated persons (primarily issuers and underwriters) to the investing public of all material information concerning the issuer and the offering.

a. Disclosure by Filing a Registration Statement

Disclosure is accomplished by requiring the issuer to file a registration statement that registers the offering of securities. As we will see, it is usually illegal to offer or sell securities before such a registration has been filed.

b. Liability for Failure to File

The 1933 Act ensures compliance by imposing civil and potentially criminal liability on those who offer or sell securities without filing a proper registration statement, as well as on those who circumvent any of the many detailed rules that specify how public offerings of securities are to be carried out.

c. Liability for Fraud and Misrepresentation

The 1933 Act also seeks to eliminate (or, at least, reduce) fraud and misrepresentation in the offering and sale of securities to the public by providing a number of liability provisions.

B. 1933 Act Section 5—Offers and Sales

1. The Challenges of Section 5

Section 5 of the 1933 Act provides rules concerning the making of *offers to sell* and the actual ***sale*** of securities through the facilities of interstate commerce. Section 5 provides a fundamental rule of securities regulation: unless the transaction or security is "exempt" from registration, it is illegal for any person to offer to sell a security unless a registration statement has been filed, and it is illegal for any person to sell a security unless a registration statement is in effect.

In order to apply Section 5 to issuers' non-exempt public offerings, it is important to make two separate classifications, which then intersect. The overall goal is to ensure that potential investors have access to important information about the issuer and its securities (like the information in the registration statement) when making investment decisions. First, we must categorize issuers into the classes in which they are regulated. These classes of issuers are subject to different rules, but the general pattern stays the same: bigger and better-known issuers tend to qualify for exceptions that are not available to smaller, less-well-known issuers because there is already significant information available to potential investors. Second, we must identify the applicable time period: the pre-filing period; the waiting period; and the post-effective period. These time periods represent stages in a public offering, from contemplation to consummation. The later the period, the more information available to potential investors; thus, the later the period, the more the issuer is permitted to solicit potential investors.

2. Classes of Issuers

To understand Section 5, one must understand the classes of issuers, because (as we will see below) some classes will qualify for exceptions from the general rules of Section 5. In general, these classes attempt to differentiate among issuers based on the amount of public information already available to potential investors about the issuer and its securities.

a. Nonreporting Issuers

This category comprises issuers that are not yet required to file periodic reports under the 1934 Act. (See below p. 108) There is relatively less information available to the market concerning these issuers, and thus the rules apply strictly to them.

b. Unseasoned Issuers

Unseasoned issuers are issuers that are required to file periodic reports under the 1934 Act, but that do not meet the eligibility requirements for using Form S-3 to register offerings of securities (see below).

c. Seasoned Issuers

Seasoned issuers are issuers that meet the eligibility requirements for using the Form S-3 registration statement but do not qualify as well-known seasoned issuers (see below). To meet these requirements, the issuer must:

(1) For the last 12 months have been required to file periodic reports under the 1934 Act, and have timely filed those reports;

(2) Have a public float (aggregate market value of common equity held by non-affiliates) of at least $75 million;

(3) In the current fiscal year, not have failed to pay any dividend or required payment on preferred stock; and

(4) In the current fiscal year, not have defaulted on debt or rent on a long-term lease, if the default is material to the financial position of the issuer.

d. "WKSIs"—Well-Known Seasoned Issuers

Well-known seasoned issuers (or "WKSIs," pronounced "wick-sees") are issuers that meet the most stringent set of requirements—and therefore get the most leeway, and the largest number of exceptions, from regulation—under Section 5. WKSIs must:

(1) Be "seasoned issuers" (see above);

(2) Satisfy one of the following:

  (i) Have a public float (aggregate market value of common equity held by non-affiliates) of at least $700 million;

  (ii) Have issued $1 billion in nonconvertible securities (i.e., securities that cannot be converted into common stock) in the last three years, and will be issuing only nonconvertible securities (and not common stock) in the proposed offering; or

  (iii) Have issued $1 billion in nonconvertible securities in the last three years, have a public float (aggregate market value of common equity held by non-affiliates) of at least $75 million, and will be issuing common stock in the offering;

and

(3) Not qualify as an "ineligible issuer," which is defined to include the issuers who:

  (i) Have not timely filed their 1934 Act reports;

  (ii) Were blank check companies (*i.e.*, companies with no business specifically identified);

  (iii) Were shell companies (*i.e.*, companies with no or nominal operations, and either no or nominal assets, or only cash assets);

  (iv) Were penny stock issuers (*i.e.*, companies with nonlisted securities that trade for less than $5/share);

  (v) Have filed for bankruptcy within the preceding three years; or

(vi) Have been found to have violated the securities laws within the preceding three years.

[SA Rule 405]

e. Emerging Growth Companies

The classification of an issuer as an emerging growth company ("EGC") was added by the Jumpstart Our Business Startups Act of 2012 (the "JOBS Act"). This Act was intended to improve access to the public markets for emerging companies.

To qualify as an EGC, an issuer's total annual gross revenues during the most recently completed fiscal year must have been less than $1,070,000,000. EGCs lose this status when the first of the following events occurs:

The last day of the fiscal year during which its total annual gross revenues are $1,070,000,000 or more;

The last day of the fiscal year following the first anniversary of the issuer's initial public offering of common equity pursuant to a registration statement;

The date on which the issuer has, during the previous three-year period, issued more than $1,000,000,000 in nonconvertible debt; or

The date on which the issuer is deemed to be a large accelerated filer.

3. Time Period Regulation

Section 5 does not expressly divide up the stages of a public offering, and it does not use the terms "pre-filing period," "waiting period," or "post-effective period." Nevertheless, a careful study of Section 5 reveals that it divides time up into three periods (which have come to be called by these names):

(i) The *pre-filing period* is the period of time when an offering is contemplated but before a registration statement is filed with the S.E.C. The general rule at this time is "no offers, no sales." (See below pp. 25 *et seq.*)

(ii) The *waiting period* is the period of time that begins when the registration statement is filed and ends when the registration is declared effective by the S.E.C. (You can think of this as the period of time when one is waiting for the registration statement to become effective.) The general rule during this time is that oral—and certain written—offers may be made, but no sales may take place. (See below pp. 31 *et seq.*)

(iii) The *post-effective period* is the period of time that begins when the registration statement is declared effective and extends indefinitely into the future. The general rule during this period of time is that both offers and sales may be made. However, there are some specific rules that require the delivery of a package of information for some period of time after the effective date. (See below pp. 36 *et seq.*)

a. Regulation During the Pre-Filing Period

During the period when an issuer is contemplating a public offering of its securities—but before a registration statement has been filed with the S.E.C.—it is unlawful for issuers, underwriters, and/or dealers ***to buy or offer to buy*** or to ***sell or offer to sell*** the issuer's securities (by any means of interstate commerce). [SA § 5(a), (c)]

(1) Rationale—No Pre-Selling

Section 5 and its related rules lay out a detailed and comprehensive scheme that regulates the offering and sale of securities by the issuer to the public. Issuers cannot simply circumvent the 1933 Act's regulatory scheme by making a sales effort just before filing a registration statement, and upon filing, reverting to the statutorily permitted offering materials. If this were allowed, issuers could lure buyers to purchase securities by using materials that do not include the full information required by the 1933 Act, and then later supply a complete information package that the buyers never read. There is, of course, never any guarantee that buyers will read the complete information package. But by prohibiting offers or sales until the package is available, fewer buyers will become vulnerable to incomplete or nonexistent disclosure. Impermissible attempts to pre-sell during this period are often referred to as "gun-jumping."

(2) Meaning of Prohibited "Offers" and "Sales"

The ban against "offers or sales" in the pre-filing period encompasses more than "offers" as defined in state contract law. Because the objective is to see that all marketing activity is conducted in accordance with the 1933 Act and its rules, the terms "offer" and "sale" in Section 5(a) and (c) have been given broader meaning than the contract concept of "offer," or "offer and acceptance." [SA Release No. 3844 (1957); SA § 2(a)(3)]

The term "offer" has been held to include the dissemination of any material that might "condition the market" prior to the actual offer of securities for public sale pursuant to a registration statement. "Conditioning the market" means whetting the public's appetite for the securities. For example, speeches by company officials, press releases, company advertising, etc., could all be "offers" in violation of Section 5(c) if they had the proscribed effect.

(3) Permitted Communications During the Pre-Filing Period

Despite the above prohibition on offers and sales during the pre-filing period, certain communications and conduct are permitted because they do not pose a significant risk of conditioning the market. Each of these is discussed below.

(a) Issuer/Underwriter Negotiations and Agreements

Preliminary negotiations and agreements between the issuer and an underwriter, or among underwriters, do not fall within the definition of "offers" or "sales" and thus are not prohibited during the pre-filing period. [SA § 2(a)(3)] An issuer is permitted to make a firm contract to sell its securities to an underwriter prior to incurring the expense of preparing the registration statement. Negotiations and agreements among underwriters are permitted also, but negotiations or agreements further downstream (*e.g.*, among underwriters and *dealers*) are *not* permitted by this provision. [*See* SA § 2(a)(3)]

(b) Communications by Issuers Made More than 30 Days Before Filing

Communications made more than 30 days before a registration statement is filed with the S.E.C. will not be considered "offers" and therefore will not be prohibited, if:

(i) The communications are made by or on behalf of the issuer (this means that communications by other participants—*e.g.*, underwriters—are not within the safe harbor);

(ii) The communications do not make any reference to the offering of securities; and

(iii) The issuer takes reasonable steps to prevent further distribution or publication of the communication during the 30 days immediately before filing the registration statement.

[SA Rule 163A]

Note, however, that there are a number of highly technical exceptions for certain kinds of offerings, issuers, and transactions, respectively, that are not eligible for the Rule 163A safe harbor.

(c) Communications by or on Behalf of Well-Known Seasoned Issuers

Well-known seasoned issuers are given the greatest latitude under the 1933 Act rules, and this extends to the actions they are permitted to take during the pre-filing period. SA Rule 163 permits WKSIs to make unrestricted oral and written offers during the pre-filing period, nearly—but not quite—doing away with the restrictions that normally apply. For such latitude to apply:

(i) The communication must be *by or on behalf of a WKSI;*

(ii) *Written offers must be filed with the S.E.C.* if and when a registration statement is ultimately filed; and

(iii) *Written offers must contain the warning legend* specified in Rule 163(b)(1).

Note that, although the S.E.C. treats WKSIs more liberally than other issuers, giving WKSIs the freedom to make oral and written offers at any time, probably an even greater benefit is given to WKSIs in the automatic shelf registration procedure, described below pp. 62 *et seq.*

(d) Communications by Seasoned and Unseasoned Reporting Issuers

Issuers filing reports under the 1934 Act are permitted to communicate regularly released "factual business information" and "forward-looking information." [SA Rule 168] This is logical because reporting issuers are required by S.E.C. rules to report these types of information regularly. However, no communication permitted under Rule 168 may contain information about the registered offering, and it may not be distributed in connection with offering activities. [SA Rule 168(c)]

(i) "Factual Business Information"

Factual business information includes factual information about the issuer and its business, as well as advertisements for its products or services, and dividend notices. [SA Rule 168(b)(1)]

(ii) "Forward-Looking Information"

Forward-looking information includes the issuer's financial projections for the future, statements about the issuer's plans and future economic performance, and descriptions of the assumptions underlying such projections and plans. [SA Rule 168(b)(2)]

(iii) Limited to Communications by or on Behalf of Issuer

As with the safe harbor for WKSIs (see above), this safe harbor is available only for communication made by or on behalf of the issuer;

communications by others, including underwriters or other participants in the offering, are not sheltered by Rule 168.

(e) Communications by Nonreporting Issuers

Even nonreporting issuers are permitted to communicate regularly released factual business information without that becoming an illegal offer. [SA Rule 169] Although Rule 169 is similar to Rule 168, it is not the same: Rule 169 does not permit the communication of forward-looking information, and the definition of "factual business information" is a little narrower, excluding dividend information and factual information contained in filings made with the S.E.C. (because there are no such filings in the case of a nonreporting issuer). Other factual information about the issuer is permitted, as are advertisements of its products and services. [SA Rule 169(b)] In general, the S.E.C. does not want unreasonably to interfere with an issuer conducting its business in a normal manner, and such activities are therefore permitted.

Note that SA Rule 169 is technically not limited to nonreporting issuers, but is available to all issuers. However, other issuers (*i.e.*, WKSIs or reporting issuers) have broader safe harbors (Rule 163 or 168, respectively) and Rule 169 in practice, therefore, is a rule for nonreporting issuers.

(f) Communications by Any Issuer Under SA Rule 135

Except for WKSIs, issuers generally are not allowed to mention the proposed offering in statements intended to qualify for a safe harbor. Rule 135, however, provides a limited opportunity for issuers (even those that are not WKSIs) to notify the public about their intention to make an offering of securities in the future. [SA Rule 135] However, Rule 135 is a checklist that must be followed rigorously, lest a communication become a prohibited offer. The notification permitted by Rule 135 is so bare-bones that it does not risk conditioning the market.

(i) Mandatory items. Certain items *must* be mentioned in the Rule 135 communication, such as the fact that the offering will be made only by means of a prospectus.

(ii) Permissible items. In addition, an issuer *may* communicate certain other facts, including the title of the security, the basic terms, the time of the offering, and the name of the issuer.

(iii) Prohibited items. Other facts, such as the identity of the underwriter, may *not* be mentioned in the Rule 135 communication.

(g) Issuer Communications with Certain Institutional Investors

Issuers are permitted to engage in some communications with certain institutional investors; these communications exempt from SA Section 5(c) and thus are permitted during the pre-filing period. [SA Rule 163B(b)(1)] In short, because these investors are presumed to be highly sophisticated, there is not a concern that they will be unduly excited by these pre-filing communications.

First, the communications must be made by an issuer or a person authorized to act on behalf of the issuer. [SA Rule 163B(b)(1)]

Second, the communications, whether oral or written, must be limited to determining whether such investors might have an interest in a contemplated registered securities offering. [SA Rule 163B(b)(1)]

Third, the potential investors must qualify as either (i) a "qualified institutional buyer" (or "QIB"); or (ii) an institution that is an "accredited investor." [SA Rule 164B(c)] Each of these types of institutional investors is discussed below.

(i) Qualified Institutional Buyer

A "qualified institutional buyer" (or "QIB") is defined in SA Rule 144A. Although there is a laundry list of institutional investors who fall within the definition, here are some key examples:

(a) A listed entity (including an insurance company or an employee benefit plan) who owns and invests on a discretionary basis at least $100 million in securities of issuers not affiliated with the entity [SA Rule 144A(a)(1)(i)]; and

(b) Any registered dealer that owns and invests on a discretionary basis at least $10 million of securities of issuers that are not affiliated with the dealer [SA Rule 144A(a)(1)(ii)].

(ii) Institution That Qualifies as an Accredited Investor

Certain individual and institutional investors qualify as "accredited" investors. [SA Rule 501(a)] This classification is particularly important when analyzing issuer exemptions from registration. [See p. 68] However, certain institutional investors who qualify as "accredited" are permitted recipients of SA Rule 163B communications. Here are some key examples:

(a) banks, registered broker-dealers, and registered investment advisors [SA Rule 144B(c)(2); SA Rule 501(a)(1)];

(b) a trust with assets in excess of $5,000,000, not formed for the specific purpose of acquiring the offered securities and directed by a "sophisticated person" [SA Rule 144B(c)(2); SA Rule 501(a)(7)]; and

(c) an entity whose equity owners all qualify as "accredited investors" [SA Rule 144B(c)(2); SA Rule 501(a)(8)].

(h) Permitted Dissemination of Information by Underwriters and Dealers

In addition to the safe harbors for issuers, the S.E.C. has established guidelines for underwriters and dealers (including those who will participate in the offering and those who will not) as to the information they may disseminate about the issuer and its securities prior to the effective date of the registration statement. In general, the S.E.C. guidelines allow underwriters and dealers to conduct their normal business operations—such as the publication of regular market reports and security analyses—as long as these do not unduly interfere with the objectives of the 1933 Act. [SA Rules 137–139]

(i) Broker-Dealers Not Participating in the Offering

Brokers and dealers that are not participating in the offering may, in the regular course of their business, publish and distribute information, recommendations, and opinions regarding the securities of an issuer, even during the pre-filing period. [SA Rule 137]

If the broker-dealer receives compensation for the report or has a special arrangement with the issuer or another participant in the distribution, the broker-dealer loses the safe harbor for ordinary-course distribution of information. [SA Rule 137(b)]

(ii) Participating Broker-Dealers

Provided the issuer is current in its required 1934 Act filings, participating broker-dealers may publish and distribute the following information regarding reporting companies:

(a) Research reports about the issuer's common stock, debt securities, or convertible preferred stock, *if* the offering is of only non-convertible debt or non-convertible, non-participating preferred stock. [SA Rule 138(a)(1)(i)]

(b) Research reports about the issuer's non-convertible debt securities or non-convertible, non-participating preferred stock, *if* the offering is of only common stock, debt securities, or convertible preferred stock. [SA Rule 138(a)(1)(ii)]

(c) Research reports about the issuer's industry or sub-industry, provided the report includes similar information with respect to a substantial number of issuers in the industry or subindustry, or contains a comprehensive list of securities recommended by the broker-dealer. [SA Rule 139(a)(2)]

Participating broker-dealers have somewhat more freedom to disseminate information about certain seasoned issuers, subject to the conditions below. If all the requirements are met, the broker-dealer can publish and distribute information regarding *any* securities of such an issuer. The requirements are that:

(a) The issuer has at least $75 million in market value of equity securities held by nonaffiliated persons or is offering only investment-grade debt securities;

(b) The broker-dealer publishes such reports in the ordinary course of its business; and

(c) the report about the issuer is not its first report about the issuer or a reinitiation after discontinuance of its reports about the issuer. [SA Rule 139(a)(1)]

In addition, pursuant to the JOBS Act, participating broker-dealers may issue research reports about emerging growth companies, *even if* the reports are about the securities to be offered. These reports are statutorily excluded from the definition of "offer." [SA § 2(a)(3)]

GILBERT

REGULATION IN THE PRE-FILING PERIOD

GENERALLY, OFFERS—INCLUDING COMMUNICATIONS TO CONDITION THE MARKET—AND SALES ARE PROHIBITED IN THE PRE-FILING PERIOD, BUT THE FOLLOWING ARE PERMITTED:

☑ Negotiations and agreements between the issuer and one or more underwriters, or among underwriters.

- ☑ Communications by or on behalf of a nonreporting issuer that: (i) are made more than 30 days before filing; (ii) contain only factual business information; or (iii) meet the requirements of the SA Rule 135 checklist.
- ☑ Communications by or on behalf of a reporting issuer (seasoned or unseasoned) that: (i) meet the conditions for nonreporting issuers; and (ii) contain only factual business information or forward-looking information.
- ☑ Communications by or on behalf of an issuer with a QIB or accredited institutional investor to determine whether such investor might have an interest in the contemplated registered offering.
- ☑ All communications made by WKSIs at any time.
- ☑ Communications by underwriters and dealers that are: (i) not participating in the offering, when the communication is made in the ordinary course of business; or (ii) participating in the offering if (a) it is a reporting issuer and the report is not about the offered security or (b) the issuer is an emerging growth company.

b. Regulation During the Waiting Period

Once the registration statement has been filed with the S.E.C., but before the S.E.C. declares it to be effective (so that the sale of securities pursuant to the statement may begin), the objective of regulation changes. Although actual sales of the securities are still not permitted [*see* SA § 5(a)] (except between the issuer and the underwriters or among the underwriters), underwriters may now arrange with brokers and dealers for their assistance in selling the issue to retail customers. In addition, both underwriters and dealers may solicit offers to purchase, so that when the registration statement becomes effective, the securities may be sold very rapidly. However, only certain types of information may be used in making selling arrangements and in conducting this pre-selling. [SA Release No. 3844 (1957)]

(1) Overview of Regulation During the Waiting Period

During the waiting period, SA Section 5(c) no longer operates, because a registration statement has now been filed. SA Section 5(a), prohibiting sales, remains in effect because the registration statement has not yet been declared effective. SA Section 5(b)(1) now becomes the focus.

During the waiting period, SA Section 5(b)(1) prohibits the use of any "prospectus" in interstate commerce, *unless* the prospectus meets the requirements of SA Section 10.

Congress's intention is to regulate written or broadcast communications, while at the same time permitting oral offers to take place.

(2) "Prospectus" Defined

The term "prospectus" includes any communication that is *written (or communicated by radio or television)* and that *offers any security for sale or confirms the sale of any security.* [SA § 2(a)(10)] Note, however, that SA Section 2(a)(10)(b) excludes certain (unexciting) written communications from the definition of "prospectus". (See p. 32)

During the waiting period, the use of any communication within the definition of "prospectus" is prohibited, unless the prospectus complies with SA Section 10. [SA § 5(b)(1)]

(3) Permitted Communications During the Waiting Period

During the waiting period, SA Section 5(a) prohibits sales, and Section 5(b)(1) prohibits the use of any prospectus that does not meet the requirements of SA Section 10. All other communications are permitted.

In sum, then, the following communications are *permitted* during the waiting period: (a) communications that are not offers (and thus not within the definition of "prospectus"); (b) offers that are not within the definition of "prospectus"; (c) communications that are exempt from SA Section 5(b)(1); and (d) prospectuses that comply with SA Section 10.

(a) Communications That Are Not Offers

Recall that communications under SA Rule 135 are, by definition, not "offers." (See p. 28) Therefore, they also cannot be "prospectuses," and as such they can be used during the waiting period.

(b) Offers That Are Not Within the Definition of "Prospectus"

(i) Oral Offers

Oral offers that are not communicated by radio or television are not within the definition of "prospectus." [SA § 2(a)(10)]. Accordingly, they are permitted during the waiting period. Section 5(b)(1) does not prohibit offers that do not fall within the definition of prospectus.

(ii) Tombstone Ads

The definition of "prospectus" excludes certain written communications that only identify the security, state the price, state by whom orders will be executed, and contain any other information that the S.E.C. permits by rule. [SA § 2(a)(10)(b)] Pursuant to this authority, the S.E.C. has adopted Rule 134, which permits so-called "tombstone" advertisements, discussed immediately below.

"Tombstone ads" and the slightly longer "identifying statements" are short announcements about a proposed offering of registered securities that typically appear in publications such as the *Wall Street Journal.* They, and other similar communications, may be published during the waiting period as long as they include:

(i) The *issuer's name;*

(ii) The *kind of security* that will be offered;

(iii) The *price* at which the security will be offered;

(iv) The *identity of the person who will be executing purchase orders*

(v) The person *from whom a prospectus may be obtained;* and

(vi) A *statement that no offer to purchase can actually be accepted* during the waiting period and that the ad itself does *not constitute a solicitation* of an indication of interest from a prospective purchaser.

[*See* SA § 2(a)(10)(b); SA Rule 134] The communication may also include a brief description of the issuer's business, the date on which the offering is expected to commence, and the like.

(c) Communications That Are Exempt from SA Section 5(b)(1)

Under SA Rule 163B, discussed above on p. 28, issuer communications with certain institutional investors (who qualify as QIBs or as accredited) to determine whether such investors have an interest in a contemplated registered offering are exempt from SA Section 5(b)(1) and thus permitted during the waiting period. [SA Rule 163B]

(d) Prospectuses That Comply with SA Section 10

SA Section 10 authorizes two kinds of prospectuses: the Section 10(a) prospectus, and the Section 10(b) prospectus. The Section 10(a) prospectus contains all of the information investors must receive under the 1933 Act. (Later, once the registration statement has been declared effective and sales have taken place, we will become concerned about meeting the requirements of SA Section 10(a).)

During the waiting period, however, participants in a public offering can deliver a less detailed Section 10(b) prospectus. The S.E.C. has authorized delivery of several different kinds of prospectuses under Section 10(b) during the waiting period: (i) the preliminary ("red herring") prospectus; (ii) the summary prospectus; and (iii) and the "free writing prospectus." Each is described below.

Because each is a prospectus that meets the requirements of Section 10(b), each is permitted during the waiting period. [*See* SA § 5(b)(1)]

(i) Preliminary ("Red Herring") Prospectus

One common kind of Section 10(b) prospectus is filed as part of the registration statement and is called either a "preliminary prospectus" or a "red herring" prospectus. (This odd nickname dates back to a former requirement that the required "subject to completion" legend in the preliminary prospectus be printed in red. Although the legend is no longer required to be in red, it still must be "prominent," and many issuers continue to use red text for the legend). [*See* Regulation S–K Item 501(10)]) The preliminary prospectus is similar to the final Section 10(a) prospectus, but it is missing some important information that is not yet available. For example, because the price of securities can change rapidly and approval of a registration statement can take a long time, the preliminary prospectus will usually not contain the offering price or any other information that is based on the price.

(ii) Summary Prospectus Prepared by Issuer

Another kind of prospectus permitted during the waiting period is a summary prospectus. [SA § 10(b); SA Rule 431] However, this variety of prospectus has become outmoded, and is seldom, if ever, used anymore.

(iii) Free Writing Prospectus

Rules 164 and 433 create another permissible type of Section 10(b) prospectus called a "free writing prospectus" (or "FWP"). Most issuers can use a FWP during the waiting period, and WKSIs can use one at any time, even before filing.

In short, a FWP is a written offer. (Recall that oral offers, other than those communicated by radio or television, are excluded from the definition of “prospectus.” [p. 32]) By definition, graphic communications count as writing for purposes of these rules. [SA Rule 405] Accordingly, offers made by electronic media, including websites and other widely distributed messages, are FWPs. Communications presented live in real-time to a live audience (like slideshows accompanying oral communications) do not qualify as FWPs as long as they are not disseminated further.

e.g. **Example:** A live presentation by corporate officers in Miami, made to investment bankers in New York, that is transmitted via the Internet and includes both video and audio, is not a “graphic communication” under this exception. Because it is not a graphic communication, it is not written, and because it is not written, it cannot be a prospectus.

FWPs are permitted during the waiting period, if the following requirements are met:

(a) If the issuer is a non-reporting or unseasoned issuer, the FWP must be preceded or accompanied by the preliminary prospectus. This can be accomplished by providing a hyperlink. [SA Rule 433(b)(2)] This requirement does not apply to seasoned issuers or WKSIs. [SA Rule 433(b)(1)] In addition, this requirement does not apply if the FWP is published or distributed by the media (*e.g.*, an article quoting the CEO). [SA Rule 433(f)(1)]

(b) The FWP must contain a legend disclosing that the issuer has filed a registration statement, recommending that potential investors read the prospectus before making an investment decision; and providing information about how to obtain these documents. [SA Rule 433(c)(2)]

(c) Although the FWP is permitted to contain information different from and supplemental to the information in the registration statement, but it cannot conflict with information in the registration statement. [SA Rule 433(c)(1)(i)]

(d) Generally, the FWP must be filed with the S.E.C. on or before the date of first use. [SA Rule 433(d)(1)] There are several exceptions to the filing requirement [SA Rule 433(d)–(f)], but the two most interesting are discussed below.

First, if the FWP is a written communication during a road show, special rules apply. If the issuer is a reporting issuer, the road show FWP is not required to be filed with the SEC. [SA Rule 433(d)(8)(i)] If the issuer is a non-reporting issuer, the issuer can either file the road show FWP with the S.E.C. or make a “bona fide electronic road show available without restriction by means of graphic communication to any person.” [SA Rule 433(d)(8)(ii)]

Second, if the FWP is published or distributed by the media, the issuer must file it with the S.E.C. within four business days after becoming aware of the publication, and the filing must contain the legend described above. [SA Rule 433(f)(1)].

(4) Impermissible Communications During Waiting Period

As in the pre-filing period, the issuer, underwriters, and dealers must be careful not to make unlawful offers—*i.e.,* by using means or materials other than those specifically permitted above. Further, no sales are permitted during the waiting period, and consequently no offers may be accepted until the registration statement has become effective. One technique often used to avoid inadvertently making a sale is to solicit offers to purchase (which must then be accepted by the offeror) rather than making offers to sell (which the customer might accept, creating a sale).

(5) Distribution of Preliminary Prospectus as Prerequisite to Acceleration

Technically, the 1933 Act merely permits, and does not require, the distribution of a preliminary prospectus during the waiting period. This is because the primary aim of the statute during the waiting period is to prevent illegal offers and sales. However, most investors make their investment decisions during the waiting period, and so the S.E.C. also wants to ensure that information about the offering is distributed to all persons who should have it. To accomplish this goal, the S.E.C. uses its ability to control acceleration of the registration statement to influence issuers to cooperate in the distribution of the preliminary prospectus.

As a practical matter, an issuer needs to have the effective date of its registration statement *accelerated* (see below). The S.E.C. will not issue an order accelerating effectiveness unless the preliminary prospectus has been distributed to certain persons.

Under the 1933 Act, a registration statement becomes effective 20 days after it is filed, unless it is amended (which starts the 20-day period anew) or unless the S.E.C. declares it effective before the end of the 20-day period. [SA § 8(a)] Usually, a registration statement is amended a number of times before it is declared effective. At approximately the time the registration statement is declared effective, a price is set for the securities, based in part on prevailing market conditions. The pricing information is either included in an amendment to the registration statement, or in some cases is simply filed later with the S.E.C. [*See* SA Rule 430A] Either way, once the price has been set, the underwriters will want to begin selling immediately, before market conditions change. If they have to wait 20 days until they can sell, the price will be "stale" and the registration statement will need another amendment—which of course starts the 20-day period over again. Thus, as a practical matter, acceleration of the effective date of a registration statement is a necessity.

The S.E.C. generally will not grant acceleration unless the preliminary prospectus has been distributed to all underwriters and dealers who can reasonably be expected to participate in the distribution. [SA Rule 460(b)(1)]

Further, if the securities are being issued by a company that has never before offered its securities to the public—and hence is not a reporting company—the S.E.C. will not accelerate the offering date unless the underwriters and dealers have sent copies of the preliminary prospectus to *all persons* who are reasonably expected to become purchasers of the securities. [SA Release No. 4968 (1969)]

REGULATION DURING THE WAITING PERIOD GILBERT

GENERALLY, SALES ARE PROHIBITED DURING THE WAITING PERIOD, BUT *ORAL* OFFERS, AND *WRITTEN* OFFERS *THAT COMPLY WITH SECTION 10*, ARE PERMITTED:

☑ Negotiations and agreements between the issuer and one or more underwriters, or among underwriters, are permitted.

☑ Written communications that only identify the security, state the price, state by whom orders will be executed, and contain any other information that the S.E.C. permits by rule (*e.g.*, Rule 134 tombstone ads) are permitted.

☑ Preliminary prospectuses under Section 10(b) must be widely distributed.

☑ Free writing prospectuses under SA Section 10(b) and Rules 164 and 433 are permitted. The rules vary depending on the kind of issuer.

c. Regulation During the Post-Effective Period

Once the registration statement is declared effective by the S.E.C., the "post-effective period" commences, and actual sale of the registered securities may (finally!) begin. The objective of the 1933 Act during the post-effective period is to ensure that all purchasers receive complete disclosure. Here is an overview of regulation during the post-effective period:

(i) Offers to purchase, and offers to sell, securities may now be accepted. As soon as there is an executory contract of sale, there is a "sale" under the Act [SA § 2(a)(3)], but "sales" are now legal [SA § 5(a)(1)].

(ii) Securities may be transported via instrumentalities of interstate commerce for the purpose of sale. [SA § 5(a)(2)] A security transported in interstate commerce must be accompanied or preceded by a Section 10(a) final prospectus. [SA § 5(b)(2)] However the S.E.C. has sharply limited the scope of this "requirement" such that "access" to a prospectus amounts to delivery of the prospectus. [SA Rule 172]

(iii) As in the waiting period, a prospectus may be carried through the mail, as long as it meets the requirements of SA Section 10. [SA § 5(b)(1)] However, the SA Section 10(b) preliminary prospectus may no longer be used. [SA Rule 430(a)—the preliminary prospectus may be used "before the effective date" of the registration statement]

(iv) Written offers (*i.e.*, any kind of sales literature) are now permitted in any form, as long as they are either accompanied or preceded by a copy of the final, statutory prospectus. [SA § 2(a)(10)(a)]

(v) When a final prospectus must be delivered, the time during which that requirement is in effect is relatively short and varies depending on the nature of the issuer.

d. Duration of Post-Effective Regulation Under Section 5

As we have seen, during the post-effective period, Section 5 continues to regulate the activities of parties to a public offering of securities, chiefly by requiring delivery of (or access to) a final prospectus. How long the requirements of Section 5 continue in effect depends on the party involved. Not everyone is subject to Section 5. Indeed, everyone is exempt from Section 5 except issuers, underwriters, and dealers. [SA Act § 4(a)(1)] How long Section 5's requirements last depends in part on whether it is an issuer, underwriter, or dealer who is asking.

(1) Issuers

Issuers are subject to Section 5 for as long as they are offering securities to the public. Moreover, each time an issuer offers securities to the public, it is subject to Section 5. Thus, simply because an issuer has registered the sale of 5 million shares of common stock to the public, it cannot sell another 1 million shares of common stock to the public without another registration statement. [SA § 5]

(2) Underwriters

Underwriters are subject to Section 5 for as long as they participate in the offering, *i.e.,* for as long as they continue to sell their allotted shares. Once the allotted shares are sold, the underwriter is no longer acting as an underwriter, although it most likely will continue to buy and sell the registered securities. In that capacity, however, it is generally acting as a dealer, rather than as an underwriter (with the possible exception of underwriters engaging in price stabilization of the security by sponging up excess demand in the market—see below pp. 195 *et seq.*) As a dealer, a former underwriter is subject to the dealer requirements, discussed immediately below.

(3) Dealers

Section 4(a)(3) of the 1933 Act *exempts* from Section 5 all transactions by a dealer *except* those taking place during the period of time in which the distribution is presumed to occur. Consider, for example, an offering in which many of the initial investors resell shortly after purchasing, in order to capture a quick profit. When they do so, they typically resell through securities dealers. Are such transactions part of the distribution? The fact is that such quick resales are indistinguishable from the sales taking place as part of the distribution, especially (but not only) when dealers that originally participated in the offering take part in the resales. For this reason, rather than attempting to trace how many retail purchasers have bought and sold a particular security, the 1933 Act simply specifies a period of time in which all dealer transactions are deemed to be part of the distribution. However, even these statutory time periods have been substantially shortened or eliminated by later S.E.C. rules. Keep in mind that these time periods specify when dealers are subject to Section 5, which includes the requirement to deliver a prospectus or, when that is excused by SA Rule 172, the requirement to deliver a notice of registration statement.

(a) Definition of "Dealer"

A dealer in this context is a person that spends all or part of its time (directly or indirectly) as an agent, broker, or principal in the offering, buying, selling, or other trading of securities issued by another person. [SA § 2(a)(12)] Note that for this purpose, dealers include brokers (who act as middlemen in transactions involving third-party buyers and sellers).

(b) Sales from Unsold Allotment—Unlimited Period

All dealers participating in the distribution are subject to Section 5, meaning that they must continue to deliver (or provide access to) a prospectus or notice of registration statement until their entire allotment is sold. [SA § 4(a)(3)(C)] There are no exceptions to this requirement, so that until a dealer's allotment is sold, Section 5 will continue to apply.

(c) Initial Public Offerings—Ninety Days

Even after a dealer has sold its allotment of securities, if the offering is an initial public offering ("IPO")—*i.e.*, the issuer has not previously sold securities to the public—then dealers continue to be subject to Section 5 beginning on the effective date of the registration statement or the commencement of the public offering, whichever is later, and ending 90 days later. [SA § 4(a)(3)]

(d) Standard Period—Forty Days

If the offering is not an IPO, then the 90-day period is shortened to 40 days. [SA § 4(a)(3)(B)]

(e) Listed Securities—Twenty-Five Days

If an issuer is offering securities that, as of the offering date, are listed on a securities exchange, then the period in which dealers are subject to Section 5 is further shortened to 25 days. [SA Rule 174(d)] This provision would apply, for example, to IPO issuers whose securities were immediately listed.

(f) Reporting Companies—Zero Days

If, immediately before filing the registration statement, the issuer is a 1934 Act reporting company (*i.e.,* is an unseasoned issuer, a seasoned issuer, or a WKSI), then dealers do not have to deliver a prospectus in connection with transactions in the security.

C. Persons Covered by the 1933 Act

1. In General

Although Section 5 of the 1933 Act provides that an offer or sale by *any person* must be registered with the S.E.C., Section 4(a)(1) of the Act *exempts* from this requirement securities transactions by persons *other than* "issuers," "underwriters," or "dealers." Thus, the registration and prospectus requirements really apply only to *"issuers," "underwriters,"* and *"dealers."*

2. Issuers

The first group covered by the Act is "issuers." Section 2(a)(4) of the 1933 Act defines "issuer" as including every person who issues or proposes to issue any security. Logically, an issuer is subject to the registration requirements of the Act whenever it makes a distribution of its securities to the public. [SA § 5]

3. Underwriters

The second group covered by the Act is "underwriters." Three classes of persons are considered "underwriters" within the meaning of the 1933 Act: (i) persons who purchase securities from the issuer with a view toward distribution; (ii) persons who offer or sell securities for an issuer in connection with a distribution; and (iii) persons who "participate" in a distribution. [SA § 2(a)(11)] One complexity is that, for purposes of this definition of "underwriter," the term "issuer" is defined more broadly than discussed above. Rather, for purposes of the definition of "underwriter," the term "issuer" *includes* so-called "control persons" of the issuer. [SA § 2(a)(11)] As a result, more parties risk being deemed "underwriters" than those who interact with the company issuing the securities. This expansion of the term "underwriter" is discussed below on pp. 40 *et seq*. The purpose of the broad definition of "underwriter" is to ensure that SA § 5's requirements continue to apply to securities distributions accomplished via an intermediary.

a. Purchasers Who Intend to Distribute Securities

One who purchases securities from an issuer with an eye toward *"distribution"* is an underwriter, provided a distribution in fact takes place.

"Distribution" essentially means a *public offering—i.e.,* an offering to a substantial number of unsophisticated investors. [SA § 2(a)(11)] The equation of "distribution" with "public offering" is essential to the so-called 4(a)(1½) resale exemption, which is discussed on p. 91.

Underwriter status frequently depends on intent. If a buyer purchases from the issuer (or a control person) with a "view to distribution," and a distribution takes place, the buyer has become an underwriter. (Note that the 1933 Act does not literally state that a distribution must occur. Under the statute, it is possible that one could become an underwriter by purchasing "with a view to distribution" and not distributing—*e.g.*, merely holding—the securities. However, it is highly unlikely a court would find underwriter status in such a transaction.)

(1) Traditional Factors Showing Investment Intent

Whether the original purchaser bought for investment or for distribution is a question of fact; *i.e.*, what was the purchaser's intent at the time of purchase? In determining intent, the following factors have traditionally been held relevant by the courts:

(a) Investment Letters

It is a common practice to require that the original purchasers give the issuer a letter indicating that they are buying for investment purposes rather than for resale. However, the purchaser's own statements on the matter are not conclusive; in particular, an investment letter will be given no weight if in fact the purchaser turns around and sells the securities shortly after purchasing them.

(b) Length of Holding Period

The longer the securities are held by the original purchasers before resale, the more likely it is that the original purchase was for investment and that the private offering exemption still applies. (At one time, the S.E.C. gave opinion letters on the subject—*i.e.*, that a one-year holding period was sufficient to show investment intent—but it no longer does so.) [SA Release No. 3825 (1957)] Here again, however, the length of time is not conclusive evidence of investment intent; the other factors must also be considered.

(c) Restrictive Legends on Stock Certificates

To show that the issuer has made a reasonable investigation, and also to establish reasonable precautions by making unlawful secondary transfers more difficult, the issuer claiming a private offering exemption often places a legend on its stock certificates to the effect that the certificates cannot be transferred without the issuer's permission. Permission to transfer is then normally conditioned on the opinion of the issuer's counsel that a transfer will not violate the securities laws. [SEA Release No. 5121 (1970)]

(2) "Change in Circumstances" Doctrine

A change in circumstances was sometimes asserted by purchasers seeking to avoid underwriter status under the 1933 Act. They purchased with an intent to invest, the argument went, but a later change in circumstances necessitated sale of the securities. This argument was seldom successful.

e.g. **Example:** G purchased convertible debentures directly from the issuer in a private placement. Ten months later, G converted the debentures into stock and sold the stock on the stock exchange. The S.E.C. brought an enforcement proceeding, claiming a violation of SA Section 5 because G was an underwriter who had publicly distributed stock in violation of SA Section 5. G argued that the issuer was losing money, and that this constituted a changed circumstance justifying his sale. The court held that G failed to establish investment intent, and G therefore was an underwriter. [**Gilligan, Will & Co. v. S.E.C**, 267 F.2d 461 (2d Cir. 1959)]

b. Persons Who Offer or Sell for an Issuer

The definition of "underwriter" also encompasses persons who actually offer or sell securities *for an issuer* in connection with the issuer's public distribution. The quintessential example is an investment bank who enters into a contract with the issuer to distribute the issuer's securities, but this definition includes whose who do so gratuitously.

e.g. **Example:** Members of a Chinese benevolent society in this country who gratuitously undertook to solicit offers for the purchase of Chinese government liberty bonds (without a contract or remuneration from the issuer) were held to be underwriters within the "selling for" definition. [**S.E.C. v. Chinese Consolidated Benevolent Association,** 120 F.2d 738 (2d Cir. 1941)]

c. Participants in a Distribution

People who participate in a distribution are underwriters of the issuer's securities within the meaning of SA Section 2(a)(11).

(1) Test of "Participation"

The test of participation is simply whether the person in question took part in some *significant* fashion in the underwriting. It does not depend on whether the person receives any monetary compensation for the services.

(2) Presumptive Underwriter Doctrine

Historically, the S.E.C. formulated an administrative shortcut—the *"presumptive underwriter doctrine"*—which provided that any person who purchased more than 10% of the securities offered in a registered public offering was presumed to qualify as an "underwriter" unless the purchaser established the requisite investment intent. However, the S.E.C. has now abandoned this doctrine.

d. Underwriters for "Control Persons"

As defined above, an "underwriter" is a person who buys from, sells for, or participates in the issuer's public distribution of securities. Section 2(a)(11) of the 1933 Act provides that for the purpose of determining who is an underwriter, the term "issuer" includes "control persons." Thus, the term "underwriter" also includes a person who buys from, sells for, or participates in a distribution for a "control person" who makes a public distribution of her stock.

(1) "Control Person" Defined

A "control person" is someone having the power to direct the management and policies of the issuer. [SA Rule 405]

(a) Source of Control

The control person's power may come through stock ownership, a position in management, influence with management, or a combination of these factors.

e.g. **Example:** Anne owns 25% of the common stock in XYZ Corp. and is on the firm's board of directors. Anne would probably be a "control person" because she is in a position to influence the management and policies of XYZ.

EXAM TIP GILBERT

On exam questions, it is important to remember that one may be deemed an underwriter not only of the main issuer of securities, but also of a control person (*e.g.*, one who has the power to direct management and policies of the issuer—through stock ownership, position in management, influence on management, or the like).

(b) Control Groups

Groups of persons who have the power to act in concert to influence the affairs of the issuer may be a "control group." Members of control groups are treated as control persons for the purposes of the 1933 Act.

(c) Control Power Need Not Be Exercised

Power to control, not exercise of the power, is what makes someone a "control person." Thus, where the principal creditor of a corporation (who was also the principal source of its business) had options to acquire the interests of others in the company, and received 90% of the company's profits, the S.E.C. found that the creditor was a "control person" even though the creditor had not actively participated in the management of the company's business. [***In re* Walston & Co.,** 7 S.E.C. 937 (1940)]

(2) Offerings by a Control Person

The public sale of securities owned by a control person or control group is called a "secondary distribution," because the stock was first issued by the issuer to the control person in the original distribution.

(3) Examples of Underwriters

Key to understanding the 1933 Act is understanding that there are several ways to be an "underwriter," as defined by the Act, and that one can inadvertently (and unknowingly) achieve underwriter status. The following are examples of statutory underwriters.

e.g. **Example:** A owns 22% of XYZ Corp. common stock, has contributed another 67% of the stock to a trust whose trustees are his sons, controls another corporation that owns an additional 2% of the XYZ stock, and is the president of XYZ. A is a control person. Thus, an offering to the public of a substantial amount of A's stock over the New York Stock Exchange is a "secondary distribution." Furthermore, any broker-dealer who participates in the public distribution on behalf of A will be held to be an underwriter. [***In re*** **Ira Haupt & Co.,** 23 S.E.C. 589 (1946)]

e.g. **Example:** XYZ sells 85,000 shares of common stock to S, the chairman of its board of directors. S already owns half of XYZ's common stock and a substantial percentage of the company's outstanding preferred stock convertible into common stock. S immediately converts the preferred stock into common stock and sells the converted stock and the newly acquired common stock to numerous persons without registration. S is a control person making an unlawful public distribution, and those selling for S in this distribution or buying from S and redistributing the stock to others are underwriters. [***In re*** **Hazel Bishop, Inc.,** 40 S.E.C. 718 (1961)]

e.g. **Example:** A, a control person owning stock in XYZ Corp., pledges his stock with a bank to secure a loan and then defaults on the loan. If the bank sells the shares publicly to repay the loan, is the bank an "underwriter" because it sold the securities to the public "for" a control person? If there is no bona fide pledge involved (*i.e.,* the "loan" is really a device to give the control person cash, and the pledgee bank intended from the beginning to sell the securities for reimbursement), the bank will be considered an underwriter. [**S.E.C. v. Guild Films Co.,** 279 F.2d 485 (2d Cir. 1960)]

e. Exemptions from Underwriter Status

The 1933 Act exempts from underwriter status certain persons who participate in distributions and might otherwise be deemed underwriters.

The most important of these exemptions from underwriter status arise in the context of resales of securities (*e.g.*, SA Rules 144 & 144A). These resale exemptions—which permit a securityholder to resell securities without being deemed an underwriter and thus without the requirement to comply with SA Section 5—are discussed on pp. 91–93.

Additional exemptions from underwriter status are discussed here:

(1) Purchasers of Unsold Securities

Persons unaffiliated with the issuer or any principal underwriter who enter into an agreement with one of the principal *underwriters* (but *not* with the issuer), to purchase all or a portion of the securities unsold after a specified period of time, are excluded from underwriter status if their purchase of the securities is for *investment purposes—i.e.,* they intend to hold the securities for a significant period as an investment. [*See* SA Rule 142]

e.g. **Example:** An institutional investor, such as an insurance company, makes an advance commitment to the underwriter to purchase those securities not otherwise sold in the issuer's public distribution. This investor may purchase the securities at a discount from the public offering price without incurring liability as an underwriter, as long as the investor purchases the securities for investment and not with a view to distribution.

(2) Dealers Selling for a Normal Commission

Dealers who are part of the selling group in an underwriting would normally come within the participation test and hence be "underwriters." However, if such dealers merely receive from the underwriter or another dealer a commission which is "not in excess of the usual and customary distributors' or sellers' commission," they are *excluded* from the definition of "underwriters." [SA § 2(a)(11); SA Rule 141]

(a) No Payment from Issuer

To qualify for this exemption, the dealer must receive the commission from an *underwriter or other dealer*; the commission may *not* be received directly from the issuer. [SA § 2(a)(11)]

(b) "Usual and Customary Commission"

In addition, the commission must be for the "usual and customary" amount (*i.e.*, it may not exceed the amount typically allowed to other persons for comparable services in similar underwritings.) Permissible commissions include remuneration commonly known as "spread"—the difference between the purchase price and the sale price (*i.e.*, the amount received by a dealer who buys and sells as a principal)—as long as this is not more than customary or normal in the circumstances.

(c) Dealers Performing Additional Functions

Note that if a dealer's function is to *manage the distribution* of all, or a substantial part, of the particular issue of securities, or if it otherwise performs the normal functions of an underwriter or underwriting syndicate, it will be deemed an underwriter regardless of the amount of its commission. [*See* SA § 2(a)(11)]

EXAM TIP GILBERT

Be sure to remember that the definition of "underwriter" extends to many persons. One who ***purchases securities from an issuer with an intent to redistribute*** them to members of the public is an underwriter if a distribution takes place, as is any person who ***offers or sells securities on behalf of the issuer,*** even if uncompensated. The term "underwriter" also includes anyone ***who participates in a distribution of securities in a significant way*** (*e.g.,* under the "presumptive underwriter doctrine," anyone who purchases a significant percentage of the securities and then resells them). Remember, however, that dealers selling for their normal commission from an underwriter or another dealer are ***not*** considered "underwriters."

4. Dealers

The third group covered by the 1933 Act are "dealers." Thus, under Section 4(a)(1), dealers are also subject to the registration and prospectus requirements of the Act.

a. Those Included as Dealers

The definition of "dealer" in Section 2(a)(12) of the Act is based on a person's general activities rather than on conduct in a particular offering. A dealer is defined as any person who, either full or part-time, is *engaged in the business* of offering, buying, selling, or otherwise dealing or trading in securities issued by another person as *agent, broker,* or *principal.* Note: this definition of dealer expressly includes those performing the function of a broker.

b. Exemptions for Dealers

(1) "Dealer's Exemption" from Section 5

Under Section 4(a)(3) of the 1933 Act, dealers are exempt from Section 5 as long as they comply with the prospectus delivery requirements of the Act.

(2) Dealer's Exemption from Underwriter Status

Note that since dealers "participate" in the underwriting process, they would usually be defined as "underwriters," and hence would be subject to Section 5 regardless of any exemption for "dealers." However, dealers are specifically *exempted* from underwriter status if they perform only normal dealer functions in return for a normal dealer's commission.

c. Exemption for Brokers

In addition to the limited exemption from registration provided for dealers, the Securities Act also provides an exemption for persons acting as brokers only. Brokers (*i.e.*, persons who sell a customer's securities for a commission) are exempt from the prospectus delivery requirement when they execute a customer's order to sell securities on any exchange or in the over-the-counter market. [SA § 4(a)(4)]

(1) Applies to Specific Transaction

The broker's exemption is only for a specific transaction. In other words, the broker need only be acting as a broker (*e.g.*, on a commission basis) in this transaction to qualify.

(2) Rationale—"Open Market" for Investors

The broker's exemption allows brokers to execute unsolicited sell orders at any time, without complying with the prospectus delivery requirements. This ensures that there is always an open market in the securities, so that they may be traded at a price reflecting their current trading value.

(3) "Usual Brokerage Function"

The broker exemption applies only if the broker is performing no more than the usual broker's function in this particular transaction. The broker's exemption is lost if the broker solicits orders to buy the seller's stock because soliciting buyers is the kind of activity normally associated with a distribution rather than a usual brokerage function. When buyers are being solicited, they should receive all of the disclosure information required by the Act.

(4) More than Usual Commission

Receipt of more than the usual brokerage commission may take the transaction beyond the usual broker's function and eliminate the exemption.

(5) Delegation of Unusual Authority

The transaction may also be deemed to be beyond the broker's function if the seller of the securities delegates unusual authority to the broker (*e.g.*, as to time and manner of executing the sell order). For example, authority to sell a "substantial block of securities" exceeds the usual brokerage function, because under such circumstances it is likely that the broker will solicit orders to buy so that he can dispose of the seller's block of securities

(6) Broker's Sales for Control Persons

The rules concerning a broker's sales for control persons are complex, mostly because for purposes of deciding who is an underwriter, control persons of issuers are deemed to be issuers. [SA § 2(a)(11)] As a result, the following rules apply:

(a) Where Control Person Has Exemption

If the control person has an exemption permitting the resale of unregistered securities (*e.g.*, under SA Rule 144; see p. 91), the broker that assists the control person in the sale may properly rely on the broker exemption in Section 4(a)(4).

(b) Where Control Person Has No Exemption

However, if the control person has no exemption, and the broker knows or has reasonable grounds for believing this fact, the broker may be acting as an "underwriter" in selling the control person's stock, in which case, the broker cannot rely on the broker's exemption.

(c) Duty to Investigate Seller's Status

Therefore, to claim the broker's exemption, the broker must make a reasonable investigation prior to any sale to determine whether the sale is for a control person and, if so, whether the control person has the requisite exemption. [SA Release No. 5168 (1971); SEA Release No. 9239 (1971)]

d. Limitation on Exemptions—Underwriters

If a dealer or broker is acting as an underwriter in a particular distribution (*i.e.,* going beyond the normal functions of a dealer or broker), the dealer or broker may *not* rely on the dealer or broker transaction exemption for transactions that are part of the distribution.

e. Customers

Even if the dealer or broker has an exemption, the selling customer must have his or her own resale exemption to avoid the prospectus delivery requirement. Usually, the selling customer is not an "issuer, underwriter, or dealer," and so is exempt under Section 4(a)(1).

D. Property Interests Covered by the 1933 Act

1. Act Applies Only to "Securities"

The 1933 Act only applies to interests that fall within the definition of "securities." Accordingly, Section 5's registration requirements, and the 1933 Act's liability provisions, only apply to certain interests.

2. Definition of "Securities"

Section 2(a)(1) of the 1933 Act defines three basic categories of "securities" subject to registration:

a. Interests or Instruments Specifically Mentioned in the Act

The 1933 Act expressly classifies certain financial instruments or interests as "securities." However, the Act also provides that its definition of securities will not apply if "the context otherwise requires." Thus, even items expressly classified as securities in the 1933 Act may not be securities if the context dictates otherwise. The Supreme Court has provided some guidance for two such items: stock and notes.

(1) Stock

If so-called "stock" *possesses the characteristics normally associated with stock—i.e.,* it carries dividend and voting rights, it is negotiable, it can be pledged, and it can appreciate in value—then it is a security under the 1933 Act.

e.g. **Example:** A purchaser of 100% of the stock in a corporation can bring a claim under the 1933 and 1934 Acts, even though the transaction involved the purchase of an entire business, and even though the parties could have structured the transaction so as to avoid transferring stock (*e.g.,* by transferring the assets of the business). [**Landreth Timber Co. v. Landreth,** 471 U.S. 681 (1985)] *Note:* It may seem obvious that stock in a corporation is a security. However, before *Landreth,* some courts had applied the "sale of business doctrine" to sales of 100% of the stock in closely held corporations. Under that doctrine, the federal securities laws did not apply.

cf. **Compare:** If so-called "stock" *lacks the normal indicia of stock,* then the courts may look to the economic realities of the situation to determine that no security is involved. Thus, the Supreme Court refused to hold that the sale of stock in a nonprofit housing cooperative involved a security. The stock lacked the usual indicia of stock: it was not transferable, there was no right to receive dividends, etc. The purchasers essentially bought living quarters for their personal use and were not investing in "stock." [**United Housing Foundation, Inc. v. Forman,** 421 U.S. 837 (1979)]

(2) Promissory Notes

Like stock, promissory notes are specifically listed as "securities" in Section 2(a)(1) of the 1933 Act. Notes, however, present a special problem, because many notes clearly are not securities (*e.g.,* the note signed by a borrower purchasing a home on credit or the note signed by a consumer buying an automobile on credit).

(a) "Family Resemblance" Test

To determine whether a note is a security, courts apply the "family resemblance" test. The test includes a presumption and exceptions to the presumption.

(i) Presumption That a Note Is a Security

Because notes are specifically mentioned as securities in the 1933 Act, there is a presumption that every note is a security.

(ii) Exception for Certain Notes

Recognizing, however, that not all notes are securities, the Supreme Court in **Reves v. Ernst & Young**, 494 U.S. 56 (1990), adopted a list of notes that are not covered by the presumption. These notes, and notes bearing a "family resemblance" to them, are deemed *not to be securities* under the 1933 Act. The list includes notes delivered in the following kinds of transactions:

a) Consumer financing;

b) Home mortgages;

c) Short-term loans secured by assets of a small business;

d) "Character" loans to bank customers;

e) Short-term secured financing of accounts receivable;

f) Short-term, open-account debts incurred in the ordinary course of business (especially when the debt is collateralized); and

g) Commercial bank loans for current operations.

(iii) Four Factors to Discern "Family Resemblance" to Non-Security Notes

If a note is not one of the notes listed above, then the note must be analyzed to determine if it bears a family resemblance to these notes. If so, then it is likewise not a security. In *Reves, supra,* the Supreme Court provided some guidance for deciding when a note bears a family resemblance to a note on the above list. Four factors should be examined:

a) *The motivations* of the seller and buyer of the note (*e.g.*, was the transaction one for investment, or instead to finance the purchase of a consumer item?);

b) *The plan of distribution* of the instrument, if any (*e.g.*, if the instrument is traded, the likelihood that it is a security increases);

c) *The reasonable expectations of the investing public* (*e.g.*, does the public reasonably expect to have the protections of the 1933 Act in this kind of transaction?);

Note: In *Reves,* the Court stated that public expectations may result in defining a note as a security *even if an economic analysis of the transaction suggests that the note is not a security;* and

d) *Finally, the existence of a comparable scheme of regulation*, which would diminish the likelihood that a note is a security in a particular case. (See further discussion of the effect of comparable regulations at p. 49)

(3) Other Interests or Instruments Specifically Mentioned in the Act

The Act also expressly classifies the following additional items as "securities":

(a) *Preorganization subscriptions* for securities;

(b) *Fractional, undivided interests in oil, gas, or other mineral rights;*

(c) *Collateral trust certificates* (a type of bond secured by collateral, frequently other securities, deposited with a trustee);

(d) *Certain types of receipts for securities,* including American depositary receipts for foreign securities (*i.e.*, where a foreign company issues receipts in this country for shares deposited in banks in the foreign country) [*see* SA § 2(a)(4)]; and

(e) *Equipment trust certificates* and certificates of interest in unincorporated investment trusts (*e.g.*, Massachusetts Trusts) [*see* SA § 2(a)(4)].

b. Investment Contracts

The broadest classification of securities in Section 2(a)(1) is the catch-all reference to "investment contracts." The S.E.C. and the courts have construed this phrase so as to apply the registration requirements of the 1933 Act to a wide variety of financial schemes.

(1) Traditional "*Howey* Test"

The traditional test for whether a property interest constitutes an investment contract is the so-called *Howey* test, set forth by the Supreme Court in **S.E.C. v. W.J. Howey** Co., 328 U.S. 293 (1946). This case holds that an "investment contract" is *any* contract or *profit-making scheme* whereby a person *invests money* in a *common enterprise* and *expects to make a profit* solely from the *efforts of the promoter* or a third party who is responsible for management.

(2) Modern Test

Drawing on *Howey*, courts have fine-tuned the test for investment contracts, expanding it slightly to capture additional interests. Under the modern test, the criteria for determining whether a particular property interest or participation in a profit-making venture is an "investment contract" are:

(a) Does the investor have an *expectation of profits?*

(b) Is there a *common enterprise?*

(c) Does the success of the enterprise depend *primarily on the efforts of persons other than the investors*?

(d) Do the investors *need the protection* of the 1933 Act?

EXAM TIP GILBERT

If your exam includes a question in which you must determine whether something is a security under the 1933 Act (and most exams do include such a question), you should ***state the traditional Howey test*** (an investment contract is any profit-making scheme whereby a person invests his money in a common enterprise and expects to make a profit solely from the efforts of others, who are responsible for management). But you should ***then note and apply the modern test*** discussed above.

(a) Expectation of Profits

This element examines whether the person is investing the money with the goal of earning a profit, as opposed to merely use or consume the item purchased. While capital appreciation and participation in earnings are examples of profit, a fixed rate of return also qualifies.

(b) Common Enterprise

This element examines whether there are a number of investors who stand in a similar relationship to a business in which they invest in common. The usual way of satisfying this element is via so-called "horizontal commonality."

(i) Horizontal Commonality

Under the so-called "horizontal" test for a common enterprise, there must be a sharing or pooling of funds or other assets by several investors and profits derived from these combined funds.

e.g. **Example:** There was *no* common enterprise where the plaintiff invested funds in a discretionary futures trading account with the defendant management firm (agreeing to share 25% of the trading profits with the defendant as compensation for its services) because there was no sharing or pooling of funds by more than one investor. [*See* **Hirk v. Agri-Research Council, Inc.,** 561 F.2d 96 (7th Cir. 1977)]

(ii) Vertical Commonality Sometimes Sufficient

Note, however, that some courts do not require horizonal commonality in order to find a common enterprise. These courts permit the common enterprise element to be met if there is only "vertical commonality." Vertical commonality depends on commonality between an investor and the promoter, as opposed to among investors.

Under a broad version of vertical commonality, a common enterprise will be found if the investor is relying on the *efforts* of the promoter to make a profit. Thus, "a common enterprise is one in which the fortunes of the investor are interwoven with and dependent upon the efforts and success of those seeking the investment." [**S.E.C. v. Glen W. Turner Enterprises, Inc.,** 474 F.2d 476 (9th Cir. 1973)] A critique of this interpretation is that it overlaps with the efforts of others element, which is discussed below.

A narrower vertical common enterprise test requires that the investment manager's fortunes rise and fall with those of the investor. For example, if a broker managing a discretionary commodities account is paid a fixed commission based on the dollar value of the trades executed (and does not participate in the profits made in the account), some courts would hold that there is *no* vertical common enterprise but only a broker providing a service; thus, there is no security. [*See* **Schofield v. First Commodity Corp.,** 638 F. Supp. 4 (D. Mass. 1985), *aff'd,* 793 F.2d 28 (1st Cir. 1986)]

(c) Efforts of Persons Other than Investors

In *Howey,* the Supreme Court noted that the test for an investment contract included a requirement that profits come *"solely"* from the efforts of others. It was perhaps inevitable that some would attempt to circumvent regulation by involving investors in the enterprise in one way or another, hoping thereby to avoid profits "solely" from the efforts of others. Courts have taken a dim view of these efforts, and the modern formulation of the *Howey* test requires only that the success of the enterprise depend *primarily* on the efforts of persons other than the investors. [*See* **S.E.C. v. Glen W. Turner Enterprises, Inc.,** *supra;* **S.E.C. v. Koscot Interplanetary, Inc.,** 497 F.2d 473 (5th Cir. 1974)]

(d) Investors' Need for the Protection of the 1933 Act

The Supreme Court has held that if a detailed scheme of federal regulation applies to a particular instrument or contract, the 1933 Act may not apply. [**Marine Bank v. Weaver,** 455 U.S. 551 (1982)]

e.g. **Example:** Plaintiffs purchased a six-year certificate of deposit from a bank. The bank then encouraged plaintiffs to pledge the certificate in a loan guarantee for one of the bank's customers. The bank never disbursed the loan but used it instead to pay off the customer's other loans and checking accounts that were in default. Four months later, the customer went bankrupt and the bank took the pledged certificate of deposit to pay off the remainder of the customer's loan. Plaintiffs sued the bank under Rule 10b–5 of the 1934 Act, but the Supreme Court held that: (i) the certificate of deposit was not a security because banks were heavily regulated and the certificate was guaranteed by the

Federal Deposit Insurance Corporation, and (ii) the agreement to guarantee a loan to one of the bank's customers was not a security because it was negotiated one on one, was private in nature, and was never intended to be publicly traded. [**Marine Bank v. Weaver,** *supra*]

e.g. **Example:** Plaintiff was a participant in a noncontributory, compulsory union pension plan. Eligibility to receive benefits under the plan was determined by years of service. When plaintiff was found ineligible to receive benefits, he sued the union under Rule 10b–5 of the 1934 Act and Section 17 of the 1933 Act. The Supreme Court held that the enactment of ERISA (which requires pension plans to disclose specified information to employees and governs the substantive terms of pension plans) made application of the 1933 and 1934 Acts unnecessary. "Whatever benefits employees might derive from the effect of the securities acts are now provided in more definite form through ERISA." [**International Brotherhood of Teamsters v. Daniel,** 439 U.S. 551 (1979)]

3. Examples

The following are illustrations of interests to which the above criteria have been applied, usually under the *Howey* test for "investment contracts." The key issues are usually whether the investor is relying "primarily on the efforts of others" and whether the investor has an "expectation of profits."

a. Crypto Interests

With the rise of various crypto interests—like cryptocurrencies, crypto tokens, and crypto coins—it is a hot topic whether these interests qualify as "investment contracts" and thus securities.

The S.E.C. has taken the position, in public statements, reports, and enforcement actions, that some of these interests are securities because they satisfy the *Howey* test. [SEC Release No. 34–81207 (2017)]

However, some cryptocurrencies, like Bitcoin, are likely sufficiently decentralized that they do not qualify as "investment contracts" because there are no "others" on whose managerial or entrepreneurial efforts the investor is relying.

b. Interests in Land

A "security" has been found where small tracts of land were sold to investors to be used for growing fruit. *Rationale:* The seller's company managed the land for the investors and was responsible for growing, harvesting, and selling the crops; and the investors received a percentage of the net profits. [**S.E.C. v. W.J. Howey Co.,** *supra*]

c. General Partnership Interests

The sale of a general partnership interest normally does *not* constitute the sale of a security, because general partners ordinarily take an active part in the management of the business (and thus the "primarily on the efforts of others" element of the *Howey* test fails).

General partnership interests may, however, be securities if one or more of the following are true:

(i) An agreement among the parties leaves so *little power in the hands of the partner* that the arrangement in fact distributes power as would a limited partnership;

(ii) The *partner is so inexperienced and unknowledgeable in business affairs that he is incapable of intelligently exercising partnership powers;*

(iii) The *partner is so dependent on some unique entrepreneurial or managerial ability* of the promoter or manager that he cannot replace the manager of the enterprise or otherwise *exercise meaningful partnership power.*

[**Williamson v. Tucker**, 645 F.2d 404 (5th Cir. 1981)]

d. Limited Partnership Interests

Limited partnership interests are usually held to be securities because limited partners usually have little or no role in managing the business. However, in an unusual circumstance, if a limited partner, pursuant to the limited partnership agreement, retains significant control over the operation of the limited partnership, the interest may not be classified as a security. [**Steinhardt Group Inc. v. Citicorp,** 126 F.3d 144 (3d Cir. 1997)]

e. Limited Liability Companies

A limited liability company ("LLC") is a kind of hybrid of a corporation and a partnership. The owners (called "members") have limited personal liability for enterprise obligations (like shareholders in a corporation), but the enterprise may be managed and taxed like a partnership. If the LLC is member-managed, the members likely exercise sufficient management and control to avoid meeting the "primarily on the efforts of others" element of the Howey test. If the LLC is manager-managed, however, the members' interests may qualify as securities.

f. Franchises

If the franchisee is active in the management of the franchise, there is normally no security. If the franchisee is passive, however, there may be a security.

e.g. **Example:** Franchisee paid $12,500 for a franchise to operate a tax center in a specified geographic area. The franchisor's participation was limited to providing initial training and assistance in establishing the center (in return for 10% of the gross sales). The court found that no security had been sold because Franchisee had to play a very active role in management. [**Wieboldt v. Metz,** 355 F. Supp. 255 (S.D.N.Y. 1973)]

g. Condominiums

There are situations in which condominiums can be securities—generally when the purchaser, in addition to buying the condominium, receives some type of investment interest. For example, condominium units have been held to be securities where there is a rental arrangement whereby the condominium project manager rents the units to others when the owners are not using them and all units share expenses and revenues from rentals on a project basis. [SA Release No. 5347 (1973)]

h. Club Memberships

Memberships in social organizations or clubs (*e.g.,* memberships in country clubs) are normally *not* considered "securities" because the members do not have an expectation of profits. However, memberships in clubs that have *some business aspect* are generally held to involve the sale of securities.

E. The Registration Statement

1. In General

Under Section 5 of the 1933 Act, prior to the original public issuance of securities, the issuer must file a registration statement with the S.E.C., the purpose of which is to disclose material facts relating to the securities being offered. The prospectus, discussed above, constitutes Part I of the registration statement and contains the most important information in the registration statement. (Part II contains supplementary information.) Ensuring that investors have access to the information in the prospectus is a principal aim of 1933 Act.

2. Preparing the Registration Statement

a. Investigation

After the issuer decides to issue the securities, the issuer and its attorney normally conduct an investigation of the proposed underwriting firm. Similarly, the underwriting firm usually does a research study of the issuer before deciding whether to underwrite the securities issue (and, if so, at what price).

b. Negotiation

The managing underwriter (on behalf of all of the underwriters) and issuer generally do not sign a formal underwriting agreement until shortly before the registration statement is to be declared effective by the S.E.C. and the actual offering price of the security to be offered is determined. However, following their investigations, the issuer and managing underwriter do negotiate the terms of the underwriting—including the tentative offering price and the underwriter's commission—and they may sign a *letter of intent* (*i.e.*, an "agreement to agree"). At this point, the parties are ready to prepare the registration statement. Recall that such an agreement does not constitute an illegal offer because it takes place between the issuer and the underwriters.

c. Drafting Process

Typically, the first step in drafting the underwriting agreement is to draw up a schedule of events assigning responsibility for each event to the various parties.

(1) Legal Responsibilities

The legal duties in preparing the offering are generally split between counsel for the issuer and counsel for the underwriters, according to the background and experience of each. Normally, counsel for the underwriters prepares the underwriting agreement while counsel for the issuer drafts the registration statement.

(2) Sources of Guidance for Drafter

Drafting a registration statement is difficult, and much of the ability required to do an effective job can be acquired only by actual practice. However, the starting point for learning what is required is the statutory guidelines and the rules and forms prescribed by the S.E.C.

(a) Applicable Sections

Sections 6 and 7 of the 1933 Act govern the registration process.

(b) Registration Forms

Next, the drafter should consult the S.E.C. has prescribed a number of forms for use in complying with the registration requirements. These forms incorporate requirements stated in Schedule A of the Act.

The S.E.C. has adopted a set of registration forms, including two basic forms:

(i) Form S-1

Form S-1 is the general form used for the registration of the securities of most companies unless another form is prescribed or authorized. This form permits the least amount of incorporation by reference of 1934 Act filing information. Domestic issuers making an initial public offering (or "IPO") must use Form S-1, as there are no other SEC reports to incorporate by reference.

(ii) Form S-3

Form S-3 requires the least amount of disclosure and incorporates by reference 1934 Act reports filed by the issuer. As you may recall, issuers qualified to use Form S-3 are deemed to be "seasoned" issuers. The requirements for issuers to qualify are discussed above on p. 24.

(c) Regulations S–K and S–X

The registration statement forms incorporate disclosure requirements detailed in Regulations S–K and S–X. Regulation S–K details how to prepare the non-financial disclosures in the registration statement, while Regulation S–X details how to prepare required financial disclosures.

(d) Additional Information Required to Make the Registration Statement Not Misleading

The form for a registration statement, along with the detailed requirements in Regulations S–K and S–X, is only the starting point for disclosure. A registration statement must contain *all additional information needed to make the registration statement, as a whole, not misleading*. [SA Rule 408] For example, it would be misleading to include required information about a particular product manufactured by the issuer but omit the fact that the issuer's management has plans to discontinue that product in the near future.

(e) Reduced Disclosure Obligations

Companies that qualify as Emerging Growth Companies or Smaller Reporting Companies have reduced disclosure obligations. These reduced obligations are intended to reduce the costs of accessing the public markets.

(i) Emerging Growth Companies

Emerging growth companies (or EGCs) are defined above on p. 25. Several of the disclosure obligations in Regulations S–K and S–X are reduced for EGCs.

(ii) Smaller Reporting Companies

Smaller reporting companies defined as issuers (1) with a public float of less than $250 million *or* (2) annual revenues of less than $200 million and a public float (if any) of less than $700 million.

Several of the disclosure obligations in Regulations S–K and S–X are reduced for smaller reporting companies. [SA Reg. S–K, Item 10(f)]

d. Required Financial Disclosures

To make a wise investment decision, a potential investor will want to project the issuer's future sales and net earnings. Thus, financial data about the issuer are obviously an important part of the information that must be disclosed in the registration statement. Required financial disclosures include the following:

(1) Balance Sheet

The issuer must release a balance sheet (*i.e.*, a statement showing its present or current financial condition) normally dated not more than *90 days* before filing; and if there is a delay in the effective date of the registration statement, the balance sheet must be updated.

(2) Audited Financial Statements

Issuer must include audited financial statements for at least the past three years (plus a statement for the year to date).

However, emerging growth companies (or "EGCs") are only required to provide audited financial statements for two fiscal years. (See p. 25)

(3) Additional Information Required to Make the Registration Statement Not Misleading

As discussed above on p. 53, a registration statement must contain *all additional information needed to make the registration statement, as a whole, not misleading*, even if it is not specifically mandated.

e. Required Non-Financial Disclosures

Regulation S–K details extensive non-financial disclosures for inclusion in the registration statement. (In addition, as discussed above on p. 53, the registration statement is required to contain all additional information needed to make the registration statement, as whole, not misleading, even if it is not specifically mandated.) Mandated disclosures include the following:

(1) Description of Business

Unsurprisingly, issuers must describe the business that it does and intends to do. [SA Reg. S–K, 101]

(2) Risk Factors

Issuers must include a section entitled "Risk Factors" in registration statements. In this section, an issuer must discuss the material factors that make an investment speculative or risky. These must be tailored to the issuer and the investment. [SA Reg. S–K, Item 105]

(3) Management's Discussion and Analysis

Issuers must include a section entitled "Management's Discussion and Analysis" ("MD&A") in registration statements. The MD&A affirmatively *requires* a certain amount of forward-looking disclosure.

The MD&A section is intended to give the investor an opportunity to look at the company through the eyes of management by providing both a short- and long-term analysis of the business of the company. It requires management to address key variables and other factors peculiar to and necessary for an understanding and evaluation of the individual company. Importantly, management must identify and disclose known trends, events, demands, commitments and uncertainties that are reasonably likely to have a material effect on financial condition or operating performance. [SA Reg. S–K, Item 303]

The S.E.C. has provided the following two-step pathway for management to determine whether a known trend, event, demand, commitment or uncertainty must be discussed in the MD&A:

Step One: Is the known trend, demand, commitment, event or uncertainty likely to come to fruition? If management determines that it is not reasonably likely to occur, no disclosure is required.

Step Two: If management cannot make that determination, it must evaluate objectively the consequences of the known trend, demand, commitment, event or uncertainty, on the assumption that it will come to fruition. Disclosure is then required unless management determines that a material effect on the registrant's financial condition or results of operations is not reasonably likely to occur. [SA Release No. 6835 (1989)]

(4) Legal Proceedings

Issuers must include a section entitled "Legal Proceedings" in registration statements. Therein, an issuer must briefly describe any material pending legal proceedings, other than ordinary routine litigation, to which the registrant or any of its subsidiaries is a part or of which any of their property is the subject. [SA Reg. S–K, Item 103]

(5) Additional Information Required to Make the Registration Statement Not Misleading

As discussed above on p. 53, a registration statement must contain all additional information needed to make the registration statement, as a whole, not misleading, even if it is not specifically mandated.

(6) Topic-Specific Examples

Periodically, the S.E.C. has released guidance about how certain significant topics (*e.g.*, climate change and cybersecurity risk) must be discussed in registration statements.

(a) Climate Change-Related Disclosures

In 2010, the S.E.C. released guidance regarding mandatory disclosures related to climate change. Those disclosures might include the impact of legislation and regulation (*e.g.*, the costs of compliance and legal risk associated with non-compliance) and the physical impacts of climate change (*e.g.*, impacts on supply, customer preferences, and insurance costs). Not surprisingly, climate change-related disclosures might be required in the Description of Business, Legal Proceedings, Risk Factors, and/or MD&A sections of the registration statement. [S.E.C. Release No. 82 (2010)] Note that, as of the time of this book's publication, the S.E.C. had proposed rules to enhance and standardize climate-related disclosures for investors. [SA Release No. 11042 (2022)] If those proposed rules are adopted, your professor will undoubtedly discuss them in class as a "hot topic."

(b) Cybersecurity Risk

In 2018, the S.E.C. published guidance regarding mandatory disclosures related to cybersecurity. Those disclosures might include the risks and costs of cybersecurity incidents and the costs of prevention. Not surprisingly, cybersecurity-related disclosures might be required in the Description of Business, Legal Proceedings, Risk Factors, and/or MD&A sections of the registration statement. [S.E.C. Release No. 10459 (2018)] Note that, as of the time of this book's publication, the S.E.C. had proposed rules to enhance and standardize disclosures regarding cybersecurity risk management, strategy, governance, and incident reporting. [SA Release No. 11038 (2022)] If those proposed rules are adopted, your professor will undoubtedly discuss them in class as a "hot topic."

(7) Forward-Looking Information

Issuers, underwriters, and others face litigation risk for misleading disclosures in registration statements. In order to encourage companies to disclose forward-looking information, there is a "safe harbor" from liability for certain forward-looking statement. This safe harbor requires the inclusion of meaningful cautionary language alongside the forward-looking statement. (See below pp. 120–122)

3. Organization of Material in the Registration Statement

In addition to requiring that certain kinds of information be disclosed, the S.E.C. closely regulates the organization of the material, including the contents of the registration statement, the use of graphs, charts, etc., to ensure that the material included is communicated clearly.

a. "Plain English" Disclosure Requirement

In 1998, the S.E.C. began to require issuers to write certain sections of the prospectus and registration statement in "plain English," in order to improve the quality of disclosure by giving investors simpler, more readable documents. [SA Release No. 7497 (1998)]

(1) Prospectus Cover Page, Summary, and Risk Factors

The prospectus cover page, summary, and risk factors sections, probably the most widely read parts of the prospectus, are required to be written in plain English. [Regulation C, Rule 421(d)]

(2) Meaning of "Plain English"

To comply with the "plain English" requirements, the S.E.C. has instructed issuers to "comply substantially with six basic principles":

(i) *Short sentences;*

(ii) *Definite, concrete, everyday language;*

(iii) *Active voice;*

(iv) *Tabular presentation or bullet lists for complex material, whenever possible;*

(v) *No legal jargon or highly technical business terms;* and

(vi) *No multiple negatives.*

[SA Release No. 7497 (1988)]

(3) Remainder of the Prospectus

Under Rule 421(b), the entire prospectus is to be clear, concise, and understandable. Although the S.E.C. has not imposed a "plain English" requirement on sections of the prospectus other than those noted above, it has announced some guidelines to make the prospectus more readable. The guidelines include some "do's" and "don't's" for effective prospectus writing [SA Release No. 7497 (1988)]:

(a) Do

(i) Present information in *clear, concise sections, paragraphs, and sentences.* Whenever possible, use short explanatory sentences and bullet lists.

(ii) *Use descriptive headings* and subheadings.

(b) Don't

(i) *Rely on glossaries* or defined terms as the primary means of explaining information in the prospectus. Define terms in a glossary or other section of the document only if the meaning is not clear from the context. Use a glossary only if it facilitates understanding of the disclosure.

(ii) *Use legal or highly technical business terminology*, or legalistic or overly complex presentations that make the disclosure hard to understand.

(iii) *Use vague boilerplate* explanations that are subject to differing interpretations.

(iv) *Include complex information copied directly from legal documents* without any clear and concise explanation of the information.

(v) *Repeat disclosure* so as to increase the size of the document without enhancing the quality of the information.

4. Liability Based on Contents of Registration Statement

Section 11 of the 1933 Act imposes civil liability on those associated with preparation of a registration statement (including the prospectus) that contains material misstatements or omissions. (This topic is discussed in detail, along with other liability provisions, on pp. 99 *et seq.*)

5. Criticisms of S.E.C. Disclosure Policy

Several commentators have criticized the S.E.C.'s policies concerning disclosure, generally on the ground that they do not achieve their goal of ensuring that an investor will receive material information concerning the offered securities. The following criticisms are among those heard most frequently.

a. Emphasis on Negative Information

There has been criticism of the fact that the S.E.C. requires the registration statement to focus on the negative aspects of the issuer (to avoid potential liability under the 1933 Act for misrepresentation), rather than allowing it to present a balanced picture of the company (relating the positive as well as the negative aspects of the company). The critics argue that because registration statements thus lack much information that is relevant to making an intelligent investment decision, and because all registration statements are uniformly negative, they may no longer be taken seriously by investors.

b. Presentation of Complex Information

Some also argue that the complex information the S.E.C. requires to be disclosed (*e.g.*, information on sophisticated products, financial information, accounting data, etc.) is impossible to present in a way that is understandable to the "average" investor. The S.E.C.'s response has been to adopt the "plain English" disclosure requirements, discussed above. The solution offered by the commentators would be to draft the registration statement for the sophisticated or expert securities analyst, to whom the average investor looks for advice, and to dispense with the charade of trying to inform the investor himself.

c. Reliance on the "Efficient Capital Market Hypothesis"

The S.E.C. policies concerning disclosure are based to some extent on the idea that the market for securities is "efficient," that is, that prices of securities in the market are affected, if not dictated, by the information available with respect to those securities. Recently, these ideas have come under scrutiny, and the impact of other factors on securities prices (such as investor "sentiment," various trading strategies that are not based on information about issuers, etc.) has been examined. Ultimately, while no one theory adequately explains pricing in the securities market, it is probably safe to assume that information about the issuer and security will continue to be viewed as an important factor and that disseminating that information will continue to be a dominant goal of securities regulation.

6. Processing the Registration Statement

a. Effective Date of Statement

The registration statement becomes effective on the *20th* day after its filing with the S.E.C, unless it is the subject of a refusal or stop order issued by the S.E.C. or becomes effective sooner by an S.E.C. acceleration order.

Often, several amendments will be required by the S.E.C. before it declares the registration statement effective. An amendment starts the 20-day waiting period running anew. However, the S.E.C. normally accelerates the effective date as soon as all of the problems with the registration statement have been worked out, so that the delay affects the offering as little as possible.

b. Review of the Registration Statement

Once the registration statement is filed, the S.E.C. determines whether, and to what extent, it will review the statement to ensure that the issuer has complied with all disclosure requirements.

(1) S.E.C. Authority

The S.E.C. cannot legally compel the issuer to amend a defective registration statement; but by commencing a formal examination or entering a "stop order" (see below), the S.E.C. can prevent the registration statement from becoming effective and thus effectively force the issuer to make the suggested amendments.

(2) S.E.C. Review Procedures

The S.E.C. employs different review procedures for examining registration statements. [SA Release No. 5231 (1972)]

(a) Deferred Review

If an initial review of the registration statement indicates that it is poorly prepared or has other serious problems, the S.E.C. will simply notify the registrant of that fact (without specific comments) and allow the registrant to consider whether to go forward, with-draw, or amend the statement.

(b) Cursory Review

If, after an initial review, the registration statement appears to be proper, the S.E.C. will indicate to the registrant that only a cursory review has been made and that the statement will be declared effective on the date and at the time requested in letters from the issuer and the managing underwriter. These acceleration requests are treated by the S.E.C. as a declaration that the various parties are aware of their statutory responsibilities under the Act. This procedure saves the S.E.C. the administrative time normally consumed in a "full review" (below) but exposes the issuer to the risk of having mistakes in the documents which a more exhaustive review by the S.E.C. might have revealed.

(c) Summary Review

This type of review means that the S.E.C. notifies the issuer that the statement will be declared effective on receipt of: (i) the same type of letters as required in a cursory review; *plus* (ii) adequate responses to limited comments made by the S.E.C. in its review.

(d) Full Review

Here the S.E.C. gives a *complete* accounting, financial, and legal review—either on its own or when the issuer refuses to agree to the more limited cursory or summary review. The S.E.C. gives a full review to all first-time issuers.

(e) Confidential review

An issuer who wishes to receive S.E.C. feedback about a registration statement out of the public eye may request confidential review of its registration statement. The S.E.C. will conduct this nonpublic review for the following registration statements only:

(i) initial public offering, if the issuer confirms in a cover letter that it will publicly file its registration statement at least 15 days prior to any road show (or, if the issuer will not conduct a road show, at least 15 days prior to the requested effective date);

(ii) initial registration of a class of securities, if the issuer confirms that it will publicly file its registration statement at least 15 days prior to the anticipated effective date of the registration statement for its listing on a national securities exchange;

(iii) offering within one year after either (i) or (ii), if the issuer confirms that it will publicly file its registration statement at least 48 hours prior to any requested effective time and date.

[S.E.C. Announcement, Draft Registration Statement Processing Procedures Expanded (June 29, 2017) (supplemented August 17, 2017 and June 24, 2020)]

Importantly, while the registration statement is undergoing confidential review, the issuer is still in the pre-filing period, with the associated prohibition on offers and sales. Only once the registration statement is public does the issuer enter the waiting period, in which offers are permitted.

c. Formal Proceedings by the S.E.C.

(1) Formal Examination

If either the S.E.C.'s initial review or the issuer's responses to that review indicate a serious problem, and the issuer appears uncooperative, the S.E.C. can institute a formal examination under SA Section 8(e). The consequences of a formal examination are grave: The 1933 Act prohibits offers and sales of securities subject to such an examination if the examination began before the registration statement was declared effective. [SA § 5(c)] This essentially returns the offering to the pre-filing period, with all its restrictions, including the prohibitions on conditioning the market.

The 1933 Act does not impose any limit on how long a Section 8(e) examination may take. Nevertheless, if the S.E.C. unreasonably delays completion of the exam, a court may compel it either to terminate the exam or to issue a stop order (discussed below). [*See* **Las Vegas Hawaiian Development Co. v. S.E.C.,** 466 F. Supp. 928 (D. Haw. 1979)]

(2) Refusal and Stop Orders

If, following an examination of the registration statement, the S.E.C. finds that the issuer has failed to comply with the Act's disclosure requirements, the S.E.C. may issue an order delaying or suspending the effectiveness of the registration statement.

(a) Refusal Order

A "refusal order" may be issued within 10 days after the filing of a statement that is clearly inadequate on its face. Such an order *delays* the effective date in order to allow the S.E.C. to take appropriate action; therefore, it must always be issued *prior to* the effective date of the registration statement. [SA § 8(b)] The impracticability of acting within 10 days after a registration statement is filed has made the refusal order rare, and the stop order (below) is the more common form of S.E.C. action.

(b) Stop Order

A "stop order" either delays the effective date *or* stops the selling of securities (if it has begun), so as to permit an investigation of the issuer and the securities offered. The S.E.C. may issue a stop order at any time—whether before or after the effective date. [SA § 8(d)]

(3) S.E.C.'s Use of Acceleration Power

As a practical matter, the S.E.C. and issuers do not resort to formal grounds to delay the effective date. Issuers simply state on the registration statement that it will not be effective until S.E.C. approval. As a quid pro quo, the S.E.C. then accelerates effectiveness to the date requested by the issuer and the managing underwriter.

d. Withdrawal of Registration Statement

If, after filing, there are problems with the issuing company or its registration statement, the issuer may simply seek to withdraw the statement—in order to avoid adverse publicity and/or potential liability under the Act.

(1) S.E.C. Approval Required

The S.E.C. will grant the issuer's application for withdrawal only if withdrawal is consistent with the public interest and protection of investors. [SA Rule 477]

(2) Timing of Request

The S.E.C. will generally honor a withdrawal request filed ***before*** the institution of stop order proceedings. (But, of course, if a stop order has been instituted in the *post-effective* period, the S.E.C. will *not* permit withdrawal—because the stock (or part of it) has already been sold.)

e. Refusal of Underwriter to Proceed—Material Misstatements

The underwriter normally conducts an independent investigation of the issuer during the waiting period to determine whether all material facts have been disclosed in the registration statement. (This relates to the underwriter's defense of "due diligence" in case there are material misstatements or omissions in the registration statement; see below pp. 96 *et seq.*) If there are material misstatements, the underwriter may *refuse* to proceed with the underwriting despite its contractual obligation to purchase and sell the issue. *Rationale:* An underwriting contract that violates the 1933 Act because of material misstatements in the registration statement is void and therefore unenforceable. [**Kaiser-Frazer Corp. v. Otis & Co.,** 195 F.2d 838 (2d Cir. 1952)]

The underwriter also usually requires that the issuer's counsel (if the drafter of the registration statement) render the underwriter a legal opinion that he has no reason to believe that the registration statement contains any material omissions or misstatements.

f. Blue Sky Qualification

In rare cases, the securities of a company going public must also be qualified under the "blue sky" or state securities laws of the states in which they are intended to be offered. Most companies going public do not need to qualify their securities under state law, however, because the securities fall within the definition of "covered securities" under the National Securities Markets Improvement Act of 1996. (See below pp. 210 *et seq.*)

g. FINRA Clearance

The issuer must also receive clearance from the Financial Industry Regulatory Authority ("FINRA") to confirm that (1) FINRA members' underwriting terms and arrangements are not unfair or unreasonable and (2) any FINRA members' conflicts of interests are prominently disclosed.

7. Post-Effective Amendments and Updates to Registration Statement

There are two possible sources of error in the registration statement: (i) an intentional or unintentional material misstatement or omission may exist at the time the registration statement becomes effective; or (ii) everything may be correct at the time the registration statement becomes effective, but subsequent events may outdate the registration statement so that it contains material misstatements or omissions at the date of use. The Securities Act provides for a way to update the registration statement and the prospectus in each of these situations.

a. Errors Existing at Time of Effectiveness

If the registration statement contains an error at the time it is declared effective, but the error is discovered only *after* the effective date, the appropriate way to update the prospectus is to file a "post-effective" amendment with the S.E.C.

b. Errors Caused by Subsequent Developments

If developments *after* the effective date of the registration statement make the information in the registration statement or prospectus misleading or false (although it was accurate at the effective date), a correction may be made simply by placing a sticker on the cover of the prospectus and supplying the correct information in the body of the prospectus.

c. Updating Requirement

Whether or not any errors are discovered, the 1933 Act requires that a prospectus still in use nine months after the effective date be updated to ensure that it contains information as of a date not more than 16 months prior to its use. The provision puts an outside limit on what can be considered "currently" accurate. [SA § 10(a)(3)]

8. Shelf Registration

Many issuers are almost constantly involved in issuing new securities. It would be convenient for such issuers to simply prepare one registration statement, thereby registering all securities that they may offer at any time in the future (a so-called "shelf registration"). In addition to convenience, registration for the shelf offers some significant advantages to issuers. Among these are the ability to take advantage of favorable market conditions by selling preregistered securities immediately and reducing expenses by allowing issuers to register large quantities of securities in a single transaction.

a. General Prohibition Against Shelf Registration

As a general rule, the 1933 Act prohibits shelf registration. SA Section 6(a) provides that a registration statement is deemed effective only as to the securities *specified* in the registration statement. *Rationale:* A single registration statement may not provide adequate disclosure to investors (*i.e.*, material events may occur subsequent to the filing of the registration statement that would make some of the information in the registration statement incorrect).

And note: the S.E.C. has indicated that it may be materially misleading for an issuer to include in a registration statement more securities than are going to be offered *presently*; *i.e.*, it is misleading to include securities that are to be offered at some remote future date. [***In re* Shawnee Chiles Syndicate,** 10 S.E.C. 109 (1941)]

b. Exceptions to Prohibition

Despite SA Section 6(a), today shelf registration is available in a wide variety of offerings.

(1) Traditional Shelf Registration

SA Rule 415 lists the traditional offerings for which the S.E.C. permits shelf registration. Rule 415 also provides that companies that are allowed to use registration Form S-3 may shelf register their securities. S-3 companies are those that are widely followed in the marketplace and that file reports pursuant to the 1934

Act. (See above p. 24) These reports may be incorporated by reference, and the information in them need not be repeated again in the prospectus delivered to investors.

(2) "Automatic" Shelf Registration for WKSIs

In addition to the "traditional" shelf registration provided in SA Rule 415, WKSIs are permitted even more flexibility, with the availability of "automatic" shelf registration. Recall that WKSIs are allowed to make written offers at any time, and in general are relieved of some of the more onerous requirements imposed on issuers during the pre-filing and waiting periods. In light of their relative freedom, it is understandable that WKSIs are also given broader freedom to register securities for the shelf.

(a) Immediate Effectiveness

An automatic shelf registration statement is effective immediately when filed with the S.E.C. [SA Rule 462(e)]

(b) Unspecified Quantities; Pay-as-You-Go

WKSIs do not need to specify the quantity of securities they are registering on an automatic shelf registration statement. Instead, they need specify only the name(s) and class(es) of the securities. [SA Rule 430B(a)] The fee for filing an automatic shelf registration statement is calculated based on the market value of the securities at the time they are actually offered (so-called "pay-as-you-go" registration). [SA Rule 456(b)]

(c) Ability to Add Securities and Classes of Securities

Unlike most registration statements, which cover only the securities specifically registered at the time of effectiveness [SA Rule 413(a)], an automatic shelf registration statement can be amended to add additional securities (if a quantity was originally specified) and even to add additional classes of securities. [SA Rule 413(b)]

(3) Three-Year Limit and Renewal Provision

Shelf registration statements are effective for three years, but the issuer can file a new registration statement covering the same securities and continue offering them on a continuous basis. [SA Rule 415(a)(5)] Any unsold securities and filing fees paid in connection with unsold securities simply transfer over to the new registration statement. [SA Rule 415(a)(6)]

(4) Disclosure in Shelf Registration

When securities are registered for the shelf, not all the information about the offering(s) is known, because they are to be conducted in the future. An issuer in a shelf registration will typically file a "base prospectus" as part of the registration statement. This base prospectus describes what documents filed by the issuer under the 1934 Act will be incorporated by reference into the registration statement, but omits most specifics about the future offerings. [SA Rule 430B] Information about particular offerings following a shelf registration is disseminated by distribution or making available a prospectus supplement that contains the additional information, or by incorporating information from 1934 Act filings into the shelf registration statement by reference, or by a post-effective amendment to the shelf registration statement. [SA Rule 430B(d)]

F. Exemptions from Registration Requirements

1. In General

The cost and time required for a registered offering are high. Expenses include the S.E.C. registration fee, accounting and legal fees, underwriting fees, printing costs (including stock certificates), state filing fees (in each state where the securities are sold), and insurance against Securities Act liabilities. The time required for a first-time issuer to complete the full registration and selling process is generally between 90 and 120 days. Therefore, if issuers can avoid having to go through the registration process, they will make every effort to do so. Thus, an issue frequently encountered under the 1933 Act is whether a particular distribution of securities qualifies under one or more of the *exemptions* from registration provided in the 1933 Act for certain types of *securities* and certain types of securities *transactions.*

2. Distinction Between Exempted Securities and Exempt Transactions

It is important to distinguish exempted securities from exempted transactions. If the security itself is exempted, as above, it can be sold and resold without ever being subject to the registration requirements of Section 5. On the other hand, if only the transaction is exempt, that transaction is not subject to Section 5, but a later transaction in the same securities might be. For example, if XYZ Corp. issues stock to A under a transaction exemption, and A later transfers the stock to B, the transfer to B may not be exempt. However, if the security issued by XYZ to A is exempt, the transfer from A to B would be exempt. Exempted transactions are covered in Section 4 of the 1933 Act and Section 3(a)(9)–(12), 3(b), and 3(c).

3. Exempted Securities

Certain types of securities are themselves exempt from registration under Section 5 of the 1933 Act (*i.e.*, they may be sold and resold without ever being subject to registration.) Most of the exemptions for securities are covered in Section 3 of the 1933 Act.

a. Bank and Government Securities

Section 3(a)(2) of the 1933 Act exempts from the registration requirements: (i) securities issued or guaranteed by the United States, its territories, or the states themselves; (ii) securities issued or guaranteed by banks; (iii) certain kinds of tax-free industrial revenue bonds; (iv) equity interests in certain trust funds maintained by banks in a fiduciary capacity; and (v) interests in insurance company "separate accounts" that fund pension or profit-sharing plans qualified under the Internal Revenue Code.

b. Short-Term Notes and Other Debt Instruments

Notes or drafts arising out of current transactions are exempt if their maturity date does not exceed *nine months.* [SA § 3(a)(3)]

c. Charitable Organizations

Securities issued by religious, educational, or charitable organizations are also exempt from registration if the organization is organized and operated for charitable purposes only. [SA § 3(a)(4)]

d. Savings and Loan Associations

Securities issued by savings and loan or related institutions are exempt if the issuer is supervised by state and/or federal authorities. [SA § 3(a)(5)]

e. Railroad Equipment Trusts

Securities issued by common carriers to finance the acquisition of rolling stock are exempt. [SA § 3(a)(6)]

f. Bankruptcy

Securities issued by a receiver or trustee in bankruptcy with the approval of the court are exempt. [SA § 3(a)(7)]

g. Insurance Policies

Finally, insurance, endowment, or annuity policies issued by companies supervised by state agencies are exempt. [SA § 3(a)(8)]

EXAM TIP GILBERT

You are very likely to see an exam question involving exemptions from 1933 Act registration. Be familiar with the rather short list of ***securities*** that are ***exempt from registration***: (i) bank and government securities, (ii) notes and drafts maturing in less than nine months, (iii) securities of charitable organizations, (iv) securities of savings and loans organizations regulated by state and/or federal authorities, (v) securities issued by common carriers to finance the purchase of rolling stock, (vi) securities issued by a receiver or trustee in bankruptcy with court approval, and (vii) insurance, endowment, and annuity policies issued by state-supervised agencies. Transactions in ***all other securities must be registered*** unless the ***transaction*** itself qualifies for an exemption (*see* below). You are more likely to be tested on transactional exemptions rather than exempt securities, but it is worth foreclosing the exempt security pathway.

---

4. Issuer's Transactional Exemptions

a. In General

Section 5 of the 1933 Act prohibits the offer or sale of securities unless a registration statement is filed with the S.E.C. Section 4(a)(1) exempts transactions by everyone *except* issuers, underwriters, and dealers from Section 5. Thus, issuers must identify another exemption from Section 5 before offering or selling securities. The key issuer transactional exemptions are reviewed below.

b. Section 4(a)(2) Private Offering Exemption

SA Section 4(a)(2) exempts "transactions by an issuer not involving any public offering" from Section 5. The contours of this statutory exemption have been fleshed out by case law. The primary case is **S.E.C. v. Ralston Purina Co.,** 346 U.S. 119 (1953), although lower courts have provided additional nuance. Despite this case law, the exemption's requirements remain somewhat vague. In response, the S.E.C. has adopted a safe harbor under Section 4(a)(2), SA Rule 506(b), which provides greater clarity to issuers. However, an issuer may rely on the Section 4(a)(2) exemption without satisfying Rule 506(b).

(1) What Is the Policy Rationale for the Exemption from Registration?

The primary question is whether, given the circumstances of the offering, potential purchasers need the protection of the registration provisions. [*See* **S.E.C. v. Ralston Purina Co.,** 346 U.S. 119 (1953)] If the offering is not "public" as interpreted by the courts, investors do not need the protection of registration.

(2) Is There a Limit on the Amount of Money an Issuer Can Raise or That a Single Investor Can Invest in the Exempt Offering?

Although there is not a strict cap on the amount of money that an issuer can raise under the Section 4(a)(2) exemption, the greater the amount raised, the more likely the offering will be viewed as public. For example, an offering of $4 million in securities looks more "public" than a $20,000 issue. [**Hill York Corp. v. American International Franchises,** 448 F.2d 680 (5th Cir. 1971)]

(3) Is There a Limit on the Number of Offerees or Purchasers?

The concept of a "private offering" also seems to imply that the offerees will be *few* in number. The Supreme Court has stated that the number of offerees is not a major factor. [**S.E.C. v. Ralston Purina Co.,** *supra*] However, lower courts have emphasized the number of offerees in classifying the offer as public or private. Thus, when the number of offerees gets very large, the offering is likely to be deemed public and subject to registration. [**Hill York Corp. v. American International Franchises,** *supra*] It is the number of *offerees—not* the number of actual *purchasers*—that is determinative.

(4) Are the Offerees or Purchasers Required to Be of a Certain Type?

The sophistication of the offerees is highly relevant to whether they need the protection of registration. Are they knowledgeable enough to ask the right questions, demand and get the information they need to make an intelligent investment decision, appreciate and bear the risk of securities investment, etc.? If so, this factor tends to support the conclusion that the offering is private.

(5) Is Certain Information Required to Be Disclosed to Offerees or Purchasers in Order to Satisfy the Exemption?

All offerees must have access to the same information as would be included in a registration statement. [SA Release No. 5487 (1974); *see* **S.E.C. v. Kenton Capital, Ltd.**, 69 F. Supp. 2d 1 (D.D.C. 1998)] Access to information can be shown in two ways:

(a) Relationship with Issuer

The first way to show access to information is to show that the offerees had a close relationship to the issuer and its management because this provides the needed access to relevant information. [**Doran v. Petroleum Management Corp.**, 545 F.2d 893 (5th Cir. 1977); **S.E.C. v. Continental Tobacco Co.**, 463 F.2d 137 (5th Cir. 1972)]

(b) Receipt of Material Information

The second way to demonstrate access to information is for the issuer to show that it actually distributed to its offerees the same type of material information as would be contained in a formal registration statement and provided access to any additional information requested. [**Doran v. Petroleum Management Corp.**, *supra*; **S.E.C. v. Continental Tobacco Co.**, *supra*]

(6) Are There Manner or Place of Sale Restrictions?

General solicitation or advertising is prohibited, lest the offering be deemed public. (See below, p. 70, for an expanded discussion of the meaning of general solicitation or advertising.)

(7) Does the Issuer Have to Satisfy Certain Qualifications?

There are no issuer qualification requirements.

(8) Is an S.E.C. Filing Required?

No S.E.C. filing is required.

(9) Are the Securities "Restricted," Such That Resale by Initial Investors Is Prohibited?

Yes. Resale of securities originally sold pursuant to the Section 4(a)(2) private placement exemption can destroy the exemption because they can be a conduit for a wider distribution (thus transforming the offering from private to public).

(10) Are State Registration Requirements Preempted?

No.

(11) How Clear Is the Exemption, and Is There Grace for Noncompliance?

The contours of the exemption are vague, and one non-complying offer destroys the exemption for the entire transaction.

c. Rule 506(b) Private Offering Exemption

In recognition of the ambiguities of the statutory Section 4(a)(2) exemption for issuers not engaged in a public offering, the S.E.C. has promulgated a safe harbor in Rule 506(b) of Regulation D. In short, if an issuer satisfies the requirements of Rule 506(b), the issuer is deemed to satisfy the Section 4(a)(2) exemption. The Rule 506(b) is the most frequently used issuer transactional exemption and, accordingly, is heavily tested on exams.

(1) What Is the Policy Rationale for the Exemption from Registration?

The Rule 506(b) exemption is a safe harbor within the statutory Section 4(a)(2) exemption. Thus, it likewise is a private offering exemption. The Rule 506(b) exemption is one of the exemptions contained in Regulation D. (The others are the Rule 506(c) and Rule 504 exemptions.) Regulation D's goals are to (a) simplify and clarify existing exemptions; (b) expand the availability of existing exemptions; and (c) achieve uniformity between federal and state exemptions.

(2) Is There a Limit on the Amount of Money an Issuer Can Raise or That a Single Investor Can Invest in the Exempt Offering?

There are no limits on the amount that can be raised by the issuer or invested a single investor.

(3) Is There a Limit on the Number of Offerees or Purchasers?

There is a cap of 35 "purchasers." [SA Rule 506(b)(2)(i)] Importantly, however, investors who qualify as "accredited" do not count toward that 35-purchaser cap. [SA Rule 501(e)(1)(iv)] Thus, an issuer can sell to an *unlimited number of accredited investors*. (See below for the definition of "accredited investor.")

(4) Are the Offerees or Purchasers Required to Be of a Certain Type?

All investors must be either (a) an accredited investor; or (b) a sophisticated investor or have a representative who is sophisticated. As noted above, an issuer can sell to an unlimited number of accredited investors but is capped at 35 non-accredited investors.

(a) Definition of "Accredited Investor"

One of the key concepts in Regulation D is the "accredited investor." In short, accredited investors are deemed to be sufficiently sophisticated not to need additional investor protections *or* sufficiently wealthy to hire someone sophisticated to advise them. Rule 501(a) defines "accredited investors" to include the following categories:

(i) institutional investors such as banks, insurance companies, and pension plans [SA Rule 501(a)(1)];

(ii) private business development companies [SA Rule 501(a)(2)];

(iii) corporations, partnerships, tax-exempt charities, and the like, in each case (i) not formed for the specific purpose of acquiring the securities in question, and (ii) with total assets exceeding $5 million [SA Rule 501(a)(3)];

(iv) directors, executive officers, and general partners of the issuer of the securities [SA Rule 501(a)(4)];

(v) natural persons with $1 million in net worth (individually, or jointly with spouse) [SA Rule 501(a)(5)];

Note: Equity in a person's primary residence is excluded from this net worth calculation. This carve-out was added by the Dodd-Frank Wall Street Reform and Consumer Protection Act of 2010 in the wake of the 2009 financial crisis, in which many homeowners lost a significant amount of the equity in their homes virtually overnight.

(vi) natural persons with $200,000 in individual annual income (or $300,000 joint income with spouse) [SA Rule 501(a)(6)];

(vii) trusts not formed for the specific purpose of acquiring the securities in question, with total assets exceeding $5 million, if directed by a "sophisticate" [SA Rule 501(a)(7)];

(viii) any entity in which all the equity owners are accredited investors [SA Rule 501(a)(8)];

(ix) any entity not listed above, not formed for the specific purposed of acquiring the securities in question, which owns investments in excess of $5 million [SA Rule 501(a)(9)];

(x) any natural person holding in good standing a professional certificate, designation, or credentials from an accredited educational institution that the S.E.C. designates as qualifying an individual for accredited investor status [SA Rule 501(a)(10)]; and

Note: This category of accredited investor was added in 2020 and is intended to expand the pool of accredited investors to include natural persons who do not satisfy the above wealth or income tests but who, by virtue of their education or experience, are sophisticated in financial and business matters. To date, the S.E.C. has designated the following individuals as accredited investors under this provision, relying on certifications and designations administered by the Financial Industry Regulatory Authority ("FINRA"): (a) Licensed General Securities Representative (Series 7); (b) Licensed Investment Adviser Representative (Series 65); and (c) Licensed Private Securities Offerings Representative (Series 82)

(xi) any natural person who is a "knowledgeable employee" (as defined by Rule 3c–5(a)(4) of the Investment Company of 1940) of the issuer [SA Rule 501(a)(11)].

(b) Definition of Sophisticated Investor

To be a sophisticate, the purchaser or investment advisor must have "such knowledge and experience in financial and business matters that he [or she] is capable of evaluating the merits and risks of the prospective investment," or the issuer must reasonably believe that the purchaser meets that description. [SA Rule 506(b)(2)(ii)]

(5) Is Certain Information Required to Be Disclosed to Offerees or Purchasers in Order to Satisfy the Exemption?

Issuers must give all investors, prior to purchase, an opportunity to ask questions and to obtain additional information that the issuer can acquire without unreasonable effort or expense. [*See* SA Rule 502(b)(2)(v)]

In addition, issuers must deliver of a written disclosure document to anyone that is not an accredited investor. (As a reminder, the issuer is capped at selling to 35 non-accredited investors.) In such a case, delivery of the information specified in Rule 502(b)(2) (see below) is required to be made to those persons that are not accredited investors. When securities are sold only to accredited investors, there is no mandatory disclosure in order to satisfy the exemption from registration. However, in such a case, the issuer is still subject to the antifraud and civil liability provisions of the federal securities laws, which may require disclosure.

(a) Overview of Disclosure Required to Non-Accredited Investors

The nature of the required disclosure varies with the kind of issuer (*i.e.*, whether or not the issuer is a 1934 Act reporting company) and the dollar amount of the offering. [*See* SA Rule 502(b)]

(b) Impact of Disclosure Required to Non-Accredited Investors

As a practical matter, because of the enhanced mandatory disclosure requirements when selling to non-accredited investors, and the cap on 35 non-accredited investors, most issuers elect not to sell to any non-accredited investors when relying on the Rule 506(b) exemption.

(6) Are There Manner or Place of Sale Restrictions?

General solicitation and advertising are prohibited. [SA Rule 502(c)] Probably the single most important factor in avoiding a general solicitation under Rule 502(c) is the presence of a substantive, preexisting relationship between the issuer and the offerees. Not just any relationship will do; the S.E.C. looks for a relationship that makes the issuer "aware of the financial circumstances or sophistication of the persons with whom the relationship exists." [Mineral Lands Research & Marketing Corp., S.E.C. No Action Letter (Nov. 4, 1985)]

The S.E.C. has approved a procedure by which accredited investors who want to review private placement memoranda can do so on the internet, without the issuer thereby violating Rule 502(c)'s prohibition against general solicitation. An investor who is interested in reviewing such materials is required to complete a questionnaire, and the responses are assessed to determine whether the investor is "accredited" under Rule 501. If so, the investor is provided a password that can be used to access private placement memoranda. [IPONET, S.E.C. No-Action Letter (July 26, 1996)]

(7) Does the Issuer Have to Satisfy Certain Qualifications?

So-called "bad actors" are barred from using the Rule 506(b) exemption. [SA Rule 506(d)]

(a) Scope of Persons to Whom the "Bad Actor" Test Applies

The "bad actor" test applies not only to the issuer but also to a laundry list of affiliated entities and individuals. That list includes the following: any predecessor of the issuer; any affiliated issuer; any director, executive officer, other officer participating in the offering, general partner of managing member of the issuer; and any beneficial owner of 20% or more of the issuer's outstanding voting equity securities; any promoter connected with the issuer at the time of sale. [SA Rule 506(d)]

(b) "Bad Actor" Test

If any person listed above on p. 70 meets the "bad actor" test, the issuer is prohibited from using the Rule 506(b) exemption. The test includes the following people:

(i) people convicted within the past ten years (or the past five years for issuers, their predecessors, and affiliated issuers) of any felony or misdemeanor in connection with the purchase or sale of any security or involving the making of any false filing with the S.E.C.;

(ii) people subject to any order, judgment, or decree of any court of competent jurisdiction, entered within the past five years, that retrains such person from engaging in any conduct in connection with the purchase or sale of any security or involving the making of any false filing with the S.E.C.;

(iii) people subject to a final order of a state securities commission, entered within the past ten years, based on a violation of any law or regulation that prohibits fraudulent, manipulative, or deceptive conduct; and

(iv) people subject to any order of the S.E.C., entered within the past five years, that orders the person to cease and desist from violations of listed federal securities laws (including the antifraud provisions and SA Section 5).

(8) Is an S.E.C. Filing Required?

Within 15 days after the first sale of securities under Regulation D, the seller must give the S.E.C. notice of the sale by filing Form D. [SA Rule 503] Although the filing of Form D is not a prerequisite to satisfying the Rule 506(b) exemption, the failure to do so may prevent the issuer from relying on the exemption in the future. [*See* SA Rule 507]

(9) Are the Securities "Restricted," Such That Resale by Initial Investors Is Prohibited?

Yes. Issuers must exercise reasonable care to assure that the purchasers are not "underwriters" as defined in 1933 Act Section 2(a)(11). Reasonable care may be demonstrated by:

(a) Reasonable inquiry to determine if the purchaser is acquiring the securities for himself or for other persons;

(b) Written disclosure to each purchaser prior to sale that the securities are restricted and cannot be resold; and

(c) Placement of a legend on the security certificates, stating that the securities have not been registered and noting the existence of restrictions on transferability and sale of the securities.

[SA Rule 502(d)] Note that while these steps evidence reasonable care by the issuers, they are not the exclusive means to demonstrate such care.

(10) Are State Registration Requirements Preempted?

Yes. [SA § 18(b)(4)(F)] Note that this is a major difference from the statutory Section 4(a)(2) exemption. If an issuer relied on the statutory Section 4(a)(2) exemption without satisfying the Rule 506(b) safe harbor, state registration requirements are not preempted.

(11) How Clear Is the Exemption, and Is There Grace for Noncompliance?

Rule 506(b) clearly states the detailed requirements to meet the exemption. In addition, Rule 508 provides that an issuer that commits an inadvertent and immaterial violation can, under some circumstances, still claim the exemption.

d. Rule 506(c) Exemption

Congress, in the Jumpstart Our Business Startups Act of 2012 ("JOBS Act") mandated that the S.E.C. promulgate a new exemption, Rule 506(c). This exemption is similar to the Rule 506(b) exemption, with three major differences: (1) general solicitation and advertising is *permitted*; (2) *all* investors must be "accredited"; and (3) the issuer must take additional "reasonable steps to verify" each investor's status as accredited.

(1) What Is the Policy Rationale for the Exemption from Registration?

The JOBS Act, which mandated the adoption of the Rule 506(c) exemption, was intended to streamline issuers' access to capital.

(2) Is There a Limit on the Amount of Money an Issuer Can Raise or That a Single Investor Can Invest in the Exempt Offering?

There are no limits on the amount that can be raised by the issuer or invested a single investor.

(3) Is There a Limit on the Number of Offerees or Purchasers?

There is no limit on the number of offerees or purchasers.

(4) Are the Offerees or Purchasers Required to Be of a Certain Type?

All investors must be accredited. [See the definition of "accredited investor" above on p. 68]

In addition, the issuer must take "reasonable steps to verify" the status of each investor is accredited. The rule provides several non-exclusive means that an issuer can use to conduct this verification, including the following:

(a) If the investor is qualifying as accredited on the basis of income, by reviewing the investor's tax returns for the past two years, accompanied by a written representation from the investor that he or she has a reasonable expectation of reaching the income level needed to qualify as an accredited investor during the current year; and

(b) If the investor is qualifying as accredited on the basis of net worth, reviewing documents that reflect assets (including bank and brokerage statements dated within the past three months), reviewing a consumer report from a nationwide consumer reporting agency dated within the past three months, and obtaining a written representation from the purchaser that all liabilities necessary to make a determination of net worth have been disclosed. [SA Rule 506(c)(2)(ii)]

(5) Is Certain Information Required to Be Disclosed to Offerees or Purchasers in Order to Satisfy the Exemption?

There is no mandatory disclosure in order to satisfy the exemption from registration. However, the issuer is still subject to the antifraud and civil liability provisions of the federal securities laws, which may require disclosure.

(6) Are There Manner or Place of Sale Restrictions?

General solicitation and advertising is permitted.

(7) Does the Issuer Have to Satisfy Certain Qualifications?

So-called "bad actors" are barred from using the Rule 506(c) exemption. (See above p. 70)

(8) Is an S.E.C. Filing Required?

Within 15 days after the first sale of securities under Regulation D, the seller must give the S.E.C. notice of the sale by filing Form D. [SA Rule 503] Although the filing of Form D is not a prerequisite to satisfying the Rule 506(c) exemption, the failure to do so may prevent the issuer from relying on the exemption in the future. [*See* SA Rule 507]

(9) Are the Securities "Restricted," Such That Resale by Initial Investors Is Prohibited?

Yes. Issuers must exercise reasonable care to assure that the purchasers are not "underwriters" as defined in 1933 Act Section 2(a)(11). (See above p. 38)

(10) Are State Registration Requirements Preempted?

Yes.

(11) How Clear Is the Exemption, and Is There Grace for Noncompliance?

Rule 506(c) clearly states the detailed requirements to meet the exemption. In addition, Rule 508 provides that an issuer that commits an inadvertent and immaterial violation can, under some circumstances, still claim the exemption.

e. Rule 504 Exemption

(1) What Is the Policy Rationale for the Exemption from Registration?

The S.E.C. originally promulgated Rule 504, which is within Regulation D, pursuant to its small issues exemptive authority in Section 3(b)(1) of the 1933 Act, which permits the S.E.C. to exempt security offerings from registration if the protection of the Act is not required and $5 million or less in securities is involved in the offering. In 2021, however, the S.E.C. amended Rule 504 to expand the permitted dollar amount raised to $10 million. The S.E.C. did so pursuant to its general exemptive authority under Section 28 of the 1933 Act. The remaining elements of the Rule exemption remained unchanged, so that the exemption still retains some attributes of a small issues exemption despite the increase in the dollar amount of funds that can be raised.

(a) Operation of Rule 504

Rule 504 is unique in that a number of the exemption's requirements disappear if an issuer complies with specified state registration/exemption requirements. It is unlikely that an issuer would elect to rely on Rule 504 without satisfying the state registration/exemption requirements.

(b) State Registration/Exemption Requirements

A number of Rule 504's requirements disappear if the issuer makes offer or sales:

(i) Exclusively in one or more states that provide for the registration of the securities, and require the public filing and delivery to investors of a substantive disclosure document before sale, and are made in accordance with those state provisions;

(ii) In one or more states that have no provision for the registration of the securities or the public filing or delivery of a disclosure document before sale, if the securities have been registered in at least one state that provides for such registration, public filing, and delivery before sale; offers and sales are made in that state in accordance with such provisions; and the disclosure document is delivered before sale to all purchasers (including those in the states that have no such procedure); or

(iii) Exclusively according to state law exemptions from registration that permit general solicitation and general advertising so long as sales are made only to "accredited investors" as defined in Rule 501(a).

[SA Rule 504(b)(1)]

(2) Is There a Limit on the Amount of Money an Issuer Can Raise or That a Single Investor Can Invest in the Exempt Offering?

Yes. The aggregate offering price for an offering of securities under Rule 504 is $10 million, less the aggregate price for all securities sold (i) in the 12 months before the start of and during the Rule 504 offering in reliance on Rule 504; or (ii) in violation of 1933 Act Section 5. [SA Rule 504(b)(2)]

(3) Is There a Limit on the Number of Offerees or Purchasers?

There is no limit on the number of offerees or purchasers.

(4) Are the Offerees or Purchasers Required to Be of a Certain Type?

Although Rule 504 does not limit offerees or purchasers to those of a certain type, as a practical matter, an issuer relying on Rule 504 will meet the state-law registration/exemptions detailed above on p. 73. As such, all offers and sales must occur only in those states.

(5) Is Certain Information Required to Be Disclosed to Offerees or Purchasers in Order to Satisfy the Exemption?

There is no mandatory disclosure in order to satisfy the exemption from registration. However, the issuer is still subject to the antifraud and civil liability provisions of the federal securities laws, which may require disclosure.

(6) Are There Manner or Place of Sale Restrictions?

General solicitation and advertising is prohibited in Rule 504 transactions, but that prohibition disappears if the issuer complies with the state registration/exemption requirements discussed above on p. 73. [SA Rule 504(b)(1)]

As a practical matter, an issuer relying on Rule 504 will meet the state-law registration/exemptions detailed above on p. 73. As such, all offers and sales must occur only in those states.

(7) Does the Issuer Have to Satisfy Certain Qualifications?

So-called "bad actors" are barred from using the Rule 504 exemption. (See above p. 70) In addition, Rule 504 is not available to issuers who are (a) reporting companies under the 1934 Act, (b) investment companies, or (c) development stage companies without a specific business plan or purpose and that have indicated a business plan to engage in a merger or acquisition of an unidentified company. [SA Rule 504(a)]

(8) Is an S.E.C. Filing Required?

Within 15 days after the first sale of securities under Regulation D, the seller must give the S.E.C. notice of the sale by filing Form D. [SA Rule 503] Although the filing of Form D is not a prerequisite to satisfying the Rule 506(c) exemption, the failure to do so may prevent the issuer from relying on the exemption in the future. [*See* SA Rule 507]

(9) Are the Securities "Restricted," Such That Resale by Initial Investors Is Prohibited?

Issuers must exercise reasonable care to assure that the purchasers are not "underwriters" as defined in 1933 Act Section 2(a)(11), but that requirement disappears if the issuer complies with the state registration/exemption requirements discussed above on p. 73. [SA Rule 504(b)(1)]

(10) Are State Registration Requirements Preempted?

No. Rule 504 relies on state registration rules.

(11) How Clear Is the Exemption, and Is There Grace for Noncompliance?

Rule 504 clearly states the requirements to meet the exemption. In addition, Rule 508 provides that an issuer that commits an inadvertent and immaterial violation can, under some circumstances, still claim the exemption.

f. Section 3(a)(11) Instrastate Offering Exemption

(1) What Is the Policy Rationale for the Exemption from Registration?

The SA Section 3(a)(11) intrastate offering exemption is designed to facilitate the raising of local capital for local businesses. The exemption is permitted on the grounds that local investors will be adequately protected both by their proximity to the issuer and by state regulations.

(2) Is There a Limit on the Amount of Money an Issuer Can Raise or That a Single Investor Can Invest in the Exempt Offering?

No.

(3) Is There a Limit on the Number of Offerees or Purchasers?

No.

(4) Are the Offerees or Purchasers Required to Be of a Certain Type?

All offerees and purchasers must be residents of one state (the issuer's state). Mere presence in the state is not sufficient to establish residence. Rather, the test is similar to that for "domicile." The purchaser must reside in the state with an intent to remain.

(5) Is Certain Information Required to Be Disclosed to Offerees or Purchasers in Order to Satisfy the Exemption?

There is no mandatory disclosure in order to satisfy the exemption from registration. However, the issuer is still subject to the antifraud and civil liability provisions of the federal securities laws, which may require disclosure.

(6) Are There Manner or Place of Sale Restrictions?

The securities may only be offered or sold in one state (the state of the issuers', offerees', and purchasers' residence). Advertising is permitted, as long as it does not become an out-of-state offer. The inclusion of disclaimer, indicating that offers are being made only to residents of the state, *may* be sufficient.

(7) Does the Issuer Have to Satisfy Certain Qualifications?

The issuer must reside in the same state as all offerees and purchasers. The issuer must meet two requirements to establish "residence" under Section 3(a)(11):

(a) Issuer's Residence in State

First, the issuer must reside in the state where the offering is made. For a corporation, the state of residence is the state of incorporation.

(b) Issuer's Business in State

Because the purpose of the intrastate exemption is to finance local business, the issuer must also be "doing business" in the state. "Doing business" is judged by (i) whether the issuer is doing a majority of its business in the state and (ii) whether the proceeds of the offering are used in the state.

e.g. **Example:** A Minnesota corporation with its only office in Minnesota sold unsecured installment notes to Minnesota residents. However, the intrastate offering exemption was not available because the proceeds of the offering were for loans to land developers outside the state. [**S.E.C. v. McDonald Investment Co.**, 343 F. Supp. 343 (D. Minn. 1972)]

(8) Is an S.E.C. Filing Required?

No.

(9) Are the Securities "Restricted," Such That Resale by Initial Investors Is Prohibited?

Eventual resales to nonresidents are possible without destroying the intrastate offering exemption, but only after the original distribution to residents is complete—*i.e.*, only after the offering has "come to rest" in the hands of state residents. Under Section 3(a)(11), whether an issue of securities has "come to rest" depends on the intent of the original purchasers. If the securities were purchased with the intention of keeping them for investment, the issue is complete and resales-to nonresidents may begin. But if the purchasers intend a further distribution or resale, the issue has not "come to rest" and any resale to nonresidents will destroy the exemption.

e.g. **Example:** A relatively long holding period of one year or more may be sufficient to prove the necessary investment intent. Conversely, a resident's resale within a short time to a nonresident supports an inference that the offering has not come to rest within the state and may defeat the exemption. An even stronger inference is created when the original sale is to a broker-dealer, who resells within a short time to out-of-state residents. [SA Release No. 4434 (1961)]

(10) Are State Registration Requirements Preempted?

No.

(11) How Clear Is the Exemption, and Is There Grace for Noncompliance?

There are some ambiguities within the Section 3(a)(11) exemption, including whether the issuer is "doing business" in the state, whether advertising risks being deemed an out-of-state offer, and whether the securities have "come to rest" with the purchasers. In addition, a single offer to a nonresident can destroy the Section 3(a)(11) exemption, regardless of how compelling the facts are. Note that the S.E.C.

has promulgated a safe harbor under Section 3(a)(11), Rule 147, that responds in part to these difficulties.

g. Rule 147 Instrastate Offering Exemption

(1) What Is the Policy Rationale for the Exemption from Registration?

Rule 147 is a safe harbor within the Section 3(a)(11) intrastate offering exemption and thus has the same policy rationale.

(2) Is There a Limit on the Amount of Money an Issuer Can Raise or That a Single Investor Can Invest in the Exempt Offering?

No.

(3) Is There a Limit on the Number of Offerees or Purchasers?

No.

(4) Are the Offerees or Purchasers Required to Be of a Certain Type?

All offerees and purchasers must be residents of one state (the issuer's state). Rule 147 provides a clear test to assess whether a purchaser is a resident. In addition, the issuer must take certain steps to ensure that no offers are made to out-of-state residents.

(a) Test to Determine Purchasers' In-State Residence

All purchasers must reside in the state of the issuer's residence. A purchaser's residence is determined as follows:

(i) If the purchaser is a business organization, it resides in the state of its principal place of business (however, if the organization is organized for the specific purpose of acquiring securities offered under Rule 147, then all beneficial owners of the organization must also be residents of the state);

(ii) If the purchaser is an individual, he or she resides in the state of his or her principal residence.

[SA Rule 147(d)]

Note: The issuer is also required to obtain a written representation from each purchaser as to his or her residence. [SA Rule 147(f)(1)(iii)]

(b) Issuer's Steps to Ensure No Out-of-State Offers

In order to prevent out-of-state offers (and sales), the issuer is required to accompany any offer, in the manner in which the offer is communicated, a prominent disclosure that sales will only be made to in-state residents and that out-of-state resales are prohibited for six months. [SA Rule 147(f)(3)]

(5) Is Certain Information Required to Be Disclosed to Offerees or Purchasers in Order to Satisfy the Exemption?

Issuers are required to make the mandatory disclosures about the in-state nature of the offer and the prohibition on out-of-state resales for six months. No additional disclosures are required in order to satisfy the exemption from registration. However, the issuer is still subject to the antifraud and civil liability provisions of the federal securities laws, which may require disclosure.

(6) Are There Manner or Place of Sale Restrictions?

All offers and sales must be in-state. Although advertising is permitted within the state, it must be accompanied by a prominent disclosure that sales will only be made to in-state residents and that out-of-state resales are prohibited for six months. [SA Rule 147(f)(3)]

(7) Does the Issuer Have to Satisfy Certain Qualifications?

The issuer must be "resident" and "doing business" in the same state as the offerees and purchasers. Rule 147 provides specific rules for determining whether an issuer is resident and doing business in the state.

(a) Determination of the Issuer's State of Residence

The issuer's state of residence is determined as follows:

(i) If the issuer is a corporation or other business entity organized under state law, the issuer is a resident of the state where it *both* (1) incorporated or organized under state law and (2) has its principal place of business; and

(ii) If the issuer is a general partnership or other form of business entity not organized under state law, the issuer is a resident of the state where it has its principal place of business.

[SA Rule 147(c)(1)]

Note: If a business entity is organized under the law of one state with its principal place of business in another state, it cannot rely on Rule 147 because it is not a "resident" of any state under this test. For example, if a corporation is incorporated in Delaware with its principal place of business in California, it is neither a resident of Delaware nor California under this test. The S.E.C. responded to this shortcoming of Rule 147 in Rule 147A, discussed below.

(b) Determination of Whether the Issuer Is Doing Business in the State

An issuer is deemed to be doing business in a state if it satisfies *one* of the following four tests:

(i) at least 80% of its consolidated gross revenues are derived from the operation of a business or property located in the state, or from the rendering of services within the state;

(ii) at least 80% of the issuer's consolidated assets are held in the state;

(iii) at least 80% of the proceeds from the securities transaction in question are to be used, and in fact are used, in the issuer's operations within the state; or

(iv) a majority of the issuer's employees are located within the state.

[SA Rule 147(c)(2)]

(8) Is an S.E.C. Filing Required?

No.

(9) Are the Securities "Restricted," Such That Resale by Initial Investors Is Prohibited?

Out-of-state resales are prohibited for six months. [SA Rule 147(e)] In addition, the issuer must take certain precautions to prevent out-of-state resales:

(a) The issuer must place a prominent legend on the certificate or other document evidencing the security stating that out-of-state resales are prohibited for six months;

(b) The issuer must issue stop transfer instructions to the issuer's transfer agent, if any; and

(c) All offers and sales must be accompanied by a prominent disclosure that sales will only be made to in-state residents and that out-of-state resales are prohibited for six months.

[SA Rule 147(f)]

(10) Are State Registration Requirements Preempted?

No.

(11) How Clear Is the Exemption, and Is There Grace for Noncompliance?

The exemption clearly defines how to determine the residence of issuers, offerees, and purchasers, although there remains some ambiguity about how to ensure that advertising (including on the internet) does not result in a prohibited out-of-state offer. (Note that Rule 147A responds to this ambiguity.) There is a little bit of grace for issuers in that they must merely "reasonably believe" that all offerees and purchasers are in-state residents.

h. Rule 147A Instrastate Offering Exemption

In 2016, the S.E.C. adopted Rule 147A. As discussed above, there are two significant limitations to the Rule 147 exemption (which a safe harbor under that statutory Section 3(a)(11) exemption): (1) it is unclear whether an issuer could comply with the prohibition on out-of-state offers while using the internet to advertise the securities; and (2) an issuer with different states of incorporation (or organization) and principal place of business cannot satisfy Rule 147's residency requirement in any state. These limitations of Rule 147 are mandated by Section 3(a)(11). In response, the S.E.C. adopted Rule 147A under its general exemptive authority (rather than under Section 3(a)(11)). [SA Section 28] Rule 147A is substantially similar to Rule 147 except that it resolves both of these limitations.

(1) What Is the Policy Rationale for the Exemption from Registration?

Rule 147A is substantially similar to the other intrastate exemptions and thus has the same policy rationale.

(2) Is There a Limit on the Amount of Money an Issuer Can Raise or That a Single Investor Can Invest in the Exempt Offering?

No.

(3) Is There a Limit on the Number of Offerees or Purchasers?

No.

(4) Are the Offerees or Purchasers Required to Be of a Certain Type?

All *purchasers* (not offerees!) must be residents of one state (the issuer's state). Rule 147A provides a clear test to assess whether a purchaser is a resident. In addition, the issuer must prominently disclose this limitation in all offers.

(a) Test to Determine Purchasers' In-State Residence

All purchasers must reside in the state of the issuer's residence. A purchaser's residence is determined as follows:

(i) If the purchaser is a business organization, it resides in the state of its principal place of business (however, if the organization is organized for the specific purpose of acquiring securities offered under Rule 147, then all beneficial owners of the organization must also be residents of the state);

(ii) If the purchaser is an individual, he or she resides in the state of his or her principal residence.

[SA Rule 147(d)]

Note: The issuer is also required to obtain a written representation from each purchaser as to his or her residence. [SA Rule 147A(f)(1)(iii)]

(b) Issuer's Disclosures to Offerees

The issuer is required to accompany any offer, in the manner in which the offer is communicated, a prominent disclosure that sales will only be made to in-state residents and that out-of-state resales are prohibited for six months. [SA Rule 147A(f)(3)]

(5) Is Certain Information Required to Be Disclosed to Offerees or Purchasers in Order to Satisfy the Exemption?

Issuers are required to make the mandatory disclosures about the in-state purchaser requirement and the prohibition on out-of-state resales for six months. No additional disclosures are required in order to satisfy the exemption from registration. However, the issuer is still subject to the antifraud and civil liability provisions of the federal securities laws, which may require disclosure.

(6) Are There Manner or Place of Sale Restrictions?

All sales (not offers!) must be in-state. Advertising is permitted within the state, as long as it is accompanied by a prominent disclosure that sales will only be made to in-state residents and that out-of-state resales are prohibited for six months. [SA Rule 147A(f)(3)]

(7) Does the Issuer Have to Satisfy Certain Qualifications?

The issuer must be "resident" and "doing business" in the same state as the offerees and purchasers. Rule 147A provides specific rules for determining whether an issuer is resident and doing business in the state. In addition, investment companies may not rely on Rule 147A.

(a) Determination of the Issuer's State of Residence

The issuer's state of residence is its principal place of business. [SA Rule 147A(c)(1)]

Note: Unlike Rule 147, the issuer's state of incorporation or organization is not relevant to its place of residence. Accordingly, a corporation that is incorporated in Delaware with its principal place of business in California is permitted to rely on Rule 147A. That issuer would be a resident of California.

(b) Determination of Whether the Issuer Is Doing Business in the State

An issuer is deemed to be doing business in a state if it satisfies *one* of the following four tests:

(i) at least 80% of its consolidated gross revenues are derived from the operation of a business or property located in the state, or from the rendering of services within the state;

(ii) at least 80% of the issuer's consolidated assets are held in the state;

(iii) at least 80% of the proceeds from the securities transaction in question are to be used, and in fact are used, in the issuer's operations within the state; or

(iv) a majority of the issuer's employees are located within the state.

[SA Rule 147A(c)(2)]

(8) Is an S.E.C. Filing Required?

No.

(9) Are the Securities "Restricted," Such That Resale by Initial Investors Is Prohibited?

Out-of-state resales are prohibited for six months. [SA Rule 147A(e)] In addition, the issuer must take certain precautions to prevent out-of-state resales:

(a) The issuer must place a prominent legend on the certificate or other document evidencing the security stating that out-of-state resales are prohibited for six months;

(b) The issuer must issue stop transfer instructions to the issuer's transfer agent, if any; and

(c) All offers and sales must be accompanied by a prominent disclosure that sales will only be made to in-state residents and that out-of-state resales are prohibited for six months.

[SA Rule 147A(f)]

(10) Are State Registration Requirements Preempted?

No.

(11) How Clear Is the Exemption, and Is There Grace for Noncompliance?

The exemption responds to the ambiguities in Rule 147. In addition, there is a little bit of grace for issuers in that they must merely "reasonably believe" that all purchasers are in-state residents.

i. Regulation CF Crowdfunding Exemption

As a key component of the Jumpstart our Business Startups Act of 2012 ("JOBS Act), Congress enacted SA Sections 4(a)(6) and 4A to authorize so-called crowdfunding. The S.E.C. implemented this statutory mandate by adopting Regulation CF.

(1) What Is the Policy Rationale for the Exemption from Registration?

When authorizing crowdfunded offerings, Congress sought to increase issuers' access to capital by permitting issuers to raise funds from disperse investors via the internet. At the same time, Congress sought to ensure that investors were sufficiently protected in light of the risky nature of these investments.

(2) Is There a Limit on the Amount of Money an Issuer Can Raise or That a Single Investor Can Invest in the Exempt Offering?

(a) Limit on Amount Raised

The current offering limit is $5 million (includes any securities sold during the 12 months preceding this transaction under this exemption).

In addition, the issuer must disclose a target offering amount and the deadline to reach that amount. If the issuer does not achieve that targeting offering amount by the deadline, no securities may be sold in the offering, and all funds must be returned to investors.

(b) Limit on Amount Invested

If the investor is "accredited" (see above p. 68), there is no limit on the amount the investor can invest in this or other crowdfunded offerings. If the investor is not accredited, however, the investor's investment is capped—*not only for this offering, but for all Regulation CF offerings during the 12 months preceding this transaction*. These investment limits depend on the investor's income or wealth:

(i) If *either* the non-accredited investor's annual income *or* net worth is less than $107,000, the investor's investment is capped at the *greater* of the following:

(1) $2,200 or

(2) 5% of the investor's annual income or net worth (whichever is greater).

(ii) If *both* the non-accredited investor's annual income and net worth *are* $107,000 or greater, the investor's investment is capped at the *lesser* of the following:

(1) $107,000 or

(2) 10% of the investor's annual income or net worth (whichever is greater).

[Reg. CF, Rule 100(a)(2)]

(3) Is There a Limit on the Number of Offerees or Purchasers?

No.

(4) Are the Offerees or Purchasers Required to Be of a Certain Type?

No.

(5) Is Certain Information Required to Be Disclosed to Offerees or Purchasers in Order to Satisfy the Exemption?

Yes, the mandatory S.E.C. filings discussed below on pp. 83–84 (the Form C: Offering Statement, the Form C: Progress Update, and the Form C: Annual Report) must be provided to all investors.

(6) Are There Manner or Place of Sale Restrictions?

Yes, issuers must conduct the Regulation CF offering only via an intermediary (*e.g.*, a funding portal) that itself complies with Regulation CF. All funding portals are required to register with the S.E.C. and meet various requirements.

(7) Does the Issuer Have to Satisfy Certain Qualifications?

The following issuers may not rely on Regulation CF: (1) reporting issuers under the 1934 Act; (2) investment companies; (3) issuers who qualify as "bad actors"; and (4) issuers who have relied on Regulation CF previously but have not provided investors with required annual reports during the two years immediately preceding this offer. [Reg. CF, Rule 100(b)]

(8) Is an S.E.C. Filing Required?

Yes, issuers are required to make three types of S.E.C. filings: the Form C: Offering Statement, the Form C: Progress Update, and the Form C: Annual Report. These filings must also be provided to investors.

(a) Form C: Offering Statement

The Form C: Offering Statement must be filed with the S.E.C. and provided to all investors. Required components include a description of the purpose and intended use of the offering proceeds, a description of the ownership and capital structure of the issuer, and financial disclosures. [Reg CF, Rule 201] The requisite financial disclosures are graduated, depending on the amount sought to be raised in the offering:

(i) If the offering (including all amounts sold under Regulation CF during the preceding 12 months) is $107,000 or less, the issuer must disclose its total income, taxable income, and total tax from the most recently completed year (if any) and provide financial statements. The principal executive officer must certify the accuracy of these disclosures.

(ii) If the offering (including all amounts sold under Regulation CF during the preceding 12 months) is more than $107,000 but not more than $535,000, the issuer must provide financial statements *reviewed* by an independent public accountant.

(iii) If the offering is more than $535,000 but not more than $1,070,000 *and if* the issuer has not previously sold securities under Regulation CF, the issuer must provide financial statements *reviewed* by an independent public accountant.

(iv) If the offering is more than $535,000 (including all amounts sold under Regulation CF during the preceding 12 months) *and if* the issuer does not fall within subpart (iii) above, the issuer must provide the financial statements *audited* by an independent public accountant.

[Reg. CF, Rule 201]

(b) **Form C: Progress Update**

The Form C: Progress Update must be filed with the S.E.C. and provided to all investors. This update must be filed no later than five business days after the dates on which the issuer reaches 50% and 100% of the target offering amount. [Reg CF, Rule 203(a)(3)]

(c) **Form C: Annual Report**

After completing an offering under Regulation CF, an issuer must file an annual report (Form C: Annual Report) with the S.E.C., as well as posting the annual report on its website. This report must include the issuer's financial statements, certified by the principal executive officer as being accurate.

This ongoing reporting requirement (which is significantly less substantial that the reporting requirements under the 1934 Act) continues until the first of the following occurs:

(i) the issuer becomes a reporting company under the 1934 Act;

(ii) since its most recent sales under Regulation CF, the issuer has filed at least one annual report and has fewer than 300 holders of record;

(iii) since its most recent sales under Regulation CF, the issuer has filed annual reports for at least the three most recent years and has total assets that do not exceed $10 million;

(iv) the issuer or another party repurchases all of the securities issued under Regulation CF; or

(v) the issuer liquidates or dissolves its business in accordance with state law.

[Reg. CF, Rule 202]

(9) **Are the Securities "Restricted," Such That Resale by Initial Investors Is Prohibited?**

Initial purchasers may not resell the securities purchased under Regulation CF for one year, unless the securities are transferred (a) to the issuer; (b) to an accredited investor; (c) as part of an offering registered with the S.E.C.; or (d) to a member of the family of the purchaser or the equivalent. [Reg. CF, Rule 501]

(10) **Are State Registration Requirements Preempted?**

Yes.

(11) **How Clear Is the Exemption, and Is There Grace for Noncompliance?**

The exemption is clear, and an issuer that commits an inadvertent and immaterial violation can, under some circumstances, still claim the exemption. [Reg. CF, Rule 502]

j. Integration of Offerings

Suppose an issuer sells $10,000 worth of securities to a single investor. The next day, the issuer sells $10,000 in securities to a different investor; the next day, to a third investor, and so on for a full year. Are these 365 separate transactions (each of which may qualify for a separate exemption from registration), or one transaction spread over a year (which must satisfy a single exemption from registration)? These facts raise the problem of *integration*: When an issuer has on separate occasions attempted several offerings under transactional exemptions, a question may arise as to whether the offerings were truly separate or only one offering disguised as multiple offerings to help the issuer evade registration. While the issuer might attempt to convey the appearance of having made two or more offerings, the S.E.C. might decide that the several offerings are *integrated* (*i.e.*, that all of the offerings are part of the same offering). The effect of having several offerings integrated into one can be disastrous for the issuer, because it is unlikely that the integrated offering will qualify for a transactional exemption. The issuer, relying on exempt status, has not registered the offering and, therefore, will violate the Securities Act.

In 2020, the S.E.C. substantially revised the integration rules, decreasing the likelihood of integration. An issuer who has made multiple offerings should follow a two-step analysis:

(1) Are the offerings within a safe harbor from integration? If so, the offerings will not be integrated. If not, proceed to step two.

(2) Will the offerings be integrated under the general principle of integration? If so, the offerings will be integrated. If not, the offerings will not be integrated.

(1) Safe Harbors from Integration

Five key safe harbors applicable to exempt offerings are discussed here:

(a) Two Consecutive Exempt Offerings, Neither of Which Permits General Solicitation

The offerings will not be integrated if:

(i) More than 30 calendar days elapsed between the termination or completion of the first offering and the commencement of the second offering.

[SA Rule 152(b)(1)]

(b) Two Consecutive Exempt Offerings, the First of Which Permits General Solicitation and the Second of Which Prohibits General Solicitation

The offerings will not be integrated if:

(i) More than 30 calendar days elapsed between the termination or completion of the first offering and the commencement of the second offering; *and*

(ii) The issuer has a reasonable belief, based on the facts and circumstances, with respect to each purchaser in the exempt offering prohibiting general solicitation, that the issuer *either* (1) did not solicit such purchaser through the use of general solicitation *or* (2) established a substantive relationship with such purchaser prior to the commencement of the exempt offering prohibiting general solicitation. [SA Rule 152(b)(1)]

(c) Two Consecutive Exempt Offerings, the First of Which Prohibits General Solicitation and the Second of Which Permits General Solicitation

The offerings will not be integrated if the second offering commences after the first offering is terminated or completed. [SA Rule 152(b)(4)]

(d) Two Consecutive Exempt Offerings, Both of Which Permit General Solicitation

The offerings will not be integrated if the second offering commences after the first offering is terminated or completed. [SA Rule 152(b)(4)]

(e) An Exempt Offering Followed by a Registered Offering

The offerings will not be integrated if:

(i) The exempt offering was pursuant to an exemption for which general solicitation is not permitted; *or*

(ii) The exempt offering was pursuant to an exemption for which general solicitation is permitted, but the offering was made only to QIBs or institutional accredited investors; *or*

(iii) The exempt offering was pursuant to an exemption for which general solicitation is permitted, but more than 30 calendar days elapsed between the termination or completion of the exempt offering and the commencement of the registered offering. [SA Rule 152(b)(2)]

(2) General Principle of Integration

If the two offerings do not fall within a safe harbor from integration, then the general principle of integration applies. The two offerings will not be integrated if each independently satisfies an exemption or the registration requirements, with the following *two caveats*:

(a) *For an exempt offering prohibiting general solicitation*, the issuer must have a reasonable belief, based on the facts and circumstances, with respect to each purchaser in the exempt offering prohibiting general solicitation, that the issuer *either* (1) did not solicit such purchaser through the use of general solicitation *or* (2) established a substantive relationship with such purchaser prior to the commencement of the exempt offering prohibiting general solicitation. [SA Rule 152(a)(1)]

(b) *For multiple concurrent exempt offerings permitting general solicitation*, general solicitation offering materials for one offering that include information about the material terms of a concurrent offering under another exemption must comply with all of the requirements for, and restrictions on, offers under *both* exemptions (*e.g.*, legend requirements). [SA Rule 152(a)(2)]

5. Resale Exemptions

SA Section 5 prohibits all offers or sales of securities absent registration. This applies not only to initial sales by the issuer, but also to resales by investors.

Most resales are exempt from Section 5's registration requirements, however, under Section 4(a)(1). Section 4(a)(1) exempts all transactions from Section 5 *except* transactions involving an issuer, an underwriter, or a dealer.

For purposes of investors seeking to resell their securities, the key is to avoid "underwriter" status for either party to the transaction (either the reseller or the buyer). If either the reseller or the buyer qualifies as an underwriter, the transaction is not exempt from Section 5. To add to the complexity, as discussed above on pp. 38 *et seq.*, the term "underwriter" is defined broadly for this purpose to include persons who sell for an affiliate (control person) of the issuer. This means that anyone who purchases from a control person and resells in a public manner (for example, through a broker) risks becoming an underwriter. In both the case of resale of securities first sold in an exempt transaction, and securities sold by a control person, a party may become an underwriter without expressly taking on the "business role" of an underwriter. Such parties are called "statutory underwriters."

Example: George acquires 50,000 shares of ABC Corp. common stock in an unregistered private placement (*e.g.*, under Rule 506(b)). One month after acquiring the stock, George resells to 500 unsophisticated investors. This transaction violates Section 5, because ABC stock is not an exempt security and George's sale transaction does not qualify, as far as we know, for any exemption from the registration requirements under the 1933 Act. George's role here is that of an underwriter: he sold for an issuer in connection with a distribution.

Example: George is the CEO (a "control person") of ABC Corp. He also owns 50,000 shares of ABC common stock that he purchased on the stock exchange, using his brokerage account. George sells all 50,000 shares from his brokerage account, to raise money for a new vacation home. This transaction violates Section 5. Although George is not an underwriter in this example (he purchased the stock on the open market), his broker has become an underwriter (purchased from a control person of the issuer—which, for this purpose, is the same thing as buying directly from the issuer—and sold publicly). So, Section 5 is violated when George's broker sold to the public. However, George is also in trouble because his transaction was not within Section 4(a)(1). It involved an underwriter, and transactions by underwriters are not exempt. [*See* **United States v. Wolfson,** 405 F.2d 779 (2d Cir. 1968), *cert. denied,* 394 U.S. 946 (1969)]

Fortunately, there are several resale exemptions which ensure that resale transactions will not involve a statutory underwriter. The key resale exemptions are discussed here.

a. The So-Called 4(a)(1½) Resale Exemption

The so-called 4(a)(1½) exemption is a judicial interpretation of the definition of "underwriter" for purposes of Section 4(a)(1) by using case law interpreting Section 4(a)(2). The nickname for this exemption recognizes this melding. The rationale for this exemption is as follows:

(1) One means of foreclosing status as an "underwriter" is to disprove a "distribution."

(2) A "distribution" is the equivalent of a "public offering" and implicates the same policy concerns.

(3) Section 4(a)(2) exempts transactions by issuers not involving a "public offering."

(4) The Supreme Court, in **S.E.C. v. Ralston Purina**, 346 U.S. 119 (1953), identified the elements that must be present for a transaction to not be a "public offering" by the issuer under § 4(a)(2) because the offering is to "those who are shown to be able to fend for themselves."

(5) Thus, if the *Ralston Purina* elements are present, then there is not a "distribution" for purposes of § 4(a)(1), because the offering is likewise to those who do not need the protections of registration.

The *Ralston Purina* elements are discussed above on pp. 65 *et seq*. Because these elements are somewhat amorphous, and because it may be difficult for a reseller to satisfy all of these elements, a reseller will likely prefer to satisfy an express resale exemption.

b. Rule 144 Resale Exemption

Rule 144 is a safe harbor within Section 4(a)(1); if the reseller complies with Rule 144, the reseller will not be deemed an "underwriter" under Section 4(a)(1). Rule 144 provides six pathways for exempt resales, depending on the statuses of the re-seller, the securities, and the issuer:

(1) an affiliate selling restricted securities of a non-reporting issuer;

(2) an affiliate selling restricted securities of a reporting issuer;

(3) an affiliate selling unrestricted securities of a non-reporting issuer;

(4) an affiliate selling unrestricted securities of a reporting issuer;

(5) a non-affiliate selling restricted securities of a non-reporting issuer; and

(6) a non-affiliate selling restricted securities of a reporting issuer.

The Rule 144 definitions of "affiliate," "restricted securities," and "reporting issuer" are provided here. Then, each pathway is summarized.

(1) Definition of "Affiliate"

An "affiliate" is "a person that directly, or indirectly through one or more intermediaries, controls, or is controlled by, or is under common control with, such issuer." [SA Rule 144(a)(1)] The term "control" means "the possession, direct or indirect, of the power to direct or cause the direction of the management and policies of a person, whether through the ownership of voting securities, by contract, or otherwise." [SA Rule 405] Affiliates potentially include shareholders with a significant ownership percentage, officers, and directors.

(2) Definition of "Restricted Securities"

Rule 144 defines "restricted securities" as including the following:

(a) securities acquired directly or indirectly from the issuer, or from an affiliate of the issuer, in a transaction or chain of transactions not involving any public offering; and

(b) securities acquired from the issuer that are subject to the resale limitations of § 230.502(d) under Regulation D.

[SA Rule 144(a)(3)]

(3) Definition of "Reporting Issuer"

A "reporting issuer" under Rule 144 is one who "is, and has been for a period of at least 90 days immediately before the sale, subject to the reporting requirements of Section 13 or 15(d) of the Securities Exchange Act of 1934." [SA Rule 144(b)(1)(i)]

(4) Affiliate Selling Restricted Securities of a Non-Reporting Issuer

The resale is exempt if:

(a) adequate public information about the issuer is available (issuers not required to report under the 1934 Act may choose to report voluntarily, in order to make Rule 144 available to their security holders);

(b) reseller has held the securities for at least one year;

(c) reseller complies with volume limits on amount of securities sold; and

(d) reseller complies with manner of sale rules.

(5) Affiliate Selling Restricted Securities of a Reporting Issuer

The resale is exempt if:

(a) issuer has filed all required reports;

(b) reseller has held the securities for at least six months;

(c) reseller complies with volume limits on amount of securities sold; and

(d) reseller complies with manner of sale rules.

(6) Affiliate Selling Unrestricted Securities of a Non-Reporting Issuer

The resale is exempt if:

(a) adequate public information about the issuer is available (issuers not required to report under the 1934 Act may choose to report voluntarily, in order to make Rule 144 available to their security holders);

(b) reseller complies with volume limits on amount of securities sold; and

(c) reseller complies with manner of sale rules.

(7) Affiliate Selling Unrestricted Securities of a Reporting Issuer

The resale is exempt if:

(a) issuer has filed all required reports;

(b) reseller complies with volume limits on amount of securities sold; and

(c) reseller complies with manner of sale rules.

(8) Non-Affiliate Selling Restricted Securities of a Non-Reporting Issuer

The resale is exempt if:

(a) reseller has held the securities for at least one year.

(9) Non-Affiliate Selling Restricted Securities of a Reporting Issuer

The resale is exempt if:

(a) issuer has filed all required reports and reseller has held securities for at least six months; or

(b) reseller has held the securities for at least one year.

c. Section 4(a)(7) Resale Exemption

In 2015, the Fixing America's Surface Transportation Act added a new resale exemption, SA Section 4(a)(7) of the Securities Act. The key requirements are as follows:

(1) all purchasers must be "accredited" under Regulation D;

(2) general solicitation or advertising is prohibited;

(3) the seller must provide certain specific information to all prospective purchasers, including financial statements of the issuer; and

(4) the reseller cannot qualify as a "bad actor" under Regulation D.

d. Rule 144A Resale Exemption

The resale is exempt under SA Rule 144A if the following elements are met:

(1) every purchaser must be a "qualified institutional buyer" ("QIB") or someone whom the seller "reasonably believes" is such; and

(2) prospective purchasers must receive specified information from the issuer, including financial statements.

Note that, pursuant to the Jumpstart Our Business Startups Act of 2012 ("JOBS Act"), general solicitation and advertising is now permitted under Rule 144A.

G. Liabilities Under the 1933 Act

1. Introduction

The liability provisions of the 1933 Act are organized around the two basic objectives of the Act: providing disclosure of material information to potential investors in newly issued securities and generally preventing fraud and/or misrepresentation in the interstate sale of securities.

Note: SEA Section 10(b) and Rule 10b–5 also prohibit fraud in the sale of securities. Therefore, this liability provision is often used in claims associated with the offer and sale of securities. This liability provision is discussed further below on pp. 115 *et seq.*

a. Conduct Resulting in Liability

Issuers and others involved in a securities transaction may be liable for violating SA Section 5. Examples of violations of Section 5 include (1) offering or selling securities without satisfying an exemption from registration or registering the securities and (2) making an improper offer during the pre-filing period.

In addition, issuers and others involved in a securities transaction may be liable for making misrepresentations or omitting required information when offering or selling securities.

b. Right to Bring Action

Some of the 1933 Act's liability provisions can be enforced by private parties (*e.g.*, injured investors). Other provisions can only be enforced by the S.E.C.

c. Procedural Requirements

If the liability provision provides a private right of action, the injured investors may seek to assert their rights as a class. In that circumstance, there are additional procedural requirements imposed, not only by the rules of civil procedure, but also by the securities laws.

d. Remedies

A wide range of remedies is available in actions under the 1933 Act, depending in the first instance on the nature of the plaintiff. That is, there are different remedies available to the S.E.C. than are available to a private plaintiff (*e.g.*, an aggrieved investor).

e. Analytical Pathway

For each private civil liability provision, it is important to analyze the following questions:

(1) Who is a potentially liable defendant?

(2) Who is a potential plaintiff?

(3) What are the elements of the claim?

(4) What defenses are available?

(5) What is the plaintiff's remedy?

(6) Are there any special procedural or jurisdictional requirements potentially applicable to this claim?

Each of these questions will be addressed in turn for the key 1933 Act private civil liability provisions.

2. Section 12(a)(1)

Section 12(a)(1) provides that any person who offers or sells a security in violation of any of the provisions of Section 5 of the 1933 Act shall be liable to the purchaser for: (i) the consideration paid (with interest) less the amount of any income received on the securities (*i.e.*, a suit for rescission); or (ii) for damages (mimicking rescission) if the purchaser no longer owns the security.

a. Who Is a Potentially Liable Defendant?

Section 12(a)(1) imposes liability on those who offer or sell a security in violation of Section 5. But the 1933 Act nowhere says who may, for these purposes, be regarded as a statutory "seller" (or offeror). Clearly the person who passes title to the security is a seller, but may anyone else be regarded as a "seller" for purposes of Section 12(a)(1)? Courts were in conflict over this question until 1988, when the Supreme Court decided **Pinter v. Dahl**, 486 U.S. 622 (1988).

(1) Facts of *Pinter v. Dahl*

Pinter, an oil and gas operator and securities broker, sold unregistered oil and gas interests to Dahl in an attempted private placement. Later, Dahl solicited some of his friends to purchase additional interests, because Dahl believed the interests were good investments. Pinter sold the interests to Dahl's friends on the strength of Dahl's representations that the friends qualified as private placement investors. It turned out that the friends were not qualified private placement investors, and when the investment became worthless, Dahl and his friends sued under Section 12(a)(1). Pinter counterclaimed, alleging, among other things, that Dahl was a "seller" under Section 12(a)(1) and therefore that Dahl was required to contribute toward the amounts awarded the other plaintiffs.

(2) Definition of "Seller"

The Supreme Court held in *Pinter* that a "seller" for Section 12(a)(1) purposes includes:

(a) The person who actually passes title for value; and

(b) A person who solicits the purchase for value, motivated at least in part by the desire to serve his or her own financial interests or those of the securities owner.

Note: Under *Pinter*, the term "seller" does not include persons whose *sole* motivation in acting is to benefit the buyer.

(3) Control Persons

In addition, persons who "control" any person liable under Section 12(a)(1) may be held jointly and severally liable with the controlled person, unless the controlling person had no knowledge of, or reasonable grounds to believe in, the existence of the facts on which the liability of the controlled person is alleged to rest. [SA § 15(a)]

b. Who Is a Potential Plaintiff?

Investors have a private right of action under Section 12(a)(1). Section 12(a)(1) imposes a condition of privity of contract between the plaintiff-purchaser and the seller-defendant. Remember, however, that persons who solicit the plaintiff's purchase, although they do not actually pass title to the security, are nevertheless held to be "sellers" in privity with the purchaser.

c. What Are the Elements of the Claim?

The plaintiff must establish a violation of SA Section 5. Such violations include selling unregistered securities absent an exemption from registration, failing to deliver a required prospectus, and making an illegal offer in the pre-filing period.

d. What Defenses Are Available?

The defendant can assert the equitable defense of "in pari delicto."

In addition, the statute of limitations is relatively short. The period of limitations is one year after the violation, but in no event more than three years after the security was *bona fide* offered to the public.

e. What Is the Plaintiff's Remedy?

The plaintiff is entitled to rescission or, if the plaintiff has already resold the securities, damages mimicking rescission.

f. Are There Any Special Procedural or Jurisdictional Requirements Potentially Applicable to This Claim?

Federal and state courts have concurrent jurisdiction over claims under SA Section 12(a)(1). [SA § 22(a); *see* **Cyan, Inc. v. Beaver County Employees Retirement Fund**, discussed below on p. 100]

If the claim is asserted as a class action in federal court, SA Section 27 applies, including the provisions regarding the appointment of lead plaintiff and the stay of discovery during the pendency of any motion to dismiss. It is an open question to what degree these provisions apply if the class action is proceeding in state court.

3. Section 12(a)(2)

Section 12(a)(2) prohibits offers or sales of securities by means of a prospectus or oral communication that contains an untrue statement or omission of material fact necessary in order to make statements therein not misleading.

a. Who Is a Potentially Liable Defendant?

Pinter v. Dahl, discussed above on p. 91, applies equally to claims under Section 12(a)(2). Thus, the following persons are potentially liable defendants:

(1) The person who actually passes title for value; and

(2) A person who solicits the purchase for value, motivated at least in part by the desire to serve his or her own financial interests or those of the securities owner.

In addition, persons who "control" any person liable under Section 12(a)(2) may be held jointly and severally liable with the controlled person, unless the controlling person had no knowledge of, or reasonable grounds to believe in, the existence of the facts on which the liability of the controlled person is alleged to rest. [SA § 15(a)]

b. Who Is a Potential Plaintiff?

Injured investors have a private right of action under Section 12(a)(2). As under Section 12(a)(1), Section 12(a)(2) imposes a privity requirement. The plaintiff must have purchased from the defendant. Remember, however, that persons who solicit the plaintiff's purchase, although they do not actually pass title to the security, are nevertheless held to be "sellers" in privity with the purchaser. Unlike under Section 11, no tracing is permitted.

c. What Are the Elements of the Claim?

The elements of a claim under Section 12(a)(2) are as follows:

(1) An Untrue Statement or Omission of Material Fact Necessary in Order to Make Statements Therein Not Misleading

(a) Materiality

In order for a false or omitted fact to form the basis for liability, it must be "material." An omitted or misrepresented fact is material if there is a substantial likelihood that a reasonable investor would consider it important in making an investment decision. Stated otherwise, an omitted or misrepresented fact is material if there is a substantial likelihood that the fact would have been viewed by the reasonable investor as having significantly altered the total mix of information made available. This is an objective standard, based on a reasonable investor.

(b) Safe Harbor for Forward-Looking Statements

The safe harbor for forward-looking statements applies only to forward-looking statements made by, or on behalf of, a reporting issuer. [SA § 27A(a)] Thus, if the Section 12(a)(2) claim is based on alleged misrepresentations associated with an initial public offering of a non-reporting issuer, the safe harbor does not apply. If the claim is based on alleged misrepresentations associated with a public offering of a reporting issuer, however, the safe harbor may shield the defendant from liability. The safe harbor is discussed further below on pp. 120–122. In short, however, a forward-looking statement cannot form the basis of liability if (1) it is identified as forward-looking and accompanied by meaningful cautionary language or (2) the plaintiff fails to prove that the forward-looking statement was made with actual knowledge that it was false or misleading. [SA § 27A(c)(1)]

(2) Plaintiff Did Not Know of the Untruth or Omission

Section 12(a)(2) states that an untruth or omission is only actionable if the following test is met: "purchaser not knowing of such untruth or omission."

(3) By Means of a Prospectus or Oral Communication in a "Public" Offering

Prior to the Supreme Court's decision in **Gustafson v. Alloyd Co.**, 513 U.S. 561 (1995), it was widely believed that Section 12(a)(2) applied to misrepresentations or omissions in connection with all securities offerings, regardless of whether the offerings were registered or exempt. In *Gustavson*, however, the Court severely limited the applicability of Section 12(a)(2) by holding that it applies only to misrepresentations or omissions in "public" offerings. Registered offerings certainly qualify as public. It is an open question whether some exempt offerings qualify as "public" for purposes of Section 12(a)(2).

(4) Defendant's Knowledge of the Untrue Statement

The plaintiff must plead that the defendant knew, or in the exercise of reasonable care should have known, of the untrue statement. However, the defendant then must bear the burden of proof on the issue (*i.e.*, that he or she did not know, and in the exercise of reasonable care could not have known, of the untrue statement). (See below p. 94 on the reasonable care defense.)

d. What Defenses Are Available?

(1) Reasonable Care Defense

A defendant can escape liability by proving that he or she "did not know, and in the exercise of reasonable care could not have known, of such untruth or omission." [SA § 12(a)(2)] This is basically a simple negligence standard.

Whether an investigation is required depends on all of the circumstances, but an underwriter probably has to make a reasonable investigation of an issuer. [**Sanders v. John Nuveen & Co.**, 619 F.2d 1222 (7th Cir. 1980), *cert. denied*, 450 U.S. 1005 (1981)]

(2) Statute of Limitations

The period of limitations for a Section 12(a)(2) cause of action is one year after discovery of the false statement or material omission, or after such discovery should have been made in the exercise of reasonable diligence, but not more than three years after the sale.

e. What Is the Plaintiff's Remedy?

Like under SA Section 12(a)(1), the plaintiff is entitled to rescission or, if the plaintiff has already resold the securities, damages mimicking rescission.

However, in an action brought under Section 12(a)(2), the defendant can avoid monetary liability to the extent that he or she can prove that all or any portion of the loss otherwise recoverable under Section 12(a)(2) was caused by something other than the defendant's alleged misstatement or omission. [SA § 12(b)]

f. Are There Any Special Procedural or Jurisdictional Requirements Potentially Applicable to This Claim?

Federal and state courts have concurrent jurisdiction over claims under SA Section 12(a)(2), even if those claims are asserted as class actions. [SA § 22(a); *see* **Cyan, Inc. v. Beaver County Employees Retirement Fund**, discussed below on p. 100]

If the claim is asserted as a class action in federal court, SA Section 27 applies, including the provisions regarding the appointment of lead plaintiff and the stay of discovery during the pendency of any motion to dismiss. It is an open question to what degree these provisions apply if the class action is proceeding in state court.

4. Section 11

Section 11 of the 1933 Act imposes liability on designated persons for materially false or misleading statements or omissions in an effective registration statement. Section 11 is the most frequently litigated liability provision in the Act.

a. Who Is a Potentially Liable Defendant?

Section 11 lists the potentially liable defendants as follows:

(1) every person who signed the registration statement (*see* SA § 6(a) for required signatories [issuer, CEO, CFO, controller, principal accounting officer, and majority of board].);

(2) every person who was a director of or a partner in issuer at time of filing;

(3) very person who, with his or her consent, is named as being or about to become a director, person performing similar functions, or partner;

(4) every accountant, engineer, or appraiser (or person with similar authority) who, with his or her consent, is named as having prepared or certified any part of the registration statement (*but only* with respect to that "expertised" portion]; and

(5) every underwriter. [SA § 11(a)(1)]

In addition, persons who "control" any person who is liable under Section 11 may be held jointly and severally liable with the liable persons, unless the controlling person had no knowledge of nor reasonable grounds to believe in the existence of the facts on which the liability of the controlled person is alleged to rest. [*See* SA § 15]

b. Who Is a Potential Plaintiff?

Any person "acquiring such security" offered pursuant to the allegedly false or misleading registration statement has standing as a plaintiff. Most courts interpret this to mean that even persons who purchased a security in the secondary market (as opposed to those who purchased the security in the issuer's public offering) can recover under Section 11, as long as they can prove that the specific securities purchased were issued in the offering registered by the defective registration statement (a procedure called "tracing" the securities). [*See, e.g.*, **Hertzberg v. Dignity Partners, Inc.**, 191 F.3d 1076 (9th Cir. 1999)]

Unlike SA Section 12(a)(2), Section 11 does not require privity of contract between the plaintiff and the defendant. In other words, a purchaser with standing may sue any person described by the statute as a potential defendant.

c. What Are the Elements of the Claim?

The elements of a claim under Section 11 are as follows:

(1) An Untrue Statement or Omission of Material Fact Necessary in Order to Make Statements Therein Not Misleading

(a) Materiality

In order for a false or omitted fact to form the basis for liability, it must be "material." An omitted or misrepresented fact is material if there is a substantial likelihood that a reasonable investor would consider it important in making an investment decision. Stated otherwise, an omitted or misrepresented fact is material if there is a substantial likelihood that the fact would have been viewed by the reasonable investor as having significantly altered the total mix of information made available. This is an objective standard, based on a reasonable investor.

(b) Safe Harbor for Forward-Looking Statements

The safe harbor for forward-looking statements applies only to forward-looking statements made by, or on behalf of, a reporting issuer. [SA § 27A(a)] Thus, if the Section 11 claim is based on alleged misrepresentations associated with an initial public offering, the safe harbor does not apply. If the claim is based on alleged misrepresentations in a registration statement of a reporting issuer, however, the safe harbor may shield the defendant from liability. The safe harbor is discussed further below on pp. 120–122. In short, however, a forward-looking statement cannot form the basis of liability if (1) it is identified as forward-looking and accompanied by meaningful cautionary language or (2) the plaintiff fails to prove that the forward-looking statement was made with actual knowledge that it was false or misleading. [SA § 27A(c)(1)]

(2) Plaintiff Did Not Know of the Untruth or Omission

The plaintiff must plead that he or she did not know of the untruth or omission. However, the defendant then must bear the burden of proof on the issue. (See below on the plaintiff's knowledge defense.)

(3) Plaintiff's Reliance

Generally, the plaintiff does not need to plead or prove reliance on the alleged untruth or omission.

If, however, the plaintiff purchased the security after the issuer made generally available to its security holders an earning statement covering a period of at least 12 months beginning after the effective date of the registration statement, the plaintiff must prove reliance on the untruth or omission. Such reliance may be established without proof of the reading of the registration statement by the plaintiff. [SA § 11(a)]

(4) In an Effective Registration Statement

The alleged untruth or omission must be in an effective registration statement. A free writing prospectus (see above p. 33) is not part of the registration statement for an offering. Consequently, SA Section 11 does not apply to statements made in a free writing prospectus.

(5) Defendant's Lack of Due Diligence

Although Section 11 is a strict liability claim (*i.e.*, the plaintiff does not have to prove that the defendant acted with a particular mental state), defendants may be able to prove a due diligence defense. (See below on the due diligence defense.)

d. What Defenses Are Available?

(1) Plaintiff's Knowledge

It is an affirmative defense to liability if the plaintiff-purchaser knew of the misleading statements or omissions and invested in the securities anyway.

(2) Defendant's Due Diligence

A defendant may be able to avoid Section 11 liability by proving his or her due diligence. The availability of this defense, and the due diligence test that applies, depends on the identity of the defendant and the type of untruth or omission. Section

11 makes a distinction between "experts" (*i.e.*, those who certify part of the registration statement as being true [such as certified public accountants who certify that the financial statements were prepared according to generally accepted accounting principles]) and "non-experts" (*i.e.*, all others who may be held liable pursuant to Section 11). Section 11 also draws a distinction between the standard of care (*i.e.*, what constitutes due diligence) required of non-experts who review material prepared by other non-experts, and that required of non-experts reviewing statements of experts.

(a) Issuer

The due diligence defense is *not* available to the issuer.

(b) Non-Expert Regarded Expertised Statement

If the alleged misrepresentation or omission is in an expertised portion of the registration statement, a non-expert may establish the due diligence defense merely by showing that he or she had "no reasonable ground to believe and did not believe" that the statement was untrue. For example, if the alleged misrepresentation is in a financial statement that was audited by an accountant, a director may be able to establish due diligence under this relatively lenient standard.

(c) Non-Expert Regarding Non-Expertised Statement

If the alleged misrepresentation or omission is not in an expertised portion of the registration, however, a non-expert may establish the due diligence defense only by showing that "after reasonable investigation," he or she had "reasonable ground to believe and did believe" that the statement was true. For example, if the alleged misrepresentation is the MD&A portion of the registration statement, a director may establish due diligence only via this more stringent standard.

Under Section 11, the test for defining the scope of a "reasonable investigation" is what a prudent person would do in the management of her own affairs. [*See* SA § 11(c)] As a practical matter, however, there is no single standard. The court looks at each individual defendant and, based on the person's position with the issuer, responsibilities relative to the issuer and the registration statement, and background, skills, training, and access to information, the court determines what the person should have done to fulfill the obligation of a "reasonable investigation." In other words, the test is really what kind of investigation a prudent person in the defendant's position, with the same responsibilities, skills, etc., would have made. [**Escott v. BarChris Construction Corp.**, *supra*] Here are some examples:

(i) Attorney Drafting Registration Statement

An attorney who is also a member of the issuer's board of directors and who drafts the issuer's registration statement (and collects facts from the issuer to do so) does not "certify" his or her work and thus is a "non-expert" as to the registration statement in general. In *BarChris*, the court indicated that the attorney-director did not have to conduct an independent audit of the issuer, but that a reasonable investigation would go beyond merely trusting the opinions and responses of the issuer's officers as to material facts. Therefore, a reasonable investigation by the attorney would include:

(a) looking at original written records (*e.g.*, written contracts) to verify statements in the registration statement;

(b) an examination of the issuer's facilities, operations, material contracts, corporate minutes and other documents, and major items important to its financial condition;

(c) use of a comprehensive questionnaire for directors and officers to elicit information required to be disclosed (such as whether they had any conflicting interests); and

(d) having an accountant check any suspicious items disclosed by the lawyer's investigation.

(ii) Underwriters

Underwriters qualify as non-experts and so must make a reasonable investigation of the non-expert portions of the registration statement. They cannot simply rely on assurances of accuracy from the issuer's management, attorneys, etc. [*See* **Escott v. BarChris Construction Corp.**, *supra*]

Note that normally the "lead underwriter" (usually the underwriting firm that first established contact with the issuer, and which structures and manages the underwriting for all of the other underwriting firms) will conduct an investigation of the issuer for all members of the underwriting syndicate to satisfy the due diligence requirement. However, if the lead underwriter conducts a faulty investigation, this does not absolve the other underwriters.

(iii) Inside Directors and Executive Officers

The standard of diligence imposed on directors who are also part of management (*i.e.*, officers of the issuer) and on the principal executive officers of the issuer is even higher than that imposed on underwriters. For example, if there are misstatements made relating to the issuer's financial condition, the issuer's chief financial officer will have a hard time sustaining his or burden of showing that he or she really did not know of the misrepresentations. [*See* **Escott v. BarChris Construction Corp.**, *supra*]

(iv) Outside Directors

Outside directors (those who are not employed by the issuer as part of management) must also meet the due diligence test for non-experts. However, their position differs from inside directors in that, although they must discharge the duty of a director, they cannot realistically be expected to do a great deal to check on the accuracy of the registration statement. Thus, the issue is how extensive is the duty of an outside director? It appears from the cases that outside directors will probably be expected to attend directors' meetings during the time registration is underway and will also be held responsible for reading directors' meeting minutes, reading the drafts of the registration statement before filing and, in a general way, questioning company management, accountants, and legal counsel. If this investigation turns up apparent misstatements, the directors must personally check into these matters and require company counsel to check into them. [*See* **Escott v. BarChris Construction Corp.**, *supra*]

(d) Expert Regarding Expertised Statement

Likewise, if the alleged misrepresentation or omission is an expertised portion of the registration, the expert may establish the due diligence defense only by showing that "after reasonable investigation," he or she had "reasonable ground to believe and did believe" that the statement was true. An expert must meet this more stringent standard to establish the due diligence defense with respect to statements that he or she expertised. (As a reminder, an expert is only potentially liable under Section 11 for the portion of the registration statement that he or she expertised.)

For their belief to be reasonable, the experts must have made a reasonable investigation into the facts supporting the statements made. Normally, this means that they must at least have performed up to the standards of their profession (*e.g.*, accountants must make an investigation of the facts that would conform to the standards of their profession and must state the issuer's financial results according to the generally accepted accounting principles set forth by the S.E.C.). [*See* **Escott v. BarChris Construction Corp.**, 283 F. Supp. 643 (S.D.N.Y. 1968)]

(3) Statute of Limitations

Under Section 11, the period of limitations is one year after discovery of the false statement, with an overall limitation of three years after the security is first bona fide offered to the public. [SA § 13] This means that if a portion of the issue remains unsold after three years, for example in a continuous offering, purchasers after that time are not protected by Section 11 of the Act.

e. What Is the Plaintiff's Remedy?

(1) Damages Calculation

The plaintiff may recover the difference *between*

(a) the amount paid for the security (not exceeding the offer price) *and*

(b) the following applicable amount:

(i) the value at the time suit is brought (if the security is not sold pre-suit); *or*

(ii) the price for which the security was sold before suit was brought (if the security was sold pre-suit); *or*

(iii) the price for which the security was sold during the pendency of the suit (*if* the damages amount is *less* than the difference if calculated at the time suit was brought). [SA § 11(e)]

Note: a plaintiff does not have a duty to mitigate damages by selling during the suit, even if it would decrease the damages recovery.

Note: In no case can the amount recovered exceed the price at which the security was offered to the public.

(2) Reduction of Damages

The defendant may reduce the damages by proving that all or some portion of the calculated damages resulted from some cause other than the misrepresentation or omission of material fact in the registration statement. [SA § 11(e)]

(3) Joint and Several Liability

All defendants (*except* outside directors) who are liable under Section 11 are jointly and severally liable, and every person who becomes liable to make any payment under Section 11 may recover contribution from any person who, if had they been sued would have been liable, unless the person who has become liable was guilty of fraudulent misrepresentation and the person who has not become liable was not. [SA § 11(f)]

Outside directors are jointly and severally liable only for knowing violations of Section 11. For all other violations of Section 11, they are liable proportionately to their respective degrees of fault. [SA § 11(f)(2)]

f. Are There Any Special Procedural or Jurisdictional Requirements Potentially Applicable to This Claim?

Federal and state courts have concurrent jurisdiction over claims under SA Section 12(a)(1), even if those claims are asserted as class actions. [SA § 22(a); *see* **Cyan, Inc. v. Beaver County Employees Retirement Fund**, 138 S.Ct. 1061 (2018)] In 2018, in *Cyan*, the Supreme Court resolved a circuit split regarding whether Securities Act claims asserted as class actions could proceed in state court, despite the Securities Litigation Uniform Standards Act ("SLUSA") [SA § 16]. The Court held that SLUSA did not deprive state courts of jurisdiction over Securities Act class actions. (SLUSA is discussed further below on pp. 212 *et seq.*) This had led to an influx of Section 11 class actions into state courts.

If the claim is asserted as a class action in federal court, SA Section 27 applies, including the provisions regarding the appointment of lead plaintiff and the stay of discovery during the pendency of any motion to dismiss. It is an open question to what degree these provisions apply if the class action is proceeding in state court.

5. Section 17—S.E.C. Enforcement

As discussed above, Sections 11, 12(a)(1), and 12(a)(2) of the 1933 Act provide plaintiffs with express causes of action based on specific types of misconduct in connection with the issuance of securities. These sections, however, are not available to the S.E.C., which is not a party to securities transactions. The Act therefore contains a provision—Section 17—which provides the S.E.C. with enforcement authority.

a. Overview of Section 17

Section 17 makes it unlawful for any person in the *offer or sale* of securities by use of any means or instruments of transportation or communication in interstate commerce or by the use of the mails, directly or indirectly:

(a) *To employ any device, scheme, or artifice* to defraud [SA § 17(a)(1)]; or

(b) *To obtain money or property* by means of any *untrue statement of a material fact* or *any omission* to state a material fact [SA § 17(a)(2)]; or

(c) *To engage in any transaction, practice, or course of business* which operates or would operate as a fraud or deceit upon the *purchaser* [SA § 17(a)(3)].

b. Culpable Conduct

Subsection 17(a)(1) requires a showing of scienter, while the two remaining subsections require only a showing of negligence. [**Aaron v. S.E.C.**, 446 U.S. 680 (1980)]

c. Administrative Proceedings

The S.E.C. has statutory authority to bring administrative proceedings to seek cease-and-desist orders for violations of the 1933 Act. [SA § 8A(a)] Cease-and-desist orders resemble injunctions, in that each directs the respondent to stop violating the Act. The cease-and-desist order is issued administratively, i.e., by the S.E.C. itself, while an injunction is issued by a federal district judge.

In connection with a proceeding for a permanent cease-and-desist order, the S.E.C. may also order the respondent to furnish an accounting and to disgorge any monies received in violation of the 1933 Act, including reasonable interest. [SA § 8A(e)]

Finally, the Dodd-Frank Wall Street Reform and Consumer Protection Act of 2010 authorized the S.E.C. to impose monetary penalties in administrative proceedings for violations of the 1933 Act. [SA § 8A(g); SEA § 21B] Note that the Fifth Circuit Court of Appeals has held that it is unconstitutional for the S.E.C. to impose monetary penalties in administrative proceedings. **Jarkesy v. S.E.C.**, 34 F.4th 446 (5th Cir. 2022).

d. S.E.C. Lawsuits

(1) Injunctive Relief

Section 20(a) of the 1933 Act authorizes the S.E.C. to conduct investigations into possible violations of the Act. Section 20(b) gives the S.E.C. the power to seek injunctive relief from the federal courts whenever it appears that the Act or the rules thereunder have been or are about to be violated.

(2) Civil Monetary Penalties

In addition to obtaining an injunction against future violations of the securities laws, the S.E.C. has the authority, in connection with any injunctive action, to seek civil monetary penalties. [SA § 20(d)]

The penalties that can be imposed are tiered as follows:

(a) Up to the greater of (i) $5,000 ($50,000 for corporations) for each violation, or (ii) the gross amount of pecuniary gain to the defendant; *or*

(b) Up to the greater of (i) $50,000 per violation ($250,000 for corporations), or (ii) the gross amount of pecuniary gain to the defendant, *if the violation involved fraud, deceit, manipulation, or deliberate or reckless disregard of a regulatory requirement*; *or*

(c) Up to the greater of (i) $100,000 per violation ($500,000 for corporations), or (ii) the gross amount of pecuniary gain to the defendant, *if the violation involved fraud, deceit, manipulation, or deliberate or reckless disregard of a regulatory requirement and directly or indirectly caused substantial losses or created a significant risk of substantial losses to other persons.*

e. Implied Civil Liability

There is a long-standing split in the federal circuit courts over whether Section 17(a) of the 1933 Act includes an "implied" civil cause of action permitting private persons to sue under the section and thereby, perhaps, avoiding some of the more onerous requirements of other sections of the 1933 and 1934 Acts that create remedies for private plaintiffs.

6. Section 24 Criminal Prosecution

The Department of Justice may criminally prosecute violations of the 1933 Act. Section 24 of the 1933 Act imposes criminal penalties upon conviction of a willful violation of any of the provisions of the 1933 Act, including violation of Section 17(a). "Willful" violation of Section 17(a) means that the defendant had the intent to defraud or that he or she made representations without knowing whether or not they were true. It need not be shown that the defendant knew that a "security" (as defined by the 1933 Act) was being sold or that defendant knew he or she was violating some specific provision of the securities laws. [**United States v. Brown**, 578 F.2d 1280 (9th Cir. 1978)]

7. Indemnification

a. Officers, Directors, and Control Persons

Officers, directors, and control persons of an issuer may be exposed to substantial liability under the securities laws and substantial litigation expenses in defense of securities actions. The laws of the various states vary as to whether and to what extent these persons (acting as representatives for the corporation) may be indemnified against such liability by the issuer.

Note: It is currently the policy of the S.E.C. that before it will accelerate the effectiveness of a registration statement, indemnification must either be waived by such persons or a statement must be made in the prospectus to the effect that the S.E.C. considers such indemnification against the policy of the 1933 Act (and therefore unenforceable) and that such persons promise to submit the question (if it arises) to a court of competent jurisdiction for a decision. [SA Reg. S–K, Item 512(h)]

b. Underwriters

Note that indemnification by the issuer of the *underwriters* is common. The S.E.C. has done nothing to discourage this, even though some scholars believe that there is no reason to make a distinction between officers and directors on one hand, and underwriters, on the other.

8. Contribution

A related question involves whether contribution is available in actions brought under sections of the 1933 Act that do not expressly provide for contribution (*i.e.,* sections other than Section 11). The courts have been friendlier to the idea of contribution in these actions than they have been to claims for indemnification.

a. Distinguish Indemnification

While indemnification is the payment of all of a party's costs and expenses, contribution involves only the allocation of the damages among the defendants.

b. S.E.C. Policy

So far, the S.E.C. has not attempted to discourage claims for contribution. Arguably, contribution does not violate the policies underlying the 1933 Act. Indeed, Section 11(f) expressly provides for contribution in a Section 11 case. In fact, contribution furthers the policies of the Act, insofar as contribution tends to ensure that all defendants will bear some of the burden of the violation.

9. Liability Insurance

Another important issue in the area of liability is whether an issuer can purchase insurance to cover potential liabilities that could *not* be properly indemnified under state law.

a. Availability of Insurance

State law varies, but many states do allow such insurance, and commercial policies are available. Insurance policies are not uniform with respect to what conduct they insure against; however, most do not insure against willful misconduct.

b. S.E.C. Policy

Thus far, the S.E.C. has drawn a distinction between indemnification and insurance and has not discouraged insurance. [SA Rule 461(c)] Arguably, this distinction is appropriate for the following reasons:

(1) If insurance were unavailable, the cost to the issuer's shareholders arising from liability could be high;

(2) Underwriters might refrain from marketing securities; and

(3) Directors and others might be unwilling to serve companies involved in the registration process.

10. Stipulations Contrary to Liability Provisions Void

Any condition, stipulation, or provision (as in contract of sale) purporting to bind any person acquiring any security to waive compliance by the seller with any of the provisions of the 1933 Act or its rules and regulations is *void.* [SA § 14]

e.g. **Example:** A sold B stock in an unregistered public offering. Later, A offered to return the money for the stock and gave BIO days in which to respond to the rescission offer. B did not respond. Still later, B sued for rescission under what is now Section 12(a)(1) of the 1933 Act. The court held that B had not waived his rights under the 1933 Act by failing to respond to A's offer of rescission. [**Meyers v. C & M Petroleum Producers, Inc.,** 476 F.2d 427 (5th Cir. 1973)]

Chapter Three

Regulation of Securities Trading—the Securities Exchange Act of 1934

CONTENTS	PAGE

Key Exam Issues 107

A. Overview of the 1934 Act 107

B. Civil Liability Under Rule 10b–5 of the 1934 Act 115

C. The Private Securities Litigation Reform Act of 1995 140

D. Insider Liability for Short-Swing Profits 144

E. Tender Offers and Repurchases of Stock 152

F. Regulation of Proxy Solicitations....157

G. Liability of Attorneys in Securities Transactions....174

H. Criminal Prosecution....178

Key Exam Issues

The previous section of this Summary dealt with the Securities Act of 1933 and its regulation of the original distribution of securities. This section will cover the Securities Exchange Act of 1934 and its regulation of the trading of securities *subsequent* to their original distribution. For example, if XYZ Corp. issues 100,000 shares of its common stock to the public and registers this stock for trading on the New York Stock Exchange, the 1934 Act will regulate many aspects of the trading of XYZ's common stock. (Note, however, that Rule 10b–5, the 1934 Act's antifraud provision, applies *both* to the issuance *and* to the subsequent trading of securities.)

This chapter covers a lot of important information. For exam purposes, the most important topics for you to study are:

1. Rule 10b–5

Rule 10b–5 is one of the most important remedy provisions of the 1934 Act. The key approach is to memorize the elements of the cause of action and then sift through the facts of your question to determine if each element is present. Remember to consider Rule 10b–5 whenever you see trading by persons having important information that is not yet available to the public.

2. Tender Offers and Repurchases of Stock

This is an important area of securities regulation law. Be sure you discuss the requirements for making a tender offer (*e.g.,* disclosure of information).

3. Proxy Solicitation

Although this topic is often covered in a Business Entities class, at least a brief review of the information on proxy contests and remedies for violation of the proxy rules would be worthwhile.

4. Short-Swing Profits on Insider Transactions

This is sometimes the subject of an exam question. Also consider Rule 10b–5 if there has been any misrepresentation or nondisclosure of significant information.

5. Liability of Attorneys in Securities Transactions

As many of you will likely be attorneys in securities transactions, it is worth reminding yourself of the potential liability that attorneys in particular face.

A. Overview of the 1934 Act

1. Purpose of the Act

The purpose of the Securities Exchange Act of 1934 ("SEA") is to protect interstate commerce and the national credit, and to ensure a fair and honest market for the trading of securities. [SEA § 2]

2. Registration and Reporting Requirements—Section 12

Section 12 of the 1934 Act requires that certain securities be registered with the S.E.C. Once a company has registered its securities, it thereafter must file reports with the S.E.C. on a periodic basis. In addition, many of the company's other activities are subject to regulation under other provisions of the 1934 Act.

a. Companies Required to Register Their Securities

Companies whose securities must be registered with the S.E.C. may be divided into two categories: *listed companies* and *over-the-counter (or "OTC") companies.* Companies of either kind that have triggered the 1934 Act registration requirements and begun to comply with the 1934 Act are typically referred to as *"registered"* or *"reporting"* companies.

(1) Listed Companies

All companies whose securities are traded on a national stock exchange must register the securities so traded. [*See* SEA § 12(a), (b)]

Example: If the common stock of XYZ Corp. is traded on a national securities exchange (such as the New York Stock Exchange), XYZ must register the stock with the S.E.C. under Section 12 of the 1934 Act.

(2) Over-the-Counter Companies

In addition to listed companies, the 1934 Act requires registration of securities of *all companies that have reached a certain size,* even if their stock is not traded on a securities exchange. "Size" is measured by reference to the company's total assets and the number of shareholders it has.

An issuer must register its securities if:

(a) it has more than $10 million in assets; *and*

(b) it has a class of equity securities held of record by either:

  (i) 2,000 persons; *or*

  (ii) 500 non-accredited investors. [SEA § 12(g)(1)]

Note: investors pursuant to Regulation CF (the federal crowdfunding exemption discussed above on pp. 81 *et seq.*) are excluded from this count as long as (1) the issuer is current in its ongoing annual reports required pursuant to Reg. CF, (2) the issuer has total assets of $25 million or less, and (3) the issuer has engaged the services of a transfer agent registered with the SEC. [SEA Rule 12g–6]

b. Information Required with Registration

Section 12 requires that the registering company supply the S.E.C. with information similar to that submitted with a Form S-1 registration statement under the 1933 Act (*i.e.,* information concerning its organization, financial structure, and the nature of its business; its securities outstanding; the names of directors, officers, underwriters, and principal shareholders, and their remuneration and material contracts with the issuer; bonus and profit-sharing arrangements; management and service contracts; options outstanding with respect to the issuer's securities; and all other material contracts and important financial statements). [SEA § 12(b)(1); *see* SEA Form 10]

c. Reporting Requirements of Registered Companies

All companies that have securities registered with the S.E.C. pursuant to SEA Section 12 must make periodic (annual and quarterly) reports to the S.E.C. [SEA Forms 10-K & 10-Q] In addition, if a significant event takes place, the issuer is required to file a "current report." [SEA Form 8-K] Form 10-K is the annual report of the issuer and requires virtually the same information that is required of an issuer registering an offering of securities on Form S-1 under the 1933 Act.

d. Reports Required of Companies Offering Their Securities to the Public

Every issuer of a security registered under the 1933 Act must also file periodic reports with the S.E.C. Like the Section 12 registration requirements, the periodic report provisions refer to SEA Section 13 for the content and nature of the reports that must be filed with the S.E.C.

e. Effect Is Registration of the Issuer

Note that technically what is registered under Section 12 of the 1934 Act is a class of securities, but the net effect, under the associated reporting requirements, is to register the issuer and subject the issuer to periodic reporting requirements of the 1934 Act. The reporting requirements are the same, whether triggered by size, listing, or 1933 Act registration.

f. Integration of the Disclosure Requirements

In 1980, the S.E.C. began a shift toward reliance on the 1934 Act and continuous reporting through that Act's monthly, quarterly, and annual reports to keep disclosure about issuers current. Since then, the requirements for disclosure under the 1933 and 1934 Acts have largely been integrated.

g. Integrity of Accounting

The S.E.C. has broad authority to regulate the accounting of publicly held companies. Regulation S–X provides detailed requirements for the accounting disclosures that issuers and registrants must make under the 1933 and 1934 Acts. In addition, SEA Section 13(b)(2), which was added by the Foreign Corrupt Practices Act and various sections of the Sarbanes-Oxley Act of 2002 ("SOXA"), also touch on public company accounting. Each of these is discussed below.

(1) Requirement to Keep Accurate Books and Records—SEA Section 13(b)(2)

SEA Section 13(b)(2) (added by the Foreign Corrupt Practices Act) requires 1934 Act reporting companies to keep accurate books and records and to maintain reasonable internal accounting controls. This provision "gives the S.E.C. authority over the entire financial management and reporting requirements of publicly held United States corporations." [**S.E.C. v. World-Wide Coin Investments, Ltd.,** 567 F. Supp. 724 (N.D. Ga. 1983)] In addition, *knowing* violations of Section 13(b)(2) are criminal offenses. [SEA § 13(b)(2)]

(2) Signatures and Certifications

(a) Signatures

The principal executive officer, financial officer, and accounting officer, as well as a majority of the board of directors, must sign the annual report on Form 10-K filed with the S.E.C. This signature requirement may produce liability for any misstatements made in the report.

(b) Certifications

Both the chief executive officer and the chief financial officer of reporting companies must certify as accurate the financial statements contained in the company's filings under the 1934 Act. [SOXA § 302] In addition, 1934 Act filings must contain officer certifications that the company has in place adequate disclosure controls and procedures, which are the processes the company uses to ensure that management knows of all information necessary for the company to meet its disclosure obligations. [SOXA § 404] These certifications have been combined into one, standard certification, separate copies of which must be executed by the CEO and CFO. These certifications must be in exactly the language prescribed by the S.E.C. and must be included in every periodic report of the company under the 1934 Act that contains financial statements. Finally, SOXA Section 906 also requires the CEO and CFO to certify that each periodic report under the 1934 Act fully complies with the reporting requirements of the Exchange Act and "fairly presents, in all material respects, the financial condition and results of operations" of the company. A false certification under Section 906 is a criminal violation. [SOXA § 906; 18 U.S.C. § 1350]

3. Registration of Securities Professionals Under the 1934 Act

In addition to the registration requirements of Section 12, other provisions of the 1934 Act require the registration of national securities exchanges, broker-dealers, information processors, and clearing agencies.

a. Registration of National Securities Exchanges

The 1934 Act defines an "exchange" [SEA § 3(a)(1)], and requires such an exchange to register with the S.E.C. unless exempt [SEA § 6].

(1) Effect of Registration Requirement

It is unlawful for any broker, dealer, or other securities exchange to employ any means of interstate commerce for the purpose of using the facilities of a national exchange unless the national exchange is registered (or exempt from registration) under the Act. [SEA § 5]

(2) Agreement to Comply

National exchanges must also agree to comply with the 1934 Act and to enact rules governing the conduct of exchange members. [SEA § 6]

(3) Regulation of Transactions

The 1934 Act also regulates various types of transactions entered into by stock exchange members. For example, the S.E.C. tries to prevent any conflicts of interest, particularly where a member of the exchange is acting as a broker (agent) *and* as a dealer (buying or selling from his own inventory) at the same time. [SEA § 11]

b. Registration of Broker-Dealers

The 1934 Act provides for the registration with the S.E.C. of all brokers and dealers who transact securities business in interstate commerce. [SEA § 15(b)]

(1) **Standards of Conduct**

The 1934 Act authorizes the S.E.C. to adopt and enforce rules for broker-dealers with respect to training, qualifications, and financial responsibility. [SEA § 15(b)]

(2) **Censure, Suspension, Revocation, or Denial of Registration**

As a means of enforcing its standards of conduct, the S.E.C. is authorized under the 1934 Act (after a hearing) to censure a broker-dealer, or to deny, suspend, or revoke its registration for various types of prohibited conduct (*e.g.,* a willful violation of the securities laws). [SEA § 15(b)(4)]

(3) **Indirect Regulation**

Not only does the S.E.C. regulate the conduct of brokers and dealers directly, but it also oversees the regulation of their conduct by regulating the organizations of which they are members. Section 15A of the 1934 Act, for example, permits self-regulatory organizations of brokers and dealers to register with the S.E.C. (one organization, the Financial Industry Regulatory Authority ["FINRA"] has done so). All brokers and dealers doing an interstate securities business must belong to FINRA, which regulates their conduct. [SEA § 15(b)(8)] Also, broker-dealers that belong to the national securities exchanges are regulated directly by the exchanges, which in turn are regulated by the S.E.C.

c. **Registration of Information Processors**

"Securities information processors" (*i.e.,* persons who distribute information about securities, price quotations, or transactions) are required to register with the S.E.C. and make periodic reports. [SEA § 11A(b)]

d. **Registration of Back-Office Agencies**

Transfer agents, clearing houses, and others involved in the mechanical completion of securities trades are also required to register and make periodic reports. [SEA § 17A]

(1) **Transfer Agents**

Banks often have stock transfer departments, and public corporations usually appoint outside transfer agents, who are responsible for keeping track of all shareholders and stock certificates and seeing that all transfers are completed properly.

(2) **Clearing Houses**

The exchanges normally have clearing houses, through which all certificates that are part of exchange transactions pass, so that proper deliveries will be made.

4. Additional Reporting Requirements Under the 1934 Act

In addition to the reports required of registered companies and 1933 Act issuers under Section 13 of the 1934 Act, other persons and entities are also required to file reports which the Commission uses to administer the provisions of the 1934 Act.

a. **Reports by Five Percent Owners of Registered Securities**

The 1934 Act requires that the purchaser of more than 5% of a class of equity security registered under the Act must file certain information with the S.E.C., the issuer of the security, and the securities exchange (if the securities are traded on a national exchange). [SEA § 13(d); *see* SEA Rule 13d–1]

(1) Information to Be Included

The report must contain information concerning the purchaser, the source of the funds used to purchase the securities, any plans the purchaser may have to acquire more of the same securities, and any plans it may have to attempt to change the issuer's business or corporate structure. [*See* SEA Schedule 13D]

(2) Purpose

This provision is aimed at regulating "tender offers," *i.e.,* transactions in which Company A makes an offer to buy the shares of Company B directly from Company B's shareholders.

b. Reports by Officers, Directors, and Ten Percent Security Holders

Officers and directors of the issuing corporation and owners of more than 10% of a class of security registered under Section 12 must file a report with the S.E.C. listing their holdings, and must also file a monthly update of any changes therein. This report helps the S.E.C. enforce Section 16(b) of the Act (which prevents insiders from making profits on short-term purchases and sales of registered securities). [SEA § 16(a)]

c. Reports by National Securities Exchanges and Associations

National securities exchanges and securities associations are required to file many reports concerning changes in their rules, discipline of their members, etc. [SEA §§ 6, 15]

d. Reports by Institutional Investors

Section 13(f) of the 1934 Act and Rule 13f–1 require investment managers (*e.g.,* banks) who exercise investment discretion over accounts having $100 million or more in exchange-traded or over-the-counter-quoted equity securities to file Form 13F annually with the S.E.C. The form reports the number of shares of each security held, the aggregate fair market value of the shares, and information about the nature of the manager's investment discretion and voting authority.

e. Liability for Filing False Reports

Filing materially false reports with the S.E.C. under the 1934 Act can result in civil and criminal liability.

5. Regulation of Practices Relating to Stock Ownership

The 1934 Act also regulates the following matters relating to stock ownership:

a. Proxy Solicitation

The Act governs the manner in which voting proxies are solicited from the shareholders of companies whose securities are registered under Section 12 of the Act. [SEA § 14]

b. Tender Offers

Sections 13 and 14 of the Act govern the practices used in making a tender offer.

6. Regulation of Accounting Records and Internal Controls

The 1934 Act also requires that reporting companies (i) make and keep books, records, and accounts which, in reasonable detail, accurately and fairly reflect the financial transactions of the issuer, arid (ii) devise and maintain a system of internal accounting controls sufficient to provide reasonable assurances that proper recording of transactions and control of assets is achieved. [SEA § 13(b)(2)]

7. A National Securities Market

The 1934 Act also establishes the goal of a "national market system" and directs the creation of a National Market Advisory Board to move the securities markets in that direction. [SEA § 11A]

8. Role of the S.E.C. in Administering the 1934 Act

As with the 1933 Act, the S.E.C. has broad power in administering the 1934 Act, including the powers to investigate, make and enforce rules, and impose penalties.

9. Role of Other Regulatory Agencies

The 1934 Act also grants power to the Board of Governors of the Federal Reserve System, the Comptroller of the Currency, and the Federal Deposit Insurance Corporation.

10. Sarbanes-Oxley Act

The Sarbanes-Oxley Act of 2002 ("SOXA") introduced detailed regulation of reporting companies' auditors and accountants. It also regulates lawyers and securities analysts, changed the nature and frequency of disclosures made under the 1934 Act, and enhanced fines and penalties for financial crimes. Where SOXA has changed the 1934 Act, the changes are discussed in the discussion of those portions of the 1934 Act.

11. Liability Provisions of the 1934 Act

Several provisions of the Securities Exchange Act provide for a private cause of action for damages resulting from a violation of its provisions.

a. Express Provision for Damages

Some of these liability provisions *expressly* provide for private damage actions. For example, Section 18 of the 1934 Act provides for the liability of anyone making false or misleading statements in any document filed pursuant to the SEA or any rule or regulation adopted thereunder (such as misstatements made in a filing pursuant to Sections 12(b) or (g)). Recovery is allowed to any person who purchased or sold a security in reliance on a false statement at a price that was affected by the statement. Additional provisions for express liability include Section 16(b) of the Securities Exchange Act, regulating short-swing trading, and Section 9 of the same Act, regulating market manipulation.

b. Implied Provision for Damages

Although other regulatory provisions do not expressly provide for private damage actions, in many instances a private right of action has been implied by the courts. The most important implied private right of action is under SEA Section 10(b) and Rule 10b–5. The trend of decisions, however, is away from implying private causes of action. This trend is reflected in the Supreme Court's strict interpretation of statutory language, the intent of Congress to avoid overlap of the federal securities laws, and the concern that in the past it has been too easy to recover under the securities laws, resulting in the filing of unwarranted suits in order to recover their settlement value.

(1) *Cort v. Ash* Test

In **Cort v. Ash,** 422 U.S. 66 (1975), the Supreme Court established a four-prong test to determine whether a private right of action would be implied from a federal statute:

(a) Is the plaintiff one of the *class for whose benefit the statute was enacted?*

(b) Is there any indication of *legislative intent,* explicit or implicit, *to create or deny such a remedy?*

(c) Is implication of a private cause of action *consistent with the underlying purposes* of the legislative scheme?

(d) Is the cause of action one *traditionally relegated to state law?*

(2) Legislative Intent Governs

In cases decided after *Cort,* the Supreme Court has emphasized the first three prongs of the test. Ultimately, the issue is whether Congress intended to create a private right of action. [*See* **Transamerica Mortgage Advisors, Inc. v. Lewis,** 444 U.S. 11 (1979); **Touche Ross & Co. v. Redington,** 442 U.S. 560 (1979)]

(3) Express Remedy

Where the securities laws provide an express remedy for a specific situation, it is unlikely that the courts will also imply an additional remedy under some other provision of the 1934 Act. [*See, e.g.,* **Cramer v. General Telephone & Electronics,** 443 F. Supp. 516, *aff'd,* 582 F.2d 259 (3d Cir. 1978)]

c. Defenses

There are a number of possible defenses to causes of action brought under the various sections of the 1934 Act. These defenses are discussed *infra* in connection with the various liability provisions to which they relate.

12. Role of the Courts

a. Jurisdiction

The district courts of the United States have *exclusive* original jurisdiction over violations of the 1934 Act or its regulations and over actions brought to enforce liabilities or duties thereunder. (Contrast this with the 1933 Act, which provides that federal and state courts have concurrent jurisdiction.) Nationwide service of process is available. [SEA § 27]

b. Court Powers

(1) Powers of Subpoena and Contempt

The district courts have the power to issue orders to appear, to give testimony, and to produce evidence. In addition, a district court can cite persons in contempt for any violations of its orders. [SEA § 21]

(2) Mandamus

Upon application by the S.E.C., the district courts may issue writs of mandamus to compel various corporate acts.

c. Judicial Review

Another function of federal courts is to review decisions of the S.E.C. These appeals are heard in the District of Columbia Circuit, or in the circuit in which the appellant resides or has its principal place of business. [SEA § 25] S.E.C. decisions must be based on a record, and the S.E.C.'s decision on factual issues is conclusive if based on "substantial evidence." Appeal from district court decisions is also to the circuit courts, then by certiorari to the United States Supreme Court.

B. Civil Liability Under Rule 10b–5 of the 1934 Act

1. Introduction

Rule 10b–5 is the most significant remedy provisions of the 1934 Act. It was adopted by the S.E.C. to strengthen the remedies provided in the 1933 Act against fraud in the purchase and sale of securities.

2. Statement of Rule 10b–5

Rule 10b–5, which was enacted by the S.E.C. pursuant to Section 10(b) of the 1934 Act, makes it unlawful, in connection with the *purchase or sale of any security,* for any person, directly or indirectly, by the use of *any means or instrumentality of interstate commerce,* or of the mails, or of any facility of any national securities exchange:

a. *To employ any device, scheme, or artifice to defraud;*

b. *To make any untrue statement of a material fact, or to omit to state a material fact* necessary in order to make the statements made, in light of the circumstances under which they were made, not misleading; or

c. *To engage in any act, practice, or course of business which operates or would operate as a fraud or deceit* upon any person.

3. Securities and Transactions Covered

a. Securities Covered

Rule 10b–5 is very broad in its application to securities transactions; however, a "security" must be involved before the rule will apply. The term "security" is broadly defined (about the same as under the 1933 Act; *see* Sections 3(a)(10) and (11) of the 1934 Act). However, the trend in the Supreme Court is to limit the scope of the federal securities laws to the regulation of public trading markets and large, interstate investment promotions. One way to do this is to narrow the definition of "security." [*See, e.g.,* **Marine Bank v. Weaver,** *supra,* p. 49—a certificate of deposit is not a security]

b. Transactions Covered

The courts have indicated that all purchases and sales of securities are covered under Rule 10b–5, whether on exchanges, over-the-counter transactions, or private transactions. [**Fratt v. Robinson,** 203 F.2d 627 (9th Cir. 1953)]

(1) Compared to 1933 Act

The antifraud provisions of the 1933 Act apply only to fraud committed *by the seller* against purchasers. Thus, prior to the adoption of Rule 10b–5, there was no general prohibition against fraud committed by a purchaser in inducing a seller to sell.

(2) Compared to Other Sections of 1934 Act

Section 9 of the 1934 Act applies to both purchases and sales, but only in the context of securities listed on a national exchange; Section 15 also applies to both, but only in securities transactions in which broker-dealers are involved. *Rule 10b–5* applies to both purchases and sales in *all contexts.*

c. Interstate Commerce Requirement

Before Rule 10b–5 will apply to a transaction, some means of interstate commerce, or the mails, or a national securities exchange must be used "in connection with" the purchase or sale of securities.

(1) Any Part of Transaction "In Commerce"

The courts have held that the misrepresentation itself need not be transmitted by these jurisdictional means; it is sufficient if *any part* of the securities transaction occurs in interstate commerce [*e.g.,* delivery of the securities). [**Fratt v. Robinson,** *supra*]

(2) Use of Interstate Means Can Be Intrastate

Any use of the interstate means is sufficient; the transaction itself need not involve more than one state. Thus, most courts have held that an intrastate telephone call is sufficient to establish jurisdiction, because the phone lines also carry interstate messages. [*See, e.g.,* **Dupuy v. Dupuy,** 511 F.2d 641 (5th Cir. 1975)]

4. Jurisdiction, Venue, and Service of Process

One of the reasons that Rule 10b–5 has been used so frequently is its broad procedural provisions.

a. Jurisdiction

The federal courts have exclusive jurisdiction over all civil actions arising under Rule 10b–5, regardless of the amount in controversy.

b. Venue

Suit may be brought in the district court of any district in which any act or transaction in violation of the rule occurred or in any district where the defendant is found, resides, or transacts business.

c. Service of Process

Process may be served anywhere in the world.

5. Elements of Cause of Action

The elements of a cause of action under Rule 10b–5 depend on whether a private plaintiff or the government (*e.g.,* the S.E.C. or the Department of Justice) is seeking to establish liability. The elements are listed, and then each element is discussed in detail.

a. Actions by Private Plaintiffs

In a private civil action, a plaintiff must prove the following elements:

(1) the plaintiff has standing to assert the claim;

(2) the defendant is a primary violator;

(3) the defendant engaged in manipulation or deception;

(4) with respect to a material fact;

(5) in connection with the purchase of sale of a security;

(6) scienter;

(7) reliance;

(8) loss causation; and

(9) damages.

Note: As a practical matter, most private Rule 10b–5 actions are asserted as class actions. Accordingly, there are additional procedural requirements imposed by the Federal Rules of Civil Procedure and the securities laws. Most important are the requirements imposed by the Private Securities Litigation Reform Act of 1995. (See below pp. 140 *et seq.*) Some of those procedural requirements interact with the substantive elements and are thus important to note alongside the elements of the claim.

b. Actions by the Government

In a government action under Rule 10b–5, the government must prove the above-listed elements with some exceptions. In particular, the government is ***not*** required to prove the following elements:

(1) the plaintiff has standing to assert the claim (the government has standing!);

(2) the defendant is a primary violator (the government *may* pursue secondary violators);

(3) reliance;

(4) loss causation; and

(5) damages.

The remaining elements are the same.

c. The Plaintiff Has Standing to Assert the Claim

In a private action under Rule 10b–5, the *plaintiff* must either be an actual "purchaser" or an actual "seller" of securities to have standing to maintain a Rule 10b–5 cause of action. [**Blue Chip Stamps v. Manor Drug Stores,** *infra*]

e.g. **Example:** Plaintiff, a shareholder of Newport Steel Corp., brought a shareholder derivative suit alleging a Rule 10b–5 violation against the president of Newport. The president had caused Newport to reject a merger proposal (which would have benefited all Newport shareholders), and then sold his own 40% controlling interest for double the market price to the same interested purchaser. The court held that the plaintiff had no standing to sue, because *neither* the corporation nor the plaintiff was a purchaser or seller as required by Rule 10b–5. [*See* **Birnbaum v. Newport Steel Corp.,** 193 F.2d 461 (2d Cir.), *cert. denied*, 343 U.S. 956 (1952)]

(1) **Purpose of Requirement**

The purpose of the "purchase or sale" requirement is to prevent vexatious litigation by ensuring that there is objective evidence of the plaintiff's transactions. [**Blue Chip Stamps v. Manor Drug Stores,** *infra*] In other words, a plaintiff cannot obtain standing by claiming that "I would have bought that stock if you hadn't lied to me." (Mere offerees do not have standing.) Likewise, a plaintiff cannot obtain standing by claiming that "I would have sold that stock if you hadn't lied to me." (Mere holders do not have standing.)

(2) **Contexts in Which the Issue Arises**

(a) **Depreciation in Value**

The "purchase or sale" issue may arise when the plaintiff has not actually sold his stock but argues that the stock has depreciated in value due to the misrepresentations made by the defendant. [*See, e.g.,* **Greenstein v. Paul,** 400 F.2d 580 (2d Cir. 1968)—plaintiff had no standing because there was no purchase or sale]

(b) **Transaction Prevented**

The issue may also arise when the plaintiff claims he would have purchased stock but for the negative statements made by the defendant. [**Blue Chip Stamps v. Manor Drug Stores,** *infra*—no Rule 10b–5 cause of action because no actual purchase or sale]

(3) **Exception for Derivative Suits**

If a plaintiff asserts a Rule 10b–5 action in a representative capacity on behalf of the corporation (*i.e.,* a shareholder derivative suit), the courts have held that the individual plaintiff shareholder need *not* be an actual purchaser or seller; it is sufficient if there is a purchase or sale *by the corporation.* [**Superintendent of Insurance v. Bankers Life & Casualty Co.,** *infra*]

d. **The Defendant Is a Primary Violator**

Private civil actions may only be asserted against primary violators. In contrast, the government may pursue secondary violators (*i.e.,* aiders and abettors). In addition, control persons of primary violators are potentially liable in both private and governmental actions.

(1) **Aiders and Abettors**

In **Central Bank of Denver, N.A. v. First Interstate Bank of Denver, N.A.,** 511 U.S. 164 (1994), the Supreme Court held that there is no implied right of action against one who merely aids and abets a violation of SEA Rule 10b–5. Therefore, only primary violators are potential defendants in a private civil action.

The S.E.C. *may* bring enforcement actions against mere aiders and abettors, however. [SEA § 20(e)] The elements of aiding and abetting are as follows: (1) primary securities violation by another; (2) substantial assistance by the alleged aider and abettor in the commission of the primary violation; and (3) the alleged aider and abettor was either knowing or reckless with respect to whether his or her conduct was improper.

In addition, the Department of Justice *may* criminally prosecute aiders and abettors of securities fraud. [18 U.S.C. § 2]

(2) Makers of Statements

Someone who *makes* an untrue statement or misleading omission (on which liability is based) is a primary violator, who can be liable in both private and governmental actions. In **Janus Capital Group, Inc. v. First Derivative Traders**, 564 U.S. 135 (2011), the Supreme Court held that the "maker" is the person with "ultimate authority over the statement, including its content and whether and how to communicate it." Someone who merely "prepares or publishes a statement on behalf of another is not its maker." (*Id.*) Thus, for example, signatories of SEC filings are likely "makers" of the statements therein who are subject to primary liability.

(3) Disseminators of Statements

In addition, someone who *disseminates* an untrue statement or misleading omission (on which liability is based) may be a primary violator, who can be liable in both private and governmental actions. In **Lorenzo v. S.E.C.**, 139 S.Ct. 1094, 1105 (2019), the Supreme Court held that a person who disseminates materially misleading statements with the intent to defraud investors can be held primarily liable under Rule 10b–5, even if that person does not "make" any statement to investors.

(4) Control Persons

Control person liability applies in both private civil suits and in government actions. If there is not a primary violator, however, there is no control person liability.

(a) Control Person Test

Every person who, directly or indirectly, controls any person liable under Rule 10b–5 can be held jointly and severally liable with and to the same extent as such controlled person. [SEA § 20(a)]

(b) Defense to Control Person Liability

It is a defense to control person liability that the controlling person (1) acted in good faith and (2) did not directly or indirectly induce the act of acts constituting the violation or cause of action. [SEA § 20(a)]

e. The Defendant Engaged in Manipulation or Deception

The conduct prohibited by Rule 10b–5 is securities fraud, which the Supreme Court has interpreted as encompassing *only* deception and manipulation. [**Santa Fe Industries, Inc. v. Green,** 430 U.S. 462 (1977)] Most Rule 10b–5 cases are premised on deception, either via a false statement or a misleading omission.

(1) Deception via False Statement

The most straightforward way to establish deception is to identify a false statement of fact by a defendant. For example, if a defendant states that "our quarterly sales totaled $1 million" when they actually totaled only $1,000, this would be a false statement of fact. (Of course, in order to be actionable, the other elements of securities fraud must also be met, including that it was a false statement about a material fact and that the defendant made the statement with the requisite scienter.)

This element is more complex if the alleged securities fraud is premised on an opinion or a forward-looking statement (*i.e.*, a prediction).

(a) Deceptive Opinions

If a defendant expresses an opinion (*e.g.*, "I believe that our sales exceeded $1 million), it actually contains two embedded statements: (1) I actually believe this; and (2) our sales exceeded $1 million. The question arises whether an opinion can be actually as securities fraud and, if so, which of these two embedded statements must be false?

The Supreme Court answered this question in **Omnicare, Inc. v. Laborers Dist. Council Const. Indus. Pension Fund**, 575 U.S. 175 (2015). (Although Omnicare was decided under Section 11 of the 1933 Act rather than Rule 10b–5, most lower courts have held that the reasoning applies equally to claims under Rule 10b–5.) The Court held that, in order for an opinion to be actionable as a false statement of fact, *both* propositions must be false. In other words, a plaintiff must prove (1) that the speaker did not actually believe the statement to be true *and* (2) that it was not in fact true. Note that the result of this is to, in effect, raise the scienter standard (see below p. 128) for opinions *from* recklessness about truth or falsity *to* disbelief.

Importantly, however, the Court in *Omnicare* also held that an opinion may give rise to a duty to disclose and thus constitute actionable deception via omission. This liability pathway is discussed below on p. 123.

(b) Deceptive Forward-Looking Statements

A forward-looking statement (*i.e.*, a prediction) is really a subset of opinions—it is an opinion about what the future holds. A prediction without any reasonable basis could be materially misleading to investors. Yet, issuers are required to disclose certain forward-looking information (*e.g.*, in the MD&A), and Congress wanted to encourage issuers to disclose this type of soft information, even if not mandated. Thus, as a component of the Private Securities Litigation Reform Act of 1995, Congress enacted a safe harbor, effectively shielding certain forward-looking statements from private civil liability. (Note that Congress enacted an identical safe harbor for forward-looking statements in both the 1933 Act and the 1934 Act. Because the safe harbor does not apply to statements made in connection with *initial* public offerings, however, its impact has been slightly less important in 1933 Act claims.) [SA § 27A; SEA § 21E]

The safe harbor only applies in private civil actions under Rule 10b–5. A defendant may not rely on the safe harbor to defend against an S.E.C. enforcement action or a criminal prosecution.

(i) Definition of Forward-Looking Statement

"Forward-looking statement" is defined to include a laundry list of predictions, including the following:

(1) a statement containing a financial projection (note, however, that statements contained within a financial statement prepared in accordance with generally accepted accounting principles are excluded from protection);

(2) a statement of the plans and objectives of management for future operations; and

(3) a statement of future economic performance.

[SA § 27A(i)(1); SEA § 21E(i)(1)]

(ii) Who May Use the Safe Harbor

The safe harbor is available to:

(1) Issuers subject to the reporting requirements of the 1934 Act;

(2) Persons acting on behalf of such an issuer;

(3) Outside reviewers retained by such an issuer; and

(4) The issuer's underwriters, with respect to information provided by the issuer or derived from information provided by the issuer.

[SA § 27A(a); SEA § 21E(a)]

(iii) Who Is Excluded

Certain issuers are excluded from using the safe harbor, even if they otherwise would qualify:

(1) Issuers of penny stock; and

(2) Issuers that, in the prior three years, have been criminally convicted of securities fraud or have been the subject of governmental decrees or orders relating to securities fraud.

[SA § 27A(b); SEA § 21E(b)]

(iv) Transactions Excluded

Likewise, forward-looking statements made in connection with certain kinds of transactions are excluded from the safe harbor, even if they would otherwise have been covered. Excluded are statements made in connection with:

(1) "Going private" transactions;

(2) Tender offers;

(3) Initial public offerings;

(4) Partnership "roll-up" transactions; and

(5) Statements made in financial statements.

[SA § 27A(b); SEA § 21E(b)]

(v) First Means of Protection: Actual Knowledge

The 1995 Act's safe harbor provides two *alternative* means of protection for forward-looking statements.

First, a private civil plaintiff cannot recover from a covered person unless the plaintiff proves that the forward-looking statement was made with *actual knowledge that it was false or materially incomplete.* Even if the plaintiff can prove actual knowledge, however, the second means of protection may still apply to protect the statement.

Note that the impact of this provision is to effectively raise the scienter standard (see below p. 128) applicable to forward-looking statements *from* recklessness about truth or falsity to *actual knowledge* of falsity.

(vi) Second Means of Protection: Accompanied by Meaningful Cautionary Language

Second, a private civil plaintiff cannot recover from a covered person if a forward-looking statement was (1) identified as a forward-looking statement and (2) accompanied by meaningful cautionary statements identifying important factors that could cause actual results to differ materially from those predicted in the forward-looking statement.

(vii) "Meaningful" Cautionary Language

" 'Boilerplate' warnings will not suffice as meaningful cautionary statements identifying important factors . . . ." [H.R. Rep. No. 369, 104th Cong., 1st Sess. 43–44 (1995)] To qualify, a statement "must convey substantive information about factors that realistically could cause results to differ materially from those projected in the forward-looking statement. . . ." [*Id.*]

Congress does not expect issuers to show perfect foresight. Thus, not all factors that could cause the results to vary must be described, and indeed, "*failure to include the particular factor* that ultimately causes the forward-looking statement not to come true *will not mean the statement is not protected* by the safe harbor." [*Id.*]

(viii) Accompaniment

If the forward-looking statement is written, the meaningful cautionary language must be in the same document.

If the forward-looking statement is oral, the meaningful cautionary language may be cross-referenced. (Thus, for example, a CEO appearing in a TV interview is not required to read a page-length statement containing meaningful cautionary language.) Rather, the oral statement is protected if the oral statement *identifies a readily available written document* that contains the "meaningful cautionary statements" described in the safe harbor for written statements. [SA § 27A(c)(2); SEA § 21E(c)(2)]

(2) Deception via Omission

An omission is only actionable as securities fraud if there was a *duty to disclose.* [**Basic, Inc. v. Levinson**, 485 US. 224 (1988)] Thus, if a plaintiff is premising a Rule 10b–5 claim on a defendant's alleged silence, the plaintiff must identify the source of the defendant's duty to speak.

(a) Statements Necessary to Make Disclosures Not Misleading

If a defendant makes a disclosure, the disclosure should be complete so as not to be materially misleading. In other words, a half-truth gives rise to the duty to tell the whole truth. For example, if a corporation is pursuing a specific business goal and announces the goal, as well as an intended approach for accomplishing it, the corporation may be required to disclose other approaches when they are under active and serious consideration. [***In re* Time Warner Inc. Securities Litigation,** 9 F.3d 259 (2d Cir. 1993)]

(b) Opinions as Source of Duty to Disclose

In *Omnicare*, *supra*, the Supreme Court recognized that an opinion may give rise to a duty to disclose. In particular, a reasonable investor may, depending on the circumstances, understand an opinion statement to convey facts about how the speaker has formed the opinion. If the real facts are otherwise, but omitted, the opinion statement will be misleadingly incomplete. For example, if a company expresses the opinion that "we believe our conduct is lawful," but the company expresses the opinion without having consulted a lawyer, the opinion could be misleadingly incomplete, giving rise to a duty to disclose the fact that a lawyer was not consulted.

(c) Mandatory Disclosures Under the Securities Laws

The 1933 Act, the 1934 Act, and the rules promulgated thereunder require issuers to make various periodic disclosures (*e.g.*, in registration statements, in annual reports, in quarterly reports, and in current reports). These rules impose a duty to disclose, and an issuer's failure to do so is actionable as securities fraud.

(d) Issuer's Duty to Correct or Update

Outside the mandatory disclosure requirements of the securities laws, issuers generally are not under a duty to disclose information, even material information. However, if an issuer makes statements that later become false or misleading, a duty to correct or update those statements may arise. The failure to correct or update in this case might be fraudulent or deceptive and, therefore, violate Rule 10b–5.

(i) Disclosure Misleading When Made

If a statement is misleading when it is made, and the speaker thereafter learns this, a duty to correct the earlier statement arises. [**Backman v. Polaroid Corp.,** 910 F.2d 10 (1st Cir. 1990)]

(ii) Disclosure Accurate When Made

Courts are divided as to whether a duty to correct exists when the issuer makes a statement that is accurate and complete at the time it is made but is rendered false or misleading by later events. Some courts have held that if the statement has a forward intent or connotation on which persons can be expected to rely, a duty to correct the earlier statement arises. [*See* **Weiner v. The Quaker Oats Co.,** 129 F.3d 310 (3d Cir. 1997); **Stransky v. Cummins Engine Co.,** 51 F.3d 1329 (7th Cir. 1995)] Other courts have held that as long as the disclosure was accurate at the time it was made, no duty to update or correct it arises later. [*See* **Grassi v. Information Resources, Inc.,** 63 F.3d 596 (7th Cir. 1995)]

(iii) Statements by Third Parties

Issuers are not required to correct or respond to rumors or inaccurate statements about them made by third parties. However, if the issuer is the source of the inaccuracy, or is responsible for disseminating the statements of third parties, the issuer may be required to correct or update the statements. [**Elkind v. Liggett & Myers, Inc.,** 635 F.2d 156 (2d Cir, 1980)]

(3) Mere Breach of Fiduciary Duty Is Not Fraud

A breach of duty under state corporate law (*e.g.,* breach of the directors' fiduciary duty of loyalty or care) is not a sufficient "fraud" for 10b–5 purposes. [**Santa Fe Industries, Inc. v. Green,** *supra*] However, cases involving breach of fiduciary duty may also involve deception, and fiduciary duty may be the source of a duty to disclose.

(4) Breach of Contract as Fraud

Ordinarily, a state-law breach of contract claim would not give rise to an action under Rule 10b–5. However, if a person sells a security with a secret intention not to honor it, then an action for fraud may lie under Rule 10b–5. [**Wharf (Holdings) Ltd. v. United International Holdings, Inc.,** 532 U.S. 588 (2001)]

(5) Manipulation

Manipulation is also prohibited under Rule 10b–5. As explained by the Supreme Court, manipulation is " 'virtually a term of art when used in connection with securities markets.' The term refers generally to practices, such as wash sales, matched orders, or rigged prices, that are intended to mislead investors by artificially affecting market activity." [*Santa Fe Indus., supra*]

(6) Insider Trading

Insider trading is a form of actionable securities fraud. The elements of Rule 10b–5 claim premised on insider trading are discussed below on pp. 132 *et seq*.

f. With Respect to a Material Fact

Rule 10b–5 requires that the misrepresentation or omission be of a *material* fact.

(1) Definition of Materiality

A fact is material if there is a *substantial likelihood* that a *reasonable investor* would consider it *significant* when making an investment decision. In other words, the materiality requirement is satisfied when there is a substantial likelihood that the disclosure of the omitted fact would have been viewed by the reasonable investor as having significantly altered the "total mix" of information made available. [**Basic, Inc. v. Levinson**, 485 US. 224 (1988); **TSC Industries, Inc. v. Northway, Inc.**, 426 U.S. 438 (1976)] This is an objective test, based on a hypothetical "reasonable" investor.

(2) Mixed Question of Law and Fact

Materiality is a mixed question of law and fact. Courts may grant defendants' motions to dismiss Rule 10b–5 claims on the basis that the alleged misstatement or omission was immaterial as a matter of law. Indeed, this is a frequent ground for dismissal of Rule 10b–5 claims.

(3) Probability/Magnitude Standard

When it is uncertain whether an event will or will not occur, the *TSC Industries* test for materiality—whether there is a substantial likelihood that a reasonable shareholder would consider the event significant—is difficult to answer. The Supreme Court has adopted a standard for such circumstances that balances two issues: First, *how likely* is the occurrence of the event? Second, if the event occurs, *how significant* would it be to the issuer (and, thus, to the investor in the issuer's securities)? [**Basic, Inc. v. Levinson,** *supra*] A relatively unlikely event might still be material if it would be very significant. Likewise, a relatively insignificant event might still be material if it is highly likely to occur.

e.g. **Example:** The stock of Company B began to trade heavily, due to rumors that B was engaged in preliminary merger negotiations with C. Officers of B were asked on several occasions whether merger negotiations were underway; each time, they denied the rumors. Eventually C made a tender offer for B, and B revealed that negotiations had in fact been underway for some time. The Court held that the proper test for materiality would balance, at the time of each denial, the likelihood that the negotiations would bear fruit against the significance (to B) of the merger if it were to take place. Thus, a very low probability (approaching zero) of success in the merger discussions would justify nondisclosure. Because the merger unquestionably would be very significant to B, however, even a small increase in the likelihood of success would make the fact of the negotiations material. [**Basic, Inc. v. Levinson,** *supra*]

(4) No Bright-Line Tests

There is a great temptation to try to apply bright-line tests for materiality, but the S.E.C. and the courts have consistently rejected such attempts.

An S.E.C. Staff Accounting Bulletin describes factors that "may well render material a quantitatively small misstatement of a financial statement item," including whether the misstatement:

(a) Arises from an item capable of precise measurement or whether it arises from an estimate and, if so, the degree of imprecision inherent in the estimate;

(b) Masks a change in earnings or other trends;

(c) Hides a failure to meet analysts' consensus expectations for the enterprise;

(d) Changes a loss into income or vice versa;

(e) Concerns a segment or other portion of the registrant's business that has been identified as playing a significant role in the registrant's operations or profitability;

(f) Affects the registrant's compliance with loan covenant or other contractual requirements;

(g) Has the effect of increasing management's compensation—*e.g.,* by satisfying requirements for the award of bonuses or other forms of incentive compensation; or

(h) Involves concealment of an unlawful transaction.

[SAB 99, 70 S.E.C. 785 (1999)]

The Supreme Court has also repeatedly rejected proposed bright-line rules for materiality. In *Basic, supra,* the Court rejected the defendant's proposed bright-line rule that preliminary merger negotiations are material only once the parties to the negotiations reach an agreement in principle. Again, in **Matrixx Initiatives, Inc. v. Siracusano**, 563 U.S. 27 (2011). The Court rejected the defendant's proposed bright-line rule that reports to the FDA of adverse events associated with a pharmaceutical company's products cannot be material absent a sufficient number of such reports to establish a statistically significant risk that the product is in fact causing the events. In both cases, the Court explained that the proposed bright-line rule would "artificially exclud[e] from the definition of materiality information . . . which would otherwise be considered significant to the trading decision of a reasonable investor."

(5) "Bespeaks Caution" Doctrine

The materiality of a particular disclosure is affected by the other disclosures that are made (*i.e.,* statements must be evaluated in context). If a prediction is accompanied by other disclosure that "bespeak caution," the prediction may be immaterial as a matter of law.

Note that many predictions are also protected via the safe harbor for forward-looking statements (see above pp. 120–122), which is a codification of the bespeaks caution doctrine.

(6) Puffery

Courts often dismiss claims based on alleged "puffery" as immaterial as a matter of law. Although these assessments are fact-specific, courts often hold that vaguely optimistic statements are immaterial puffery on which no reasonable investor would rely on mere "corporate cheerleading" when making an investment decision.

g. In Connection with the Purchase of Sale of a Security

Rule 10b–5 requires that the defendant's misrepresentation or deception be "in connection with" the purchase or sale of a security.

(1) "In Connection with" Test

An alleged fraud is "in connection with" a purchase or sale of a security if it is "material to a decision by one or more individuals (other than the fraudster) to buy or to sell" a security. [**Chadbourne & Parke LLP v. Troice**, 571 U.S. 377 (2014)] Although *Chadbourne* involved an interpretation of the "in connection with" language in the Securities Litigation Uniform Standards Act, the Court relied on authority interpreting the same language in Section 10(b) and Rule 10b–5.

(2) Defendant Need Not Be an Actual Purchaser or Seller

Although a private plaintiff in a Rule 10b–5 action must be a purchaser or seller of securities, the *defendant need not have engaged in a purchase or sale.* Rather, the defendant's fraudulent activity need only be "in connection with" the purchase or sale of securities.

e.g. **Example:** A defendant corporation was held liable for a misleading press release on which reasonable investors might have relied in the purchase or sale of the company's securities. [**S.E.C. v. Texas Gulf Sulphur Co.,** 401 F.2d 833 (2d Cir. 1968)]

(3) Problem of Remoteness

The most common issue in this area is whether the fraud or deception is so remote from the plaintiff's purchase or sale transaction as to sever the requisite "connection."

(a) Fraud as Part of the Securities Sales Transaction

If the defendant's fraud occurs as part of the securities transaction itself, it is clear that a sufficient connection exists. For example, A sells securities to B, without disclosing material inside information. Assuming fraud, the necessary connection with B's purchase exists.

(b) Fraud Separate from the Sales Transaction

The more difficult cases are those in which the defendant's fraud is not directly related to, and does not involve the terms of, the securities transaction itself. It is not clear how close to the sale of securities the fraud must be in order to meet the "in connection with" requirement. We can say that if the purchase or sale is merely incidental to the fraud, then the fraud is not "in connection with" the securities transaction. On the other hand, it is clear that the defendant's fraud does not have to be about the value of securities.

e.g. **Example:** A stockbroker induced an elderly man to invest more than $400,000 in a discretionary brokerage account, over which the broker had investment control and a power of attorney. The broker engaged in a series of transactions that left the account empty. The transactions, themselves were not fraudulent, in the sense that the prices of purchases and sales were the market prices. The account was emptied by the broker's diverting the proceeds of the transactions to his own accounts, by writing checks on the account that were paid by liquidating a sufficient quantity of securities to cover the checks. The Court held that this fraud was in connection with the purchase or sale of securities. While the transactions, in isolation, appear not to be fraudulent, they were conducted in furtherance of a scheme to defraud the investor. While it is not automatically a violation of Rule 10b–5 to steal money from a brokerage account, in this case, the securities transactions were initiated and concluded in furtherance of a scheme to defraud. [**S.E.C. v. Zandford,** 535 U.S. 813 (2002)]

e.g. **Example:** W Corp. sold U Corp. an option to purchase stock in T Corp. W Corp. never intended to honor the option, if U should attempt to exercise it. The Court held that this was a fraud "in connection with" the purchase or sale of a security, and not merely a breach of contract (the option) to sell securities in the future. The option itself is a security, and the sale with the secret intent not to honor the option was fraudulent, "in connection with" the sale of the option. [**Wharf (Holdings) Ltd.,** *supra*]

(4) Privity Not Required

The "in connection with" requirement ***does not require privity***, and there is no ***requirement*** that the plaintiff and defendant be in privity with one another in an action under Rule 10b–5. [**Superintendent of Insurance v. Bankers Life & Casualty Co.**, 404 U.S. 6 (1971)]

h. Scienter

For liability to exist under Rule 10b–5, it must be shown that the defendant had "scienter."

(1) Test for Scienter

In **Ernst & Ernst v. Hochfelder,** 425 U.S. 185 (1976), the Supreme Court held that scienter is required, which does not include mere negligence. Something *more* than negligence is required. The Court in *Hochfelder* reserved the question whether a defendant who lacked actual knowledge of a fraud, but acted recklessly, might be liable under Rule 10b–5. Circuit courts addressing the issue after *Hochfelder*, however, have uniformly held that a defendant's *recklessness* is enough to establish liability under Rule 10b–5.

Reckless conduct has been defined as "highly unreasonable [conduct], involving not merely simple, or even inexcusable negligence, but an extreme departure from the standards of ordinary care, and which presents a danger of misleading buyers or sellers that is either known to the defendant or is so obvious that the actor must have been aware of it." [**Sundstrand Corp. v. Sun Chemical Corp.,** 553 F.2d 1033 (7th Cir.), *cert. denied*, 434 U.S. 875 (1977)]

(2) Heightened Scienter for Forward-Looking Statements

As discussed above on p. 121, if the safe harbor for forward-looking statements applies, a private plaintiff cannot recover for a fraudulent forward-looking statement unless it was made with *actual knowledge* of its falsity. [SEA § 21E; SA § 17A]

(3) Heightened Scienter for Opinions

As discussed above on p. 120, if a plaintiff is alleging that an opinion constituted a false statement of fact, the plaintiff must prove that the speaker disbelieved the opinion expressed (as opposed to merely being reckless about its truth or falsity). [*Omnicare*, *supra*]

(4) Requirement to Plead Scienter with Particularity

Under the Federal Rules of Civil Procedure, allegations of fraud must be pleaded with particularity. Excluded from this particularity requirement, however, is the defendant's mental state. [FRCP 9(b)]

However, Congress has statutorily imposed a heightened pleading requirement for allegations of securities fraud in private civil litigation. The Private Securities Litigation Reform Act of 1995 ("PSLRA") states that, in any private action arising under the 1934 Act in which the plaintiff may recover money damages only with proof that the defendant acted with a particular state of mind, the complaint shall "state with particularity facts giving rise to a strong inference that the defendant acted with the required state of mind." [SEA § 21D(b)(2)(A)]

(a) Adequacy of Pleading Scienter Assessed via Motion to Dismiss

In any private action under the 1934 Act, the court shall, on the motion of the defendant, dismiss the complaint if the plaintiff has not pleaded a strong inference of scienter. [SEA § 21D(b)(3)(A)]

(b) Analysis to Determine Whether Scienter Is Pleaded with Particularity

In **Tellabs, Inc. v. Makor Issues & Rts., Ltd.,** 551 U.S. 308 (2007), the Supreme Court provided the following analytical pathway to determine whether scienter is pleaded with particularity:

(i) The court must, as with any motion to dismiss for failure to plead a claim on which relief can be granted, accept all factual allegations in the complaint as true.

(ii) The court must consider the complaint in its entirety, including documents incorporated by reference and matters of which a court may take judicial notice.

(iii) Based thereon, the court must assess *both* the inference of scienter *and* the inference of non-scienter and then compare the two inferences.

(iv) The complaint will survive dismissal *only if a reasonable person would deem the inference of scienter cogent and at least as compelling as any opposing inference one could draw from the facts alleged.*

(c) Impact of Discovery Stay

The PSLRA also imposes a discovery stay in any private litigation under the 1934 Act during the pendency of any motion to dismiss. [SEA § 21D(b)(3)(B)] Thus, a private civil plaintiff cannot rely on discovery to gather information to support the pleading of a strong inference of scienter. Rather, a plaintiff must rely on other sources of information in order to satisfy the requirement to plead a strong inference of scienter, including whistleblowers.

i. Reliance

In private civil actions, in addition to the elements the government must prove, the plaintiff must show that he or she *relied* on the material fact that was misrepresented or omitted. This reliance element is sometimes referred to as "transaction causation."

(1) Proving Individualized Reliance

An individual investor can prove by reliance by demonstrating that (i) he or she that actually *believed* the misrepresentations, and (ii) that belief was a substantial factor the plaintiff's entering into the transaction. [**List v. Fashion Park, Inc.,** 340 F.2d 457 (2d Cir.), *cert. denied sub nom.* **List v. Lerner,** 382 U.S. 811 (1965)]

(2) Individualized Reliance Would Prevent Class Certification

Private civil actions under Rule 10b–5 are often brought as class actions. If each member of the class were required to prove his or her individualized reliance, however, it would defeat class certification because "questions of law or fact common to class members" would not "predominate over any questions affecting only individual members." [FRCP 23(b)(3)] Courts, however, have identified two presumptions of reliance, which can be asserted on a class-wide basis without preventing class certification.

(3) Presumption of Reliance on Omissions

If the defendant failed to disclose a material fact, *reliance by the plaintiffs is generally presumed.* This is so because of the difficulty of proving that the plaintiff "relied" on something that was not said. The presumption of reliance can be rebutted by showing that the plaintiff did *not* rely. [**Affiliated Ute Citizens v. United States,** 406 U.S. 128 (1972)] This presumption has been construed narrowly by courts as applying only in so-called "pure omissions" cases rather than in cases alleging both misstatements and omissions.

(4) Presumption of Reliance on Misstatements

The fraud-on-the market presumption of reliance, if successfully invoked, establishes class-wide reliance on alleged misstatements and omission.

(a) Fraud-on-the-Market Presumption of Reliance

The fraud-on-the-market presumption of reliance actually contains two embedded presumptions: (1) that the fraud affected the market price; and (2) that the plaintiff relied on the integrity of the market price when making an investment decision.

In order to invoke the first embedded presumption (that the fraud affected the market price), the plaintiff must show (1) that the alleged misrepresentations were publicly known, (2) that they were material, and (3) that the stock traded in an efficient market.

In order to invoke the second embedded presumption (that the plaintiff relied on the integrity of the market price when making an investment decision), the plaintiff must prove that the plaintiff traded the stock between the time the misrepresentations were made and when the truth was revealed.

[**Halliburton Co. v. Erica P. John Fund, Inc.,** 573 U.S. 258 (2014)]

(b) Efficient Capital Markets Theory

The first embedded presumption (that the fraud affected the market price) is based on the efficient capital markets theory. Under this theory, in an efficient capital market (*i.e.,* a market in which pricing reflects all publicly available information about a security), material misrepresentations or omissions cause a distortion in the price.

(c) Plaintiff's Required Showing at the Time of Class Certification

In order to invoke the fraud-on-the-market presumption of reliance, the plaintiff must establish that the allegedly material misrepresentation was publicly disseminated and that the market was efficient.

Courts have identified five factors as useful in determining whether the market for a security was efficient:

(i) A large weekly trading volume;

(ii) The existence of a significant number of reports by security analysts;

(iii) The existence of market makers and arbitrageurs in the security;

(iv) The issuer's eligibility to file an S-3 registration statement under the 1933 Act; and

(v) A history of immediate movement in the price of the security in response to unexpected corporate events or financial developments.

[**Cammer v. Bloom,** 711 F. Supp. 1264 (D.N.J. 1989)]

(d) Rebutting the Fraud-on-the-Market Presumption of Reliance

Defendants may rebut the fraud-on-the-market presumption of reliance by undercutting its two embedded presumptions (*i.e.*, that the fraud affected the market price and that the plaintiff relied on the integrity of the market when making an investment decision). The timing of that rebuttal depends on the aspect sought to be rebutted, however. At the time that the plaintiff seeks to certify the class, the defendant may prevent class certification by showing that the alleged fraud did *not* affect the market price. A defendant may not defeat class certification by proving that the alleged misrepresentations were immaterial, however. That showing must wait for the merits stage.

(i) Defendants May Prevent Class Certification by Proving the Lack of Price Impact

Defendants may prevent class certification by proving that an alleged misrepresentation did not actually affect the market price of the stock.

[**Halliburton Co. v. Erica P. John Fund,** Inc., 573 U.S. 258 (2014)] Defendants must prove the lack of price impact by a preponderance of the evidence. [**Goldman Sachs Grp., Inc. v. Arkansas Tchr. Ret. Sys.,** 141 S.Ct. 1951 (2021)] Defendants usually seek to disprove price impact by introducing "event studies" (regression analyses) that seek to show that the market price of the stock did *not* respond to the alleged misrepresentations. Plaintiffs usually introduce competing event studies seeking to show that the market price of the stock responded to the alleged misrepresentations.

(ii) Defendants May Not Prevent Class Certification by Disproving Materiality

Defendants must wait for the merits stage of the case to litigate materiality, however. Although materiality is a prerequisite for invoking the fraud-on-the-market presumption, the Supreme Court held that it should be left to the merits stage because it does not bear on the predominance requirement of Rule 23(b)(3). Materiality is an objective issue susceptible to common, class-wide proof. If a plaintiff fails to prove materiality, it would defeat every plaintiff's claim on the merits (because materiality is an element of claims under Rule 10b–5). Thus, if a plaintiff fails to prove materiality, it would not simply preclude invocation of the presumption (and thereby cause individual questions of reliance to predominate over common ones). [**Amgen Inc. v. Connecticut Ret. Plans & Tr. Funds,** 568 U.S. 455 (2013)]

j. Loss Causation

Loss causation is a necessary element in a private civil action for damages under Rule 10b–5. That is, the defendant's action must have proximately caused economic loss to the plaintiff.

Proof that the plaintiff purchased the security at an inflated purchase price is insufficient to establish loss causation. [**Dura Pharms., Inc. v. Broudo**, 544 U.S. 336 (2005)] Where the value of the security does not actually decline as a result of an alleged misrepresentation, there is no economic loss attributable to that misrepresentation. In the absence of a correction in the market price, the cost of the alleged misrepresentation is still incorporated into the value of the security and may be recovered at any time simply by reselling the security at the inflated price. [**Semerenko v. Cendant Corp.**, 223 F.3d 165, 184 (3d Cir. 2000)] Plaintiffs often seek to prove loss causation by showing, not only that the price was inflated by the misrepresentation, but also that the share price fell after the truth became known.

e.g. **Example:** C Corp. made a tender offer for A Corp., which caused the price of A stock to rise. During the course of the tender offer, C discovered accounting irregularities that eventually caused C to restate its financial statements for several years and that turned ostensible profits into actual losses. Throughout the several months in which C investigated its accounting problems, C issued statements to the effect that it was financially healthy and that it remained committed to the merger. Eventually C abandoned the merger, and the price of A stock declined substantially. The court held that the element of loss causation was adequately pleaded on these facts. [**Semerenko v. Cendant Corp.**, *supra*]

k. Damages

The usual measure of damages in a private civil suit is out-of-pocket damages—*i.e.*, the difference between the inflated price paid and the actual value at the time of purchase.

The PSLRA imposes a cap on damages, which seeks to ensure that damages are not inflated by a temporary fluctuation in the stock price. Damages are capped at the difference between (1) the price paid or received by the plaintiff (as appropriate) and (2) the mean trading price during the 90-day period after the corrective disclosure. [SEA § 21D(e)]

Punitive damages are not available under Rule 10b–5.

l. Burden of Proof

In private civil causes of action for damages, the burden of proof is on the plaintiff to prove the Rule 10b–5 cause of action by a *preponderance of the evidence.* [**Herman & MacLean v. Huddleston,** 459 U.S. 375 (1983)]

6. Insider Trading

Trading on the basis of material, nonpublic information is *sometimes* actionable under Rule 10b–5. There is not a general prohibition on trading on the basis of material, nonpublic information. Rather, trading on the basis of material, nonpublic information is actionable under Rule 10b–5 *only if* the trading was in breach of a duty of trust or confidence owed to the issuer, its shareholders, or the source of the information.

a. A Duty Not to Trade on the Basis of Material, Nonpublic Information

The typical insider trading case consists of a purchase or sale by the defendant over an exchange without disclosing inside information. In such cases, the Supreme Court has held that no violation of Rule 10b–5 occurs *unless* the defendant breaches a duty in so trading. [**United States v. O'Hagan**, 521 U.S. 642 (1997); **Chiarella v. United States**, 445 U.S. 222 (1980)]

This duty arises in two paradigmatic scenarios: (1) where the person trading is an "insider"; and (2) where the person trading is a "misappropriator." In addition, under certain circumstances, "tippers" who are insiders or misappropriators can be liable, even if they themselves do not trade; and "tippees" of an insider or misappropriator sometimes inherit their tipper's duty.

(1) Insiders

An "insider" is an officer, director, controlling shareholder, or corporate employee of an issuer. There are two key elements of insider status:

(1) The person must have a relationship that gives access—directly or indirectly—to information about the issuer's securities intended only for business purposes and not for personal benefit; and

(2) There must be an inherent unfairness resulting from the insider taking advantage of the information, knowing that it is unavailable to those with whom the insider is dealing.

In addition to traditional insiders, courts treat persons such as accountants, lawyers, investment bankers, and others as "insiders" when they enter "into a special confidential relationship" with the issuer "and are given access to information solely for corporate purposes," with an expectation that the information will be kept confidential. [**Dirks v. S.E.C.**, 463 U.S. 646 (1983)] e.g. **Example:** An investment banker, working on a proposed public offering for the issuer, received material nonpublic information about the issuer and traded on the basis of that information. The court held that the investment banker (and his employer) were liable as insiders. [**Shapiro v. Merrill Lynch, Pierce, Fenner & Smith, Inc.**, 495 F.2d 228 (2d Cir. 1974)]

(2) Misappropriators

Persons who misappropriate material nonpublic information for securities trading purposes, in breach of a duty to the source of the information, may be liable for insider trading.

(a) *United States v. O'Hagan*

In *O'Hagan*, a law firm was retained by the purchaser in a tender offer. O'Hagan, a lawyer with the firm, learned of the tender offer and purchased securities of the target, later selling them for a profit of more than $4.3 million. O'Hagan was a constructive insider of the *purchaser*, not of the *target*. Thus, O'Hagan did not owe a duty to abstain from trading on the basis of his insider status.

However, the Supreme Court, applying the misappropriation theory, held that O'Hagan violated Rule 10b–5. A person violates Rule 10b–5 when he or she misappropriates confidential information for securities trading purposes in breach of a duty to the source of the information. [**United States v. O'Hagan**, 521 U.S. 642 (1997)]

(b) Rule 10b5–2

In 2000, the S.E.C. adopted Rule 10b5–2 to help clarify application of the misappropriation theory in family or personal relationships. Rule 10b5–2 sets out three nonexclusive circumstances in which a person has a duty of trust or confidence that will be breached if that person uses information for personal gain or reveals it to a third party. The breach of this duty, in turn, will support a cause of action under the misappropriation theory of insider trading. The circumstances in which such a duty exists include:

(i) When the recipient of the information agrees to maintain the information in confidence;

(ii) When the source of the information and the recipient have a history, pattern, or practice of sharing confidences, so that the recipient knows or should know that the source expects the information to remain in confidence; and

(iii) When the recipient of the information obtains the information from her spouse, parent, child, or sibling, unless the recipient can demonstrate that she did not know, nor reasonably should have known, that the information was expected to be kept confidential and that there was no actual agreement to keep it confidential.

[SEA Rule 10b5–2]

(3) Tippers and Tippees

"Tippers" (i.e., insiders who, in breach of a duty, provide material nonpublic information to others, who then trade on that information) may be liable under Rule 10b–5, even if they do not themselves trade on the information. Likewise, "tippees" (i.e., persons who receive a tip from insiders and subsequently trade securities related to the tipped information) may inherit their tippers' duty not to trade.

(a) Test for Tipper/Tippee Liability

Tippers and tippees may be liable under Rule 10b–5 under certain circumstances for a tippee's trade. Recall that liability under Rule 10b–5 for insider trading is premised on the breach of a duty of trust and confidence owed to the issuer, its shareholders, or the source of the information. Clearly an insider breaches such a duty by trading with a shareholder of the issuer, but in most cases a *tippee, as an unrelated party, is not bound by such duties.* What, then, supports a tippee's liability for insider trading?

(b) *Dirks v. S.E.C.*

The Supreme Court held that tippee liability is premised on breach by the tipper of a duty; *i.e.*, the tippee derivatively breaches the tipper's duty. Dirks, a stock analyst, was told by a corporate insider that the assets of the issuer were vastly overstated. The insider was not motivated by any personal gain but sought only to reveal the corporate fraud. Dirks gave this information to his clients, who then sold the issuer's stock to unknowing purchasers.

The Supreme Court held that neither the insider (the tipper) nor Dirks (the tippee) violated Rule 10b–5. A tippee is liable for acting (either trading, or tipping others) on a tip only if, in giving the tip:

(i) The insider-tipper has *breached duties owed to the issuer or its shareholders;*

(ii) The insider-tipper has *acted from a motive of "personal benefit";* and

(iii) The tippee knew, or should have known, that the information was provided by the tipper in breach of a duty.

(c) The "Personal Benefit" Requirement

The requirement that the insider act to receive a "personal benefit" is satisfied if the insider receives a pecuniary gain or a reputational benefit that might translate into future earnings.

The Supreme Court in *Dirks* stated that this requirement is also met when an insider makes a *gift of confidential information to a trading relative or a friend.* According to the Supreme Court, such a "tip and trade resemble trading by the insider himself followed by a gift of the profits to the recipient." The Court reaffirmed this in *Salman*: "In such situations, the tipper benefits personally because giving a gift of trading information is the same thing as trading by the tipper followed by a gift of the proceeds." [**Salman v. United States**, 580 U.S. 39 (2016)]

b. "On the Basis of" Material, Nonpublic Information

Suppose a person is in possession of material nonpublic information with respect to a security, and then trades, but proves that the information did not cause the trade (*i.e.,* that the trade would have taken place even if the person had not learned the information)? In other words, does a person violate Rule 10b–5 merely by trading while in possession of material nonpublic information, or must the person actually use the information before a violation takes place?

(1) Rule 10b5–1

Prior to 2000, there was some conflict in the cases on the "use v. possession" question. In 2000, however, the S.E.C. adopted Rule 10b5–1, under which a person will be deemed to have purchased or sold a security on the basis of material nonpublic information if the person was aware of the information when purchasing or selling.

(2) "Awareness of" Information

Rule 10b5–1 does not indicate the circumstances under which a person is "aware of" material nonpublic information. Often it will be clear, for example when the C.E.O. of an issuer makes a business decision that will affect the company's stock price, and then buys or sells the company's stock. In other cases, however, there may be only indirect evidence of awareness, for example when the defendant's telephone records reveal calls to persons with inside information, but there is no direct proof that inside information was discussed.

(3) Scienter and Rule 10b5–1

Rule 10b5–1 does not modify the requirement that scienter be established before Rule 10b–5 is violated. It merely defines trading "on the basis of" material nonpublic information to include all trading taking place while the defendant is aware of such information.

(4) Affirmative Defenses Under Rule 10b5–1

Rule 10b5–1 includes two affirmative defenses, either of which will shield the defendant from liability for trading "on the basis of" material nonpublic information. As with all affirmative defenses, the defendant must carry the burden of proof to establish the defense.

(a) Prearranged Trading

The first affirmative defense requires proof that the challenged trading took place pursuant to a binding contract, trading instruction, or written *plan that existed before the defendant became aware of material nonpublic information.* [SEA Rule 10b5–1(c)(1)]

(b) Institutional Trading

The second affirmative defense is available to anyone *other than a natural person.* For this defense, the defendant must prove that:

(i) The individual making the investment decision for the institution was *not aware of the material nonpublic information;* and

(ii) The institution had *reasonable policies* in place to ensure that the individuals making investment decisions would not violate the insider trading rules.

[SEA Rule 10b5–1(c)(2)]

c. Scienter in Insider Trading Cases

Insider trading is only actionable under Rule 10b–5 if the defendant acted with scienter. Pleading and proving scienter in insider trading cases is often easier than in other cases. It can still be difficult, however, if the plaintiff cannot prove that an insider had material nonpublic information, but instead relies on the timing of the insider's trades to raise the inference that the insider had such information. One court has concluded that "insider trading is suspicious only when it is dramatically out of line with prior trading practices at times calculated to maximize the personal benefit from undisclosed inside information." [**Ronconi v. Larkin**, 253 F.3d 423 (9th Cir. 2001)]

d. "Selective Disclosure" and Regulation FD

Dirks appeared to condone at least one kind of activity that the S.E.C. considers unlawful—the selective disclosure by insiders of material nonpublic information to securities analysts. Recall that, under *Dirks,* disclosure by an insider gives rise to a cause of action under Rule 10b–5 only if the insider acts from a motive of personal benefit. Thus, an insider can reveal material nonpublic information, as long as there is no quid pro quo. The S.E.C. has long been suspicious that, in many cases where insiders selectively disclose material nonpublic information to securities analysts, there actually is a benefit back to the issuer, such as favorable reports concerning the issuer by the analyst. There have been few cases brought claiming this as a violation of Rule 10b–5, however, in part because it would be very difficult to prove the illicit benefit obtained by the issuer. To remedy the problem of selective disclosure, in 2000, the S.E.C. adopted Regulation FD (for "Fair Disclosure"), which is are summarized below.

(1) Requirements—in General

The essence of Regulation FD is that if a disclosure of material nonpublic information is made by a regulated person and to a regulated person, the issuer must simultaneously (in the case of an intentional disclosure) or promptly (in the case of an inadvertent disclosure) make the information public.

(2) Applies to 1934 Act Reporting Companies

Regulation FD is a reporting provision, rather than an antifraud provision. Thus, it applies to most companies that are required by either SEA Section 13(a) or Section 15(d) to file reports with the S.E.C.

(3) Persons to Whom Disclosures Are Subject to Regulation

A disclosure of material nonpublic information is subject to Regulation FD if it is made by the issuer (or by a regulated person on its behalf) to:

(a) A broker-dealer;

(b) An investment adviser:

(c) An investment company;

(d) Persons associated with any of the above; or

(e) Holders of the issuer's securities, if it is reasonably foreseeable that the holders will buy or sell securities on the basis of the disclosed information.

(4) Excluded Persons

Specifically excluded from the list of regulated disclosees are:

(a) Ratings agencies that publish their ratings, if disclosure is made solely for rating purposes;

(b) Persons subject to a duty of confidentiality; and

(c) Persons who agree to keep the information confidential.

(5) Persons by Whom Disclosures Are Subject to Regulation

Disclosures are regulated if made by senior officials of the issuer or by anyone else who regularly communicates with any of the persons to whom disclosures are regulated.

(6) Timing of Public Disclosure

The key obligation under Regulation FD is to make the information available to the public. How long the issuer has to accomplish this depends on whether the regulated disclosure was intentional or unintentional.

(a) Intentional Disclosures—Simultaneous Public Disclosure Required

A regulated disclosure is intentional if the regulated person making the disclosure knew, or was reckless in not knowing, that the information disclosed was material and nonpublic. The obligation in this case is to make the information public simultaneously with the disclosure to the regulated disclosee.

(b) Unintentional Disclosures—Prompt Public Disclosure Required

A regulated disclosure is unintentional if the regulated person making the disclosure did not know, and was not reckless in not knowing, that the information disclosed was material and nonpublic. When an unintentional disclosure happens, the issuer must make the information public "as soon as reasonably practicable."

e. Specific Insider Trading Legislation

The securities markets of the 1980s were turbulent and produced two significant statutes dealing with insider trading: the Insider Trading Sanctions Act of 1984 and the Insider Trading and Securities Fraud Enforcement Act of 1988.

(1) Insider Trading Sanctions Act

In 1984, Congress gave the S.E.C. additional enforcement powers against insider trading by enacting the Insider Trading Sanctions Act of 1984. Under this statute, the S.E.C. can seek a civil penalty of up to *three times* the amount of the insider's ill-gotten profits (or avoided losses). There are many unanswered questions under this Act, for example, would successive actions under the Act and for criminal violations violate the constitutional prohibition against double jeopardy? In view of the Act's provisions establishing the possibility of penalties at three times the insider's trading profits, would a nontrading tipper be covered by the Act? [*See* SEA § 21A]

(2) Insider Trading and Securities Fraud Enforcement Act of 1988

In 1988, Congress adopted the Insider Trading and Securities Fraud Enforcement Act (the "1988 Act"). This statute, which added Section 20A to the 1934 Act, provides a cause of action to persons who sold or purchased a security in the market at the time that the defendant purchased or sold a security of the same class, if the defendant's transaction violated "any provision of [the 1934 Act and the rules thereunder]."

(a) Establishes Cause of Action

The 1988 Act does not prohibit any activity; instead, it relies on the existing provisions of the 1934 Act to establish a violation. Once a violation is established, however, the 1988 Act establishes a cause of action in favor of contemporaneous traders in the market.

(b) Remedies Under the 1988 Act

The 1988 Act limits the amount recoverable to the *defendant's profit gained or loss avoided.* This amount is then further reduced by the amount of any profits the defendant has already disgorged relating to the same securities transactions. [SEA § 20A(b)(1), (2)]

f. Liability of Multiple Defendants

If there are multiple defendants in a Rule 10b–5 action, two questions arise: First, what is the individual liability of each defendant? And second, can one defendant recover from another (that is, is there a right of contribution)?

(1) Liability of Each Defendant

Until 1995, the liability of multiple defendants under Rule 10b–5 was joint and several—*i.e.,* all defendants were individually liable for the total damages. In 1995, however, Congress enacted the PSLRA, which added Section 21D(f) to the 1934 Act. Section 21D(f) provides that in *private actions* under the 1934 Act: (i) persons who knowingly commit securities fraud are jointly and severally liable; and (ii) all others are liable in proportion to their respective fault.

(2) Contribution

In 1993, the Supreme Court confirmed the holdings of numerous lower courts that a defendant in a private action under Rule 10b–5 has a right of contribution against other defendants found liable in the case. [**Musick, Peeler & Garrett v. Employers Insurance Co.,** 508 U.S. 286 (1993)]

g. S.E.C. Actions

When the S.E.C. brings an action under Rule 10b–5, it may seek remedies different from those sought by private plaintiffs. The S.E.C. may itself sue for an injunction or to recover trading profits made by the defendants. [**S.E.C. v. Texas Gulf Sulphur Co.,** *supra,* p. 191] Where the S.E.C. sues a defendant that purchased securities based on inside information, the proper measure of damages is the difference between the price paid (*e.g.,* $5/share) and the price at which the security traded within a short time after the material information was disclosed to the public (*e.g.,* $10/share). [*See* **S.E.C. v. MacDonald,** 699 F.2d 47 (1st Cir. 1983)] In addition, the S.E.C. may recommend a criminal action to the Justice Department under Rule 10b–5.

7. Defenses

The following defenses are available to a defendant in a Rule 10b–5 action.

a. Statute of Limitations

The Sarbanes-Oxley Act of 2002 for the first time created an express statute of limitations that applies to private actions under Rule 10b–5. Under SOXA Section 804, a Rule 10b–5 action must be brought within *two years after the discovery of the facts constituting the violation, and in no case later than five years after the violation occurred.* [SOXA § 804; 28 U.S.C. § 1658(b)]

Because plaintiffs must bring suit within two years of "discovery" of the facts constituting the violation, it is important to know when "discovery" of these facts has taken place. The Supreme Court has interpreted this to mean either (1) actual discovery *or* (2) when a reasonably diligent plaintiff would have discovered the facts constituting the violation, whichever is earlier. [**Merck & Co. v. Reynolds**, 559 U.S. 633 (2010)] In addition, because scienter is a prerequisite to a violation of Rule 10b–5, the period does not begin to run until discovery of facts supporting scienter (as well as the other facts necessary to plead a claim). (*Id.*)

b. Other Common Law Defenses

Other common law defenses, such as in pari delicto (*i.e.*, equal fault), may be applicable to Rule 10b–5 actions. However, courts are careful to subordinate such defenses to the primary objective of seeing that the purposes and policies of the securities acts are carried out. [*See* **Bateman Eichler, Hill Richards, Inc. v. Berner**, 472 U.S. 299 (1985)]

e.g. **Example:** In *Bateman*, the Court held that the defense of in pari delicto did *not* prevent a tippee (who had been given false information) from suing the corporate insiders who passed on the false information. The Court reasoned that barring such private actions would result in fraudulent schemes going undetected by the S.E.C., because there would be no incentive for plaintiff-tippees to bring such actions.

8. Class Actions Under Rule 10b–5

Rule 10b–5 actions are frequently brought as class actions because many shareholders may be similarly injured by the same Rule 10b–5 violation and yet, because of the expenses of litigation, no single shareholder would have the incentive to bring a claim on his or her own.

a. "Class Action" Defined

The class action is a suit in which a representative plaintiff presses his or her own claim and the claims of others similarly situated in a single action to establish the liability of the defendant and the gross amount of damages. It is in some respects an ideal method for enforcement of private Rule 10b–5 rights. It contributes to the efficient use of limited judicial resources; ensures that the interests of all plaintiffs (which may otherwise be too small to be asserted economically in individual actions) are given vindication in the courts; and thereby contributes to the effective enforcement of the federal securities laws.

b. Federal Court Jurisdiction

The 1934 Act vests exclusive jurisdiction in the federal district courts over violation of its provisions and over all suits to enforce any liability or duty created by it or the rules and regulations thereunder. [SEA § 27]

c. Preconditions to the Existence of a Class

The federal courts must apply the Federal Rules of Civil Procedure in all procedural matters; therefore, the Federal Rules apply to class actions brought under the federal securities laws. Federal Rule 23(a) lists four mandatory preconditions to the existence of a class of plaintiffs:

(1) The class must be so *numerous* that joinder of all members is impracticable;

(2) There must be *questions of law or fact common to the entire class* of plaintiffs;

(3) The claims or defenses of the representative parties must be *typical* of the claims or defenses of the entire class; and

(4) The representative parties must *fairly and adequately protect* the interests of the entire class.

Even assuming that the above preconditions to the existence of a class are met, Federal Rule 23(b) imposes an additional requirement that the class representative (plaintiff) plead and show the existence of one of the following special circumstances:

(1) That *inconsistent, varying, or disadvantageous judgments* are likely if a class action is not permitted; or

(2) That final *injunctive or declaratory relief* is appropriate; or

(3) That the *questions of law or fact common to class members predominate* over any questions affecting only individual members, and that a class action is superior to other available methods for the fair and efficient adjudication of the controversy.

As discussed above on p. 134, class actions under Rule 10b–5 generally proceed under Rule 23(b)(3), requiring that questions of law or fact common to class members predominate over questions affecting only individual members. This explains why establishing class-wide reliance is imperative to class certification.

d. Exclusion from the Class

Under Federal Rule 23(c)(2), potential class members can avoid being bound by any judgment rendered in a class action by requesting exclusion from the class.

e. Private Securities Litigation Reform Act of 1995

As discussed in the next section, the PSLRA has made it considerably more difficult for private plaintiffs to bring securities fraud class actions.

C. The Private Securities Litigation Reform Act of 1995

1. Introduction

We have already discussed the Private Securities Litigation Reform Act of 1995 ("PSLRA"), which made important changes to the securities laws, mainly dealing with the conduct of securities litigation by private parties. This section provides an overview of these changes. Impetus for the PSLRA arose from the perception that abuse was widespread in securities litigation brought by private plaintiffs. As early as 1975, the Supreme Court noted that litigation under the federal securities laws "presents a danger of vexatiousness different in degree and in kind from that which accompanies litigation in general." [**Blue Chip Stamps v. Manor Drug Stores,** *supra*] The PSLRA may be the most significant federal statute on the subject of securities litigation since the New Deal. The PSLRA received overwhelming congressional support (it was passed over President Clinton's veto).

2. Limitations of the 1995 Act

The 1995 Act *does not apply* to:

a. Actions brought by the federal government (including the S.E.C.);

b. Actions brought by the securities self-regulatory organizations;

c. Actions brought by private plaintiffs under other federal laws (except that private civil RICO actions based on securities law violations are limited by the 1995 Act);

d. Actions brought by private plaintiffs under state law (including common law fraud and state securities laws; or

e. Actions brought by state securities regulators.

Note: Although actions brought by private plaintiffs under state law are excluded from the PSLRA, the Securities Litigation Uniform Standards Act, discussed below on p. 212, precludes most such class actions to proceed, thus forcing securities class actions to be governed by the PSLRA's provisions.

3. Major Provisions of the PSLRA

The PSLRA's major provisions are summarized below:

a. Scope

Keep in mind that the 1995 Act does not affect actions brought by the government, whether by the S.E.C. or by the Justice Department. The 1995 Act applies only to litigation filed by private plaintiffs.

b. Safe Harbor for Forward-Looking Statements

As discussed above on pp. 120–122, the PSLRA provides a safe harbor from liability for certain forward-looking statements.

c. Heightened Scienter Pleading Requirements

As discussed above on p. 128, the PSLRA requires plaintiffs to plead a strong inference of scienter.

d. Special Verdict

The PSLRA provides that a court hearing fraud claims by a private plaintiff must, on motion of the defendant, submit written questions to the jury regarding the defendant's state of mind. [SA § 27(d); SEA § 21D(d)]

e. Class Action Reform

Class action lawsuits were among those perceived as most abusive under the former law; accordingly, the PSLRA made some important changes in the way class action securities litigation is conducted.

(1) Notice to Class Members

Within 20 days after a securities class action complaint is filed, the plaintiff must notify the members of the purported plaintiff class of the lawsuit. Up to 60 days after the filing, any member of the class can move the court to be named the lead plaintiff. [SA § 27(a)(3)(A); SEA § 21D(a)(3)(A)]

(2) Lead Plaintiffs Must Meet Certain Criteria

The motion filed by a would-be lead plaintiff must be decided by the court within 90 days after the filing of the complaint. The court must designate, as lead plaintiff for the class, the "most adequate plaintiff," *i.e.*, the class member or members "that the court determines to be the most capable of adequately representing the interests of all class members." [SA § 27(a)(3)(B); SEA § 21D(a)(3)(B)] The lead plaintiff "shall, subject to the approval of the court, select and retain counsel to represent the class." [*Id.*]

(a) Congress's Rationale

When a class of investors has been harmed by a securities law violation, it is often uneconomical for the holder of a small stake to sue, even when the defendant's liability is clear, because the cost of bringing such a case to judgment (or even to settlement) can easily exceed the value of the small investor's investment. Consequently, such cases are typically filed as class actions. Moreover, class action litigation often results in awards of attorneys' fees to the plaintiffs' attorneys. Historically, this led some members of the plaintiffs' bar to race to the courthouse to file a class-action lawsuit, naming as the lead plaintiff a "professional plaintiff," who was often paid a "bounty" for his or her willingness to serve. Such plaintiffs are not good class representatives, because their entire interest in the litigation is limited to the bounty payment. The PSLRA, by requiring the appointment of the "most adequate plaintiff," sought to change the status quo by ensuring that the lead plaintiff will fairly represent the interests of the plaintiff class—rather than the interests of the plaintiffs' counsel.

(b) Presumption That Large Stake Equals Adequacy

There is a rebuttable presumption that the plaintiff with "the largest financial interest in the relief sought by the class" is the most adequate plaintiff. [SA § 27(a)(3)(B)(iii); SEA § 21D(a)(3)(B)(iii)]

(c) Number

More than one lead plaintiff can be appointed, especially when there is a logical group of plaintiffs to represent the plaintiff class, such as when two or more readily identifiable plaintiffs collectively have the largest financial interest in the relief sought. [***In re*** **Cephalon Securities Litigation,** 1996 WL 515203 (E.D. Pa. 1996)]

(d) Grounds for Challenging Appointment

While the defendant may challenge the appointment of a lead plaintiff on procedural grounds (for example, that the appointed lead plaintiff failed to file a certification with the complaint or failed to serve notice to the class members), the defendant lacks standing to challenge the appointment of a lead plaintiff based on failure to meet the criteria set out by the PSLRA. [**Greebel v. FTP Software, Inc.,** 939 F. Supp. 57 (D. Mass. 1996)]

(3) Certain Payments Are Prohibited

"Bounty" payments to the lead plaintiff, and similar arrangements, are prohibited. [SA § 27(a)(4); SEA § 21D(a)(4)]

(4) Restrictions on Repeat Plaintiffs

A person may serve as lead plaintiff in no more than five securities class actions brought in any three-year period, unless the court grants permission to serve in additional class actions. [SA § 27(a)(3)(B)(vi); SEA § 21D(a)(3)(B)(vi)]

f. The Securities Litigation Uniform Standards Act of 1998

One of the results of the class action reforms adopted in the PSLRA was the migration of securities fraud class actions to the state courts, perhaps to avoid the new, more onerous requirements of the federal securities laws. In response, Congress passed the Securities Litigation Uniform Standards Act of 1998, which precludes class actions (and similar consolidated proceedings) based on state law if the action alleges misrepresentation or omission of a material fact, or the use of a manipulative or deceptive device or contrivance, in connection with the purchase or sale of a security. In effect, state securities fraud litigation is precluded if it is a class action or involves consolidated actions of more than 50 plaintiffs. (See below p. 212)

g. Discovery

(1) Stay of Discovery

The PSLRA provides for *a stay of discovery* upon the filing of a motion to dismiss by the defendant. [SA § 27(b); SEA § 21D(b)(3)]

(a) Rationale

Before the PSLRA, critics of the status quo often asserted that the merits of a case had little relevance to the "settlement value" of the case. Plaintiffs in private securities litigation were typically allowed to conduct extensive discovery of an issuer's top management, even while a motion to dismiss the case was pending. Because such discovery consumes a lot of the managers' time, it can end up costing the issuer a great deal of money. Issuers confronting such scenarios sometimes found it cheaper to settle the cases, even if they were frivolous. The PSLRA's stay of discovery provision responds by staying discovery while the court considers the defendant's motion to dismiss.

(2) Exceptions

Along with the stay of discovery, the PSLRA provides for two limited exceptions, when discovery will not be stayed. [SA § 27(b); SEA § 21D(b)(3)]

(a) The "Undue Prejudice" Exception

The exception to staying discovery for "undue prejudice" is available if the plaintiff *would suffer improper or unfair detriment even if less than irreparable harm.* [**Medical Imaging Centers v. Lichtenstein,** 1996 WL 156926 (S.D. Cal.), *aff'd,* 917 F. Supp. 717 (S.D. Cal. 1996)]

(b) The "Loss of Evidence" Exception

The PSLRA also permits an exception to the stay of disclosure if the loss of evidence might result; however, the plaintiff must provide some proof. If the plaintiff merely makes speculative assertions regarding the loss of evidence, the stay of discovery will not be lifted. [**Novak v. Kasaks**, 1996 WL 467534 (S.D.N.Y. 1996)]

h. Damages Capped

As discussed above on p. 132, the PSLRA caps damages in actions brought under the 1934 Act to the difference between the price paid by the plaintiff (or, in case of a sale by the plaintiff, the price received) and the average trading price of the security during the

90-day period beginning on the day corrective information (*i.e.*, the truth) is disseminated to the market. [SEA § 21D(e)]

i. Contribution and Proportionate Liability

Before the PSLRA, plaintiffs in securities cases sometimes searched for the "deepest pocket"; *i.e.*, they would look for and sue the defendant able to pay the largest amount, even if that defendant's actions were merely collateral to the fraud. (Of course, the absence of aiding and abetting liability in private civil securities fraud cases limits the effectiveness of strategy.) This strategy was arguably encouraged by the rule of joint and several liability, which provides that any defendant can be required to pay the entire amount of a judgment. The PSLRA sharply reduces the applicability of joint and several liability:

(1) In actions brought under the *1934 Act*, joint and several liability is limited to those who *"knowingly commit"* a violation of the securities laws.

(2) In actions brought under *Section 11* of the 1933 Act, joint and several liability of *outside directors* is limited to those who *"knowingly commit"* a violation of the securities laws.

(3) In actions brought under either the *1933 or the 1934 Acts*, "knowingly commit" is defined as having *actual knowledge* of the falsity or fraud.

(4) In actions brought under either the *1933 or the 1934 Acts, defendants are provided express rights of contribution.*

[SA § 11(f)(2); SEA § 21D(f)]

j. Settlement Terms

The PSLRA requires that plaintiffs' counsel provide extensive disclosure of the terms of any settlement. In addition, counsel fees for plaintiffs' counsel are limited. [SA § 27(a)(5)–(7); SEA § 21D(a)(5)–(7)]

k. Mandatory Sanctions

In a case brought under the 1933 or the 1934 Acts, if the court finds that there was a violation of Federal Rule of Civil Procedure 11(b) as to the complaint, any responsive pleading, or any dispositive motion, the court *must* impose sanctions under Rule 11 against the party or attorney responsible. (Rule 11(b), among other things, prohibits presenting papers for an improper purpose and requires legal and factual contentions in papers to be supportable.) In addition, the court may require a bond against any sanctions to be imposed under Rule 11. [SA § 27(c); SEA § 21D(c)]

D. Insider Liability for Short-Swing Profits

1. Introduction

Section 16 is designed to prevent corporate insiders from using inside information about their companies to make short-swing profits by buying and then selling, or selling and then buying, securities of their corporation within a six-month period. It is a prophylactic supplement to Rule 10b–5's prohibition on insider trading. This summary provides an overview of the rules.

a. Basic Rule—Reporting and Disgorgement

SEA Section 16 accomplishes its goal of deterring the use of inside information by requiring insiders to: (i) *file periodic reports* of their holdings of the issuer's securities [SEA § 16(a)], and (ii) *disgorge any profits* resulting from any combination of sales and purchases taking place within six months of each other [SEA § 16(b)].

b. Makes Short Sales by Insiders Unlawful

In addition, Section 16(c) makes it unlawful for insiders to engage in short sales of their company's equity securities.

A "short sale" is a sale of securities that the seller does not yet own, but plans to purchase just in time to cover the obligations of the sale. This strategy can be thought of as a "bet against the company"—the short seller sells at today's price, hoping that later, when he or she has to cover the sale by delivering the securities, he or she will be able to purchase the securities more cheaply.

c. Distinguish—Rule 10b–5 "Insider Trading"

Although both Rule 10b–5 and Section 16 are sometimes said to prohibit "insider trading," the provisions operate entirely differently. A Rule 10b–5 case is based on a fraudulent misrepresentation or failure to disclose (see above pp. 132 *et seq.*). Section 16, on the other hand, is based on the amount of time elapsed between a purchase and sale (or a sale and purchase) of the issuer's securities by an insider. If the amount of time is too short, the insider must give up his or her "profits," regardless of whether information was misrepresented or withheld. The presence or absence of fraud is irrelevant to a Section 16 case.

d. Limitations of Section 16

Section 16 is not intended to be a comprehensive solution to the problem of insider trading. In fact, its narrow focus on short-swing trades makes it oblivious to even the most outrageous intentional frauds, as long as there are no purchases and sales within six months of one another.

e.g. **Example:** A, a director of X Corp., has owned 100 shares of X Corp. stock for three years. At a board meeting, A becomes aware that X Corp. is about to suffer a large loss of business. Before the news becomes public, A sells her X Corp. shares. A has not incurred any liability under Section 16 (although she would likely be liable under Rule 10b–5).

Note: Rule 10b–5 and Section 16(b) *can* apply to the same transaction. In the example above, had A owned the X Corp. stock for only three weeks, she could be liable to X Corp. under Section 16(b) for her short-swing profits and concurrently liable under Rule 10b–5 in an action by the S.E.C. or by contemporaneous purchasers of X Corp. shares.

2. Nature of a Section 16 Cause of Action

Section 16(a) and (c) are enforceable only by the S.E.C. and not by private plaintiffs. However, any shareholder of the issuer can bring a lawsuit under Section 16(b) to recover for the issuer an insider's profit from short-swing trading.

3. Elements of a Section 16(b) Cause of Action

Section 16(b) provides that:

(a) Any officer, director, or owner of more than 10% of any class of an equity security registered under Section 12;

(b) Who realizes any profit;

(c) From a purchase and sale, or sale and purchase, of;

(d) Any nonexempt equity security of the issuer;

(e) Within any period of less than six months;

(f) Shall be liable to the corporation for the profits made from the trading.

These elements are discussed further below.

a. Any Officer, Director, or Owner of More than 10% of Any Class of an Equity Security Registered Under Section 12

Section 16 applies to officers and directors of a corporation with a class of equity securities registered under Section 12 of the Act *and* all persons who beneficially own more than 10% of any class of the corporation's equity securities registered under Section 12.

(1) Officers and Directors

Whether a potential defendant was an officer or director at a particular point in time is in most cases readily established through the corporate minute book.

(a) "Officer" Defined

An officer is defined as an issuer's president, principal financial officer, principal accounting officer (or, if there is no such accounting officer, the controller), any vice president of the issuer in charge of a principal business unit, division, or function (such as sales, administration, or finance), any other officer who performs a policy-making function, or "any other person who performs similar policy-making functions for the issuer." [SEA Rule 16a–1(f)]

(b) Timing Issues

Section 16 raises three timing issues with respect to officers and directors: (1) What happens if a person was not an officer or director at the time of the first transaction (purchase or sale), but becomes one by the time of the second transaction (sale or purchase)? (2) What is the result in the reverse situation; i.e., the person was an officer or director at the time of the first transaction, but is no longer one at the time of the second? (3) And finally, what happens if an officer or director of a company is not subject to Section 16, because the company has no equity securities registered, and then the person becomes subject to Section 16 when the company registers a class of equity securities?

(i) Transaction Before Person Becomes an Officer or Director

If a transaction takes place before the person becomes an officer or director, the policy underlying Section 16 does not apply because such a person generally has no access to inside information. The S.E.C. adopted this view in 1991 and dropped an earlier requirement that persons report all transactions taking place six months before becoming officers or directors.

(ii) Transaction After Person Ceases Being an Officer or Director

A transaction that takes place after the person ceases to be an officer or director is subject to Section 16 only if it takes place within six months of a transaction that happened while the person was an officer or director.

(iii) Officer or Director Becomes Subject to Section 16

The last timing issue arises when an officer or director is not initially required to report a transaction, because the issuer has not registered a class of equity securities under the 1934 Act. If the issuer then registers a class of security, must the insider report the earlier transaction (and be liable for any profit when the transactions are matched)? The answer is yes, if (i) the insider engaged in the second transaction after becoming subject to the reporting requirement (*i.e.*, after the issuer registered a class of equity securities), and (ii) the second transaction took place within six months of the first transaction. [SEA Rule 16a–2(a)]

This rule is designed to trap transactions by insiders taking place shortly before the issuer goes public. The S.E.C. believes that in general, insiders of companies that are about to go public know about those plans far enough in advance to plan for Section 16. In addition, the possibilities for abuse just before the company goes public are greater than they are later, when a market price has been established for the company's securities.

(2) Beneficial Owner of More than 10%

To qualify as an "insider" by virtue of stock ownership, a person must beneficially own more than 10% of some class of *registered* equity security. But once qualified as an "insider" (either by owning more than 10% of a registered equity security, or by being an officer or director of a company with a class of registered equity security), purchases and sales of *any equity security of the issuer*—whether or not it is registered—may give rise to liability.

(a) Beneficial Owners

The concept of "beneficial ownership" is critical in analyzing Section 16 questions. A person may beneficially own securities to which he or she does not have record title; this is the usual case, for example, when a person purchases securities through a brokerage firm. Record title to the securities is held by the brokerage, while the buyer is the beneficial owner—meaning the benefits of ownership belong to the buyer, although the legal title is in the brokerage. For purposes of Section 16, record title is not important: it is beneficial ownership that counts. Under Section 16, there are two separate tests for determining beneficial ownership, depending on the purpose of the determination:

(b) Beneficial Ownership of More than Ten Percent of a Class of Registered Equity Security

In deciding whether a person is the holder of more than 10% of a class of registered equity security, and is therefore an "insider" subject to Section 16, all securities of that class beneficially owned by that person are counted. *For this purpose only,* beneficial ownership means having *voting power* with respect to those securities. In other words, all securities of that class which the person has the right to vote will be counted. [SEA Rule 16a–1(a)(1)]

(c) **All Other Section 16 Purposes**

For all other Section 16 purposes (*e.g.*, in reporting ownership of securities under Section 16(a), or in calculating the profits from securities transactions under Section 16(b)), beneficial ownership means having a direct or indirect *pecuniary interest in the shares.* [SEA Rule 16a–1(a)(2)]

(d) **Both Methods May Apply to One Situation**

Suppose a person is the beneficial owner of more than 10% of a class of registered equity security based on voting power. The consequence of this is that he or she is required periodically to report ownership under Section 16(a). However, the only securities reported under Section 16(a) are the securities in which he or she had a direct or indirect pecuniary interest, which might be more (or less) than the securities over which he or she has voting power. [SEA Rule 16a–1(a), note]

(e) **Timing of Ownership**

Although officers and directors need not occupy their positions at the time of both purchase and sale, the language of the statute indicates that 10% shareholders can be liable only if such ownership exists both at the time of purchase and at the time of sale.

e.g. **Example:** A owns no stock in X Corporation. On March 3, A buys X Corporation common shares (which are registered under the 1934 Act) in an amount sufficient to make A an 11% shareholder. On May 1 (less than six months later), A sells all the X Corporation common shares. Result: Although A must report the May 1 sale under Section 16(a), A is not liable to disgorge any profit under Section 16(b). The purchase by which A became a more-than-10% shareholder is not counted for Section 16(b) purposes, because at the time of that purchase, A was not a more-than-10% shareholder. [**Foremost-McKesson, Inc. v. Provident Securities Co.**, 423 U.S. 232 (1976)]

b. **Who Realizes Any Profit**

The profit of the defendant under Section 16(b) is calculated according to the statute and is unrelated to any real-world notion of buying low and selling high.

(1) **Any Purchase or Sale May Be Matched**

Section 16(b) may be applied to any matched "purchase" and "sale" (or "sale" and "purchase"), if the matched transactions occur within a period of less than six months.

e.g. **Example:** A, a director, buys 100 shares of XYZ stock on June 1 for $10 per share. On July 1, A sells the stock for $9 per share. On August 1, A buys 100 shares for $8 per share. Finally, on September 1, A sells the stock for $7 per share. In three months, A has lost a total of $200, but is still liable under Section 16(b), since the $9 sale can be matched with the $8 purchase (providing a $100 profit).

(2) **"Profit" from a Sale Followed by a Purchase**

Section 16 profit can be earned not only from a purchase followed by a sale, but also from a sale followed by a purchase.

e.g. **Example:** B, a director of G Corp. (which has its common stock registered under Section 12), sells 100 shares of G common stock on June 1, at $10 per share. Two months later, on August 1, B purchases 100 shares of G common stock at $5 per share. B is liable to G Corp. for her profit of $5 per share.

(3) Profit Maximized

The matching of purchase and sale transactions that will produce the maximum profit is used, and there is no attempt made to trace particular securities bought and sold. For example, if 100 shares are purchased at $1 per share and 100 at $2 per share, and five months later 100 shares are sold at $10 per share, the recoverable profit is $9 per share.

(4) Loss Transactions

Any transactions in the six-month period that produce losses are ignored.

c. From a Purchase and Sale, or Sale and Purchase

To establish liability under Section 16(b), there must be a matching purchase and sale, or sale and purchase. The general rule is that for purposes of Section 16(b), a "purchase" occurs when the purchaser undertakes an irrevocable obligation to take and pay for the stock, and a "sale" occurs when the seller undertakes an irrevocable obligation to deliver and accept payment for the stock. Although these rules are easily stated, there are several types of stock transactions where it may not be clear if a "purchase" or "sale" has actually occurred. Many of these transactions involve the exchange of stock either for property or for other stock.

(1) Stock Options

When determining whether there has been a purchase or sale of a security, the acquisition of a stock option (or other derivative security), rather than its exercise, is the significant event. Exercise of the option is viewed by the S.E.C. as merely a change from indirect to direct beneficial ownership, with no particular significance under Section 16. [S.E.C. Release No. 34–23369 (1991)] Rationale: The S.E.C.'s position recognizes that derivative securities (for instance, stock options) are functionally equivalent to the underlying equity securities. The S.E.C.'s position with respect to stock options is that the critical event—the one providing the opportunity to profit from inside information—occurs when the person has the legal right to receive (or to deliver) the underlying equity security at a fixed price.

The practical effect of the rules is that a purchase of an option is treated as the purchase (or sale, as appropriate) of the underlying security, and will be matched against any counterpart transaction—in the underlying security or in a derivative of the underlying security—to create a "profit" recoverable under Section 16.

(a) Exercise of an Option

The exercise of an option in most cases amounts to neither a purchase nor a sale under Section 16. The opportunity for profit is created when the option is acquired, and its exercise, because it does not create a new opportunity for profit, is exempt.

(b) Exception—Exercise of "Out-of-the-Money" Options

There is an exception to the rule that the exercise of an option is exempt: exercise by an insider of an out-of-the-money call option may constitute a purchase of the underlying security.

An option is in the money if its exercise price represents a profit opportunity for the option holder. Thus, a call option is in the money if its exercise price is less than the current market price of the underlying security. An option is out of the money when its exercise would produce a loss to the option holder. (Options that are out-of-the money are also sometimes referred to as "under water.") The S.E.C.'s reluctance to treat the exercise of an out-of-the-money option as exempt from Section 16 appears to be based on a general suspicion of such transactions, rather than on a specific perception of danger. In support of its decision, the S.E.C. noted merely that "there appears to be little economic justification for an insider to exercise an out-of-the-money option" and referred to unspecified "concerns as to the reasons that an insider would" do so. [S.E.C. Release No. 34–23369, *supra*]

(2) Stock Appreciation Rights

Stock appreciation rights ("S.A.R.s") give officers a cash bonus equal to the increase in value of a specified number of the issuer's shares over the period of time between the grant of the S.A.R. and its exercise. In most cases, S.A.R.s are exempt from Section 16, as are most awards pursuant to employee benefit plans and most employee compensation.

(3) Gifts

A bona fide gift of stock is not a purchase by the donee under Section 16. [**Shaw v. Dreyfus**, 172 F.2d 140 (2d Cir. 1949)]

d. Any Nonexempt Equity Security of the Issuer

Section 16 applies to transactions in equity securities. The 1934 Act defines "equity security" as "any stock or similar security; or any security convertible, with or without consideration, into such a security"; as well as certain "acquisition rights" to such securities; and "any other security which the Commission shall deem to be of a similar nature and consider necessary or appropriate . . . to treat as an equity security." [SEA § 3(a)(11)]

(1) Convertible Securities

A security convertible into an equity security (*e.g.*, a debenture convertible into common stock) is an equity security for the purposes of Section 12. Thus, a holder of more than 10% of such a security is an "insider" and, therefore, is subject to the reporting requirements of Section 16(a) and the disgorgement provisions of Section 16(b).

(2) Calculating Ten Percent of Convertible Securities

However, for purposes of determining whether the holder of convertible securities is a more-than-10% shareholder under Section 16(b), the court will consider the relative amount of the underlying security (that is, of the security into which the convertible security can be converted) owned by the shareholder, not the relative amount of the convertible security itself. [SEA Rule 16a–4(a); *see* **Chemical Fund, Inc. v. Xerox Corp.**, 377 F.2d 107 (2d Cir. 1967)]

e.g. **Example:** In *Chemical Fund, supra,* an investment company held more than 10% of the corporation's convertible debentures. These debentures, however, if converted into common stock and added to the already outstanding common, would equal less than 3% of the corporation's common stock. The court held that the investment company was not a beneficial owner of more than 10% within the meaning of Section 16.

Rationale: Section 16 applies to more-than-10% holders because they have the opportunity to control (or at least to substantially influence) the corporation through voting. Thus, the court reasoned, it makes sense to consider the position of the shareholder after conversion and to disregard percentage ownership of unconverted, nonvoting securities. This reasoning has now been adopted by the S.E.C. [S.E.C. Release No. 34–28869, note 36 (1991)]

e. Within Any Period of Less than Six Months

For Section 16(b) to apply, the matching purchase and sale must occur within a period of *less than* six months. For Section 16 purposes, a fractional day counts as a full day. Because a fractional day counts as a full day, the Section 16 "period of less than six months" can be generically defined as a period that begins at any time on day 1 and ends at midnight on the day that is two days before the corresponding date six months later. This result follows because if the period were to extend to the following day, that entire day would be counted, and therefore the period would be exactly six months, rather than "less than six months" as the statute requires. In other words, because any fraction of a day counts as a full day, the statutory term "less than six months" amounts to "six months less at least one full day."

f. Shall Be Liable to the Corporation for the Profits Made from the Trading

The corporation may sue under Section 16 for the profit made by its insider or, if the corporation declines to proceed, any security holder of the corporation may bring a derivative action on behalf of the corporation. (Note that the S.E.C. has no authority to seek injunctive or other relief for the violation of Section 16(b).) A security holder may sue under Section 16(b) only if the issuer shall fail or refuse to bring such suit within 60 days after request or shall fail diligently to prosecute the same thereafter.

g. Statute of Limitations

Section 16(b) provides for a statute of limitations of two years from the date when the profit is realized by the insider. The statute is tolled, however, if the insider has not filed the reports required by Section 16(a), until such time as the profits are discovered or with reasonable diligence should have been discovered.

h. Strict Liability

The general rule is that there are no defenses to a Section 16(b) action if all elements of the cause of action are present (*i.e.*, an "insider," registered equity securities, and a matching purchase and sale within the required time period). Thus, it makes no difference that the insider cannot be shown to have had access to any inside information or to have used any inside information in effectuating the matching purchase and sale.

i. Exemptions

There are a number of exemptions from Section 16(b) liability, including the following:

(1) Securities Received in Foreclosure on a Debt

Section 16(b) exempts a security acquired in good faith in connection with a debt previously contracted. Thus, the receipt of securities in connection with a foreclosure is not a "purchase" within the meaning of Section 16(b).

(2) Gifts and Inheritance

By rule, the S.E.C. has exempted bona fide gifts and transfers of securities by will or intestate descent. [SEA Rule 16b–5]

(3) Employee Benefit Plans and Compensation

In general, transactions taking place between the issuer and its officers and directors are exempt from Section 16(b) if they are either approved by the issuer's board of directors (or a committee containing at least two outside directors), or approved by the issuer's shareholders. [SEA Rule 16b–3(d), (e)] Transactions with an employee benefit plan are treated like transactions with the issuer. [SEA Rule 16b–3(a)]

E. Tender Offers and Repurchases of Stock

1. Introduction

A "tender offer" is an offer by a person (the "bidder") to purchase the securities of a corporation (the "target"), made directly to the shareholders of the target. The purchase price may be paid *in cash, in securities*, or in a combination of both. The offer may be made with (a "friendly" offer) or without (a "hostile" offer) the cooperation of the target's management.

Due to the limitations in the coverage of other provisions of the federal securities laws, in 1968 Congress passed the Williams Act (named after Senator Harrison Williams of New Jersey) specifically to regulate tender offers. The Williams Act added to the 1934 Act Section 13(d) and (e), and Section 14(d), (e), and (f).

a. Jurisdiction to Regulate

Jurisdiction of the federal government over tender offers is based on their effect on interstate commerce and on the use of the mails or other means of interstate commerce to effect the transaction.

b. Overview of SEA Regulation of Tender Offers

The following sections of the 1934 Act apply to tender offers:

(1) Reporting Requirement

Section 13(d) requires any party who acquires 5% or more of an equity security registered under Section 12 of the 1934 Act to report the acquisition and the party's intentions with respect to the issuer of the security. [*See also* Schedule 13D—sets forth the reporting requirements of Section 13(d) in more detail]

(2) Disclosure Requirements

Section 14(d) is the basic section that regulates the making of tender offers. Under this section, the bidder must make an appropriate disclosure prior to commencing the tender offer. [*See also* Schedule TO] In addition, Section 14(d)(4) requires disclosure by anyone making a "solicitation or recommendation to the holders of [the target's securities] to accept or reject a tender offer." [*See also* Schedule 14D-9] Rule 14e–2 requires the target's management to disclose its position on the tender offer; this disclosure triggers the target's obligation to file a Schedule 14D-9.

(3) Antifraud Provision

Section 14(e) is an antifraud provision that makes it unlawful for any party making a tender offer—or defending against one—to make untrue statements of material fact (or to omit to state material facts), or to engage in any fraudulent, deceptive, or manipulative act or practice in connection with any tender offer.

c. Relationship to Section 16(a) of the 1934 Act

The provisions of Sections 13(d) and 16(a) of the 1934 Act overlap somewhat. Section 13(d) requires that ownership of *5%* or more of a registered equity security be reported, whereas Section 16(a) requires the reporting of holdings by officers, directors, or persons owning 10%, including a purchase by a person who thereby becomes the owner of 10%.

d. Implied Private Rights of Action

(1) By the Target Company

Courts generally agree that a target company has an implied private right of action against the bidder for a violation of Section 13(d) (*e.g.*, for filing a false statement). [*See, e.g.*, **Gearhart Industries, Inc. v. Smith International, Inc.,** 741 F.2d 707 (5th Cir. 1984)]

(a) Target's Remedies Under Section 13(d)

Target companies suing under Section 13(d) typically obtain a temporary injunction against the bidder, pending corrective disclosure. [*See, e.g.*, **Florida Commercial Banks v. Culverhouse,** 772 F.2d 1513 (11th Cir. 1985)] Although the target usually would prefer an order directing the bidder's divestment of target stock, or "sterilization" of the bidder's target stock (*i.e.*, a prohibition on voting that stock), several courts have held that such remedies are *not* available. [**Liberty National Insurance Co. v. Charter Co.,** 734 F.2d 545 (11th Cir. 1984); **Dan River, Inc. v. Icahn,** 701 F.2d 278 (4th Cir. 1983)]

(2) By the Shareholders of the Target Company

Shareholders of the target company have standing pursuant to Section 13(d), but damages are not available. [*See, e.g.*, **Kamerman v. Steinberg,** 891 F.2d 424 (2d Cir. 1989)]

2. Actions for Misstatements or Insufficient Disclosure—Section 14(e)

Under Section 14(e) it is unlawful for any person to make untrue statements or to omit to state material facts, *or* to engage in any scheme of deception or fraud in connection with any tender offer or in opposition thereto. (Note the similarity of language between Section 14(e) and Section 10(b) and Rule 10b–5, discussed *supra.*)

a. Private Remedies for Violation of Section 14(e)

Section 14(e) may be enforced by private persons (*e.g.*, shareholders of the target denied the opportunity to tender their stock by management's actions, or the bidder denied the opportunity to take over the target) or by the S.E.C. Private plaintiffs have three possible remedies: *damages, a temporary injunction* (usually to force corrective disclosure), *or a permanent injunction* (which may be sought by the target to prevent the bidder from going forward with the offer). Each remedy requires the plaintiff to prove different elements, and each is considered below.

b. Private Action for Damages

A private plaintiff seeking damages for violation of Section 14(e) must prove: (1) standing to sue; (2) misstatements, nondisclosure, or some other species of fraudulent act; (3) materiality; (4) (maybe) reliance (*i.e.*, transaction causation); (5) (maybe) causation; and (6) (maybe) scienter.

(1) Standing

In **Piper v. Chris-Craft Industries, Inc.,** 430 U.S. 1 (1977), the Supreme Court held that a defeated bidder does not have an implied *damages* remedy under Section 14(e).

(a) *Piper*

In *Piper*, Chris-Craft had sought control of Piper Aircraft through several tender offers. It eventually gained 42% of Piper's stock, partly as the result of exchanging some of its shares for Piper shares in a tender offer. But a rival bidder, Bangor Punta, eventually gained control (slightly over 50%) of Piper. Chris-Craft alleged (and two lower courts agreed) that Piper, Bangor Punta, and Bangor Punta's underwriter had made material misstatements or omissions in connection with the tender offer. Nevertheless, the Court held that Chris-Craft had no cause of action for damages. The Court reasoned that Congress's intent in passing the Williams Act was *to protect shareholders of the target*, who prior to the Williams Act had been essentially at the mercy of "corporate raiders"; there was no evidence of intent to protect the defeated bidder. Furthermore, the Court held that application of the principles announced in **Cort v. Ash** (see above p. 114) suggested that a private damages remedy was inappropriate for a defeated bidder.

(b) Bidder and Shareholder

Many bidders are already shareholders of the target at the time they launch the tender offer. *Piper* left open the possibility that such a bidder would have standing, but one circuit court has held that a bidder that was also a shareholder would be considered merely a bidder for standing purposes, and hence would be barred from a damages action under *Piper.* [**Kalmanovitz v. G. Heileman Brewing Co.,** 769 F.2d 152 (3d Cir. 1985)]

(2) Misstatements, Nondisclosure, or Fraudulent Acts

For a cause of action to exist under Section 14(e), there must be a misstatement of a material fact, a failure to disclose a material fact, or some other scheme of fraud or deception. The Supreme Court has stated that the purpose of Section 14(e) is to see that shareholders receive full disclosure, not to allow the courts to oversee the substantive fairness of tender offers. [**Schreiber v. Burlington Northern, Inc.,** 472 U.S. 1 (1985)]

(3) Materiality

The misrepresented or undisclosed fact must be material. The test for materiality is whether there is a *substantial likelihood that a reasonable shareholder would consider the information important* in deciding whether to accept the tender offer.

[**Seaboard World Airlines, Inc. v. Tiger International, Inc.,** 600 F.2d 355 (2d Cir. 1979)]

(a) Application

In applying this standard, the courts have indicated that the marketplace conditions under which a tender offer takes place must be considered in testing materiality. The essential objective of the tender offer rules is to assure fair and honest dealing, not to impose an unrealistic requirement of "laboratory conditions." [**Electronic Specialty Co. v. International Controls Corp.,** 409 F.2d 937 (2d Cir. 1969)]

e.g. **Example:** Parties to a tender offer often act quickly, impulsively, and in angry response to the actions of the opposing party. They are not required to follow through on all statements of intent or preference (as long as the statements are truthful at the time given); neither are they required to correct erroneous reports in the news media. [**Electronic Specialty Co. v. International Controls Corp.,** *supra*]

(4) Reliance—Transaction Causation

At present, courts are split as to whether the plaintiffs must show their individual reliance on a misrepresentation or omission. [*See, e.g.*, **Plaine v. McCabe,** 797 F.2d 713 (9th Cir. 1986)—reliance in a § 14(e) case may be inferred from a showing that shareholders in general were misled into approving the transaction; **Lewis v. McGraw,** 619 F.2d 192 (2d Cir. 1980)—§ 14(e) cause of action fails absent a showing of individual reliance] In the future, it is likely that reliance will be handled in much the same way as it now is under Rule 10b–5; *i.e.*, on a case-by-case basis, with certain presumptions that apply in cases where a reliance requirement seems incongruous (*e.g.*, in cases of fraudulent omission).

(5) Loss Causation

As with reliance, the status of the law on loss causation in Section 14(e) cases is uncertain.

(a) *Piper*

Piper, supra, was decided by the majority on the issue of standing. Justice Blackmun, concurring, would have decided the case against the plaintiffs, because in his view they had not shown loss causation. A court might follow Justice Blackmun and hold that loss causation is a requirement in Section 14(e) cases.

(6) Standard of Culpability

The Supreme Court has not addressed the question whether Section 14(e) requires a showing of scienter. There are two analogous provisions that could influence a court deciding this question: Section 17(a) of the 1933 Act and Rule 10b–5 under the 1934 Act.

(a) Language in Sections 17(a), 14(e) and Rule 10b–5

The language used in Section 17(a) of the 1933 Act is very similar to that used in 1934 Act Section 14(e) and, for that matter, in Rule 10b–5 under the 1934 Act. In other words, all three provisions are drafted in essentially the same way (although the paragraph structure varies among them).

(b) Significance

The Supreme Court has held that 1933 Act Section 17(a)(1) requires a showing of scienter, while subsections (a)(2) and (a)(3) do not. [**Aaron v. S.E.C.,** *supra*] On the other hand, the Court has held *that all three parts of Rule 10b–5 require a showing of scienter.* [**Ernst & Ernst v. Hochfelder,** *supra*] A court confronting the question whether Section 14(e) requires a showing of scienter might follow *Aaron*, and hold that some parts of Section 14(e) require scienter while others do not; or the court might follow *Hochfelder,* and hold that Section 14(e) always requires scienter.

(c) Majority View

Most courts adopt the analogy to Rule 10b–5 and require a showing of scienter in all Section 14(e) cases. [*See, e.g.,* **Connecticut National Bank v. Fluor Corp.,** 808 F.2d 957 (2d Cir. 1987)]

(7) Damages

See the discussion of the measure of damages in connection with Rule 10b–5.

3. Private Action for Injunction

A plaintiff who is injured by a violation of the tender offer rules may, as an alternative to an action for damages, also sue for a temporary or permanent injunction.

a. Permanent Injunctions

Before a court will permanently enjoin the making or consummation of a tender offer, the plaintiff must show that it will suffer *irreparable injury* as a result of the defendant's violation of the tender offer rules. Permanent injunctions are exceedingly rare in tender offer cases.

e.g. **Example:** An action was brought under Section 13(d) for the defendant's failure to file the required report after acquiring 5% of the plaintiff's stock. Although the defendant had intended to make a tender offer, it had not actually done so at the time the plaintiff's action was brought. The Supreme Court found that the violation was not willful and that no irreparable injury resulted. [**Rondeau v. Mosinee Paper Corp.,** *supra*, p. 211] Under these circumstances, the Court held that a permanent injunction would not issue against a mere *technical violation* of the tender offer rules. The Court stated that the plaintiff (the potential target company) would have to show that it would suffer an irreparable injury that could not be remedied at law, before an injunction would issue to bar the defendant from voting the shares it had acquired and from acquiring any more shares for a period of five years.

b. Preliminary Injunctions

Unlike permanent injunctions, preliminary injunctions are fairly common in tender offer litigation and generally issue pending improved or corrective disclosure by the defendant. However, in some cases, the issuance of a preliminary injunction effectively is the end of the offer. A plaintiff seeking a preliminary injunction must meet the burden of showing either (i) probable success if the case were to go to trial on the merits *and* the possibility of irreparable injury, *or* (ii) the existence of serious questions going to the merits *and* a balance of hardships in the plaintiff's favor. [**Stark v. New York Stock Exchange, Inc.,** 466 F.2d 743 (2d Cir. 1972)]

e.g. **Example:** The plaintiff (the target company) was granted a preliminary injunction upon showing that the defendant had failed to disclose its intentions regarding the disposition of the plaintiff's assets if the tender offer were successful, and that the defendant had also failed to disclose that the English government had the statutory power to control the disposition of the plaintiff's assets. [**General Host Corp. v. Triumph American, Inc.,** 359 F. Supp. 749 (E.D. Wis. 1973)]

c. **Bidder's Standing to Seek Injunctions**

The question whether a bidder has standing to seek an injunction is unresolved at present.

(1) **Recap—Action for Damages**

Recall that the bidder has *no* standing under Section 14(e) to bring a lawsuit for damages. [**Piper v. Chris-Craft Industries, Inc.,** *supra*]

(2) **Injunctive Relief**

While *Piper* did not specifically address injunctions, the Court's opinion can be read to support the bidder's right to seek injunctive relief. A lower court has so held. [*See* **A&K Railroad Materials, Inc. v. Green Bay & Western Railroad,** 437 F. Supp. 636 (E.D. Wis. 1977)—bidder has standing to sue for an injunction, but mere negligence is insufficient to support the action; *and see* **Humana, Inc. v. American Medicorp, Inc.,** 445 F. Supp. 613 (S.D.N.Y. 1977)]

4. Enforcement by the S.E.C.

The S.E.C. may use several means to enforce the tender offer rules:

(a) Injunctions;

(b) Criminal prosecutions;

(c) Cease-and-desist proceedings; or

(d) Orders for compliance with Section 13 or 14.

F. Regulation of Proxy Solicitations

1. Federal Proxy Rules—an Introduction

Because it favors the solicitation of proxies by corporate management, the proxy system is an effective tool for maintaining control over a large, public corporation. Due to the tremendous number of shares such a corporation will have outstanding, purchasing a majority of the outstanding voting stock—*e.g.*, in a tender offer—is often prohibitively expensive. Soliciting proxies from the many individual shareholders whose aggregate votes constitute the needed majority is not cheap, either—but it is far less expensive than purchasing a majority of the outstanding voting stock. Also, in most cases, state law permits management to use *corporate funds* to pay for the solicitation. To prevent abuses in the proxy solicitation process, authority to regulate proxies relating to securities registered under the 1934 Act has been given to the S.E.C. in Section 14(a) of that 1934 Act.

a. Objectives of the S.E.C. Rules

Pursuant to its authority under Section 14(a), the S.E.C. has adopted rules for the regulation of proxy solicitations. [*See* SEA Regulation 14A] These rules are designed to accomplish three objectives:

(1) To Encourage Full Disclosure

Those who solicit proxies (or attempt to dissuade shareholders from granting them) must fully disclose all material facts to the shareholders being solicited. [SEA Rules 14a–3—14a–6]

(2) To Prevent Fraud

The federal rules specifically prohibit the use of fraud in the solicitation of proxies. [SEA Rule 14a–9]

(3) To Provide for Shareholder Proposals

The S.E.C. rules require management to include in its proxy statement proper shareholder proposals. [SEA Rule 14a–8]

b. "Proxy" Defined

A proxy is a power of attorney to vote shares owned by someone else. At common law, proxies were illegal, but today they are permitted and regulated both by state statutes and by the Securities Exchange Act. A proxy establishes an agency relationship that is revocable at any time, except under certain limited conditions. Under state law, a proxy that is expressly made irrevocable *and* is "coupled with an interest" generally is irrevocable. For example, when a shareholder borrows money and pledges her stock as security, granting the lender an irrevocable proxy to vote the pledged shares, the proxy is coupled with an interest and is therefore irrevocable. State statutes usually limit the duration for which even an irrevocable proxy coupled with an interest may be given (*e.g.*, to a period of five years).

c. What Constitutes a Proxy Solicitation

Under federal law, a "solicitation" is any communication to the shareholders reasonably calculated to result in the granting, withholding, or revocation of a proxy. [SEA Rule 14a–1(*l*)] Every "solicitation" of a proxy is governed by Regulation 14A, but certain solicitations are exempt from some of its requirements.

(1) Proxy Voting Advice Is a "Solicitation"

The definition of "solicitation" explicitly includes proxy voting advice if:

(a) the advice makes a recommendation to a security holder as to its vote, consent, or authorization on a specific matter for which security holder approval is solicited;

(b) the advice is furnished by a person that markets its expertise as a provider of such proxy voting advice, separately from other forms of investment advice; and

(c) the person sells such proxy voting advice for a fee.

[SEA Rule 14a–1(*l*)(1)(iii)(A)]

However, as discussed below, proxy voting advice businesses are exempt from the proxy delivery and filing requirements if certain conditions are met.

(2) Regular Financial Reports Not a "Solicitation"

An issuer may distribute its regular annual, semi-annual, or quarterly financial report and not have it deemed a "proxy solicitation." Indeed, the proxy rules *require* most issuers subject to the 1934 Act to send the annual report to their shareholders. [SEA Rule 14a–3]

(3) Statement of Intended Vote Not a "Solicitation"

The proxy rules exclude from the definition of "solicitation" a communication by a security holder, who does not otherwise engage in a nonexempt solicitation, stating how the security holder intends to vote and the reasons therefor. [SEA Rule 14a–1(*l*)(2)(iv)]

(a) Requirements

To be excluded from the definition of "solicitation," at least one of the following must be true of the statement of intended vote:

(i) Communication Made in Public Medium

The communication will be excluded if it is made in a public medium (i.e., the communication is made by means of speeches in a public forum; press releases; published or broadcast opinions; or statements or advertisements appearing in a broadcast medium, newspaper, magazine, or other bona fide publication disseminated on a regular basis).

(ii) Communication Made by a Fiduciary to Beneficiary

A communication directed to persons to whom the security holder owes a fiduciary duty in connection with the voting of securities of the registrant held by the security holder is excluded.

(iii) Communication Made in Response to Unsolicited Request

A communication made in response to unsolicited requests for additional information with respect to a prior exempt communication made under (a) or (b), above, is exempt.

(iv) Response to Unprompted Request for Proxy Voting Advice

Proxy voting advice is exempt only if furnished in response to an unprompted request.

(b) Persons Eligible

The exclusion from the definition of "solicitation" is available to all shareholders, including officers and directors of the registrant, as long as they do not otherwise engage in a regulated solicitation.

(c) Antifraud Provisions May Not Be Applicable

One interesting effect of excluding these communications from the definition of "solicitation" is that the antifraud provisions of the proxy rules are apparently not applicable to such communications. Rule 14a–9, by its terms, applies only to "solicitations" subject to Regulation 14A.

2. Proxy Disclosure Requirements

There are two kinds of required disclosure under the proxy rules: the proxy statement and the annual report. Each is discussed below.

a. The Proxy Statement

The proxy rules set forth what information must be disclosed in the proxy statement, essentially all material facts regarding matters to be voted on by the security holders and identification of the participants in the solicitation. [*See* SEA Schedule 14A]

What if the issuer is not soliciting proxies? For example, there might be insiders of the issuer who control enough votes to constitute a quorum (and, perhaps, a majority of the votes present at any shareholder meeting). Can the issuer avoid the disclosure otherwise required under the proxy rules? The answer is no, because SEA Section 14I requires the issuer to "file with the [SEC] and transmit to [the security holders] information substantially equivalent to the information which would be required to be transmitted if a solicitation were made . . . ." [*See* SEA Schedule 14C]

b. The Annual Report

The second component of required proxy disclosure is the issuer's annual report. If directors are to be elected, before the meeting at which the election is to take place, the registrant must provide shareholders with an annual report. The contents of the annual report are specified in the proxy rules. [*See* SEA Rule 14a–3]

c. Antifraud Provisions

The proxy rules contain antifraud provisions in SEA Rule 14a–9. These provisions apply to all proxy "solicitations" as defined in Rule 14a–1, whether or not the particular solicitation is exempt from the delivery or filing requirements. If the activity in question is part of a solicitation, the antifraud rules apply to all materials used and statements made by the parties. [*See* SEA Rule 14a–9]

3. Proxy Statement Delivery Requirements

In addition to specifying what information must be disclosed to shareholders when their proxies are solicited, the proxy rules specify the manner in which the information must be disclosed: by delivery of a preliminary or definitive proxy statement and, if directors are to be elected, an annual report.

a. Solicitation Prohibited Without Delivery of Proxy Statement

A solicitation subject to the proxy rules is not permitted to begin unless *each person solicited* has been furnished with a *written proxy statement containing the information required by Schedule 14A.* [SEA Rule 14a–3]

(1) Proxy Statement May Be Preliminary

Note, however, that the written proxy statement required before a solicitation can begin *need not be in definitive form*—a preliminary proxy statement will meet the S.E.C.'s requirements, as long as it contains the information required by Schedule 14A. [*See* SEA Rule 14a–3(a)]

(2) Proxy Card Prohibited Until Definitive Proxy Statement Delivered

Even though the proxy solicitation can begin before the definitive proxy statement is delivered, *the person soliciting* proxies may *not* deliver a proxy card (called the "form of proxy"—*i.e.*, the actual form on which the shareholders grant authority to vote their shares and specify how the shares are to be voted) *until a definitive proxy statement has been delivered* to the shareholders. [SEA Rule 14a–4(f)]

(3) Exceptions to Delivery Requirements

The proxy statement delivery requirements do not apply to certain solicitations.

(a) Public Solicitation

Solicitations made by public broadcast, speech, advertisement, etc., need not be preceded or accompanied by delivery of a written proxy statement as long as:

(1) No form of proxy, consent, or authorization or means to execute such a document are provided in connection with the communication; and

(2) At the time the communication is made, a definitive proxy statement is on file with the S.E.C.

[SEA Rule 14a–3(f)]

(b) Soliciting Person Not Seeking Proxy Authority

Similarly, if the person soliciting is not the issuer and is not actually seeking a proxy from the shareholders, no written proxy statement need be delivered. [SEA Rule 14a–2(b)(1)] Note, however, that proxy voting advice is exempt under this provision only if additional conditions are met.

(c) Solicitation of Ten Persons or Fewer

Anyone (other than management) may solicit proxies from 10 or fewer persons without having to comply with the proxy rules. [SEA Rule 14a–2(b)(2)]

(d) Proxy Voting Advice

Proxy voting advice is exempt from the delivery requirements only if the following five conditions are met:

(i) One of the following two conditions is met;

  (a) the proxy advisor is not actually seeking a proxy from the shareholders; or

  (b) the proxy advisor furnishes the advice to a person with whom the advisor has a business relationship, the advisor renders financial advice in the ordinary course of business, the advisor discloses to the recipient of the advice any significant relationships and material interests, and the advisor is not furnishing advice on behalf of a person soliciting proxies in opposition to the election or removal of directors;

(ii) The proxy advisor discloses in its proxy voting advice any material conflicts of interest;

(iii) the proxy advisor discloses any policies and procedures used to identify material conflicts of interest and the steps taken to address any identified conflicts;

(iv) the proxy advisor has adopted and publicly disclosed policies and procedures designed to ensure that registrants that are the subject of the proxy voting advice have that advice made available to them prior to, or simultaneously with, the clients; *and*

(v) the proxy advisor provides its clients with a mechanism by which they can reasonably be made aware of a registrant's responses to the proxy voting advice prior to the meeting.

[SEA Rule 14a–2(b)(1), (3) & (9)]

(e) General Exception and Proxy Contests

Proxy contests are high-stakes contests for corporate control. Because both sides in a proxy contest often need to act quickly, the proxy rules contain a general exception permitting solicitation before a proxy statement is filed. [SEA Rule 14a–12] Such solicitations are permitted if:

(i) Each written communication to shareholders includes:

(1) The identity of the participants in the solicitation and a description of their interest, or a prominent legend describing where such information is available; and

(2) A prominent legend advising security holders to read the proxy statement when it becomes available;

(ii) A definitive proxy statement is provided to security holders at the same time, or before, the form of proxy is provided; and

(iii) All material used under this exception is filed with the S.E.C.

4. Proxy Statement Filing Requirements

All written materials used in a solicitation must be filed with the S.E.C. [SEA Rule 14a–6] Some materials must be filed in preliminary, "draft" form before definitive copies are disseminated to the shareholders. Other materials need not be filed with the S.E.C. until final, definitive versions have been prepared and are actually disseminated.

a. Varieties of Written Proxy Materials

Written materials distributed to shareholders in connection with a proxy solicitation may be loosely grouped into three categories: the proxy statement, the form of proxy, and other soliciting materials.

b. Advance Filing Requirements

The S.E.C. requires preliminary versions of both the proxy statement and the form of proxy must be filed with the S.E.C. *at least 10 days before the definitive versions are disseminated* to shareholders. [SEA Rule 14a–6(a)]

(1) Exception to Advice Filing Requirements

The issuer need not file preliminary copies of the proxy statement or the form of proxy if the solicitation relates to any meeting of security holders at which the *only* matters to be acted upon are:

(i) The *election of directors*;

(ii) Election, approval, or ratification of *accountants*;

(iii) A proposal by a security holder included pursuant to *SEA Rule 14a–8*;

(iv) A *shareholder nominee for director* included pursuant to SEA Rule 14a–11;

(v) The approval or ratification of a plan of *executive compensation*;

(vi) *Certain matters affecting investment companies* registered under the Investment Company Act of 1940; or

(vii) A *shareholder advisory vote on executive compensation*.

[SEA Rule 14a–6(a)]

(2) Other Soliciting Materials

Materials other than the proxy statement and the form of proxy need not be filed in advance of their dissemination to shareholders.

c. Filing Requirements for Definitive Versions

All materials used in a solicitation must be filed (or mailed for filing) with the S.E.C. and with each national securities exchange on which securities of the registrant trade *no later than the day on which they are first used.* If the materials have been filed in preliminary form, the final versions are prepared with a view to the S.E.C.'s comments on the previously filed versions.

d. Exceptions to Filing Requirements

Some solicitations are exempt from both the delivery and filing requirements. In particular, solicitations where the person is not seeking proxy authority (see above p. 161), solicitation of ten persons or fewer (see above p. 161), and proxy voting advice (if specific conditions are met) (see above p. 161) are exempt from the filing requirement.

e. Antifraud Provisions Applicable

Note that whether or not the S.E.C. requires advance filing of particular solicitation documents, the antifraud provisions of the 1934 Act apply to all materials used and statements made by the parties. [*See* SEA Rule 14a–9]

5. The Proxy Statement

The following information must be included in the proxy statement (or the information statement, if proxies are not solicited):

a. Details About Solicitation

A statement identifying for whom the solicitation is being made, the means (mail, etc.) being used, who bears the cost, the amount already spent, and an estimate of the total amount to be spent in the proxy solicitation. [Schedule 14A]

b. Details About Director Election

In addition, if directors are to be elected at the shareholders' meeting, the proxy statement must name and give detailed information about (i) the nominees of the person who is soliciting the proxy, (ii) other directors whose terms of office continue beyond the meeting, and (iii) the officers of the registrant. The statement must include information regarding transactions during the past year between the specified persons and the registrant. [Schedule 14A]

c. Details About Specific Matters

Detailed information must be disclosed relating to the specific matters for which the proxy is being solicited. [Schedule 14A] Specific rules cover the information required in situations of merger, sale of corporate assets, liquidation or dissolution, or the purchase of another company.

d. Details About Executive Compensation

If the solicitation is made on behalf of the registrant, the proxy statement must also disclose details about the registrant's compensation of its executive officers. Information is required about the person serving as chief executive officer, the four most highly compensated officers other than the CEO, and up to two persons for whom disclosure would have been provided but for the fact that they were no longer serving as executive officers at the end of the most recent fiscal year. [Schedule 14A; Regulation S–K Item 402(a)(3)]

e. Details About General Matters

There are some general matters that must also be disclosed, including significant changes in control, the fact that securities owned by control persons have been pledged as collateral for loans, the vote required on each issue, the shares entitled to vote, and the record date for voting. [Schedule 14A]

6. Shareholder Proposals

Under certain circumstances, a shareholder may compel management to include a shareholder proposal in the registrant's proxy statement to be submitted to shareholders for a vote. [SEA Rule 14a–8] Management will in almost every case attempt to exclude the proposal from the proxy statement, relying on SEA Rule 14a–8(c), which provides a list of permissible reasons for not including an otherwise proper shareholder proposal.

a. Requirements

To be included in the registrant's proxy statement, a shareholder proposal must meet the requirements of SEA Rule 14a–8(a) and (b), which are briefly outlined below.

(1) Eligible Shareholders

The proponent of the proposal must meet one of the following requirements:

Have continuously held at least $2,000 in market value of the company's securities entitled to vote on the proposal for at least three years; or

Have continuously held at least $15,000 in market value of the company's securities entitled to vote on the proposal for at least two years; or

Have continuously held at least $25,000 in market value of the company's securities entitled to vote on the proposal for at least one year.

(2) Procedural Requirements

Shareholder proposals must be submitted in accordance with the following procedures.

(a) Length; Number of Proposals

A proponent may submit only one proposal, together with an accompanying statement in support. The proposal together with the supporting statement may not exceed 500 words.

(b) Shareholder Information

Together with the proposal, the proponent must provide his or her name and address, the number of voting securities she holds of record or beneficially, the dates on which she acquired the securities, and documentary evidence of beneficial ownership.

(c) Attendance at Meeting

Either the proponent or his or her representative (if allowed to present the proposal under state law) must attend the meeting and present the proposal.

(d) Timeliness

The proponent must submit the proposal far enough in advance to permit the registrant to consider it, and potentially to include it in the printed proxy statement sent to the shareholders.

(i) Annual Meetings

Proposals that are to be presented at the registrant's annual meeting of shareholders must be received by the registrant 120 days before the date corresponding to the day and month on which the proxy statement was delivered to shareholders for the previous year's annual meeting.

(ii) If There Was No Annual Meeting in the Previous Year

If the registrant had no annual meeting in the previous year, or if the current year's meeting date was changed by more than 30 days from the previous year's, the proponent of the proposal must deliver the proposal to the registrant a reasonable time before the solicitation is made.

(iii) Other Meetings

Proposals to be presented to shareholders at meetings other than annual meetings must be delivered to the registrant a reasonable time before the solicitation is made.

b. Management's Omission of Shareholder Proposals

If management opposes the shareholder proposal, it must file the proposal and the reasons for opposing it with the S.E.C. [SEA Rule 14a–8(j)] The S.E.C. staff will review the proposal and give an indication of whether it agrees or disagrees with management (*i.e.*, whether it would recommend an enforcement action or, alternatively, "no action" if management omits the proposal from its proxy solicitation). Note, however, that a "no action" position expressed in the staff's letter is not binding on the proponent of the proposal, who remains free to litigate the propriety of excluding the proposal in federal court. Management may properly omit shareholder proposals in the following situations [SEA Rule 14a–8(i)]:

(1) Improper Under State Law

A proposal may be excluded if it is not a proper subject for action by shareholders under the laws of the state of incorporation.

Note that some proposals are not considered proper if they would be binding on the company of approved by the shareholders. (Such binding proposals may usurp the board's role in governing the corporation.) If the proposal is drafted as a recommendation or request, however, it likely will not be improper under state law.

(2) Illegal

Management need not include a proposal that, if implemented, would require the registrant to violate any state or federal law or the law of any foreign jurisdiction to which the registrant is subject.

(3) Violation of Proxy Rules

If the proposal or its supporting statement violates any of the proxy rules (including Rule 14a–9, prohibiting false or misleading statements), it need not be included in the registrant's proxy statement.

(4) Personal Grievance

Management need not include proposals that are designed primarily to further some personal interest of the proponent not shared with other shareholders in general, *e.g.*, redressing a grievance against the registrant.

(5) Insignificant Operations of the Registrant

Management need not include a proposal that relates to insignificant operations. To establish that the shareholder proposal relates to operations that are not significantly related to the registrant's business, two elements must be shown:

(a) No Economic Significance

The operations in question must account for *less than* 5% of the registrant's *total assets* at the end of its most recent fiscal year, and less than 5% of its *net earnings* and *gross sales* for its most recent fiscal year; *and*

(b) No Other Significance

The operations *must not be significant in some other way* to the registrant's business.

e.g. **Example:** Acme Corp. had revenues last year of $141 million and profits of $6 million. One Acme line of business is the importation and sale of pate de foie gras. Its pate sales last year grossed $79,000, with a net loss of $3,126. A shareholder sought to include in Acme's proxy statement a proposal that Acme form a committee to study the methods by which its French supplier produced pate and to determine whether the geese used in production were mistreated. Acme attempted to exclude the proposal on the ground that it was insignificant to its business. When the dispute arrived in court, the court held that Acme could not exclude the proposal. Although the economic insignificance of the pate business to Acme was clear, the court ruled that the proposal might raise policy questions important enough to be considered "significantly related" to Acme's business. The court held that the rule is not limited to economic significance—the absence of policy significance must be shown before a proposal can be excluded. [**Lovenheim v. Iroquois Brands, Ltd.,** 618 F. Supp. 554 (D.D.C. 1985)]

(6) Proposal Deals with Matter Beyond Registrant's Power

Management need not include proposals relating to issues or situations over which the registrant has no control.

(7) Proposal Deals with Ordinary Business Operations of Registrant

Management may exclude proposals relating to the conduct of the ordinary business operations of the registrant. [SEA Rule 14a–8(i)(7)] *Rationale:* Matters related to the ordinary business operations of the registrant are the business of either the registrant's board of directors or its management; they are not matters over which shareholders have authority.

(8) Proposal Relates to Election to Board

Management may exclude proposals relating to an election to the registrant's board of directors; shareholders have a say in such matters simply by voting for or against the candidate (or by staging a proxy fight).

(9) Proposal Counter to Proposal to Be Submitted by Registrant at the Meeting

Similarly, if the proposal runs counter to a proposal to be submitted by the registrant, the shareholders initially will have their say by voting for or against management's proposal. In such a case, it generally adds little to put a second proposal on the agenda, and management is permitted to exclude such proposals.

(10) Proposal Moot

Proposals that are moot (*e.g.*, because they have already been substantially implemented) need not be included in the proxy statement.

(11) Proposal Duplicative

If the proposal would substantially duplicate another proposal previously submitted by another proponent, and the earlier proposal will be included in the registrant's proxy materials, the later proposal need not be included.

(12) Proposal Previously Rejected

If the proposal deals with substantially the same subject matter as a proposal submitted at any shareholder meeting (regular or special) in the preceding five years, it may be omitted from the proxy materials for any shareholder meeting held within three years after the latest such submission *if*:

(a) The proposal was submitted at only *one such prior meeting* and it received *less than 3%* of the vote;

(b) The proposal was submitted at *two such prior meetings*, and at the time of its second submission, it received *less than 15%* of the vote; *or*

(c) The proposal was submitted at *three or more* such prior meetings, and at the time of its latest submission, it received *less than 25%* of the vote.

(13) Proposal Relates to Specific Amounts of Cash or Stock Dividends

State corporation law provides that dividends are within the board's discretion. Dividends are also of particular interest to shareholders. To avoid inundation by proposals to censure the board for slashing the dividend, or demanding that the board consider raising the dividend, such proposals may be excluded.

7. Participation of Broker-Dealers in Proxy Contests

a. Stock Held in "Street Name"

A substantial majority of corporate stock in the United States is held in "street name," *i.e.*, registered on the books of the corporation in the name of a bank or brokerage firm, rather than that of the beneficial owner. S.E.C. rules require that the corporation take certain steps to see that proxy solicitation material is forwarded by banks and brokers to these beneficial owners. [SEA Rule 14a–13]

(1) Broker-Dealer Rules

The S.E.C. has also adopted rules requiring banks and broker-dealers holding securities in street name to forward promptly to the beneficial owner any proxy material received from the registrant. [SEA Rules 14b–1, 14b–2]

(2) Exchange Rules

The national exchanges (and FINRA with respect to its member firms that trade over-the-counter securities) have also adopted solicitation rules pertaining to securities held in street name.

(a) *If stock is held by the broker-dealer in a fiduciary capacity* (*e.g.*, as trustee), the broker-dealer can give the proxy without soliciting the consent of the beneficial owner.

(b) *However, if the stock is held in street name merely for safekeeping* on behalf of the beneficial owner, the broker-dealer must transmit all solicitation material to the beneficial owner and secure the beneficial owner's direction as to giving the proxy. For example, the rules of the New York Stock Exchange provide that if there is a proxy contest involving a security listed on the exchange, the broker-dealer must get appropriate instructions from the beneficial owner.

b. Solicitations by Broker-Dealers

A broker-dealer must be careful in communicating with shareholders during a proxy contest because the broker-dealer risks becoming involved as a "participant" in a solicitation. If the broker-dealer is a participant, the proxy statement used by the registrant will be defective, because it will not disclose the broker-dealer's status as a participant or the information required by SEA Schedule 14A about the broker-dealer.

(1) "Participant" in a Solicitation

The term "participant" is defined in Schedule 14A, item 4, instruction 3. The definition *includes the registrant and anyone who solicits proxies, or finances their solicitation*, but it *excludes persons who merely transmit soliciting materials.* Thus, it is especially risky for a broker-dealer to contribute anything to the text of materials that are sent, because to do so might make the "merely transmits" exclusion unavailable.

(2) Asking Instructions Not a Solicitation

The broker-dealer does not violate this rule by asking instructions of the beneficial owner on how to give the proxy. [SEA Rule 14a–2(a)(1)(iii)] But if the broker-dealer were to give favorable treatment to one soliciting party (*e.g.*, by delaying sending the materials of another), there would be a violation of the proxy rules (and also of the national exchange and FINRA rules).

(3) Providing Advice May Not Be a Solicitation

The broker-dealer may advise its customers how to respond to a proxy solicitation if there has been an unsolicited request for such advice. [SEA Release No. 7208 (1964)] And Rule 14a–2(b)(3) exempts *financial advisers* who furnish unsolicited proxy voting advice from the informational and filing requirements of Rules 14a–3 through 14a–6, 14a–8, and 14a–10 through 14a–14. However, advisers must disclose to the recipient of any advice: (i) any significant relationship with the registrant, an affiliate, or shareholder proponent; and (ii) any material interest of the adviser in the matter to which the advice relates. In addition, the adviser may not receive remuneration for providing the advice, except from the recipient. However, this exemption does not apply to advice furnished on behalf of anyone soliciting proxies or a candidate in an election contest for directors under Rule 14a–11. (In addition, if the broker-dealer qualifies as a proxy voting advise business under Rule 14a–1(*l*)(1)(iii)(A), the broker-dealer must *also* satisfy the additional conditions in Rule 14a–2(b)(9).)

8. Enforcement Provisions

An action may be brought for any violation of the proxy rules, and the courts will fashion whatever relief is appropriate under the circumstances.

a. Implied Private Cause of Action

As with 1934 Act Section 10(b) and Rule 10b–5, *supra*, neither Section 14(a) nor the proxy rules explicitly confer a private right of action for violation of the proxy rules. However, in 1964 the Supreme Court held that *there is a private right of action for violation of the proxy rules.* [**J.I. Case Co. v. Borak,** 377 U.S. 426 (1964)]

b. Antifraud Provisions

Most actions claiming violation of the proxy rules are brought under SEA Rule 14a–9, the antifraud rule relating to the solicitation of proxies. The purpose of the antifraud provisions is to ensure accurate disclosure to shareholders of material facts necessary to support an intelligent decision on matters in which proxies are solicited, thus protecting the shareholders and the integrity of the shareholder voting process. The elements of a cause of action under Rule 14a–9 are: (1) a misrepresentation or misleading omission, (2) of a material fact, (3) made at least negligently, if not recklessly or intentionally. In addition, private plaintiffs must establish causation, which, as we will see, is—for purposes of the proxy rules—defined in terms of materiality. These elements are discussed in detail below.

(1) Misrepresentations or Misleading Omissions of Fact

Solicitations that are made by any proxy statement, form of proxy, notice of meeting, or other communication, either written or oral, and that contain an affirmative misrepresentation or misleading omission of a material fact, are prohibited.

(a) Examples

Rule 14a–9 includes the following examples of potential material misrepresentations or omissions of fact:

(i) Predictions of specific future market prices for the issuer's shares;

(ii) Statements that impugn character, integrity, or personal reputation or that make charges concerning illegal, immoral, or improper conduct, without factual foundation;

(iii) Proxy statements, forms of proxy, or other soliciting materials that fail to distinguish themselves clearly from the soliciting material of others soliciting for the same meeting or subject matter;

(iv) Claims made prior to a shareholders' meeting concerning the results of the proxy solicitation; and

(v) Failure to disclose material information about proxy voting advice, such as proxy voting advice business's methodology, sources of information, or conflicts of interest.

[SEA Rule 14a–9]

(b) Misleading Opinions

(i) Facts of *Virginia Bankshares*

In *Virginia Bankshares*, proxies were solicited in connection with a proposed merger of First American Bank of Virginia ("the Bank") into Virginia Bankshares, Inc. ("VBI"). VBI owned about 85% of the voting stock of the Bank, making the merger a "freeze-out" merger in which the votes of the minority shareholders were not required by state law or by the corporate charter or bylaws. Nevertheless, the directors of the Bank solicited the proxies of the minority shareholders. The proxy solicitation materials contained the statement that "The Plan of Merger has been approved by the Board of Directors because it provides an opportunity for the Bank's public shareholders to achieve a high value for their shares." The materials also contained the statement that the merger plan was "fair" to the minority shareholders. Plaintiff claimed that the statements by the Bank's directors were false because the directors believed neither that the $42 price was high nor that the merger terms were fair to the minority shareholders.

(ii) When Actionable

The Supreme Court held that a statement of opinion (here, that the merger price provided "high value") can be actionable if:

(a) The board did not in fact hold the opinion stated; *and*

(b) The fact underlying the opinion is also misrepresented.

e.g. **Example:** The statement, "The Plan of Merger has been approved by the Board of Directors because it provides an opportunity for the Bank's public shareholders to achieve a high value for their shares," is actionable on a showing that:

(a) The board did not approve the plan because they believed it provided a high price to minority shareholders, but rather they approved the plan because they wanted to keep their jobs; *and*

(b) In fact, $42 is not a high price for the Bank's shares.

The Court specifically held that it is not enough to prove that the board did not believe the statement in the soliciting materials. If the facts underlying the statement of opinion or belief are correctly stated, no cause of action will lie.

(c) Misleading Omissions

Rule 14a–9 prohibits not only affirmative misstatements of fact but also misleading omissions. In particular, the rule prohibits any omission "to state any material fact necessary in order to make the statements therein not false or misleading or necessary to correct any statement in any earlier communication with respect to the solicitation of a proxy for the same meeting or subject matter which has become false or misleading." [SEA Rule 14a–9(a)]

(i) Information Already in the Other Party's Possession

There is no requirement to disclose information to the other party that the other party already has, or that is already well-known in the securities market. [***In re* Apple Computer Securities Litigation,** 886 F.2d 1109 (9th Cir. 1989), *cert. denied sub nom.*, **Schneider v. Apple Computer, Inc.,** 496 U.S. 943 (1990); **Seibert v. Sperry Rand Corp.,** 586 F.2d 949 (2d Cir. 1978)]

(ii) Uncharged Misconduct

Misconduct that is not expressly required to be disclosed by an S.E.C. rule most often does not have to be disclosed. Thus, information that would support an inference of market manipulation does not have to be disclosed in the absence of a charge of market manipulation. [*TSC Industries, Inc., supra*]

(iii) Conflicts of Interest

The existence of an actual or potential conflict of interest is almost always materially misleading if not disclosed. Thus, a parent company must disclose that it is considering spinning off an operating company subsidiary, reducing the likelihood that the parent would continue to support the operations of the subsidiary (even absent any legal obligation to do so). [**Kronfeld v. Trans World Airlines, Inc.,** 832 F.2d 726 (2d Cir. 1987), *cert. denied*, 485 U.S. 1007 (1988)]

(d) Safe Harbor for Forward-Looking Statements

The PSLRA safe harbor for forward-looking statements, discussed above on pp. 120–122, applies to private civil actions under Rule 14a–9.

(2) Materiality

The misrepresentation or omission must be of a *material* fact.

(a) Materiality Test

The Supreme Court has stated that the test for materiality is whether there is a *substantial likelihood* that a reasonable shareholder would consider the fact of significance in determining how to vote. [**TSC Industries, Inc. v. Northway, Inc.,** *supra*] The Court stated that this does *not* require proof of a substantial likelihood that disclosure would have caused the reasonable shareholder to change her vote, but only that the omitted fact would have had *actual significance* to the voter.

(b) The "Total Mix" of Information

In determining materiality, not only the information disclosed in the proxy statement is considered. Stockholders may be assumed to be aware of other information as well, and the "total mix" of information available to stockholders must be considered in deciding whether a statement or omission is misleading. This total mix includes "information already in the public domain and facts known or reasonably available to the shareholders." This information, however, does not necessarily include everything filed by a company under the 1934 Act: "Corporate documents that have not been distributed to the shareholders entitled to vote on the proposal should rarely be considered part of the total mix of information." [**United Paperworkers International Union v. International Paper Co.,** 985 F.2d 1190 (2d Cir. 1993)]

(3) Standard of Culpability

Section 14(a) of the 1934 Act offers no explicit standard of liability for proxy fraud. The courts that have considered the issue have come to different conclusions.

(a) Corporation—Negligence Suffices

Courts have indicated that a corporation conducting a proxy solicitation can be held to have violated the proxy rules on a finding of negligence. [**Gerstle v. Gamble-Skogmo, Inc.,** 478 F.2d 1281 (2d Cir. 1973)]

(b) Officers, Directors, and Employees—Negligence May Suffice

Officers, directors, and employees may be liable upon a finding of negligence. [*See* **Gerstle v. Gamble-Skogmo, Inc.,** *supra*]

(c) Outside Accountants—Scienter May Be Required

A court has also held that in a private (*i.e.*, nongovernment) lawsuit brought against the outside accounting firm responsible for putting false financial statements in the proxy statement, liability could only be found if scienter was present. [**Adams v. Standard Knitting Mills,** 623 F.2d 422 (6th Cir. 1980)]

(4) Loss Causation

To establish a cause of action under the antifraud provisions, the plaintiff must prove that the misrepresentation or omission of material fact was the cause of his or her loss.

(a) Question of Fact

The courts have held that the issue of causation is one of fact, to be determined at trial.

(b) Defined in Terms of Materiality

Initially, plaintiffs were required to prove both reliance (*i.e.*, transaction causation) and loss causation (*i.e.*, that the misleading facts or omissions had actually caused their damages). These requirements, however, posed complex problems of proof for the plaintiffs (who typically sue in a class action). To require each member of the class to establish causation specific to that member is to make class certification impossible, because the individual question of causation will dominate the common questions. The problem is much the same as that raised by the requirement that the plaintiffs establish reliance and loss causation in an action under Rule 10b–5. In 1970, the Supreme Court held that the causation required in an action under Rule 14a–9 is defined in terms of *materiality*. [**Mills v. Electric Auto-Lite Co.,** 396 U.S. 375 (1970)]

(i) Solicitation an "Essential Link"

Once materiality is shown, the plaintiff can prove causation simply by showing that the proxy solicitation itself was an essential link in effecting the transaction. In other words, the plaintiff need only show that the party soliciting the proxies needed the votes represented by the proxies to carry the proposition.

e.g. **Example:** In *Mills*, defendant, which owned 54% of the stock of A Corp., solicited proxies to get the two-thirds vote of the A shareholders required to effect a merger (*i.e.*, solicitation was necessary to accomplish the transaction). However, defendant failed to disclose to A's shareholders that it controlled 54% of A's stock. The Court held that causation was established by proof (i) of the materiality of the omission and (ii) that the solicitation was an essential link in the transaction.

(ii) Where Solicitation Not Required for Transaction

Suppose that the party soliciting the proxies has enough votes by itself to approve the transaction, but nevertheless conducts a proxy solicitation, and there is a material misrepresentation or omission in the proxy statement. The Court took a relatively strict view of causation in such a case, holding that the causation required in a Rule 14a–9 case *had not been established* when the plaintiffs' (minority shareholders') votes were not needed, under state law or corporate bylaw, to approve a merger, and the plaintiffs' vote did not foreclose any remedy that would otherwise have been available. [**Virginia Bankshares, Inc. v. Sandberg,** *supra*]

c. Remedies for Violation of the Proxy Rules

(1) Actions by the S.E.C.

The S.E.C. may bring an action for an *injunction* to prevent the solicitation of proxies, to prevent the voting of proxies obtained through improper solicitation, to require re-solicitation of proxies.

(2) Implied Private Actions

The courts will fashion whatever relief is appropriate to remedy the loss caused by the proxy violation, *e.g.*, damages, rescission of the transaction, etc. [**J.I. Case Co. v. Borak,** *supra*]

(a) Derivative and Class Actions

A shareholder may bring a direct cause of action or join with others to bring a class action; or, alternatively, the shareholder may bring a derivative suit on behalf of the corporation. [**J.I. Case Co. v. Borak,** *supra*]

(b) Merger Cases

In *J.I. Case*, which involved a merger, the Court indicated that an appropriate remedy might be to *unwind* the merger. One factor to be considered in the decision whether to rescind a merger is the "fairness" of the terms of the transaction. However, practically speaking, rescission is seldom if ever feasible in merger cases. For example, if the merger involved public companies, it would be difficult or impossible to trace back and return all of the shares traded at the time of the merger, since trading of the stock would inevitably have taken place since the time of the merger. A case subsequent to *J.I. Case* indicated that, at least in that case, it was not feasible to unwind the merger. Hence, the plaintiffs were allowed to recover their share in the profits realized after their company was merged into the defendant and the assets of their company sold at a substantial profit. [**Gerstle v. Gamble-Skogmo, Inc.,** *supra*]

G. Liability of Attorneys in Securities Transactions

1. Overview

In the traditional view of the lawyer's role, lawyers are responsible chiefly to their *clients.* In contrast, the S.E.C. occasionally suggests that securities lawyers ought to assume a "watchdog" function. This view emphasizes the lawyer's responsibilities to the *public.* It is a response to the role that some lawyers have played in securities fraud—many complex fraudulent schemes would not have been possible without the diligent efforts of counsel. In particular, after the financial scandals of 2001–2002, SOXA extended regulation of securities lawyers beyond anything that had come before. In this section, we will look first at the liability of lawyers to clients and third parties, and then we will focus on the responsibilities of lawyers to the public as reflected in SOXA.

2. Liability to Clients for Malpractice

Lawyers have always had the responsibility of performing competently for their clients; consequently, they may be liable to their clients for a knowing or negligent failure to do so.

3. Liability as Principals

A lawyer may also be liable for a violation of the securities laws as a principal in a business transaction. For example, a lawyer may own securities and make a material misrepresentation in connection with their sale, or purchase securities using material, nonpublic information.

4. Liability to Those Affected by Securities Transactions

In addition, a lawyer may in some situations be liable to parties affected by a securities transaction. When such liability is alleged, it is important to determine whether it is claimed to result from the lawyer's involvement as a participant or as an aider and abettor.

a. Liability as a Director

For instance, when the lawyer who drafted the issuer's registration statement is also a director of the issuer, the lawyer may be liable to purchasers of the issuer's securities under 1933 Act Section 11. [*See* **Escott v. BarChris Construction Corp.,** *supra*] Likewise, if a lawyer-director signs an S.E.C. filing containing a material misrepresentation or omission, he or she may be liable as a "maker" of that statement under Rule 10b–5.

b. Liability as an Expert

Similarly, lawyers participate in some transactions not as advisers to a party, but instead as experts with respect to a particular subject matter. For instance, a lawyer might render an opinion that title to real property has been passed to the issuer, and this opinion might be referred to in the registration statement. This can result in the lawyer's liability, not as a lawyer per se, but as an expert whose certification was material to the transaction. [SA § 11]

c. Liability as a "Seller"

Occasionally, lawyers are alleged to be liable under 1933 Act Section 12 as "sellers" of securities. To sustain such a claim, the lawyers would have to be heavily involved in the solicitation process. [*See* **Pinter v. Dahl,** *supra*]

5. Liability as an "Aider and Abettor"

Although aiders and abettors of securities fraud are not subject to private civil liability under Rule 10b–5, the S.E.C. may pursue enforcement actions against aiders and abettors. The most common factual basis for a lawyer's liability as an aider and abettor is the delivery of a legal opinion letter. Because the delivery of such letters is usually made a condition to closing a securities transaction, it is relatively easy to point to the delivery of the letter as a *sine qua non* of the transaction, and with hindsight, to find that the lawyer "must have" known her client's (fraudulent) intentions. [*See, e.g.*, **S.E.C. v. Spectrum Ltd.,** 489 F.2d 535 (2d Cir. 1973)—S.E.C. action for an injunction against lawyer who delivered opinion letter to the effect that a securities transaction did not require 1933 Act registration]

6. Professional Responsibility of Lawyers Under SOXA

SOXA addresses the professional responsibility of lawyers. Under SOXA, the S.E.C. has adopted 17 C.F.R. part 205, Standards of Professional Conduct for Attorneys, which codifies and extends prior law. Part 205 is discussed below, together with other relevant provisions addressing the responsibilities of securities lawyers.

a. "Up-the-Ladder" Reporting

SOXA mandates "up-the-ladder" reporting of if an attorney has evidence of a material violation of securities law, breach of fiduciary duty, or similar violation by the issuer or any of its agents.

(1) Triggering up-the-Ladder Reporting

Up-the-ladder reporting is not triggered until the lawyer has "evidence of a material violation of securities law or breach of fiduciary duty or similar violation." [SOXA § 307] This phrase is critical, as it triggers the requirement to report up the ladder.

(a) "Material Violation"

A "material violation" is "a material violation of an applicable United States federal or state securities law, a material breach of fiduciary duty arising under United States federal or state law, or a similar material violation of any United States federal or state law." [17 C.F.R. § 205.2(i)] "Breach of fiduciary duty refers to any breach of fiduciary or similar duty to the issuer recognized under an applicable federal or state statute or at common law, including but not limited to misfeasance, nonfeasance, abdication of duty, abuse of trust, and approval of unlawful transactions." [17 C.F.R. § 205.2(d)]

(b) "Evidence of Material Violation"

"Evidence of a material violation" is "credible evidence, based upon which it would be unreasonable, under the circumstances, for a prudent and competent attorney not to conclude that it is reasonably likely that a material violation has occurred, is ongoing, or is about to occur." [17 C.F.R. § 205.2(e)]

(2) Mandatory Reporting

(a) First Rung of the Ladder

Up-the-ladder reporting means that the lawyer who becomes aware of evidence of a material violation must first report it to the chief legal officer of the issuer. [17 C.F.R. § 205.3(b)(1)]

(b) Second Rung of the Ladder

If that person does not provide an "appropriate response" within a reasonable time, the lawyer must then report the evidence of a material violation to the audit committee or another board committee composed of only independent directors. [17 C.F.R. § 205.3(b)(3).]

(i) "Appropriate Response"

The term "appropriate response" is important because if the reporting lawyer determines that the response he or she receives is not appropriate, she is required to go further up the ladder to the audit or other board committee. For purposes of the professional conduct rules, "appropriate response" means a response to an attorney regarding reported evidence of a material violation as a result of which the attorney reasonably believes:

(a) That *no material violation* (as defined above) has occurred, is ongoing, or is about to occur;

(b) That the issuer *has taken appropriate measures* to remedy or prevent violations; or

(c) That the issuer has *retained or directed an attorney to review* the reported evidence of a material violation and either:

   (i) Has *substantially implemented any remedial recommendations* made by the attorney; or

   (ii) The attorney *may assert a colorable defense* on behalf of the issuer or agent in any proceeding relating to the reported evidence of a material violation.

[17 C.F.R. § 205.2(b)]

(3) Attorney-Client Privilege

SOXA's up-the-ladder reporting requirement preserves attorney-client privilege because reporting remains within the corporate client (*e.g.*, to chief legal officer, to audit committee, etc.), which has not thereby waived the privilege.

(4) Optional Disclosure to S.E.C.

An attorney may, without the issuer's consent, reveal confidential related to the representation to the extent the attorney reasonably believes necessary:

(a) to prevent the issuer from committing a material violation that is likely to cause substantial injury to the financial interest or property of the issuer or investors;

(b) to prevent the issuer, in an S.E.C. investigation or administrative proceeding, from committing or suborning perjury or from committing an act likely to perpetrate a fraud upon the S.E.C.; or

(c) to rectify the consequences of a material violation by the issuer that caused, or may cause, substantial injury to the financial interest or property of the issuer or investors in the furtherance of which the attorney's services were used.

[17 C.F.R. § 205.3(d)(2)]

b. Role of the "Qualified Legal Compliance Committee" ("QLCC")

Issuers that form a "qualified legal compliance committee" ("QLCC") may place much of the responsibility for legal compliance on the committee. The QLCC need not contain any lawyers, but perhaps that is not surprising because up-the-ladder reporting will in most cases terminate with the issuer's audit committee, which likewise need not contain any lawyers.

(1) Advantages of a QLCC

Most issuers will probably establish a QLCC because such a committee is more likely to prepare a coordinated response to evidence of securities law problems than the chief legal officer, who may not have procedures developed in advance to deal with such issues. In addition, a QLCC involves the issuer's board at an early stage of the response, perhaps making an adequate response more likely.

(2) Procedure for Invoking the QLCC

A QLCC comes into play in two situations: (a) when the reporting lawyer elects to report directly to the QLCC rather than to the chief legal officer; or (b) the reporting lawyer reports the matter to the chief legal officer, who instead of taking action personally, refers the matter to the QLCC.

(3) Composition of the QLCC

The QLCC must include at least one member of the issuer's audit committee and two or more members of the issuer's board of directors who are not employed, directly or indirectly, by the issuer. [17 C.F.R. § 205.2(k)(1)]

(4) QLCC Authority

A QLCC must have *at least* the following authority [17 C.F.R. § 205.2(k)(3)]:

(a) To *inform* the issuer's chief legal officer and chief executive officer of reports of evidence of a material violation;

(b) To *determine whether an investigation is necessary* regarding any report of evidence of a material violation and, if it determines an investigation is necessary or appropriate, to:

(i) Notify the audit committee or the full board of directors;

(ii) Initiate an investigation, which may be conducted either by the chief legal officer (or the equivalent thereof) or by outside attorneys;

(iii) Retain such additional expert personnel as the committee deems necessary; and

(iv) At the conclusion of any such investigation, to (a) recommend, by majority vote, that the issuer implement an appropriate response to evidence of a material violation; and (b) inform the chief legal officer and the chief executive officer (or the equivalents thereof) and the board of directors of the results of any such investigation under this section and the appropriate remedial measures to be adopted; and

(v) To take all other appropriate action, including notifying the Commission in the event that the issuer fails in any material respect to implement an appropriate response that the QLCC has recommended the issuer to take.

c. Sanctions for Violation of the Attorney Conduct Rules

The S.E.C. may censure a violating lawyer, or deny the violator the privilege of appearing and practicing before it. [17 C.F.R. § 205.6(b)] In addition, the S.E.C. may "subject such attorney to the civil penalties and remedies for a violation of the federal securities laws available to the Commission in an action brought by the Commission thereunder." [17 C.F.R. § 205.6(a)] This could potentially bring into play the full spectrum of remedies available to the S.E.C. in civil or administrative proceedings.

H. Criminal Prosecution

1. Overview

When most people think of criminal conduct under the securities laws, they think of insider trading or complex stock frauds. In fact, the criminal provisions of the 1933 and 1934 Act cover much more than fraud and insider trading. *Willful violation of any provision* of either statute, or of any rule or regulation promulgated under either statute, is a *felony.* In addition, a "knowing and willful" false statement in a filing under the 1934 Act is a criminal offense. Each violation of the 1933 Act is potentially punishable by five years' imprisonment, and the penalty for violating the 1934 Act is even more severe: each infraction can result in up to 20 years in prison. [SA § 24; SEA § 32(a)]

a. Other Statutes

Charges arising from securities transactions are often brought under provisions other than the securities laws. Sometimes this is done to avoid difficult issues that have cropped up under the securities laws. Thus, for example, in **Carpenter v. United States,** 484 U.S. 19 (1987), the prosecution charged violations of SEA Section 10(b) and Rule 10b–5 and also of the federal mail and wire fraud statutes. Ultimately, the securities law convictions were affirmed by an equally divided Court, but the mail and wire fraud convictions were affirmed unanimously.

b. Impact of Sarbanes-Oxley

In 2002, SOXA created several new crimes and enhanced the penalties for others. These changes are discussed below.

2. Commencing a Criminal Action

The S.E.C. does not have the authority to bring a criminal action, which can be done only by the United States Attorney's office in the relevant jurisdiction(s). Nevertheless, the S.E.C. is obviously heavily involved in, and very knowledgeable about, illegal securities activities, and securities prosecutions are usually the result of an informal referral from the S.E.C.'s

Enforcement Division. A formal referral under 1934 Act Section 21(d) is also possible, although such referrals (which require a vote of the Commission) are relatively rare.

a. Parallel Proceedings

There is a good deal of cooperation between the Justice Department and the S.E.C., and frequently both agencies pursue a defendant at the same time. Such parallel proceedings may raise troublesome procedural issues, as when the S.E.C. seeks discovery in its civil action and the defendant resists, claiming that the Justice Department (which will have access to everything the S.E.C. discovers) is improperly broadening the scope of its criminal discovery by "hiding behind" the S.E.C.'s civil discovery request. This argument, however, has not succeeded for defendants in securities cases. [*See, e.g.*, **S.E.C. v. Dresser Industries, Inc.,** 628 F.2d 1368 (D.C. Cir. 1980)]

b. Fifth Amendment

Defendants in parallel proceedings may exercise their Fifth Amendment privilege and refuse to testify. In a civil proceeding, however, the factfinder is allowed to draw an adverse inference from the refusal to testify and asserting this right might cost the defendant the case. On the other hand, if the defendant testifies, a transcript of the testimony will be made available to the Justice Department and can be used to impeach the defendant in later criminal proceedings.

3. Standard of Culpability

Both the 1933 Act and the 1934 Act make it a criminal offense to "willfully" violate a provision of the statute, or of an S.E.C. rule or regulation thereunder. [SA § 24; SEA § 32(a)] The 1934 Act, however, goes on to provide that a false statement made in a 1934 Act filing is criminal if it is made "willfully and knowingly." Finally, the 1934 Act provides that if the defendant can prove lack of knowledge of the statute or rule allegedly violated, no prison term can be imposed. The crimes defined under SOXA have standards of culpability varying from "knowing" conduct, to "willful and knowing" conduct, to "corrupt" conduct.

a. Culpability Under the 1933 Act

The provisions of the 1933 Act relating to criminal intent are relatively straightforward: a "willful" violation is a crime. "Willful" under the Act means the intent to do the act charged, together with knowledge that the act is wrongful. It does not mean that the defendant knew that the act violated any particular provision of a statute, or even that the act was unlawful. In a fraud case in which scienter is required, "willfulness" includes the intent to deceive, but not necessarily the intent to violate the securities laws.

e.g. **Example:** The defendant was charged with violating Securities Act Section 17(a) by fraudulently selling securities. On appeal, he argued that the government had not met its burden of proving that he knew the items sold were "securities" under the Act. The court held that the government did not need to prove that the defendant knew the items were securities; it was enough to show that the items were in fact securities, and that the defendant intended to deceive the buyers in connection with the sales. [**United States v. Brown,** 578 F.2d 1280 (9th Cir.1978)]

b. Culpability Under the 1934 Act

The 1934 Act sets up two possible standards of culpability: "willfulness," relevant to any violation of the statute or rule; and "willful and knowing," relating to false statements made in filings under the statute or rules.

(1) "Willful" Violation of the 1934 Act or Rules

"Willfulness" under the 1934 Act means much the same thing as it does under the 1933 Act; *i.e.*, intentional conduct and knowledge that the act is wrongful, but not necessarily that it is unlawful, nor that it violates any particular rule or regulation. [**United States v. Dixon,** 536 F.2d 1388 (2d Cir. 1976)]

(2) "Willful and Knowing" False Statements in Filings Under 1934 Act

The courts have not reached a consensus on what the addition of the word "knowing" means in prosecutions for false filings under the 1934 Act. It might signify an intent to deceive, or perhaps specific knowledge of the provision of law that was violated. However, the former has rarely appeared in the cases, and courts have rejected the latter. [*See, e.g.*, **United States v. Dixon,** *supra*]

(3) The 1934 Act "Lack of Knowledge" Defense

The 1934 Act also includes a provision that a defendant who proves that he or she did not know of the rule or regulation violated may not be sentenced to prison. The courts have construed this provision restrictively, holding that it is satisfied only if the defendant establishes that he or she had what amounts to a good faith belief that his or her conduct was lawful. The provision will not apply in a fraud case, in which proof of scienter forecloses the possibility of the innocence required for the "no knowledge" defense. [*See* **United States v. Lilley,** 291 F. Supp. 989 (S.D. Tex. 1968)]

c. SOXA-Defined Crimes

The crimes defined by SOXA have varying standards of culpability. Each of these standards is discussed below in relation to the crimes to which it applies.

(1) Crimes Committed "Knowingly"

The following offenses are committed when the actions taken are done "knowingly."

(a) Tampering with or Destruction of Documents

SOXA created a new crime of knowingly tampering with, falsifying, or destroying any tangible object (or record or document) with the intention of impeding, obstructing, or influencing the investigation or proper administration of any matter within the jurisdiction of any agency or department of the United States, or any case under Title 11 (bankruptcy), or relating to or in contemplation of any such case or matter. The penalty for violation of this provision is a fine and up to 20 years in prison. [SOXA § 802; 18 U.S.C. § 1519]

(b) Defrauding Shareholders of Public Companies

Another crime created under SOXA is knowingly committing or attempting fraud in connection with a security of any issuer that has a class of securities registered under SEA Section 12, or that reports under SEA Section 15(d). The punishment is a fine and up to 25 years in prison. [SOXA § 807; 18 U.S.C. § 1348]

(2) Crimes Committed "Knowingly and Willfully"

The following offenses are committed when the actions taken are taken "knowingly and willfully." The first requires knowing and willful conduct; the second can be committed "knowingly" only, but the penalty is doubled if the defendant acted both knowingly and willfully.

(a) Failure to Maintain Audit Records and Workpapers

Accountants are required to maintain all records related to an audit for five years after the audit. Knowing and willful failure to do so may result in a fine and imprisonment for up to 10 years. [SOXA § 802; 18 U.S.C. § 1520(a) & (c)]

(b) Knowing False Certification

We have already encountered SOXA's requirement that the CEO and CFO of public companies certify the financial statements of their employers. In addition, a false certification, made knowingly, is a criminal offense with a penalty of a fine of up to $1 million and a prison term of up to 10 years. [SOXA § 906(a); 18 U.S.C. § 1350(c)(1)]

(c) Knowing and Willful False Certification

If the certification referred to immediately above is knowingly and willfully false, the penalty is increased to a fine of up to $5 million and a prison term of up to 20 years. [SOXA § 906(a); 18 U.S.C. § 1350(c)(2)]

(3) Crimes Committed "Corruptly"

Finally, SOXA amends the existing crime of "tampering with a record or otherwise impeding an official proceeding" by broadening it to include "corrupt" actual or attempted alteration, destruction, or concealment of a record or other object to impair its availability for use in an official proceeding, or other actual or attempted obstruction of or influence on an official proceeding. This crime is punishable by a fine and up to 20 years imprisonment. [SOXA § 1102; 18 U.S.C. § 1512(c)]

d. Statute of Limitations

The relevant statute of limitations for criminal prosecutions under the securities laws is five years; it is not contained in the securities statutes, but rather appears in the criminal code. [*See* 18 U.S.C. § 3282]

4. Mail Fraud and Wire Fraud

The mail fraud and wire fraud statutes [18 U.S.C. §§ 1341 & 1343] are often used to prosecute persons for securities transactions, because most securities transactions involve the mails and wires. These statutes operate somewhat as catch-all fraud crimes, without some of the requirements of securities-specific crimes.

a. Elements of Mail or Wire Fraud

To make out a case of mail fraud or wire fraud, the prosecution must prove:

(1) A *scheme to defraud;*

(2) *Specific intent to defraud*; and

(3) The *mailing of a letter, or sending a wire,* in furtherance of the scheme.

(1) Person Mailing Need Not Be Defendant

Note that while it is a requirement that a letter (or wire) be sent, *it is not required that the defendant he the one sending the letter.* A scheme in which the defendant, in face-to-face meetings, fraudulently convinces others to send him money through the mail is mail fraud, even though all the mailings were done innocently.

(2) Defendant Need Not Have Specific Intent to Use Mail

The government does not need to establish the defendant's specific intent to use the mail (or cause the mail to be used); it is enough if the *use of the mail was reasonably foreseeable.*

b. "Intangible Business Property" and the "Intangible Right of Honest Services"

If a securities transaction is prosecuted as mail fraud, a problem may arise in identifying just what the victim was defrauded of. Insider trading cases, for instance, raise this issue. Prosecutors can make one of two arguments:

(1) Intangible Business Property

This idea is closely linked to the "misappropriation" theory of insider trading (discussed above). Essentially, the argument is that the tipper deprived the source of the exclusive use of the information. [*See* **Carpenter v. United States,** *supra*]

(2) Intangible Right of Honest Services

Alternatively, the prosecution can argue that the tipper (and the tippee) schemed to deprive the source of the information of her "intangible right of honest services." In 1988, Congress amended the criminal code specifically to add this possibility to the prosecutors' arsenal, by defining "scheme or artifice to defraud" to include "a scheme or artifice to deprive another of the intangible right of honest services." [*See* 18 U.S.C. § 1346] As interpreted by the Supreme Court, the deprivation of the intangible right to honest services is limited to the following two scenarios: (1) bribery; and (2) kickbacks. [**Skilling v. U.S.**, 561 U.S. 358 (2010)]

c. Enhanced Penalties for Mail and Wire Fraud

SOXA increased the prison sentences for mail and wire fraud from five years to 20 years. [SOXA § 903; 18 U.S.C. §§ 1341 & 1343]

Chapter Four

Regulation of the Securities Markets

CONTENTS	PAGE

Key Exam Issues 184

A. Regulation of the National Securities Exchanges 184

B. Regulation of the Over-the-Counter Market 189

C. Regulation of Market Manipulation and Stabilization 192

D. Regulation of Securities Analysts 199

E. Regulation of Broker-Dealers 200

Key Exam Issues

The regulation of the national securities exchanges is very important to the well-being of the securities markets, but it is seldom tested on law school exams. However, you should learn the material in this chapter so that you have a basic understanding of how the securities markets work.

The topic most likely to appear on an exam concerns the regulation of trading activities of broker-dealers. In this area, you should watch for possible conflicts of interest between the brokers and their clients, and also be familiar with the rules that brokers must follow in working with clients.

A. Regulation of the National Securities Exchanges

1. Introduction

As part of its purpose of regulating interstate trading of securities subsequent to their original distribution, the Securities Exchange Act of 1934 includes provisions regulating the "national securities exchanges" where many such securities are traded.

a. "Exchange" Defined

An "exchange" is any organization, association, or group of persons providing a marketplace or facilities for bringing together purchasers and sellers of securities. [SEA § 3(a)(1)]

(1) Requirement of Registration

It is unlawful for a broker or dealer to use any means of interstate commerce for the purpose of trading or reporting the trade of a security on an exchange unless the exchange is registered with the S.E.C. as a "national securities exchange" or exempted from registration. However, the S.E.C. may exempt an exchange from registration if the volume of transactions on the exchange is so small that regulation is not necessary for the protection of the public interest or investors. [SEA § 5]

(a) Section 6

The terms and conditions with which a national securities exchange must comply are set forth in Section 6 of the 1934 Act (*e.g.,* the rules of the exchange must be designed to prevent fraudulent and manipulative practices).

b. Listing Securities for Trading

To trade its securities on an exchange, an issuer must "list" the security with the exchange. The exchanges have rules under which an issuer can qualify its securities for trading (*e.g.,* requisite size of the firm in terms of sales and assets, net worth, etc.).

(1) Registration with the S.E.C.

Once the issuer has listed a security with a national securities exchange, the security must then be registered with the S.E.C. under Section 12 of the 1934 Act.

c. Exchange Membership

Each national securities exchange sells memberships to securities firms or individuals in the securities business. Membership carries with it the privilege of executing transactions over the exchange.

d. Exchange Disseminates Price Information

Each exchange has developed an information system for disseminating information to market participants about the prices at which various securities have been bought and sold over the exchange. This information is sold and is becoming an important source of revenue for securities exchanges.

2. Competition of Markets for Trading of Securities

a. Competing Markets

Many markets compete for the trading of securities.

(1) NYSE and Regional Exchanges

For example, a security may be listed for trading on the New York Stock Exchange ("NYSE") and on one or more of the regional exchanges, such as the Pacific Coast Stock Exchange.

(2) Over-the-Counter Markets

In addition, broker-dealers who are not members of an exchange may engage in buying and selling securities that are listed on an exchange in "over-the-counter" (*i.e.*, nonexchange) transactions.

(3) Institutional Trading

The institutions that own large amounts of securities may also engage in buying and selling securities directly with other such institutions.

(a) Alternative Trading Systems

Institutional investors trade directly with one another on alternative trading systems, which are simply computerized facilities for bringing together buyers and sellers and disseminating information about price and availability. These trading systems increasingly compete with the more-established exchanges, and their growth has been fueled by rapid advances in, and deployment of, communications and information processing technology.

(i) Regulation as Broker-Dealers

Historically, the S.E.C. was willing to permit alternative trading systems to operate without registration as securities exchanges, as long as they registered as broker-dealers. [*See* S.E.C. Release No. 34–38672 (1997)] Although the more-established markets occasionally sued to overturn the S.E.C.'s decisions, those efforts were generally unsuccessful. [*See, e.g.*, **Board of Trade v. S.E.C.,** 923 F.2d 1270 (7th Cir. 1991)]

(ii) Rapid Growth Produced Additional Regulation

In 1998, the S.E.C. estimated that almost 30% of the orders in over-the-counter stocks, and almost 5% of the orders in NYSE-listed securities, were handled by alternative trading systems. This heavy volume alerted the S.E.C. to the need to revisit its approach to alternative trading systems, and in 1998, the Commission promulgated Regulation ATS, and revised certain rules under the 1934 Act to allow alternative trading systems to choose either registration as exchanges, or registration as broker-dealers and compliance with the new Regulation ATS. [S.E.C. Release No. 34–40760 (1998)].

(4) Privatization of the Established Markets

Responding to the competitive threat from alternative trading systems, both the NYSE and Nasdaq have become private, for-profit corporations. The change is intended to enable them to streamline decisionmaking and thereby compete more effectively. These developments raise some thorny problems, notably whether self-regulation can be effectively carried out by an entity that is simultaneously seeking to maximize shareholder gain.

b. Development of National Market System

Congress has directed the S.E.C. to use its authority under the 1934 Act to facilitate the establishment of a "national market system" for securities. [SEA § 11A]

(1) Projected Elements of the National Market System

The following items have been suggested by Congress and the S.E.C. as important aspects of the national market system:

(a) *A nationwide system for disclosure* of market information so that price and volume information is available in all markets.

(b) *Elimination of artificial impediments to dealing* in the best available markets created by exchange rules or otherwise.

(c) *Establishment of terms and conditions* under which qualified broker-dealers could negotiate access to all exchanges.

(d) *An auction trading market* that would provide price and time priority protection for all public orders.

(e) *The type of securities to be included in the system* would be dependent on their characteristics (trading volume, etc.) and not on where they are traded (*i.e.,* which exchange, etc.). [*See* SEA Release No. 14416 (1978)]

(2) Progress Toward the National Market System

Progress toward a national market system, in which there is intermarket competition, has been unsteady at best. However, overall there is far more price competition in the equity markets today than there was in 1975, when a national market system became a policy goal. This is primarily the result of technological and regulatory changes that facilitate the rapid dissemination of price information. Consequently, most investors today have access to timely and reliable information about securities prices, which tends to promote competition.

3. Self-Regulation of Exchanges v. S.E.C. Supervision

a. Registration with the S.E.C.

A broker-dealer is prohibited from effecting transactions on a securities exchange unless the exchange has registered with the S.E.C. pursuant to Section 6 of the 1934 Act or is exempted from registration by other provisions of the Act. [SEA § 5]

b. Self-Regulation of Exchanges

Section 3(a)(26) of the 1934 Act provides that the national exchanges are self-regulatory organizations ("SROs") that have the power to regulate their members' activities and business practices. [SEA § 6]

(1) Rules, Policies, and Procedures

The exchange may propose rules and adopt policies and procedures for implementing its rules.

(2) S.E.C. Review

Any proposed rule or change to an existing rule must be filed with the S.E.C., which then goes through an administrative notice and comment procedure, giving the public the right to comment on the proposal. [SEA § 19(b)] In addition, the S.E.C. can, by its own rulemaking procedures, abrogate, add to, and delete rules from the rules of a self-regulatory organization. [SEA § 19(c)]

(3) Disciplinary Action

If the exchange imposes any disciplinary sanction on an exchange member, or denies membership to a firm, the exchange must notify the S.E.C., which may then review (either on its own motion or on the motion of the aggrieved party) the actions taken by the exchange. [SEA § 19(d)]

(4) S.E.C.'s Power to Sanction

Finally, the 1934 Act empowers the S.E.C. to impose sanctions on the exchanges, exchange members, and persons associated with exchange members for violation of the federal securities laws. [SEA § 19(h)]

4. Regulation of Off-the-Exchange Transactions

In addition to regulating trading on the national securities exchanges by exchange members, the S.E.C. and the national exchanges also regulate the trading in listed securities by exchange members *off the exchange.*

a. Background

Historically, the stock exchanges sharply limited trading in listed securities elsewhere than on the exchange floor. The reason for this was simple: If a security was available only on the exchange floor, from an exchange member, a customer who wanted to buy or sell the security had no choice but to pay the usual commission on the transaction. In the 1970s, however, large customers (*e.g.,* financial institutions like banks, trusts, and insurance companies) began to apply pressure to exchange members to participate in off-exchange transactions. As long as the exchanges were unwilling to permit member firms to participate in off-exchange transactions, financial institutions that wanted to avoid paying broker's commissions had to deal directly with one another and with nonmember firms. As the number of participants in this market grew, it became known as the "third market."

b. Block Transactions

Many exchange member firms also found that they were unable to handle in normal exchange transactions the purchase or sale of the large blocks of securities being traded by financial institutions. These firms found that to facilitate such transactions for their customers, they often had to negotiate the transaction off the exchange—either by finding off-the-exchange brokers or dealers willing to participate, or by finding other institutions in the third market that wished to participate.

c. NYSE Rule 390

The New York Stock Exchange eventually responded to the pressure from members and their customers, and on the recommendation of the S.E.C, the Exchange amended its Rule 390 to permit member firms, at least in theory, to engage in off-exchange transactions. Such transactions, however, were subject to strict requirements.

d. S.E.C. Permission to Trade off the Exchange

The S.E.C. viewed the amended Rule 390 as merely an interim measure and, in the late 1970s, adopted Rules 19c–1 and 19c–3. These rules preempted portions of Rule 390 of the New York Stock Exchange as it then existed and eliminated some of the restrictions on off-exchange trading by member firms.

(1) Where Member Firm Acts as Broker

When acting as a broker (*i.e.,* agent), a member firm may effect an off-exchange transaction in a listed security. [SEA Rule 19c–1]

(2) Where Member Firm Acts as Principal

Where, however, the member firm acts as a *principal* in the transaction (*e.g.,* by selling securities it owns in its investment account), the member firm must comply with exchange rules regulating off-the-exchange sales.

(3) Newly Listed Securities

The S.E.C. has also adopted a rule removing off-exchange trading restrictions on securities first listed after April 26, 1979. [SEA Rule 19c–3] This allows exchange-member brokerage firms to compete directly with exchange specialists on transactions involving these stocks.

5. Civil Liability for Violations of Exchange or FINRA Rules

In a number of cases, a plaintiff has brought a *private action* against an exchange or a member firm, alleging an implied federal cause of action based on violation of a stock exchange or FINRA rule.

a. Pre-*Blue Chip* View

The older cases hold that under limited circumstances, such an action was possible. [*See, e.g.,* **Buttrey v. Merrill Lynch, Pierce, Fenner & Smith, Inc.,** 410 F.2d 135 (7th Cir.), *cert. denied,* 396 U.S. 838 (1969)]

b. Modern View

After the Supreme Court decided the *Blue Chip* case (cutting back implied liability under the securities laws) (see above p. 117) the lower courts have refused to recognize implied actions based on violations of stock exchange or FINRA rules. [*See, e.g.,* **Carrott v. Shearson Hayden Stone, Inc.,** 724 F.2d 821 (9th Cir. 1984)]

B. Regulation of the Over-the-Counter Market

1. In General

Securities that are traded outside the exchanges are said to be traded "over-the-counter." This trading, like that which occurs on the national securities exchanges, is also subject to regulation under the 1934 Act.

2. Role of Securities Firms

Securities firms act as the agents (*i.e.,* as brokers) of the buyer and seller in over-the-counter securities transactions. And sometimes the securities firms may act as principals (*i.e.*, as dealers) as well, owning the security and acting as either buyer or seller in the transaction.

3. Transaction Information Systems

A key challenge is to disseminate information about the prices at which over-the-counter ("OTC") securities are bought and sold. An important source of price information about OTC securities are the so-called "pink sheets," published by the National Daily Quotations Bureau.

4. Regulation of Broker-Dealers

The 1934 Act provides for the registration with the S.E.C. of all broker-dealers transacting a securities business in interstate commerce. [SEA § 15] This requirement applies to essentially all broker-dealers, including those in the OTC market, because it is difficult for a broker to avoid using instrumentalities of interstate commerce.

a. Self-Regulation Required

In addition to registering with the S.E.C., broker-dealers must be members of a national securities association which is itself registered with the S.E.C. Only one such association exists today: Financial Industry Regulatory Authority ("FINRA"). (This association was formerly called the National Association of Securities Dealers ("NASD").)

b. Authority of FINRA

FINRA is authorized by the Act to adopt and enforce rules for member broker-dealers addressing a wide variety of matters, including training, broker qualifications, and capital requirements. [SEA § 15(b)] The S.E.C., however, continues to exercise authority over both the FINRA itself and over FINRA members. [SEA § 15A]

(1) FINRA*'s proposed rule additions, deletions, or changes must first be approved by the S.E.C.* [SEA § 19(b)]

(2) *In addition, the S.E.C. may exercise its power to abrogate, add to, delete, or amend the rules* of FINRA when necessary to ensure its fair administration and to accomplish the purposes of the Act. [SEA § 19(c)]

(3) *If FINRA imposes any disciplinary sanction on any member, or denies membership* to a broker-dealer, FINRA must inform the S.E.C. The S.E.C. may then review the actions taken by FINRA, either on its own motion or on the motion of an aggrieved party. [SEA § 19(d)]

(4) *Finally, the S.E.C. has the power to sanction FINRA members* and persons associated with members. [SEA § 19(h)] The S.E.C. may exercise this authority even after a FINRA member has been sanctioned by FINRA and may impose its own penalties for conduct that has already been the subject of FINRA discipline. [**Jones v. S.E.C.,** 115 F.3d 1173 (4th Cir. 1997)]

c. Regulation of Dealer Markups

One issue that frequently arises with respect to OTC securities involves the amount of profit a dealer may make on a sale. FINRA's Rules of Fair Practice require dealers to "buy or sell at a price which is fair, taking into consideration all relevant factors." Informally, FINRA has a guideline of 5% as a reasonable markup, but in some cases, a 5% markup may be unreasonable.

(1) FINRA Sanctions

A dealer that marks up prices excessively is subject to FINRA discipline. [*See, e.g.,* **Lehl v. S.E.C.,** 90 F.3d 1483 (10th Cir. 1996)]

(2) S.E.C. Sanctions

In addition, the S.E.C. has brought administrative actions under Rule 10b–5 against dealers charging excessive markups, based on the failure to disclose the excessive markup to the customer. [*See, e.g.,* **Trost & Co.,** 12 S.E.C. 531 (1942)]

(3) Private Actions

Finally, the customer who has paid an excessive markup may succeed in a private action against the dealer, usually based on Rule 10b–5. [*See, e.g.,* **Ettinger v. Merrill Lynch, Pierce, Fenner & Smith, Inc.,** 835 F.2d 1031 (3d Cir. 1987)]

5. Regulation of the "Penny Stock" Market

A significant segment of the OTC market is composed of "penny stocks," low-priced (under $5 per share) stocks of small, new companies with little or no operating history. Congress reacted to widespread fraud and abuse in the penny stock market by passing the Securities Enforcement Remedies and Penny Stock Reform Act of 1990.

a. Administrative Sanctions and Registration Provisions

The 1990 Act provides for several administrative remedies and stringent regulations governing the distribution of securities issued by "blank check" companies.

b. Broker-Dealer Regulation Under the 1990 Act

The 1990 Act also provides for extensive regulation of brokers and dealers who deal heavily in penny stocks and authorizes the S.E.C. to make rules regulating participants in the penny stock market. [SEA § 15(g)]

(1) Suspensions and Bars

Under the 1990 Act, the S.E.C. may suspend or bar persons from "being associated with any broker or dealer, or from participating in an offering of penny stock," if they have violated the 1933 or 1934 Acts in connection with a penny stock offering.

[SEA § 15(b)(6)(A)] It is illegal for such persons to work for a broker or dealer, or participate in a penny stock offering, in violation of the bar. [SEA § 15(b)(6)(B)(i)] Likewise, it is illegal for a broker or dealer to hire such persons. [SEA § 15(b)(6)(B)(ii)]

(2) Risk Disclosure Document

A broker or dealer selling penny stock to a retail customer is required to deliver a document containing the information in Schedule 15G, which sets out in detail many of the risks and dangers associated with an investment in penny stocks. [SEA Rule 15g–2]

(3) Written Purchase Agreement

The dealer must obtain from the customer an agreement to purchase the stock, setting forth the identity and quantity of the penny stock to be purchased. [SEA Rule 15g–9(a)(2)(ii)]

(4) Price Information

Penny stock dealers must also disclose to the customer available "inside" price information (the *wholesale* bid and asked prices) for the security sold. If the inside price is not available (*e.g.,* because the dealer has not consistently traded the security with other dealers), that fact and the reasons therefor must be disclosed. [SEA Rule 15g–3]

(5) Dealer Compensation Disclosure

Penny stock dealers must disclose to the customer the aggregate amount of all compensation received in connection with the penny stock transaction. [SEA Rule 15g–4]

(6) Salesperson Compensation Disclosure

In addition to disclosing the dealer's compensation, *supra*, the individual salesperson must disclose to the customer the total amount of compensation that she will receive from all sources (including the issuer or other promoters). [SEA Rule 15g–5]

(7) Account Statements

Penny stock dealers must provide their customers with a monthly account statement setting out price information for each penny stock owned by the customer. [SEA Rule 15g–6]

(8) Customer Suitability

Finally, before a broker-dealer is permitted to engage in any penny stock transaction with a customer, the *dealer must approve the customer's account.* This requires that the dealer obtain from the customer *information about the customer's financial situation, investment experience, and investment objectives.* Once that information is obtained, the dealer must determine, based on the information, that penny stock investments are suitable for the customer, and that the customer is capable of evaluating the risks of such an investment. Finally, the customer's financial information must be summarized in a written document and presented to the customer for signature, along with the statement that the broker-dealer is required by law to do so. [SEA Rule 15g–9]

C. Regulation of Market Manipulation and Stabilization

1. Introduction

The previous two sections of this Summary discussed the general regulations relating to the two principal markets for the trading of securities—the national stock exchanges and the OTC market. This section concerns the prohibitions in the 1934 Act against manipulation of the trading that occurs in these markets.

2. Regulation of Short Sales

Short sales are one of the more controversial kinds of trading activities. Although an outright ban on short sales was considered in 1934, ultimately Congress decided to let the S.E.C. determine what kinds of short-selling practices to forbid.

a. Short Sale Defined

A short sale is a sale of securities that the seller does not own, or any sale consummated by the delivery of a security borrowed by or for the seller.

b. Why Sell Short

Traders sell securities short because they believe that the price of the security will drop. Thus, a short sale is a "bet" that the market price of the securities will fall and is sometimes cited as one way in which a sophisticated trader can make money even in a falling market.

e.g. **Example:** Cathy does not own any Acme Corp. stock, but she believes that Acme stock will fall in price. Her trading strategy, then, might be to sell short Acme stock. She will sell, say, 1,000 shares of Acme stock today. Under normal market practice, her sale will not "settle" (and Cathy will not have to deliver the Acme stock) until three business days after the contract date. If Cathy is correct, and the price of Acme stock falls, she can "cover" her sale of three days ago with cheaper stock purchased today. You may wonder how Cathy can obtain Acme stock for delivery the same day in order to cover her earlier short sale. The answer lies in the ability of traders to borrow stock from one another: to implement her short-sale strategy, Cathy will borrow enough shares of Acme stock to cover the short sale. This borrowed stock is available to her when she needs it, at the then-current market price.

c. Pros and Cons of Short Sales

Short sales increase the volatility of market prices and can incentivize short-sellers to participate in a concerted effort to drive down the price of a security, using techniques like spreading rumors. Short sales can also play an important role, however, in furthering market efficiency, by ensuring that there is downward pressure on securities prices in response to negative public information.

Selling short may be an appropriate strategy for a sophisticated investor, but it is risky. The chief danger is that the short seller is exposed to liability that increases every time the price of the security goes up, until the sale is covered. Unlike an investor with a "long" position, whose risk is limited to the amount invested, the short seller's risk is hard to measure and is limited only by the potential increases in the price of the security.

d. Regulation of Short Selling

To mitigate somewhat the potential dangers of unlimited short selling, the S.E.C. has promulgated rules governing the practice in Regulation SHO, 17 C.F.R. § 242.200 *et seq.*

(1) Short Sales Must Be Identified

All sales of equity securities must be identified as "long" or "short." [17 C.F.R. § 242.200(g)]

(2) Short Sales Restricted After Significant Price Declines

Trading centers are required to have policies and procedures in place to restrict short selling when a covered security has experienced a price decline of at least 10% in one day. (This is commonly referred to as "triggering the circuit breaker.") [17 C.F.R. § 242.201(b)]

(3) Short Sales Prohibited During Distributions

During a distribution of securities, the influx of new securities into the market tends to depress the price. Because the price is likely to decline at least a little, the short-seller's risk is reduced. Short sales were thus more likely to occur during a distribution. On the other hand, short sales during a distribution may make it impossible for the issuer to complete the distribution. In response, the S.E.C. adopted Rule 105 of Regulation M, 17 C.F.R. § 242.105. The rule applies after the filing of a registration statement, relating to the class of securities sold short, and prohibits covering a short sale made in the five days before an offering is priced with securities purchased from an underwriter or broker participating in the offering.

e. Comment

The short sale regulations may discourage abuses, but they cannot prevent them. Virtually anything that can be accomplished by selling short can also be accomplished by using derivative securities, such as options, which do not carry similar restrictions. Nevertheless, the short sale regulations may be valuable if only because they tend to inhibit short sales by investors who lack the financial sophistication to understand and manage the risks that short sales entail.

3. Prohibition of Market Manipulation

Market manipulation is an attempt to set stock prices—or other important criteria of stock market performance, such as the volume of shares traded—by entering into transactions for the specific purpose of such manipulation. There is a series of provisions in the 1934 Act aimed at prohibiting market manipulation.

a. Manipulation of Listed Securities Prohibited—Section 9

Section 9(a) of the 1934 Act prohibits "any person" from using the instrumentalities of interstate commerce or the facilities of "any national securities exchange" to engage in certain specified manipulative activities with respect to securities listed on a national securities exchange. Although SEA Section 9 applies only to listed securities, its prohibitions are incorporated into Sections 10(b) and 15(c), and thus the substance of the Act's anti-manipulation provisions applies to both listed and unlisted securities. [*See* **S.E.C. v. Resch-Cassin & Co.,** 362 F. Supp. 964 (S.D.N.Y. 1973)]

(1) Per Se Violations

A series of "per se violations" are listed in Section 9. These include activities such as attempting to create a misleading appearance of active trading; effecting a series of transactions on the exchange creating the appearance of active trading, to induce a purchase or sale of a security by others; and disseminating misleading information with respect to the listed security. [SEA § 9(a)(1)–(6)]

(2) Violation of S.E.C. Rules

Other types of market transactions may also violate the 1934 Act if effected in contravention of rules adopted by the S.E.C. [SEA § 9(a)(6), (b) & (c)]

(a) Section 9(a)(6)

Section 9(a)(6) relates to "market stabilization," and makes it unlawful to engage in transactions in a listed stock for the purpose of "pegging, fixing, or stabilizing the price of such security" in contravention of such rules as may be adopted by the S.E.C. The S.E.C. regulates stabilization in Regulation M.

(3) Limited Use of Section 9

Section 9 has received only limited use by the S.E.C., due to several factors.

(a) Applies Only to Listed Securities

One reason for its limited use is that Section 9 applies only to securities listed on a national securities exchange. Other sections that are used because of their broader coverage are Rule 10b–5, which applies to both listed and over-the-counter securities, and Rule 15c1–2 (which is limited, however, to broker-dealer transactions).

(b) Must Show "Intent" or "Willfulness"

Under Section 9, the S.E.C. must prove the defendant's "intent" or "purpose" to engage in an unlawful act before it can obtain injunctive relief. And a plaintiff in a private damage action must be able to show defendant's "willfulness." [SEA § 9(f)]

b. General Prohibition Against Market Manipulation—Rule 10b–5

Rule 10b–5—a general prohibition against fraud in the purchase and sale of securities—applies to both listed and over-the-counter securities. Because of this, and the burdensome requirement of proving intent or willfulness under Section 9, Rule 10b–5 has had broad application in market manipulation cases. Moreover, the specific prohibitions of Section 9 with respect to listed securities have been held to be incorporated in Rule 10b–5. [**S.E.C. v. Resch-Cassin & Co.,** *supra*]

c. Liability Provisions Applicable to Broker-Dealers—Section 15(c)

Section 15(c) is a general fraud provision worded similarly to Section 9 and Rule 10b–5, but specifically applicable to transactions involving broker-dealers in the over-the-counter market.

(1) S.E.C. Rules

Pursuant to Section 15(c), the S.E.C. has adopted rules prohibiting certain manipulative and deceptive practices in securities trading. [SEA Rules 15c1–2—15c1–9]

(2) No "Willfulness" Element

Note that the specific element of "willfulness" (required in a private damage action brought under Section 9) is *not* present in a Section 15(c) action. [*See* SEA § 15(c)]

(3) S.E.C. Enforcement Powers

In addition to private damages actions that may be brought under Section 15(c), the S.E.C. has specific enforcement powers against broker-dealers for any violations of its rules adopted pursuant to Section 15(c). In addition, it may review disciplinary proceedings brought by FINRA against any of its broker-dealer members.

d. Manipulation During a Distribution—Regulation M

Before and during an offering of securities, the issuer, underwriters, and other participants in the offering may have an incentive to manipulate the price of the offered securities by making purchases. For example, an issuer that already has securities trading in the market would normally offer additional securities at the current market price of the securities already issued. That price could be raised, however, if the issuer or others connected with the offering were to purchase sizeable quantities of the securities just before commencing the new offering. Or, in the case of an initial public offering, the issuer or underwriters might wish to maintain the price of the securities at the offering price by making purchases even as the offering is underway. These practices have been heavily regulated by the S.E.C., first by Rule 10b–6, and, beginning in 1997, by Regulation M, 17 C.F.R. § 242.100 *et seq.*

(1) What Is Regulated

Persons subject to Regulation M may not purchase or bid for securities that are being distributed until their participation in the distribution is over.

(2) Who Is Regulated

Regulation M applies to issuers, underwriters, participating brokers and dealers, and affiliated purchasers (including persons acting in concert with any of the foregoing).

(3) When the Prohibition Begins

The beginning "restricted period" during which persons may not purchase or bid depends on how heavily traded the security is.

(a) Heavily Traded Securities—One Day

If the security has an average daily trading volume ("ADTV") of at least $100,000 and a public float (*i.e.*, the aggregate market value of all outstanding securities) of at least $25 million, the restricted period begins one business day before the offering is priced (or, if later, the day on which the person becomes a participant in the offering).

(b) Other Securities—Five Days

If the security does not meet the above criteria, the restricted period begins five business days before the offering is priced (or, if later, the day on which the person becomes a participant).

(4) Exceptions

There are a number of exceptions to Regulation M, three of which are of primary interest here:

(a) Very Heavily Traded Securities

Securities with an ADTV of at least $1 million and a public float of $150 million are not subject to the trading restrictions of Regulation M. The price of such securities is difficult, if not impossible, to manipulate by making purchases, so the prohibitions are not needed.

(b) Stabilization

Stabilization of the price of securities during an offering is a common, if manipulative, practice. Stabilizing activities and their regulation are discussed below.

(5) Regulation M Not a Safe Harbor

Finally, note that Regulation M is not a safe harbor. That is, if the S.E.C. can prove manipulative intent, even activity complying with Regulation M would be a violation of Rule 10b–5 or another, more specific, prohibition. This is the result of Regulation M's structure, which broadly prohibits activities contravening its provisions, without insulating compliant activities from S.E.C. enforcement.

4. Regulation of Market Stabilization

Market stabilization is a specific form of potential market manipulation and, as such, is regulated under the 1934 Act. [*See* SEA § 9(a)(6); Regulation M, Rule 104]

a. "Stabilization" Defined

"Stabilization" is an attempt to maintain a fixed market price for a security by purchasing all of the shares that are offered at a price lower than the desired price.

(1) Occurs in Original Public Distributions

Market stabilization usually occurs in connection with an original public distribution of shares, where the underwriters stabilize the price until the entire issue is sold. It is critical to maintain the market for a new issue at the offering price until the entire issue is sold out, particularly in situations where securities of the same class are already outstanding.

(2) May Determine Success of Public Offering

Stabilization can be extremely important to a successful public offering of securities, which ultimately depends on whether the underwriter is able to sell the securities to the public at the offering price.

Even when the underwriter is able to quickly sell the entire issue, there is *always* some immediate reselling by purchasers before the entire issue is sold out. The early purchasers may change their minds about owning the stock, or they may have bought purely for speculation, with the hope of selling immediately for a profit in the case of an early price rise. If such reselling is not absorbed through public buying pressure, the market price of the remaining stock will drop below the initial offering price, and the entire issue will not be sold at the price originally set. For this reason, the ability of the underwriters to purchase the resold shares as they come to the market, thereby stabilizing the market at the initial offering price, is of critical importance to a successful public offering.

b. Regulation of Stabilization in Public Distributions

The 1934 Act prohibits transactions for the purpose of pegging or stabilizing the price of a security *only* when such transactions are in violation of the rules and regulations adopted by the S.E.C. [SEA § 9(a)(6)] The S.E.C. has adopted Rule 104 of Regulation M to regulate stabilization in distribution situations.

Note: while Regulation M generally does not operate as a safe harbor, in the case of stabilization, *Rule 104 is a safe harbor*. If a party complies with Regulation M, the party is insulated from violating Rule 10b–5.

(1) Trading Generally Prohibited

Regulation of stabilization begins with a fundamental rule: Any stabilization in contravention of Regulation M, Rule 104 is prohibited.

(2) Stabilization Permitted to Prevent Price Decline

Stabilization in support of a public distribution is permitted "for the purpose of preventing or retarding a decline in the market price of a security." [Regulation M, Rule 104(b)]

(a) Stabilizing Price Level

Stabilization may not be made at a price higher than the highest independent bid price for the security. In no event may stabilization be made at a price higher than the offering price. The stabilizing bid may follow the market up and down, provided it does not exceed the offering price or the highest independent bid price. Offerings made "at the market," *i.e.*, at other than a set price, may not be stabilized. [Regulation M, Rule 104]

(b) Disclosure of Stabilizing

The fact that the underwriters may be stabilizing the price of an issued security must be disclosed to a purchaser at or before the completion of the transaction. In addition, if stabilization is contemplated, a specific disclosure of that fact must be made in the prospectus. The stabilizer must also report all actual stabilizing transactions to the S.E.C. [Regulation M, Rule 104(h); Regulation S–K, Item 502]

5. The "Hot Issue" Problem

a. "Hot Issue" Defined

A "hot issue" is a security offered through a public distribution for which there is tremendous demand. Thus, a "hot issue" will typically be over-subscribed (*i.e.*, there will be more initial offers to purchase than there are shares available).

b. "Hot Issue" Problems

Normally, a "hot issue" rises immediately to a premium price over the initial offering price at which it comes to the market. Underwriters and dealers may attempt to profit from this situation, to the detriment of the public, by:

(1) *Holding back a portion of the initial issue* to be sold, so that it can be sold later at higher prices;

(2) *Allocating part of the issue to employees, relatives,* etc., for later sale;

(3) *Allocating part of the issue to other broker-dealers*—who will immediately put quotes in the quotation services raising the price of the issue—and then, as demand rises, all parties (*i.e.*, the underwriters and cooperating broker-dealers) will sell to the public at a substantial premium over the stated offering price;

(4) *"Laddering"*—allocating shares in a hot issue only to customers who agree to purchase shares in the secondary market after the initial offering. This gives the aftermarket price a boost as customers fulfill their promises in the days after an offering. Customers who agree to such aftermarket purchases are not harmed by this practice, but it may injure the public, which purchases at the market price, knowing nothing of these contractual arrangements to maintain that price; or

(5) *"Spinning"*—allocating shares in a hot issue to those whom the underwriter wishes to court, because they might bring underwriting business back to the underwriter. For example, an underwriter might want to allocate generous portions in hot issues to the CEO of a company that will conduct a significant offering later in the year, or to partners of venture capital firms that can steer IPO business to the underwriter.

c. Violation of the Securities Acts

The S.E.C. and FINRA consider all of the above practices to be violations of the securities acts. [SEA Release No. 6097 (1959)]

(1) Note

Possible violations include violation of Sections 11 and 12(a)(2) of the 1933 Act (for misrepresenting that the offering will be made *to the public,* at the offering price, and for not identifying the trading firms as underwriters) and the antifraud provisions of the 1934 Act (including Rules 10b–5 and 15c1–8, and Regulation M).

(2) Distinguish

It is not a violation of the "hot issue" rules for the dealers to sell the issue to relatives and friends where the stock (which appreciated rapidly) was held for investment (at least six months) and maintained or increased in price even after the original purchasers sold (*i.e.*, no one was left "holding the bag"). [*See* ***In re*** **Institutional Securities of Colorado,** S.E.C. Admin. Proc. File No. 3–5104 (1978)]

D. Regulation of Securities Analysts

1. Introduction

In addition to regulating accountants and lawyers, SOXA regulates securities analysts. The problems that arose during 2001–2002 regarding analysts were independent of the problems regarding financial reporting, but they came at about the same time.

a. The Analysis and Research Scandal

In spring 2001, New York state investigators announced an investigation of securities analysts at several major securities firms. The analysts were allegedly compensated in part by fees generated from investment banking deals with the issuers: the more successful an issuer was in the markets, the more investment banking business the issuer would bring to the securities firm. Analysts, thus, were caught in a conflict of interest—favorable recommendations of an issuer's securities would generate business for the analyst's employer, in turn generating substantial bonuses and salary increases for the analyst. In this way, analysts were transformed from impartial researchers of a company's prospects to promoters of the company's stock. After the market bubble burst in 2000, analysts continued to issue optimistic forecasts for securities whose prices were plunging, prompting an investigation by the Attorney General of New York that was ultimately joined by federal regulators. Among other things, the investigators made public certain emails among analysts and other brokerage employees in which the analysts spoke derisively of securities they were simultaneously recommending to public investors. The ensuing scandal severely eroded investor confidence in the markets, and ultimately led to a settlement between regulators and the securities firms totaling approximately $1 billion.

2. Analysts and Regulation AC

Reacting to the analyst scandal, SOXA includes provisions addressing analyst conflicts of interest. Section 501 of SOXA requires either the S.E.C. or the SROs to adopt rules regulating securities analysts and research reports. In spring 2003, the S.E.C. adopted Regulation AC ("Analyst Certification"), pursuant to SOXA and the antifraud provisions of the 1933 and 1934 Acts. [Regulation AC, 17 C.F.R. § 242.500 *et seq.*] Among other things, Regulation AC requires:

a. Certification in Written Statements

Written research reports must include:

(i) A certification that all of the views expressed in the research report *accurately reflect the analyst's personal views* about any and all of the subject securities or issuers; and

(ii) A statement attesting that the *analyst's compensation is not related to the specific recommendations or views expressed* in the research report, or, if that is not the case, *accurate disclosure of the source, amount, and purpose of such compensation*, and that the compensation could influence the recommendations or views expressed in the research report.

[Regulation AC, Rule 501]

b. Certification Regarding Public Appearances

In addition to providing written research, analysts also often appear publicly to speak about their views of particular securities and issuers. In some respects, public appearances are even more fraught with danger than written reports; it is possible that investors would respond even more rapidly to a public appearance, for example on television, than to a written report. Accordingly, Regulation AC *prohibits outright any analyst compensation based on the views the analyst expresses in a public appearance.* Under Regulation AC, analysts must certify once each calendar quarter that:

(i) The views expressed by the analyst in all public appearances during the quarter accurately reflected the analyst's personal views at that time about any and all of the subject securities or issuers; and

(ii) That no part of the research analyst's compensation was, is, or will be, directly or indirectly, related to the specific recommendations or views expressed by the research analyst in the public appearances.

[Regulation AC, Rule 502]

E. Regulation of Broker-Dealers

1. Registration of Broker-Dealers with the S.E.C.

The 1934 Act provides for registration with the S.E.C. of all broker-dealers who engage in securities transactions in interstate commerce (unless they deal exclusively in exempt securities).

a. Definition of Broker and Dealer

Section 3 of the 1934 Act defines "broker" and "dealer."

(1) *A broker* is a person engaged "in the business of" effecting transactions in securities for the account of others. [SEA § 3(a)(4)]

(2) *A dealer* is a person engaged "in the business of" buying and selling securities for his own account, but does not include such persons when they are not doing so as part of "a regular business." [SEA § 3(a)(5)]

(3) *What is a "regular business"* is a fact question, but the buying and selling would have to be fairly regular to qualify. Thus, a single, isolated transaction does not qualify. [**De Bruin v. Andromeda Broadcasting Systems Inc.**, 465 F. Supp. 1276 (D. Nev.1979)]

b. A "Security" Must Be Sold

For the provisions of the 1934 Act relating to brokers and dealers to apply, a "security," as defined in the 1934 Act, must be involved. The definition in the 1934 Act is only slightly different from that of the 1933 Act. [*See* SEA § 3(a)(10)].

c. Requirement of Registration

Section 15(a) of the 1934 Act forbids a broker or dealer who does any interstate business to use the mails or any means or instrumentality of interstate commerce to effect any transaction in, or to induce or attempt to induce the purchase or sale of, securities (other than securities exempted under the 1934 Act), unless the broker or dealer is registered with the S.E.C. under Section 15(a) of the Act.

d. Regulation by the S.E.C.

Under Section 15(b) of the 1934 Act, the S.E.C. has established qualification standards for registration of all brokers and dealers and any persons associated with them. Registration subjects the registrant to certain standards of operational capability, training, experience, and competence. It also subjects the broker-dealer to the requirement of passing certain examinations relating to the securities business and to maintaining certain financial stability standards. Registered broker-dealers must also file periodic reports with the S.E.C. Finally, the S.E.C. may, on notice and after a hearing, censure, suspend, or revoke the registration of any broker or dealer for statutory violations.

2. Sources of Authority to Regulate

Besides direct regulation by the S.E.C., broker-dealers may also be subject to indirect regulation through the regulation of organizations of which the broker-dealers are members.

a. Self-Regulation

The 1934 Act provides for the self-regulation of registered broker-dealers through a registered national securities association, FINRA, subject to supervision and review by the S.E.C. [SEA § 15(a)]

b. Regulation by National Stock Exchanges

The 1934 Act requires national securities exchanges to regulate their members, and the S.E.C. exercises supervisory power over such regulation.

c. Regulation of Investment Advisers

An "investment adviser" is one who engages in the business of advising others whether to invest in, purchase, or sell securities. While investment advisers do not perform the same functions as broker-dealers, they do occupy an important position in the securities business where they are trusted by, and able to take advantage of, those purchasing and selling securities. For this reason, the S.E.C. regulates the activities of such advisers pursuant to the Investment Advisers Act of 1940.

3. Regulation Under General Antifraud Provisions

Section 17(a) of the 1933 Act, 1934 Act Rule 10b–5, and 1934 Act Rule 15c1–2 all prohibit fraud by broker-dealers in the purchase and sale of securities.

4. Regulation "Best Interest"

In 2019, the S.E.C. adopted a new Regulation Best Interest ("Regulation BI") to enhance the obligations that apply when a broker-dealer makes recommendations to retail customers and to reduce the potential for harm to such customers from conflicts of interest. [Reg. BI, 17 C.F.R. § 240.15*l*–1] These new rules are summarized below:

a. Obligations When Making a Recommendation

Prior to the adoption of Regulation BI, broker-dealers were subject to a mere "suitability" standard when making recommendations to investors. The S.E.C. considered imposing a fiduciary duty standard (identical to the duties owed to clients by investment advisors), but the S.E.C. rejected that in favor of a new "best interest" standard that draws from the duties owed by investment advisors.

In short, a broker-dealer, when making a recommendation to a retail investor, must exercise reasonable diligence, care, and skill to do the following:

(1) based on an understanding of the potential risks, rewards, and costs associated with the recommendation, have a reasonable basis to believe that the recommendation could be in the best interest of at least some retail customers;

(2) have a reasonable basis to believe that the recommendation is in the best interest of a particular retail customer based on that retail customer's investment profile and the potential risks, rewards, and costs associated with the recommendation;

(3) not place the financial or other interest of the broker-dealer ahead of the interest of the retail customer;

(4) have a reasonable basis to believe that a series of recommended transactions, even if in the retail customer's best interest when viewed in isolation, is not excessive and is in the retail customer's best interest when taken together in light of the retail customer's investment profile; and

(5) not place the financial or other interest of the broker-dealer making a series of recommendations ahead of the interest of the retail customer.

[17 C.F.R. § 240.15*l*–1(a)(ii)]

b. Conflict of Interest Prevention

In addition, in order to prevent conflicts of interest when broker-dealers make recommendations to retail customers, Reg. BI requires broker-dealers to establish, maintain, and enforce written policies and procedures reasonably designed to do the following:

(1) identify and either disclose or eliminate all conflicts of interest associated with a recommendation;

(2) identify and mitigate any conflicts of interest that create an incentive for a natural person associated with a broker-dealer to place the interest of the broker-dealer or the associated person ahead of the interest of the retail customer;

(3) identify and disclose any material limitations placed on the securities or investment strategies involving securities that may be recommended to a retail customer and any conflicts of interest associated with such limitations;

(4) prevent such limitations and associated conflicts of interest from causing the broker-dealer or natural person associated with the broker-dealer to make recommendations that place the interest of the broker-dealer or associated person ahead of the interest of the retail customer; and

(5) Identify and eliminate *any sales contests, sales quotas, bonuses, and non-cash compensation* that are based on the sales of specific securities or specific types of securities within a limited period of time.

[17 C.F.R. § 240.15*l*–1(a)(iii)]

5. Civil Liability for Violations of FINRA, Stock Exchange, or S.E.C. Rules

There have been a number of instances where a plaintiff has brought a cause of action against a defendant broker-dealer for the defendant's violation of a FINRA, national stock exchange, or S.E.C. rule. The recent trend of court opinions, however, has been to limit sharply the implication of private remedies under various sections of the securities laws, as well as pursuant to FINRA or stock exchange rules.

Chapter Five

Application of Federal Securities Laws to Multinational Transactions

CONTENTS	PAGE

Key Exam Issues 204

A. Registration Under the 1933 Act 204

B. Application of the 1934 Act 206

Key Exam Issues

Many securities transactions involve investors and firms in foreign countries as well as in the United States. Questions may arise about (1) whether a United States law applies to extraterritorial conduct; (2) whether United States courts have subject matter jurisdiction to hear cases involving extraterritorial conduct (subject matter jurisdiction); and (3) whether United States courts obtain personal jurisdiction over the parties involved in the transaction. The first two questions are discussed in this chapter. See the Conflict of Laws Summary for discussion of personal jurisdiction over foreign defendants.

A. Registration Under the 1933 Act

1. Introduction

The 1933 Act confers jurisdiction over multinational transactions whenever United States facilities of interstate commerce are used to effect a securities transaction. The 1933 Act defines "interstate commerce" to include commerce between any foreign country and the United States. [SA § 2(a)(7)]

2. Territoriality as Basis for Application of 1933 Act

The registration requirements of the 1933 Act are limited by geography: offerings taking place within the United States must comply with the 1933 Act, regardless of the nationality of the issuer. Offerings outside the United States need not be registered under the 1933 Act, again irrespective of the issuer's nationality.

a. Offshore Offerings

The above leaves open the question whether a particular offering in fact is outside the United States. It is easy to imagine an offering in which all the initial buyers are located overseas, but those buyers promptly resell to United States persons. To clarify some of the questions relating to offshore offerings, the S.E.C. adopted Regulation S in 1990.

(1) Regulation S

Regulation S was intended in part to clarify that the registration requirements of the 1933 Act do not apply to offers and sales made outside the United States.

(2) Rule 144A and Resale of Regulation S Securities

Simultaneously with the adoption of Regulation S, the S.E.C. adopted Rule 144A. In conjunction with Regulation S, Rule 144A makes it possible for a foreign issuer in two steps to effect a distribution to "qualified institutional buyers" (defined *supra*) in the United States. In the first step, the foreign issuer sells its securities abroad. In the second step, the overseas buyers resell under Rule 144A to "qualified institutional buyers" in the United States.

b. United States Offerings

With what regulations must a foreign issuer comply to conduct a registered offering in the United States? At one time, the United States capital markets were seen as so desirable that the S.E.C. did not concern itself much with the convenience of foreign issuers. However, the increasingly competitive nature of the global economy makes it essential that the United States accommodate foreign capital to the extent that this is consistent with the protection of United States investors. This is gradually being accomplished by efforts to streamline and harmonize domestic regulation with regulation in other countries.

(1) Registration Forms

There are two principal kinds of foreign issuers: sovereign issuers (*i.e.*, foreign governments) and private issuers (foreign corporations and other business entities).

(a) Foreign Sovereign Issuers

Schedule B to the 1933 Act specifies the information required to be included in a 1933 Act registration statement by a foreign sovereign. Note that the S.E.C. has never adopted a form for use by foreign sovereign issuers.

(b) Foreign Private Issuers

The S.E.C. has adopted Forms F-1, F-2, F-3, and F-4 for foreign private issuers. These forms are intended to parallel those used by American domestic issuers, and in most cases are comparable to Forms S-1, S-2, S-3, and S-4 used by domestic issuers.

(2) Financial Disclosure by Foreign Issuers

Probably the most difficult hurdle that a foreign issuer needs to clear before conducting an offering in the United States is the requirement that its financial statements be reconciled to United States generally accepted accounting practices ("GAAP") and the S.E.C's Regulation S–X. Often, foreign accounting practices vary substantially from those prevalent in the United States, and reconciliation is a lengthy (and expensive) task. To mitigate the burden somewhat, the S.E.C. recognizes two methods of reconciliation:

(a) Full Reconciliation

Full reconciliation requires that essentially all data (including geographic and industry segment data) be reconciled to GAAP and Regulation S–X. Although full reconciliation is not required for periodic reports under the 1934 Act, it is required for 1933 Act registration statements.

(b) Measurement Item Reconciliation

In cases where full reconciliation is not required, the S.E.C. accepts reconciliation of measurement items only—*i.e.*, of income statement and balance sheet data. While this is considerably less burdensome than full reconciliation, it nevertheless entails significant expense and potential delay.

3. American Depositary Receipts ("ADRs")

One technique has been used since the 1920s to attempt to avoid extensive regulation under the 1933 Act. Under this approach, an American bank purchases (in exempt secondary-market transactions) shares of foreign issuers. The shares are held in a trust or other custodial arrangement by the bank, which then issues receipts evidencing beneficial ownership of a stated number of shares. ADRs are popular with investors—in 1990 the dollar volume of ADRs traded, $125 billion, was almost 70 times what it had been only seven years earlier.

a. Regulation of ADRs

ADRs are, technically, securities issued by the depositary bank. Consequently, the bank must register the securities under the 1933 Act. Compliance with the 1934 Act, however, is the responsibility of the foreign issuer. If the ADRs are neither listed on a stock exchange nor traded in Nasdaq, filing of 1934 Act reports may be excused under Rule 12g3–2. If the ADRs are listed on a stock exchange, the issuer must report under the 1934 Act (usually on Form 20-F).

4. Multi-Jurisdictional Disclosure

The S.E.C. has proposed a number of possibilities for multi-jurisdictional disclosure, *i.e.*, a system of registration and disclosure that would satisfy the regulatory requirements of two or more nations at the same time. To date, however, only Canada and the United States have agreed to a system of multi-jurisdictional disclosure. [*See* SA Release No. 33–6902 (1991)]

B. Application of the 1934 Act

1. Introduction

Like the 1933 Act, the 1934 Act defines "interstate commerce" to include commerce between any foreign country and the United States. [*See* SEA § 3(a)(17)]

2. Regulation Under the 1934 Act

The registration requirements of the 1934 Act [SEA § 12(b), (g)] do not distinguish between foreign and domestic registrants. On its face, therefore, the Act seems to require registration and periodic reporting if a foreign issuer has securities listed on a United States exchange [SEA § 12(b)] or has at least 500 shareholders and more than $10 million in assets [SEA § 12(g)].

a. Exemption

Under Rule 12g3–2(b), however, all such foreign issuers are exempt from registration *if* they file with the S.E.C. all information that they make public abroad (*e.g.*, stock exchange reports, filings required by the laws of their domicile, voluntary statements released to shareholders, etc.) and if their securities are not on any United States exchange. [SEA Rule 12g3–2(b)]

b. Foreign Corrupt Practices Act

Finally, if a foreign issuer registers a class of securities under the 1934 Act, the issuer becomes subject to the Foreign Corrupt Practices Act ("FCPA"). [SEA § 30A *et seq.*]The FCPA imposes criminal penalties for certain corrupt practices (bribery of government officials and the like) and also requires the issuer to keep accurate and fair books and records and to devise a system of internal accounting controls to ensure that such payments are not being concealed.

3. International Securities Fraud

The preceding section focused on regulation of foreign entities and their securities transactions. Other international issues arising under the securities laws involve misconduct and the extent to which United States authorities can pursue (or prosecute) those responsible. The Supreme Court significantly limited the reach of Rule 10b–5 in **Morrison v. Nat'l Australia Bank Ltd.**, 561 U.S. 247 (2010).

a. Holding in *Morrison*

In *Morrison*, the Supreme Court considered the extraterritorial reach of Rule 10b–5. The Court started with the presumption that Congress intends to regulate domestically and then considered whether that presumption was overcome with respect to Rule 10b–5. In short, the Court answered "no." The Court held that SEA Section 10(b) and Rule 10b–5 prohibit securities fraud "only in connection with the purchase or sale of a security listed on an American stock exchange, and the purchase or sale of any other security in the United States." [**Morrison**, *supra*]

b. Dodd-Frank Provision in Response to *Morrison*

In 2010, shortly after *Morrison* was decided, Congress enacted the Dodd-Frank Wall Street Reform and Consumer Protection Act, which amended the jurisdictional provision in the 1934 Act to state as follows:

> The district courts of the United States and the United States courts of any Territory shall have jurisdiction of an action or proceeding brought or instituted by the Commission or the United States alleging a violation of the antifraud provisions of the title involving—
>
> (1) conduct within the United States that constitutes significant steps in furtherance of the violation, even if the securities transaction occurs outside the United States and involves only foreign investors; or
>
> (2) conduct occurring outside the United States that has a foreseeable substantial effect within the United States.

[SEA § 27(b)]

c. Impact of Dodd-Frank

It is an open question whether Dodd-Frank overruled *Morrison* so as to enable the S.E.C. to enforce securities fraud extraterritorially. *Morrison* was based on an interpretation of the conduct prohibited by Section 10(b) and Rule 10b–5, not on the 1934 Act's jurisdictional provision. However, the Tenth Circuit has held that Congress "affirmatively and unmistakably" overruled *Morrison* to apply the antifraud provisions of the federal securities acts extraterritorially when the statutory conduct-and-effects test is met. [**S.E.C. v. Scoville**, 913 F.3d 1204 (10th Cir. 2019), *cert. denied*, 140 S.Ct. 483 (2019)]

Note: even if Dodd-Frank overruled *Morrison* to allow the S.E.C. and the D.O.J. to pursue securities fraud extraterritorially (as the Tenth Circuit held in *Scoville*), Dodd-Frank did *not* overrule *Morrison* for private civil plaintiffs.

Chapter Six

Regulation of Securities Transactions by the States

CONTENTS PAGE

Key Exam Issues 210

A. Uniform Securities Act 210

B. Preemption of State Securities Laws 210

C. Secondary Distribution of Securities 212

Key Exam Issues

This chapter summarizes the state laws regulating securities and explains how federal and state securities laws interface. For more than 60 years, the Securities Act and the Securities Exchange Act preserved the power to the states to regulate securities. Every state had adopted some form of securities regulation, requiring issuers and other parties to comply not only with federal law, but also with the laws of the various states that might have contact with the transaction. All this changed in 1996, with the adoption of the National Securities Markets Improvement Act of 1996 ("NSMIA"). This chapter will give you a very brief overview of the Uniform Securities Act, which is the model for many states' securities laws, and then discuss how federal laws have severely restricted state regulation of securities.

A. Uniform Securities Act

1. Structure of Act

The Commissioners on Uniform State Laws have adopted the Uniform Securities Act, divided into sections addressing (i) fraud in general, (ii) broker-dealer registration, (iii) registration of new securities offerings, and (iv) remedies. Of these, (ii) and (iii) have been largely preempted by NSMIA, and (i) has been partially preempted by the Securities Litigation Uniform Standards Act of 1998 ("SLUSA"), discussed below.

2. Adoptions by the States

In drafting their own securities laws, most of the states have adopted some part of the Uniform Securities Act, have used some of the concepts found in the federal acts, and have added some provisions of their own choosing. In cases not preempted by federal law, nearly all the states regulate both the original distribution of securities and their subsequent trading (including the registration of broker-dealers).

B. Preemption of State Securities Laws

1. Introduction

NSMIA (codified in SA Section 18) effectively preempts most state securities laws (so-called "blue sky laws"), although the states had voluntarily ceded a good deal of power to the federal government before Section 18 was enacted by adopting broad exemptions from state regulation for many distributions. In addition, SLUSA precludes state-law securities fraud class actions. Both Acts are discussed below.

2. Structure of NSMIA

Section 18 describes four broad classes of securities ("covered securities") and prohibits the states from requiring registration or qualification of any covered security. In addition, the states are prohibited from imposing any conditions on the use of offering documents prepared by the issuer, or on disclosure documents that must be filed with the S.E.C. relating to a covered security or to the issuer of a covered security. [SA § 18]

3. Four Classes of Covered Securities

Section 18 exempts from blue sky regulation four classes of security:

a. Securities of Issuers Registered Under the Investment Company Act of 1940

Any investment company registered with the S.E.C. under the 1940 Act may issue securities free of blue sky regulation.

b. Listed Securities

Even before NSMIA, most states had already exempted from state registration securities listed or approved for listing on national securities exchanges, under the so-called blue chip or marketplace exemptions. Section 18 makes this common state exemption a federal requirement.

c. Offers or Sales to "Qualified Purchasers"

This exemption remains to be fleshed out by the S.E.C. Note that offers and sales to sophisticated institutions, such as "qualified institutional buyers" ("QIBs") under Rule 144A were already exempt under the laws of most states.

d. Certain Offers and Sales Exempt Under the 1933 Act

Section 18 also preempts state regulation of:

(1) Transactions exempt under Securities Act Section 4(a)(1) (transactions by any person other than an issuer, underwriter, or dealer) in securities of an issuer that is a 1934 Act reporting company;

(2) Transactions exempt under Securities Act Section 4(a)(4) (brokers' transactions);

(3) Transactions in securities exempt under Securities Act Section 3(a), *except:*

  (a) Securities of religious or charitable organizations;

  (b) Securities issued in intrastate offerings; and

  (c) Municipal securities offered in the state of their issue;

(4) Private placements made pursuant to rules adopted under Securities Act Section 4(a)(2) (Rules 506(b) and 506(c) of Regulation D); and

(5) Crowdfunded offerings under Regulation CF.

4. Left to the States

Clearly, SA Section 18 removes a substantial amount of authority from state securities regulators. However, the states still have authority to:

a. Regulate penny stocks (which are a significant source of securities fraud litigation);

b. Regulate many small, intrastate, and other offerings exempt from federal regulation under the 1933 Act;

c. Bring actions against brokers for fraud and other illegal conduct relating to securities and securities transactions; and

d. Require notice filings (*i.e.*, notifications of the sale of securities within the state) and the payment of fees to the state for such notice filings.

5. SLUSA Precludes State-Law Class Actions

An unintended result of the class action reforms adopted in the Private Securities Litigation Reform Act of 1995 (the "PSLRA") was the migration of securities fraud class actions to the state courts, perhaps to avoid the new, more onerous requirements of the federal securities laws. In response, Congress passed SLUSA, which precludes class actions (and similar consolidated proceedings) based on state law if the action alleges misrepresentation or omission of a material fact, or the use of a manipulative or deceptive device or contrivance, in connection with the purchase or sale of a security. In effect, state "blue sky" fraud litigation is precluded if it is a class action or involves *consolidated actions of more than 50 plaintiffs.* [*See* SA § 16(b); SEA § 28(f)]

a. Individual Lawsuits Not Precluded

Individuals may still sue under state law for securities fraud, but if more than 50 persons sue and the actions are consolidated, the resulting litigation will be precluded.

b. Derivative Actions Not Preempted

SLUSA does not preclude derivative actions brought by shareholders in the name of the corporation (see Corporations Summary), or certain other claims based on breach of fiduciary duty by a corporation's management.

c. SLUSA Applies Only to "Covered Securities"

SLUSA applies only to lawsuits alleging fraud with respect to a "covered security," as defined in Securities Act Section 18(b). (See above)

C. Secondary Distribution of Securities

1. General Fraud Provisions

Many states have statutory provisions that regulate the trading of securities subsequent to their original distribution, as does the Securities Exchange Act of 1934. Nearly every state has some general provision against fraud, and a few states have provisions similar to Rule 10b–5 of the 1934 Act. However, class actions under such provisions are precluded by SLUSA.

2. Registration of Broker-Dealers

Many states also have provisions requiring the qualification and registration of persons involved in the securities business as broker-dealers. [Uniform Securities Act § 204] Such laws have for the most part been preempted by NSMIA.

Review Questions and Answers

Review Questions

FILL IN ANSWER

1. Megacorp has issued 100,000 shares of common stock. This stock is listed for trading on the New York Stock Exchange. Megacorp's articles of incorporation authorize 200,000 shares, and so Megacorp now wishes to issue an additional 50,000 shares in a public offering. Will the 50,000 new shares be offered in the primary market? ____________

2. Abbey buys and sells securities for her customers on a commission basis. Would Abbey generally be designated as a "dealer" under the securities acts? ____________

3. The two basic purposes of the Securities Act of 1933 are (i) to ensure disclosure of material facts concerning issuers in new offerings and (ii) to prevent fraud and misrepresentation in the interstate sale of securities. True or false? ____________

4. Megacorp offers a $15 million issue of debt securities to the public. Does Megacorp have to comply with both the Securities Act of 1933 and the Trust Indenture Act of 1939? ____________

5. Microcorp has $3 million in assets and 496 non-accredited stockholders who own its common stock. (These investors did not acquire the stock pursuant to Regulation CF.) Its stock is traded on the New York Stock Exchange. Must Microcorp regularly file Forms 10-K and 10-Q with the S.E.C.? ____________

6. Nucorp sells a new issue of its securities to the public without registration under the 1933 Act. Nucorp does not use the facilities of interstate commerce to make the offering. Does the 1933 Act nevertheless apply to this transaction? ____________

7. In a "firm commitment" underwriting, does the issuer directly sell its own securities to the public? ____________

8. Xavier owns 2,500 of the 100,000 shares of Megacorp. He is not an issuer, underwriter, or dealer, as those terms are defined in the 1933 Act, and he holds no position with Megacorp. Xavier purchased the shares over the New York Stock Exchange. When Xavier goes to sell these shares to the public, must Xavier register them under the 1933 Act? ____________

9. Issuer Corp. has decided to conduct an initial public offering of its common stock. When the offering is complete, Issuer will have approximately 3,000 stockholders and assets worth $30 million. When issued, the common stock is expected to trade on the Nasdaq. The issue price will be in the

neighborhood of $10 per share. Issuer has contacted Underwriter Bros., a securities underwriting firm, to underwrite the offering on a "firm commitment" basis. Using the telephone, fax machines, and email, Issuer and Underwriter negotiate over the terms of a letter of intent describing the proposed transaction and the role that each of the parties will play. Has either Issuer or Underwriter violated Section 5 of the 1933 Act? ____________

10. Issuer and Underwriter in question 9, above, execute a letter of intent. Does the letter violate Section 5 of the 1933 Act? ____________

11. Issuer from question 9, above, publishes an ad in the local newspaper, stating that Issuer plans a public offering of one million shares at $10 per share and that Underwriter will serve as underwriter. Has Issuer violated Section 5? ____________

12. Issuer calls several rich individuals on the telephone and invites them to participate in the Issuer offering under the facts in question 9. Has Issuer violated Section 5? ____________

13. Assume that Issuer from question 9, above, rather than planning its initial public offering ("IPO"), instead is planning another offering, to take place six months after its IPO. Issuer publishes an ad in the local newspaper, stating that Issuer plans a public offering of one million shares at $10 per share and that Underwriter will serve as underwriter. Has Issuer violated Section 5? ____________

14. Assume that the issuer from question 9 completed its IPO 16 months ago and is eligible to use Form S-3 for the proposed offering. Issuer publishes an ad in the local newspaper, stating that Issuer plans a public offering of one million shares at $10 per share and that Underwriter will serve as underwriter. Has Issuer violated Section 5? ____________

15. Assume that Issuer from question 9 completed its IPO 20 years ago and, in the interim, has conducted numerous additional public offerings of its stock. Today, Issuer has outstanding over $1 billion in common stock, nearly all of it held by persons unaffiliated with Issuer, and meets all the requirements to use Form S-3 for the proposed offering. Issuer publishes an ad in the local newspaper, stating that Issuer plans a public offering of one million shares at $10 per share and that Underwriter will serve as underwriter. Has Issuer violated Section 5? ____________

16. Under Section 5 of the 1933 Act, may actual sales to investors be made during the waiting period (after filing but before the registration statement has become effective)? ____________

17. Assume that Issuer (in questions 9–15, above) has filed the registration statement for its IPO, but the registration statement has not yet been declared effective by the S.E.C. Issuer's CEO takes a potential investor out to lunch and asks whether the investor would like to participate in the offering. Has Issuer violated Section 5? ____________

18. Underwriter (from the facts above) emails copies of a preliminary prospectus for Issuer's IPO to dealers throughout the United States. In some cases, the emails have attachments that contain the prospectus; in others, the emails contain a link to a page on Underwriter's website where the Issuer prospectus can be viewed. In many cases the emails include an invitation to the recipient to reply with an indication of whether the dealer might be interested in participating in Issuer's IPO after the registration statement is declared effective. Do the emails violate Section 5? ____________

19. Dealer (from the facts above), having indicated it will participate in the Issuer IPO and that it will purchase 10,000 shares of Issuer stock, telephones Customer and offers to sell 1,000 shares of Issuer's stock at the public offering price. Customer accepts. Does this violate Section 5? ____________

20. Assume (under the facts above) that Issuer, instead of filing the registration statement for its IPO, has filed the registration statement for another offering to take place six months after its IPO. Dealer Corp., a securities dealer, intends to accept an invitation from Underwriter to participate as a retail dealer in the Issuer offering. Dealer lists Issuer's industry in its monthly report on "growth industries investors should watch." Has Dealer violated Section 5? ____________

21. Assume (under the facts above) that the registration statement for Issuer's IPO has been declared effective. Dealer calls another of its customers and offers the customer 1,000 shares of Issuer stock from its unsold allotment, and the customer accepts. Does this violate Section 5? ____________

22. After the events described in question 21, above, Dealer emails a confirmation of sale to the customer. Nothing else is mentioned in the email. Does this violate Section 5? ____________

23. One week after mailing the confirmation of sale in question 22, above, Dealer delivers to the customer the stock certificates for the Issuer stock. Nothing else is included in the envelope. Does this violate Section 5? ____________

24. Issuer has filed a registration statement, but it is not yet effective. Issuer's CEO meets in-person with a number of rich individual investors to discuss the offering. She accompanies her oral remarks with a PowerPoint slideshow, but she does not make that slideshow available to the investors in electronic or written form. Issuer does not file the slideshow with the SEC. Has Issuer violated the 1933 Act? ____________

25. Muriel purchases 100,000 shares of Siebco's common stock from Siebco, with the intent of reselling these shares immediately to the public. Is Muriel an underwriter? ____________

26. Alfred has a position on the board of directors of Batcorp and owns 25% of its outstanding common stock. Alfred originally formed the corporation, although he no longer is an officer or active in its day-to-day management. Alfred proposes to sell his 25% interest to the public through a brokerage firm. The stock is traded over the New York Stock Exchange. Must Alfred register his stock under the 1933 Act? ____________

27. Would a subdivision of lots, where most purchasers are buying the lots for speculation, later to resell them for a profit, be an offering of a "security" under the 1933 Act? __________

28. Astrid purchased a large section of land, then subdivided it into very small parcels and leased it to many investors. The leases included an obligation by Astrid to drill test wells for oil. Is it likely that a court would find that Astrid had marketed a "security" to the lessees? __________

29. Are general partnership interests usually securities under the 1933 Act? __________

30. What is the general registration form to be used by commercial and industrial companies in registration under the 1933 Act where another form does not specifically apply? __________

31. Must the following facts about Regco be disclosed in its registration statements under the 1933 Act?

    a. The recent earnings history of the company (its net profits). __________

    b. A five-year projection of its net earnings made by the company's vice president of finance. __________

    c. The fact that, if there is a drought in the Western United States, Regco's supply chain will be significantly disrupted. __________

32. If the S.E.C. makes a registration statement effective, the S.E.C. guarantees the accuracy of the facts represented in the registration statement or the prospectus. True or false? __________

33. Does an amendment filed by the issuer to a registration statement under the 1933 Act normally start the 20-day waiting period for effectiveness running again? __________

34. Shelfco wishes to register all of the securities it will issue in the future at one time, in order to avoid the expense of drafting and filing multiple registration statements under the 1933 Act. Is it true that such a registration procedure will probably not be permitted by the S.E.C.? __________

35. Ishco issues its stock to the public through a registration statement and prospectus under the 1933 Act. A free writing prospectus, which was distributed to investors during the waiting period, contained a material misrepresentation. May Alex, an investor in the Ishco securities, bring an action under Section 11 for this misrepresentation? __________

36. If a security is exempt from registration under the 1933 Act, it may be sold and resold and never have to be registered, even if resold by a control person. True or false? __________

37. There are no hard and fast rules for determining whether an issuance of securities is a private offering. True or false? __________

38. One of the tests the S.E.C. uses for determining whether a security is being offered to the "public" is whether the purchasers thereof need the protection of the 1933 Act. True or false? __________

39. Privco contemplates a private offering of its securities under Section 4(a)(2). It offers and ultimately sells its securities to 11 people. Is the offering certain to be a private offering? __________

40. Privco makes an offering of its common stock on January 1 under Rule 506(c) and a second offering on January 20 under Rule 506(b). Are these offerings in danger of losing their exempt status? __________

41. Blue Corp. issues 100,000 shares of its common stock pursuant to Rule 147. Warren buys 50,000 of these and holds them for two years. He then wishes to resell his shares in a public distribution. Because he has met his investment intent pursuant to the rule, although he is a control person, may he sell without registration under the Act? __________

42. Sameco makes an intrastate offering pursuant to Rule 147. All purchasers are residents of the same state as Sameco, but one of the offerees is not. Is the exemption therefore lost? __________

43. Sameco makes an intrastate offering pursuant to Rule 147A. All purchasers are residents of the same state as Sameco, but one of the offerees is not. Is the exemption therefore lost? __________

44. Issuer wants to raise an unlimited amount of funds by selling securities nationwide, using general solicitation and advertising, without satisfying state registration requirements. What is the best exemption for Issuer to use, and are there additional requirements in order for Issuer to satisfy that exemption? __________

45. XYZ Corp. sells to A, B, and C in a private offering. A and B (although representing that they are taking for investment) violate their representations and A sells to D through G, and B sells to H through L. Are A and B underwriters under the 1933 Act if the total offering amounts to a public offering? __________

46. Stern issues stock to Abbey in a private offering. Abbey is a control person who establishes her investment intent with respect to the offering. Abbey then sells all of her control stock through a broker over the stock exchange, without registration, to many purchasers. Has Abbey violated the 1933 Act by making a public distribution without registration? __________

47. Smith is the owner of 25% of the common stock of Corporation, which is not a reporting company, and sits on its board. None of the stock that Smith owns is restricted stock. Smith has held the stock for six months and now desires to sell it. May Smith use Rule 144? __________

48. Ronen Corp. has registered a public offering of its stock. Alex buys some stock and resells to Becky within a two-month period of the offering. There

are material misrepresentations in the registration statement. Becky does not read the registration statement and knows nothing of the misrepresentations. However, when the misrepresentations are made public, Ronen stock goes down. Becky discovers the fraud and sues Ronen. Can Becky recover under Section 11 of the 1933 Act? ______________

49. Seiko sells stock to the public pursuant to a registration statement. The offering price is $10 per share. An hour after the offering begins, all of the stock has been sold for the first time, and the stock is trading at $15 per share. Matsuo buys 100 shares at $15. There is a material misstatement in the prospectus. A month later, when the stock has fallen to $10 per share, Matsuo sells. Thereafter, Matsuo discovers the misrepresentation and sues Sellco. Under SA Section 11, what amount per share can Matsuo recover? ______________

50. Ginsu Corp. sells stock directly to the public in a public distribution without registration. Penelope is one of the purchasers. Ginsu has never heard of Section 5 of the 1933 Act; neither has Penelope. Penelope becomes disenchanted with the stock and sues under Section 12(a)(1) of the Act to rescind the transaction. Will Penelope win? ______________

51. Goldenco recruits an advisory board of influential business and civic leaders to advise the company about new marketing plans and ideas. Goldenco raises money through an intended private offering, which turns out to be a public offering. In the offering memorandum, the name, background, and experience of each member of the advisory board appear, and the memorandum states that offerees may call these people for recommendations about the company. Several offerees do so and receive assurances that the company is sound, as well as invitations to purchase Goldenco securities. The memorandum contains several material misstatements in its financial statements, and, in fact, the company is broke. May the purchasers sue the members of the advisory board under SA Section 12(a)(2)? ______________

52. Fraudco has no securities registered under Section 12 of the 1934 Act and is not subject to 1934 Act periodic reporting. Fraudco engages in a fraudulent securities transaction. May it be sued under Rule 10b–5 of the 1934 Act? ______________

53. For Rule 10b–5 to apply, there must be a sufficient connection between the activity complained of (*i.e.*, a misrepresentation, etc.) and the purchase or sale of securities. True or false? ______________

54. Issuer issues a press release announcing that it has signed a major contract with a new client. Issuer does not disclose that, simultaneously, it has lost a client of the same importance. Is this omission actionable under Rule 10b–5? ______________

55. Rule 10b–5 requires strict privity between plaintiff and defendant. True or false? ______________

56. Delco, which has securities traded on the NYSE and is issuing additional securities, chooses to predict its future earnings for the coming year. The

prediction is inaccurate and carelessly made. Is Delco subject to liability in a private civil suit under Rule 10b–5 on the basis of having misrepresented a material fact? ______________

57. Cleopatra is a long-time shareholder of Nile.com. She claims that her stock has depreciated in value in the market due to a series of misrepresentations made by the management of Nile.com to the public. Cleopatra claims that, had she known the truth, she would have sold her stock rather than holding it. Cleopatra sues Nile.com under Rule 10b–5. Does Cleopatra have standing to bring the suit? ______________

58. In the audit of Ronen Corp., the auditing firm (Artie Anson & Co.) fails to accurately account for the corporation's liabilities from outstanding warranties given on Ronen Corp. products. As a result, Ronen Corp.'s published financial statements are substantially inaccurate. A shareholder who bought Ronen Corp. stock in the market at $100 per share sues when the stock drops to $50 per share after the true facts are published. One of the named defendants in the Rule 10b–5 suit is Artie Anson & Co. At trial it is shown that Artie Anson & Co.'s omission of the material fact was the result of negligence. May the shareholder recover under Rule 10b–5 against Artie Anson & Co.? ______________

59. Ronen Corp. issues a materially false press release concerning its financial condition. Peter buys Ronen Corp. stock over the stock exchange at $10 per share. Later, when Ronen Corp. corrects the press release and discloses its true financial condition, the stock drops to $7 per share. Shortly thereafter, Ronen Corp. announces that merger discussions it has been carrying on with another corporation have terminated, at least for the present time. Peter then sues Ronen Corp. under Rule 10b–5 in an individual suit on the basis of the false press release. At trial, Peter does not prove reliance on the false press release, but simply proves that Ronen Corp.'s financial condition was a material fact. Ronen Corp. proves that, in fact, Peter did not rely on the financial condition of the corporation, but would have bought the stock anyway (because Peter had inside information about the merger discussions, in which a bidder was considering the purchase of Ronen Corp. stock for $25 per share). Is this a valid defense to Peter's lawsuit? ______________

60. Indicate whether the following persons are "insiders" of Bigco, as the term has been defined by the courts, for purposes of insider trading liability under Rule 10b–5:

    a. Controlling shareholder of Bigco who is briefed by the corporation on all major developments. ______________

    b. Directors of Bigco. ______________

    c. Officers of Bigco. ______________

61. If a defendant violates Rule 10b–5 by trading on inside information over an exchange, it is clear that the courts will allow unlimited recovery by all

injured plaintiffs no matter what their total damages, even when the defendant's total profits are substantially less than the plaintiff's damages. True or false? ______________

62. The statute of limitations for Rule 10b–5 actions is two years from the date the untruth or omission is actually discovered by the plaintiff. True or false? ______________

63. Acquireco offers cash to the shareholders of Target Corp. for their common stock in Target Corp. If the common stock of Target Corp. is registered under Section 12 of the 1934 Act, would this be a tender offer for the purposes of Section 14(d) of the 1934 Act? ______________

64. Between February and April of this year, Acquireco acquires more than 5% of the 1934 Act registered common stock of Target Corp. It is Acquireco's intention to attempt to gain control of Target Corp. through a tender offer. Must Acquireco disclose this information to the management of Target Corp.? ______________

65. Acquireco makes a tender offer for the common stock of Target Corp. Target Corp. sends out a letter to its shareholders which misrepresents the financial condition and the experience of Acquireco's management. Does Acquireco have standing in federal court to bring an action for damages against Target Corp. under Section 14(e) of the SEA? ______________

66. In the above question, could Acquireco get an injunction against the mailing of such a letter? ______________

67. For the federal proxy rules to apply, must a company have a class of its equity securities registered under Section 12 of the 1934 Act? ______________

68. Mergeco has a class of its equity securities registered under Section 12 of the SEA of 1934. It schedules its annual meeting of shareholders, where one issue to be voted on is the merger of Mergeco into Consolid Corp. No proxies are solicited. Under the federal proxy rules, must Mergeco file with the S.E.C. and distribute to its shareholders prior to the shareholders' meeting the same information that would have been included in a proxy statement had proxies been solicited? ______________

69. The antifraud provisions of the federal proxy rules do not apply to oral representations made in the course of a proxy solicitation. True or false? ______________

70. Under the antifraud provisions of the federal proxy rules, in cases where proxies are needed to secure affirmative action on a matter proposed to the shareholders, the plaintiff in a private damage action need only show that a misstatement or omission was "material" in order to substantially meet the requirement that the proxy materials be shown to have caused the damage for which the complaint seeks relief. True or false? ______________

71. Tish owns 15% of the common stock of Bankco. The common stock is registered under Section 12 of the 1934 Act. Tish also owns 15% of the

convertible preferred stock of Bankco, which is not registered under Section 12. Tish buys and then sells shares of the convertible preferred stock within six months at a profit. May a shareholder of Bankco Sue Tish in a derivative action for the profit under Section 16(b)? ____________

72. Martha owns 8% of the registered common stock of L-Mart Corp. She buys an additional 4% at $10 per share on March 1. On April 1, she sells 4% at $20 per share. Is Martha liable as an "insider" under Section 16(b) of the 1934 Act for her profit in the sale on April 1? ____________

73. Directors and officers may be held liable under Section 16(b) as "insiders," even though they were not insiders both at the beginning and at the end of the matched purchase and sale (or sale and purchase), as long as they held office at either the time of the purchase or at the time of the sale. True or false? ____________

74. As a general rule, for an insider to be liable under Section 16(b) of the 1934 Act, she must be shown to have actually received and unfairly used "inside" information. True or false? ____________

75. Abbey is a lawyer. She does not represent Macrosoft Corp., but she is a good friend of Macrosoft Corp.'s president, Bill. Macrosoft Corp. is having trouble selling a private offering of its securities. Bill asks if Abbey will help him market the issue, and Abbey agrees. Abbey takes no compensation for her services. Abbey calls several of her clients and suggests that they buy Macrosoft Corp. stock, providing them with a copy of the investment memorandum. They do so. In fact, the Macrosoft Corp. investment memorandum contained material misrepresentations concerning Macrosoft Corp.'s financial position. May the clients of Abbey successfully sue Abbey under Rule 10b–5? ____________

76. McCall is a lawyer representing Nationsco in a registration under the 1933 Act. In conferences with the president of the corporation, it is disclosed to McCall that the backlog of orders which Nationsco has stated that it has is really not as large as indicated. McCall considers this a material misstatement of fact in the draft of the registration statement. He asks the president to correct it, and the president declines, feeling that the sale of the stock issue depends on showing favorable prospects for the future. McCall must report the matter to Nationsco's chief legal officer. True or false? ____________

77. Maria has a short position in the stock of ABC Corp., which is listed on the New York Stock Exchange In order to drive down the price to allow her to cover her short position with a profit, she intentionally spreads a false rumor that ABC Corp. is under S.E.C. investigation, using social media. Is this illegal? ____________

78. Market stabilization is always illegal market manipulation. True or false? ____________

79. Smith Blarney is an underwriting firm selling a new issue of Sellco to the public in a registered offering. It plans to hold back 50,000 of the 500,000

shares being offered in the hopes that demand will lift the stock almost immediately above its $25 per share offering price. Once the price rises above $25, Smith Blarney will begin selling the 50,000 shares for its own account. Are such sales by Smith Blarney unlawful? ____________

80. Sheerson, a broker-dealer, buys 100 shares of Seiko on March 1 for $5 per share and sells the shares to its retail customers the same day for $10 per share. Could this be a violation of FINRA rules? ____________

81. Two foreign nationals met in New York to discuss a potential transaction involving securities of a foreign issuer. The securities are not listed on an American Stock Exchange. They consummated the transaction the following month at a meeting in the U.K. One of the parties has filed suit against the other in federal district court, seeking damages under Rule 10b–5. The party argues that the court has jurisdiction because conduct within the United States constituted significant steps in furtherance of the violation. The other party has filed a motion to dismiss the suit. Should the court grant the motion to dismiss? ____________

82. ABC Inc. conducts an initial public offering. Several investors in the offering bring a suit under 1933 Act Section 11 for alleged misrepresentations in the audited financial statements included in the registration statement. Named as defendants are ABC Inc., Directors who signed the registration statement, and the Auditor who audited the financial statements. Each has asserted the "due diligence" defense. What is the standard that the court will apply when analyzing this defense asserted by:

    a. ABC Inc. ____________

    b. Directors ____________

    c. Auditor ____________

83. The shareholders of XYZ Corp. have filed a class action against XYZ Corp. for violating Rule 10b–5. XYZ Corp. has filed a motion to dismiss the suit? What is one ground for dismissal that XYZ Corp. has almost certainly argued? ____________

84. XYZ Corp. is listed on the New York Stock Exchange. The shareholders of XYZ Corp. have filed a class action in Idaho state court, asserting common law fraud claims against XYZ for allegedly false statements made in an S.E.C. filing. What will XYZ Corp. likely file next? ____________

85. A shareholder of ABC Corp. has submitted a shareholder proposal, requesting an advisory vote of the shareholders on whether ABC Corp. should start using paper straws instead of plastic straws in all of its restaurants. This decision would have a de minimus impact on ABC Corp.'s earnings. Although the shareholder meets the holding requirements to submit the proposal, ABC Corp. wishes to exclude it. Can ABC exclude the proposal from its proxy statement? ____________

86. ABC Corp. wants to use the internet to sell securities to a large number of non-accredited investors, each of whom is investing only a small amount of money. Is there an exemption that would permit this offering? ______________

87. A broker complies with her duties to retail investors by recommending only securities that she believes are "suitable" for them. True or false? ______________

Answers to Review Questions

1.	**YES**	The primary markets are the facilities for the first issuance of securities to the public. [p. 4]
2.	**NO**	The securities acts define the terms "broker" and "dealer" in specific contexts. But, in general (in functional terms), a *broker* is one who buys or sells securities as an agent, for a commission. [p. 6]
3.	**TRUE**	True. [p. 11] Material disclosures are required in the registration statement and prospectus. SA Sections 11, 12(a)(2), and 17 prohibit fraud and misrepresentation in the interstate sale of securities.
4.	**YES**	The 1933 Act applies to offering and sale of all nonexempt securities (including debt securities), and the Trust Indenture Act applies to specified large issues of debt securities. [pp. 13, 45 & 64]
5.	**YES**	The registration provisions of the 1934 Act apply to (i) securities listed on a national securities exchange, and (ii) equity securities that are held by 500 or more shareholders, if the issuer has over $10 million in assets. [p. 108] Issuers with a class of securities registered under the 1934 Act must make periodic reports under that Act, including annual reports on Form 10-K and quarterly reports under Form 10-Q. [p. 108] Here, Microcorp has stock traded on the NYSE, so it is subject to 1934 Act registration and reporting.
6.	**NO**	Interstate commerce must be involved. However, it is *extremely* unlikely that a public offering could be made without using some means of interstate commerce. [p. 23]
7.	**NO**	A firm commitment underwriting is one where the underwriter buys the issuer's securities, marks them up, and sells them to the public. [p. 21]
8.	**NO**	Section 4(a)(1) of the Act indicates that Section 5's registration requirement applies only to transactions involving issuers, underwriters, or dealers. Xavier is none of these. [p. 38] And, because he is not a control person, there is no risk that his buyer might be classified as an underwriter. [pp. 38–41]
9.	**NO**	During the pre-filing period, the 1933 Act allows the issuer and the underwriters to conduct negotiations. Such negotiations are expressly excluded from the definitions of "offer" and "sale." This is true for all categories of issuers, even nonreporting issuers (which is what Issuer currently is).

It also applies to underwriters acting among themselves. [p. 26]

10. **NO** Although the letter may constitute a contract (it is hard to know for sure without carefully analyzing its specific terms), even contracts between issuers and underwriters (or among underwriters) are allowed during the pre-filing period. [p. 26]

11. **YES** Issuer is a nonreporting company, which has the most severe limitations on what it is allowed to do during the pre-filing period. In this case, Issuer is allowed to make certain statements not referring to the proposed offering (*e.g.*, statements made more than 30 days before filing, under Rule 163A, and statements of regularly communicated factual business information, under Rule 169). [pp. 26 & 28] Here, however, Issuer mentioned the offering. Consequently, the statement must be within Rule 135 or it is a violation. Rule 135 does not allow Issuer to name the underwriters; hence, the ad violates Section 5. [p. 28]

12. **YES** The calls are unlawful offers during the pre-filing period. Issuer is not a WKSI, so Rule 163 does not apply. [p. 27] Although certain communications with institutional investors are permitted, rich individuals are not institutional investors. [p. 28]

13. **YES** In this case, Issuer is an unseasoned issuer, rather than a nonreporting issuer, [p. 24] Such issuers are permitted to communicate factual business information, plus forward-looking information, during the pre-filing period. [p. 27] However, the offering must not be mentioned, or Section 5 is violated. Rule 135 still applies, as it did to a nonreporting issuer, but it does not permit naming the underwriter. [p. 28]

14. **YES** In this case, Issuer is a seasoned issuer [p. 24], but the limitations on its activities during the pre-filing period are the same as those that apply to an unseasoned issuer. The ad violates Section 5. [pp. 27 & 28]

15. **PERHAPS NOT** In this case, Issuer is a WKSI (well-known seasoned issuer) [p. 24], and as such Issuer has nearly—but not quite—unrestricted ability to make oral and written offers, even during the pre-filing period. Here, the conditions that the ad would have to meet are: (i) it must be filed with the S.E.C. if and when a registration statement ultimately is filed; and (ii) it must contain the warning legend specified by Rule 163(b)(1). Even if these conditions are not met, however, the offer may not be considered illegal if Issuer can show that it made a good faith and reasonable effort to comply with the conditions. [p. 27]

16. **NO** However, certain *offers* are permissible in this period. [p. 31]

17. **NO** Oral offers (not communicated by radio or television) are permitted during the waiting period. [p. 32].

18. **NO** Emails, websites, and the like are all within the definition of "graphic communications" and are regulated the same as other written materials. Widespread distribution of the preliminary prospectus is not only allowed, it is *required* in order to obtain acceleration of the effective date of a registration statement. [p. 35] That leaves the other statements in the emails. These, too, are treated as writings. In this case, such writings would qualify as free writing prospectuses, and as long as they contain the appropriate statements and copies are filed with the S.E.C., free writing prospectuses are legal. [p. 33]

19. **YES** The problem here is that sales are not allowed until the registration statement is effective. Although no sale has been consummated here, on the facts the parties have formed an executory contract of sale, and under the 1933 Act that is defined as a sale. [p. 35]

20. **NO** In general, participating dealers may publish reports on the industries of issuers that are 1934 Act reporting companies, provided the issuers are current in their reporting obligations. [p. 30]

21. **NO** The executory contract of sale created between Dealer and the customer amounts to a sale under the 1933 Act, but offers and sales are permitted in the post-effective period. [p. 36] The Dealer is required, however, to deliver (or provide access to) a prospectus or notice of registration statement. [p. 37]

22. **NO** A confirmation of sale may be sent to the customer as long as the requirements of Rule 172 are met, which means essentially that a registration statement has been declared effective, a final prospectus has been filed with the S.E.C., and no S.E.C. stop orders or examinations are pending regarding the offering or the participants in the offering. [p. 37]

23. **NO** As with confirmations, Dealer does not need to deliver a prospectus as long as the requirements of Rule 172 are met. [p. 37]

24. **NO** Oral offers are permitted during the waiting period. [p. 32] The slideshow, because it was not disseminated further, does not qualify as a free writing prospectus that must be filed with the S.E.C. [p. 33]

25. **YES** Muriel meets the definition of "underwriter" in Section 2(a)(11) of the 1933 Act. [p. 38]

26. **YES** Alfred is a "control person," and therefore the brokerage firm with which he deals will be deemed an "underwriter" under

the 1933 Act. Consequently, the exemption provided in SA Section 4(a)(1) will not be available to Alfred, because his transaction will involve an underwriter. [pp. 40–41] Alfred's alternative to registration is to sell under the provisions of SA Rule 144 (as an affiliate selling unrestricted securities of a reporting issuer). [p. 87]

27.	**DEPENDS**	It is possible that these interests would be classified as "investment contracts" under the *Howey* test. Such a plan, although dealing with a commodity (real estate) that is not normally thought of as a security, has the elements associated with a security—profit-making and services by central management (subdivision). However, if resales are totally the responsibility of the buyers, then perhaps there is no security because there is substantial involvement in management by the investors. [pp. 47–50]
28.	**YES**	Under the *Howey* test, it appears to be an investment contract, with management provided by Astrid. [pp. 47–50]
29.	**NO**	General partnership interests are not usually securities under the 1933 Act because the partners' management and control rights preclude the "primarily on the efforts of others" element of the *Howey* test. However, if the holder of the interest has no real partnership power or is expected to delegate most power, a general partnership interest may be treated as a security. [p. 50]
30.	**FORM S-1**	The 1933 Act provides a number of forms for use by particular types of companies or for special types of securities offerings. S-1 is the general form. [p. 53]
31.a.	**YES**	As part of the financial statements. [p. 54]
b.	**NO**	However, the S.E.C. encourages disclosure of earnings projections, with appropriate cautionary statements. [p. 56]
c.	**YES**	This is a material risk facing the business that must be disclosed. [pp. 54 & 55]
32.	**FALSE**	The S.E.C. does not make such a guarantee. The issuer and specified persons involved with the offering must take responsibility for any material inaccuracies. [pp. 35 & 99]
33.	**YES**	But the S.E.C. may, on request, shorten this period and declare the statement effective. [p. 35]
34.	**DEPENDS**	This is a "shelf registration," which is available to many issuers under certain circumstances and is automatically available to WKSIs. [p. 62]
35.	**NO**	Section 11 applies only to misrepresentations in the registration statement at the time it is declared effective. [p.

96] Note, however, that Alex may have a claim under Section 12(a)(2) for this misrepresentation. [p. 92]

36. **TRUE** This is true because the security *itself* is exempt. [p. 64] However, most exemptions under the 1933 Act are transactional exemptions. With a transactional exemption, only the specific transaction is exempt. Later resales (as by a control person) must be registered or satisfy their own transactional exemption. [p. 86]

37. **IN GENERAL, TRUE** Under Section 4(a)(2) of the Act, the S.E.C. and the courts look at a number of variables in making the private offering determination. [pp. 65–67] There are, however, specific "safe harbor" rules with objective criteria for determining whether an offering is a private one. [*See, e.g.,* Rule 506(b)] [pp. 67–71]

38. **TRUE** This is the foundation of the Supreme Court's interpretation of the Section 4(a)(2) exemption in *S.E.C. v. Ralston Purina*. [p. 65]

39. **NO** The S.E.C. and the courts consider several variables in deciding whether an offering is private and, therefore, exempt under SA Section 4(a)(2). While the number of offerees and the number of purchasers are both relevant, neither figure is determinative. An offering could be public, notwithstanding that it was made only to 11 offerees and purchasers. For example, if the purchasers were unsophisticated and not provided access to the types of information that would be available in a registration statement, Section 4(a)(2) likely does not apply. [pp. 65–67]

40. **YES** These offerings pose a high risk of being integrated. (If so, they will be treated as one single offering, and it's unlikely that they would satisfy a single exemption in light of the differential requirements of Rule 506(b) and Rule 506(c).) The first step is to determine whether the two offerings are within a safe harbor from integration. Rule 506(c) permits general solicitation, while Rule 506(b) does not. Accordingly, they will be within the safe harbor only if more than 30 days have elapsed between the two offerings, among other requirements. [p. 85] Here, where only 20 days elapsed, the two offerings are not within a safe harbor from integration. Thus, the second step is to apply the general principle of integration. Integration will depend on whether, with respect to *each* purchaser in the Rule 506(b) offering, the issuer has a reasonable belief that the purchaser was not solicited through the use of general solicitation or that the issuer had established a substantive relationship with the purchaser prior to the commencement of the offering. [p. 86]

41.	**NO**	Rule 147 is an issuer transactional exemption and does not cover resales. [p. 77] Warren must identify a resale exemption.
42.	**YES**	All offerees and purchasers must be residents of the same state under Rule 147. [p. 77] (If the issuer "reasonably believed" that the one out-of-state offeree was a resident of the same state as Sameco, the exemption would not be lost, however.) [p. 79]
43.	**NO**	Only purchasers (not offerees) are required to be residents of the issuer's state Rule 147A. [p. 80]
44.	**Rule 506(c)**	The following exemptions do not meet Issuer's requirements: (1) § 4(a)(1) and Rule 506(b) prohibit general solicitation and advertising; (2) Regulation CF and Rule 504 includes limits on the amount of money that can be raised; (3) Section 3(a)(11), Rule 147, and Rule 147A are instrastate offerings and do not preempt state registration requirements. Rule 506(c) does not limit the amount of money that can be raised, permits general solicitation and advertising, permits nationwide offers and sales, and preempts state registration requirements. However, Issuer must take reasonable steps to verify that all purchasers are accredited investors, must exercise reasonable care to ensure that purchasers are not underwriters, and must ensure that issuer is not barred as a "bad actor." [pp. 71–73]
45.	**YES**	The distribution continues until it comes to rest in the hands of those taking for investment. A and B have participated in a public distribution. [pp. 38–40]
46.	**YES**	It makes no difference that Abbey established investment intent. When a control person (an "affiliate of the issuer") sells through a broker, the broker becomes an underwriter and the 1933 Act Section 4(a)(1) exemption for transactions not involving an underwriter is not available. [pp. 40–41]
47.	**MAYBE**	Smith is likely an affiliate of Corporation. [p. 91] In order for an affiliate to sell unrestricted securities of a non-reporting issuer, Rule 144 does not impose a holding period. However, Rule 144 does require adequate public information about the issuer and compliance with volume limits and manner-of-sale rules. [p. 89]
48.	**YES**	Most courts hold that persons who purchase a security in the secondary market can recover under Section 11, as long as they can prove that the specific securities purchased were issued in the offering registered by the defective registration statement. [p. 95] A plaintiff under Section 11 does not need to prove reliance on the alleged misrepresentations. [p. 96]
49.	**$0**	Under SA Section 11, when securities are sold before suit, the measure of damages is the price paid for the security (but not

more than the offering price), less the price at which the security was sold. [p. 99] Applying this measure, Matsuo cannot recover damages under Section 11, because the price at which Matsuo sold was the same as the offering price: $10 per share.

50.	**YES**	It is a violation of Section 5 to make a public offering without registration absent an exemption. Section 12(a)(1) relates to any violation of Section 5. It makes no difference that Ginsu Corp. did not intentionally violate the Art. [pp. 91–92]
51.	**YES**	The issue is whether the advisory board members are "sellers" under Section 12(a)(2). Because the advisory board members solicited the purchases for value, motivated at least in part by the desire to serve the interests of the issuer, the board members here become sellers. [p. 92] Penelope satisfies the privity requirement [p. 93], and the offering is public [p. 93].
52.	**YES**	Rule 10b–5 applies to all types of securities and securities transactions, not just those securities registered under the 1934 Act. There is an interstate commerce requirement, but that is almost always met in a securities transaction.
53.	**TRUE**	Otherwise, nearly any fraud could somehow be connected with a purchase or sale of securities, and there would be no limitation on Rule 10b–5 causes of action.
54.	**YES**	The issuer had a duty to disclose the lost client in order to make its disclosure about the new client not misleading. [p. 122] In addition, this would likely be material because there is a significant likelihood that a reasonable investor would consider the lost client to be important when making an investment decision. [p. 124]
55.	**FALSE**	There is no privity requirement under Rule 10b–5. Rather, the plaintiff must be *a* purchaser or seller. [p. 117]
56.	**PROBABLY NOT**	First, Rule 10b–5 requires scienter, which requires at least recklessness. The facts state that the prediction was made "carelessly," which sounds more like mere negligence. [p. 127] Moreover, the prediction may qualify as a forward-looking statement for purposes of the safe harbor in the PSLRA. Under the safe harbor provision, no private plaintiff can bring a lawsuit under Rule 10b–5 unless he or she can show actual knowledge that the statement was materially false or incomplete. [pp. 121 & 128]
57.	**NO**	For a plaintiff to bring a 10b–5 cause of action, she must be an actual purchaser or seller of securities. [pp. 117–118]
58.	**NO**	This is a double no. First, there is no private cause of action against mere aiders and abettors of securities fraud under Rule

10b–5. [p. 118] Second, Rule 10b–5 requires scienter; mere negligence is not sufficient. [p. 127]

59. **YES** The fraud-on-the-market presumption of reliance is rebuttable by severing either of the following two constituent presumptions: (1) that the fraud affected the market price, and (2) that the plaintiff relied on the integrity of the market price when making an investment decision. Here, this proof would sever the second constituent presumption by showing that Peter was not relying on the integrity of the market price (but rather was speculating about the success of the merger talks). [p. 130]

60. **YES as to all** These persons are all insiders. [p. 150]

61. **FALSE** The trend is to limit damages to the plaintiff's gain (or avoided loss). [p. 138]

62. **FALSE** This is doubly false. Although the limitations period is two years, it is not triggered by the plaintiff's actual discovery of the untruth or omission. First, the standard is (1) actual discovery or (2) when a reasonable diligent plaintiff would have discovered. Second, it is triggered only when this test is met with respect to the facts constituting the violation. An untruth or omission is one fact, but there would also need to be discovery of facts supporting scienter. [p. 138]

63. **YES** A tender offer is an offer directly to a company's shareholders for their stock. Section 14(d) is the basic section that regulates the making of tender offers.

64. **YES** When a person acquires more than 5% of the registered equity securities of a company, that person must disclose his or her intentions with regard to the company to the management of that company. [p. 152]

65. **NO** A bidder has no standing to bring a damages action in this circumstance. [p. 154]

66. **MAYBE** A bidder may have standing to seek injunctive relief under Section 14(e). [p. 157]

67. **YES** The proxy rules apply only to companies reporting under the 1934 Act. [p. 158]

68. **YES** If a matter requires a shareholder vote, an information statement must be filed and distributed, even if proxies are not solicited. [p. 160]

69. **FALSE** Oral misrepresentations made by one soliciting proxies in the course of such solicitation are prohibited by Rule 14a–9 of the proxy rules. [p. 169]

70. **TRUE** The Supreme Court has indicated in the *Mills* case that causation is proved by showing materiality in a case where the proxy solicitation was an essential link in the accomplishment of the transaction. [p. 172]

71. **YES** Tish qualifies as an "insider" under Section 16 by virtue of her 15% ownership of a registered class of equity securities. Thereafter, purchases and sales of any equity security (*i.e.,* the convertible preferred stock), even if not registered, are covered by Section 16. [p. 147]

72. **NO** Section 16(b) requires that an insider for stock ownership must be a 10% owner at the time of a "purchase" *and* at the time of a "sale," if the purchase and sale are to be matched for Section 16(b) purposes. Here, the purchase on March 1 does not qualify because Martha did not own 10% on that date. [p. 148]

73. **FALSE** Transactions taking place *before a person becomes an officer* or director are not reportable and *will not be matched* with transactions taking place after the person takes office. However, transactions taking place *after the person leaves office will be matched* with transactions taking place less than six months previously, while the person was in office. [p. 146]

74. **FALSE** Section 16(b) applies if its specific requirements are met, whether or not inside information was actually used in the trading of securities by an insider. [p. 151]

75. **MAYBE** There is no implied private right of action against one who merely aids or abets a violation of Rule 10b–5. [p. 118] Therefore, the question is whether Abbey is a primary violator. She is not a "maker" of the alleged misrepresentations. [p. 119] However, under *Lorenzo,* she may qualify as a "disseminator," if she disseminated materially misleading statements with the intent to defraud investors. [p. 119]

76. **TRUE** SOXA mandates up-the-ladder reporting of material violations of the securities law. [p. 175]

77. **YES** This is market manipulation prohibited by both Rule 10b–5 and SEA Section 9(a). [pp. 124 & 193–194]

78. **FALSE** Although market manipulation is prohibited by the 1934 Act [pp. 124 & 193–194], market stabilization is permitted if compliant with Regulation M. [pp. 196 *et seq.*]

79. **YES** The S.E.C. regulates such "hot issues" and prohibits Smith Blarney's conduct and similar conduct which gives the appearance that a stock is being offered at a specific price when in fact part of the offering is not really being sold to the public at the offering price at all. [pp. 197–198]

80. **YES** FINRA requires dealers to buy or sell at a price that is fair, taking into consideration all relevant factors. Informally, 5% is a guideline for a reasonable markup. However, Sheerson could try to prove that 100% was not unreasonable if the actual market for the stock had moved up that much from the time it purchased the stock. [p. 190]

81. **PROBABLY** In *Morrison*, the Supreme Court limited the reach of Rule 10b–5 to fraud "in connection with the purchase or sale of a security listed on an American stock exchange, and the purchase or sale of any other security in the United States." [p. 207] Here, the security was not listed on U.S. exchange, and the sale occurred abroad. Although the Dodd-Frank Act amended SEA Section 27(b) to afford U.S. district courts jurisdiction over securities fraud suits where the conduct within the U.S. constituted significant steps in furtherance of the violation, this provision would not help this plaintiff. [p. 207] First, Section 27(b) only applies to actions instituted by the S.E.C. or the Department of Justice, not private plaintiffs. Second, there is some question about to what degree Section 27(b) successfully overruled Morrison, even for governmental suits. [p. 207] Therefore, the court should probably dismiss the suit.

82a. **TRICK QUESTION** The issuer does not have a "due diligence" defense. [p. 97]

b. **NON-EXPERT** The alleged misrepresentations were in the expertised portion of the registration statement. The Directors, as non-expert defendants, must merely establish that they had "no reasonable ground to believe and did not believe" that the statements were untrue. [p. 97]

c. **EXPERT** The alleged misrepresentations were in the expertised portion of the registration statement, and Auditor is the expert. As such, Auditor can establish the due diligence defense only if it can show that "after reasonable investigation" it had "reasonable ground to believe and did believe that statement was true." [p. 97]

83. **SCIENTER** The PSLRA requires dismissal unless the plaintiffs have pleaded a strong inference of scienter. [p. 128] This stringent pleading standard is difficult to achieve, particularly because the plaintiffs do not have the benefit of discovery (which is stayed during the pendency of the motion to dismiss). [p. 129] XYZ Corp. has almost uncertainly argued that the plaintiffs failed to meet this pleading standard. Under *Tellabs*, the court will survive dismissal only if a reasonable person would deem the inference of scienter cogent and at least as compelling as any opposing inference one could draw from the facts alleged. [p. 128]

84. **REMOVE/DISMISS** SLUSA precludes class actions based on the statutory or common law of any state alleging misrepresentations with

respect to the purchase or sale of a covered security. Stock-exchange-listed securities are covered securities. Thus, this action is precluded. XYZ Corp. will likely file a motion to dismiss the case under SLUSA or remove the case to federal court and then file a motion to dismiss it under SLUSA. [pp. 212 & 211]

85. **MAYBE** ABC Corp.'s strongest arguments for exclusion are that it has no economic significance [p. 166] and that it deals with ordinary business operations [p. 167]. The shareholder's strongest argument is that it is significant to ABC Corp.'s operations to become more environmentally sustainable [p. 166], and that a decision like this rises above ordinary business decisions [p. 167].

86. **YES** Regulation CF is an exemption that permits crowdfunding. ABC Corp. would have to comply with Regulation CF's various requirements, however. [pp. 81–84]

87. **FALSE** Regulation BI replaces the "suitability" standard with a "best interest" standard. [pp. 201–202]

Exam Questions and Answers

Question I

Without complying with the registration requirements of the Securities Act of 1933, XYZ Co. advertises in newspapers and over radio and television to find distributors for its product, a line of cosmetics. The distributors come from all walks of life, having had a great variety of former jobs, income levels, and educational backgrounds. Each distributor pays a fee of $5,000 for his or her "franchise," for which he or she receives an inventory of products which may be resold at a suggested retail price of $7,500. Also, the distributors receive the right to find other distributors, for which a finder's fee of $1,000 will be paid. Each distributor signs a contract with XYZ, which provides that the distributor is an "independent contractor." The company agrees to provide each new distributor with a one-week training course on how to recruit other distributors and for a fee will provide brochures, inspirational tape recordings, etc., which can be used in the recruiting meetings. But XYZ holds no meetings to assist its franchisees to recruit new distributors. All of XYZ's written materials and advertising allude to the tremendous profits that can be made under its program. But orally, before having the distributor sign a contract, the company warns potential distributors that selling the product and recruiting distributors is very hard work. The company acknowledges that the product line is really nothing special, and that the real money is to be made in recruiting other distributors. Actual results by distributors to date indicate that most have not earned their investment back; but a few have made substantial profits, mostly by selling other distributorships. One of the disgruntled distributors seeks advice as to whether he can get his $5,000 investment back if he returns the inventory unused. Consider only whether a "security" is involved under the 1933 Act.

Question II

QRS Corp., which is a 1934 Act reporting company, registers an offering of its stock for public distribution through an underwriter. In the prospectus it indicates that its earnings for the coming year will be "nominal." The stock is sold at $20 per share, which is the market price at the time of the offering. At the end of the year, the company announces that it has a loss of $25 million, or about one-third of its net worth. Immediately, the stock's price drops to $5 per share and remains there. Those who purchased QRS stock in the public offering bring a lawsuit to recover for material misstatements in the prospectus. At trial it is shown that the projection of earnings was done by the company's vice president of finance and accounting and that it was based on an "optimistic" outlook for the company's performance on existing government contracts which were behind schedule and experiencing cost overruns at the time the projection was made. Considering only Section 11 of the 1933 Act, can the purchasers recover from QRS? (Do not consider the amount of damages.)

Question III

A is a successful promoter. She has a number of very wealthy friends who invest in the deals she puts together. She gets ideas, finds management, raises the money, puts the corporation together, and then, after several years of operation, merges the companies into larger companies.

A has a new idea for the manufacture of rotating widgets. She finds B (president), C (vice president of finance), D (vice president of marketing), E (vice president of manufacturing), and hires F as her attorney. F incorporates X Co., and for 10 cents per share, F issues common stock as follows:

A = 50% or 50,000 shares
B = 20% or 20,000 shares
C = 9% or 9,000 shares
D = 9% or 9,000 shares
E = 9% or 9,000 shares
F = 3% or 3,000 shares

Prior to the issuance of the stock, A explains to B, C, D, E, and F the basic idea, showing some feasibility studies concerning the development of the product, hands out some articles on the industrial applications involved, and talks about the plan for issuing stock and financing the company. B, C, D, and E are all experienced executives who have participated in forming companies before; they ask no more questions, simply trusting in A's track record. A has hired F because F's fees are low; this is F's first incorporation, and being impressed with the 3,000 shares offered, F asks no more questions. Also, A gives the impression that she does not want to hear any questions—the investors can simply take the deal or leave it. The group discusses the financing plans; all agree that this should be covered in the business plan which is to be written. All persons taking the common stock sign investment letters; F sees that a restrictive legend is placed on the shares and issues instructions to the transfer agent that no shares are to be transferred without an opinion from F. All shareholders become members of the board of directors. State and resolve all issues raised by the above facts under Section 4(a)(2) of the Securities Act of 1933.

Question IV

XYZ is a drug manufacturer. It is a public company, traded on the New York Stock Exchange. A, the head of research, has been working on a cure for cancer for 15 years. The company has spent \$5 million on this research. The only other person in the company who knows about all of the ramifications of the project is B, the company president. On January 1, A mentions to B, while they are having lunch together, that she has made an interesting but puzzling breakthrough. Using an extract from cancerous cells of cattle, she had injected various cancerous animals and found that in some cases she has cured them. B becomes very excited. The stock of the company has been doing very poorly in the market, and B is under pressure from some shareholders and the board of directors to improve performance. A, however, has been down many blind alleys before, and she succeeds in calming B down, indicating that there are so many variables involved that it may be as long as five years before he knows "whether they have really discovered anything.

Shortly thereafter, B is responding to analysts' questions during a public conference call. An analyst asks about the status of the research. B states: "We have not made any significant progress."

S is a shareholder. On February 1, five days after the conference call, S sells 1,000 shares of XYZ at \$5 per share. This is a transaction over the New York Stock Exchange.

B, however, feels "in his bones" that A is on the verge of a dramatic breakthrough in cancer therapy. On February 10, he buys 1,000 shares on the exchange at \$5 per share.

On the morning of March 1, A bursts into B's office with news that, working nonstop, she has miraculously succeeded in separating an element from the cancerous cells that, when injected into dogs with eye cancer, seems immediately to go to work curing the diseased cells. Word has already leaked out to the research staff; by midafternoon, the XYZ stock is trading at \$10 per share.

XYZ issues a careful news release indicating that, as of March 1, the company has made progress in separating an element from cancerous cells of cattle that seems to have an effect in curing eye cancer in animals, but that nothing is known in the way of definitive research or what the possible effect may be on human beings.

The news release is sent to all shareholders and given to the major news services. By March 15, the stock has gone to \$20 per share. By March 30, it is \$25 per share. S checked with her broker on March 1 about her holdings and was told that XYZ stock had taken off, based on some cancer research breakthrough.

After checking into the facts, S hires you as an attorney and asks you to sue XYZ under Rule 10b–5. By the time the suit is brought, the stock of XYZ is selling at \$30 per share.

Discuss the merits of S's lawsuit against XYZ under Rule 10b–5. Do not consider the measure of damages, if any.

Answers to Question I

The issue is whether a security is involved.

The first question is whether this interest is specifically listed in Section 2(a)(1) of the Act (*e.g.*, stock or note). It is not.

However, the interest might nonetheless qualify as a security under the catch-all of "investments contracts." Under Howey, there are four elements to analyze:

First, are distributors investing money with an expectation of profits? Yes. The distributors are paying $5,000, not really for the right to resell products at a slight profit, but for the right to earn substantial profit by recruiting additional distributors.

Second, is there a common enterprise? It depends. It does not appear that there is horizontal commonality because the various distributors' profits are not derived from pooling or sharing. In a jurisdiction that recognizes vertical commonality, however, there appears to be both broad and narrow versions. There is broad vertical commonality because the fortunes of the investor are interwoven with the efforts of XYZ Co. There is narrow vertical commonality because the fortunes of the investor and XYZ Co. are intertwined.

Third, are the investors' profits dependent primarily on the efforts of others? Maybe. On the one hand, the efforts of the company are an important part of this recruiting process. On the other hand, the investors have to do their own recruiting to make a profit. Investors are even called "independent contractors" and warned of the difficult work involved. They are given recruiting materials but are not assisted in the actual recruiting.

Finally, do the investors need the protection of the Act? Yes. The persons enlisted here appear to be relatively unsophisticated, and the program involves a large number of people.

There is at least a colorable argument that this is a security subject to the 1933 Act.

Answers to Question II

This question raises two key issues: First, was this alleged misstatement "material"? Second, was this alleged misstatement protected by the safe harbor for forward-looking statements?

First, a misstatement is material only if there is a substantial likelihood that a reasonable investor would consider it important when making an investment decision. Here, the term "nominal" is rather vague, so it is possible that it is immaterial under the puffery doctrine. In addition, if this prediction of nominal earnings was accompanied by warnings, it is possible that it was rendered immaterial under the bespeaks caution doctrine.

Second, because QRS is a 1934 Act reporting company, it is eligible for the safe harbor for forward-looking statements. Because this statement contains a financial projection, it is within the definition of "forward-looking statement." Accordingly, under the safe harbor, the private plaintiffs must prove that the defendant had actual knowledge that the forward-looking statement was false or materially incomplete. The vice president's "optimistic" outlook appears to fall short of actual knowledge of falsity. In addition, the forward-looking statement would be protected if it was (1) identified as a forward-looking statement and (2) accompanied by meaningful cautionary language. Here, it will be helpful to QRS if it fully disclosed that its government contracts were behind schedule and experiencing cost overruns and the possible impact of continued schedule difficulties and overruns. Boilerplate warnings will not suffice for QRS. All in all, it seems unlikely that the plaintiffs will win unless they can make the difficult "actual knowledge" showing.

Answers to Question III

The issue here is whether this is a private offering of securities pursuant to Section 4(a)(2) and thereby exempt from registration under Section 5 of the 1933 Act. The availability of the Section 4(a)(2) exemption turns on whether, considering all the circumstances of the offering, the potential purchasers need the protection of the 1933 Act. That question, in turn, depends on a number of factors:

1) Manner of offering and number of offerees: First, was the offering conducted in a "public" manner, reaching a large number of offerees (which would make it likely that at least some of the offerees need 1933 Act protection)? Here, it seems that the offering was not conducted in a public manner: No advertising was used, and there was no general solicitation. Likewise, the number of offerees was relatively small.

2) Sophistication of the offerees: Also relevant to the need for 1933 Act protection is the relative sophistication of the offerees, i.e., their knowledge, experience, ability to bear the risk of the investment, and their ability to properly evaluate the merits of the securities offered. Here, there seem to be some questions that might be raised, especially with respect to F: B, C, D, and E have all participated in similar transactions before, and are "experienced executives" who presumably know a great deal about the risks of transactions like this one. F, however, has never incorporated a business, and evidently is far less experienced than the others. On the other hand, F is investing only $300 (3,000 x 10 cents), and therefore very likely can easily bear the risk of the investment. Moreover, F is a lawyer, and perhaps even a relatively unsophisticated lawyer is more savvy in business matters than a layperson.

3) Type of information provided: Another important factor examined in Section 4(a)(2) cases is the nature and amount of information provided. If the information is both qualitatively and quantitatively equivalent to the information that would be contained in a 1933 Act registration statement, or if the offerees at least had access to such information on request, the offering will be more likely to qualify under Section 4(a)(2). Here, however, that does not seem to be the case. Certainly, F does not have access to this kind or amount of information, and it is at least questionable whether B, C, D, and E had such access. On balance, the information requirement has not been met in this case.

4) Resale restrictions: The facts indicate that a restrictive legend was placed on all share certificates and that the transfer agent was instructed not to transfer shares without F's approval. Therefore, appropriate restrictions on resale have been imposed on the securities to prevent their secondary distribution to the public by the initial participants.

5) Other factors: The remaining factors favor the exemption's availability in this case. The total dollar value of the offering is relatively small ($10,000); the securities were offered only to a reasonably homogenous group; and the securities, while marketable in theory, because they are relatively cheap, have been restricted and therefore are essentially unmarketable without the called-for legal opinion.

In conclusion, while not all the requirements of Section 4(a)(2) were met here, many businesses are formed this way. Given the small dollar amount involved and the nature of the participants, all of whom have some professional tie to the issuer, it is likely that a court would apply 1933 Act Section 4(a)(2) and find the transaction exempt from registration.

Answers to Question IV

Let's analyze each element of S's claim in turn.

First, did S have standing to assert this claim? Yes, she sold XYZ securities.

Second, was XYZ a primary violator? Yes, B was speaking for XYZ when making the alleged misstatement or omission.

Third, was there a deceptive statement? Here, it appears to be based on B's failure to disclose the progress of the research. Was there a duty to disclose this progress? Arguably, it was misleading for B to state that "we have not made any significant progress" without disclosing the news shared by A.

Was the omission material? The question is whether there is a significant likelihood that a reasonable investor would find the omitted information important when making an investment decision. The probability/magnitude test helps here. The impact of a cancer cure would be phenomenal, even if the probability of the cure becoming a reality remained small. Here, where this was the first progress in 15 years, it would likely be material.

Was the omission in connection with the purchase or sale of a security? Yes, assuming materiality, it would have been material to a decision by one or more individuals to buy or sell the stock.

Did B have scienter? B had direct knowledge of A's progress. And, it is an especially bad fact that B traded on the basis of it without disclosing it to the public. S can likely establish the element of scienter.

Can S establish reliance? Here, S may be able to rely on the Affiliated Ute presumption of reliance afforded to omissions. Even if this is viewed as a mixed misstatement/omission, S will likely be able to invoke the fraud-on-the market presumption of reliance. XYZ stock was traded on the NYSE, and thus it was likely an efficient market.

Can S establish loss causation? She will have to show that she sold at a price deflated by the fraud. Here, S can point to the price increase after disclosure of the breakthrough, although that is not a direct measure of loss, as it reflects the much more exciting later development.

Table of Cases

A&K Railroad Materials, Inc. v. Green Bay & Western Railroad, 157
Aaron v. S.E.C., 100
Adams v. Standard Knitting Mills, 172
Affiliated Ute Citizens v. United States, 129
Amgen Inc. v. Connecticut Ret. Plans & Tr. Funds, 131
Apple Computer Securities Litigation, In re, 171
Backman v. Polaroid Corp., 123
Basic, Inc. v. Levinson, 122, 124
Bateman Eichler, Hill Richards, Inc. v. Berner, 139
Birnbaum v. Newport Steel Corp., 117
Board of Trade v. S.E.C., 185
Brown, United States v., 102, 179
Buttrey v. Merrill Lynch, Pierce, Fenner & Smith, Inc., 188
Cammer v. Bloom, 130
Carpenter v. United States, 178
Carrott v. Shearson Hayden Stone, Inc., 189
Central Bank of Denver, N.A. v. First Interstate Bank of Denver, N.A., 118
Cephalon Securities Litigation, In re, 142
Chadbourne & Parke LLP v. Troice, 126
Chemical Fund, Inc. v. Xerox Corp., 150
Chiarella v. United States, 132
Connecticut National Bank v. Fluor Corp., 156
Cort v. Ash, 114
Cramer v. General Telephone & Electronics, 114
Cyan, Inc. v. Beaver County Employees Retirement Fund, 100
Dan River, Inc. v. Icahn, 153
De Bruin v. Andromeda Broadcasting Systems Inc., 200
Dirks v. S.E.C., 132
Dixon, United States v., 180
Doran v. Petroleum Management Corp., 66, 67
Dupuy v. Dupuy, 116
Dura Pharms., Inc. v. Broudo, 131
Electronic Specialty Co. v. International Controls Corp., 155
Elkind v. Liggett & Myers, Inc., 123
Ernst & Ernst v. Hochfelder, 127
Escott v. BarChris Construction Corp., 99
Ettinger v. Merrill Lynch, Pierce, Fenner & Smith, Inc., 190
Florida Commercial Banks v. Culverhouse, 153
Foremost-McKesson, Inc. v. Provident Securities Co., 148
Fratt v. Robinson, 115
Gearhart Industries, Inc. v. Smith International, Inc., 153
General Host Corp. v. Triumph American, Inc., 157
Gerstle v. Gamble-Skogmo, Inc., 172, 174
Gilligan, Will & Co. v. S.E.C, 40
Goldman Sachs Grp., Inc. v. Arkansas Tchr. Ret. Sys., 131
Grassi v. Information Resources, Inc., 123
Greebel v. FTP Software, Inc., 142
Greenstein v. Paul, 118
Gustafson v. Alloyd Co., 93
Halliburton Co. v. Erica P. John Fund, Inc., 130, 131
Hazel Bishop, Inc., In re, 42
Herman & MacLean v. Huddleston, 132
Hertzberg v. Dignity Partners, Inc., 95
Hill York Corp. v. American International Franchises, 66
Hirk v. Agri-Research Council, Inc., 49
Humana, Inc. v. American Medicorp, Inc., 157
Institutional Securities of Colorado, In re, 198
International Brotherhood of Teamsters v. Daniel, 50
Ira Haupt & Co., In re, 42
J.I. Case Co. v. Borak, 169
Janus Capital Group, Inc. v. First Derivative Traders, 119
Jarkesy v. S.E.C., 101
Jones v. S.E.C., 190
Kaiser-Frazer Corp. v. Otis & Co., 61
Kalmanovitz v. G. Heileman Brewing Co., 154
Kamerman v. Steinberg, 153
Kronfeld v. Trans World Airlines, Inc., 171
Landreth Timber Co. v. Landreth, 46
Las Vegas Hawaiian Development Co. v. S.E.C., 60
Lehl v. S.E.C., 190
Lewis v. McGraw, 155
Liberty National Insurance Co. v. Charter Co., 153
Lilley, United States v., 180
List v. Fashion Park, Inc., 129
List v. Lerner, 129
Lorenzo v. S.E.C., 119
Lovenheim v. Iroquois Brands, Ltd., 166
Marine Bank v. Weaver, 49, 115
Matrixx Initiatives, Inc. v. Siracusano, 125
Medical Imaging Centers v. Lichtenstein, 143
Merck & Co. v. Reynolds, 139
Meyers v. C & M Petroleum Producers, Inc., 103
Mills v. Electric Auto-Lite Co., 173
Morrison v. Nat'l Australia Bank Ltd., 207
Musick, Peeler & Garrett v. Employers Insurance, Co., 138
Novak v. Kasaks, 143
O'Hagan, United States v., 132, 133
Omnicare, Inc. v. Laborers Dist. Council Const. Indus. Pension Fund, 120
Pinter v. Dahl, 91
Piper v. Chris-Craft Industries, Inc., 154, 157
Plaine v. McCabe, 155
Reves v. Ernst & Young, 46
Ronconi v. Larkin, 136
S.E.C. v. Chinese Consolidated Benevolent Association, 40
S.E.C. v. Continental Tobacco Co., 66
S.E.C. v. Dresser Industries, Inc., 179
S.E.C. v. Glen W. Turner Enterprises, Inc., 49
S.E.C. v. Guild Films Co., 42
S.E.C. v. Kenton Capital, Ltd., 66
S.E.C. v. Koscot Interplanetary, Inc., 49
S.E.C. v. MacDonald, 138
S.E.C. v. McDonald Investment Co., 76
S.E.C. v. Ralston Purina Co., 65, 66, 87
S.E.C. v. Resch-Cassin & Co., 193
S.E.C. v. Scoville, 207
S.E.C. v. Spectrum Ltd., 175

S.E.C. v. Texas Gulf Sulphur Co., 126, 138
S.E.C. v. W.J. Howey Co., 48
S.E.C. v. World-Wide Coin Investments, Ltd., 109
S.E.C. v. Zandford, 127
Salman v. United States, 134
Sanders v. John Nuveen & Co., 94
Santa Fe Industries, Inc. v. Green, 119
Schneider v. Apple Computer, Inc., 171
Schofield v. First Commodity Corp., 49
Schreiber v. Burlington Northern, Inc., 154
Seaboard World Airlines, Inc. v. Tiger International, Inc., 155
Seibert v. Sperry Rand Corp., 171
Semerenko v. Cendant Corp., 131
Shapiro v. Merrill Lynch, Pierce, Fenner & Smith, Inc., 133
Shaw v. Dreyfus, 150
Shawnee Chiles Syndicate, In re, 62
Skilling v. United States, 182
Stark v. New York Stock Exchange, Inc., 156
Steinhardt Group Inc. v. Citicorp, 51
Stransky v. Cummins Engine Co., 123
Sundstrand Corp. v. Sun Chemical Corp., 128
Superintendent of Insurance v. Bankers Life & Casualty Co., 127
Tellabs, Inc. v. Makor Issues & Rts., Ltd., 128
Time Warner Inc. Securities Litigation, In re, 122
Touche Ross & Co. v. Redington, 114
Transamerica Mortgage Advisors, Inc. v. Lewis, 114
TSC Industries, Inc. v. Northway, Inc., 124
United Housing Foundation, Inc. v. Forman, 46
United Paperworkers International Union v. International Paper Co., 172
Walston & Co., In re, 41
Weiner v. The Quaker Oats Co., 123
Wharf (Holdings) Ltd. v. United International Holdings, Inc., 124
Wieboldt v. Metz, 51
Williamson v. Tucker, 51
Wolfson, United States v., 87

Table of Securities Act of 1933

§ 2(a)(1) 45, 46, 47, 240
§ 2(a)(3) 26, 30, 36
§ 2(a)(4) 38, 47
§ 2(a)(7) 14, 204
§ 2(a)(10) 31, 32
§ 2(a)(10)(a) 36
§ 2(a)(10)(b) 31, 32
§ 2(a)(11) 38, 39, 40, 42, 43, 44, 71
§ 2(a)(12) 37, 43
§ 3 .... 64, 200
§ 3(a) 211
§ 3(a)(2) 64
§ 3(a)(3) 64
§ 3(a)(4) 65
§ 3(a)(5) 65
§ 3(a)(6) 65
§ 3(a)(7) 65
§ 3(a)(8) 65
§ 3(a)(9)–(12) 64
§ 3(a)(10) 115
§ 3(a)(11) 75, 76, 77, 79, 115, 230
§ 3(b) 64
§ 3(b)(1) 73
§ 3(c) 64
§ 4 64
§ 4(a)(1) 36, 38, 43, 45, 65, 86, 87, 211, 225, 230
§ 4(a)(2) 65, 66, 67, 71, 87, 211, 218, 229, 239, 240, 241
§ 4(a)(3) 37, 38, 43
§ 4(a)(3)(B) 38
§ 4(a)(3)(C) 37
§ 4(a)(4) 44, 45
§ 4(a)(6) 81
§ 4(a)(7) 89
§ 4A 81
§ 5 .... 11, 22, 23, 24, 25, 36, 37, 38, 40, 43, 44, 45, 52, 64, 65, 71, 74, 86, 87, 90, 91, 214, 215, 216, 225, 226, 231, 240
§ 5(a) 25, 26, 31
§ 5(a)(2) 36
§ 5(a)(l) 36
§ 5(b)(1) 31, 32, 33
§ 5(b)(2) 22, 36
§ 5(c) 25, 26, 28, 31, 60
§ 6 52
§ 6(a) 62, 95
§ 7 52
§ 8(a) 35
§ 8(b) 60
§ 8(d) 60
§ 8(e) 60
§ 8A(a) 101
§ 8A(e) 101
§ 8A(g) 101
§ 10 33
§ 10(a) 33, 36
§ 10(a)(3) 62
§ 10(b) 33, 36
§ 11 .... 11, 20, 57, 93, 94, 95, 96, 97, 99, 100, 102, 120, 144, 174, 175, 217, 218, 223, 225, 228, 230, 231, 238
§ 11(a) 96
§ 11(a)(1) 95
§ 11(c) 97
§ 11(e) 99
§ 11(f) 100, 102
§ 11(f)(2) 100, 144
§ 12 175
§ 12(a)(1) 11, 91, 92, 93, 94, 100, 103, 219, 231
§ 12(a)(2) 11, 20, 92, 93, 94, 100, 198, 225, 229, 231
§ 12(b) 94
§ 13 99
§ 14 103
§ 15(a) 91, 92
§ 16 100
§ 16(b) 212
§ 17 .... 11, 50, 100, 225
§ 17(a) 101, 102, 155, 179, 201
§ 17(a)(1) 100, 156
§ 17(a)(2) 100, 156
§ 17(a)(3) 100, 156
§ 17A 128
§ 18 .... 210, 211
§ 18(b) 212
§ 18(b)(4)(F) 71
§ 20(a) 101
§ 20(b) 101
§ 20(d) 101
§ 22(a) 92, 94, 100
§ 24 .... 102, 178
§ 27 .... 92, 94, 100
§ 27(a)(3)(A) 141
§ 27(a)(3)(B) 141
§ 27(a)(3)(B)(iii) 142
§ 27(a)(3)(B)(vi) 142
§ 27(a)(4) 142
§ 27(a)(5)–(7) 144
§ 27(b) 143
§ 27(c) 144
§ 27(d) 141
§ 27A 120
§ 27A(a) 93, 96, 121
§ 27A(b) 121
§ 27A(c)(1) 93, 96
§ 27A(c)(2) 122
§ 27A(i)(1) 121
§ 28 .... 73, 79

Table of Securities Exchange Act of 1934

§ 2 ... 107
§ 3(a)(1) ... 110, 184
§ 3(a)(4) ... 200
§ 3(a)(5) ... 200
§ 3(a)(10) ... 200
§ 3(a)(11) ... 150
§ 3(a)(17) ... 14, 206
§ 3(a)(26) ... 187
§ 5 ... 15, 110, 184, 187
§ 6 ... 12, 15, 110, 112, 184, 187
§ 6(b)(5) ... 15
§ 9 ... 11, 113, 193
§ 9(a) ... 193, 233
§ 9(a)(1)–(6) ... 194
§ 9(a)(6) ... 194, 196, 197
§ 9(b) ... 194
§ 9(c) ... 194
§ 9(f) ... 194
§ 10(b) ... 90, 113, 115, 169, 178, 193, 207
§ 11 ... 110
§ 11A ... 113, 186
§ 11A(b) ... 111
§ 12 ... 11, 107, 112, 184
§ 12(a) ... 108
§ 12(b) ... 108, 113, 206
§ 12(b)(1) ... 108
§ 12(g) ... 113, 206
§ 12(g)(1) ... 108
§ 13 ... 11, 88, 109, 112
§ 13(a) ... 136
§ 13(b)(2) ... 109, 113
§ 13(d) ... 112, 152, 153
§ 13(e) ... 152
§ 13(f) ... 112
§ 14 ... 11, 112, 157
§ 14(a) ... 157, 158, 169, 172
§ 14(d) ... 152, 221, 232
§ 14(d)(4) ... 152
§ 14(e) ... 152, 153, 155
§ 14(f) ... 152
§ 14I ... 160
§ 15 ... 12, 112, 116, 189
§ 15(a) ... 200, 201
§ 15(b) ... 110, 111, 189, 201
§ 15(b)(4) ... 111
§ 15(b)(6)(A) ... 191
§ 15(b)(6)(B)(i) ... 191
§ 15(b)(6)(B)(ii) ... 191
§ 15(b)(8) ... 15, 111
§ 15(c) ... 193, 194, 195
§ 15(d) ... 88, 136, 180
§ 15(g) ... 190
§ 15A ... 12, 15, 111, 189
§ 15A(b)(6) ... 15
§ 16 ... 11, 144
§ 16(a) ... 112, 145, 153
§ 16(b) ... 112, 113, 145, 148, 149, 150, 151, 152, 221, 222, 233
§ 16(c) ... 145
§ 17A ... 111
§ 18 ... 8, 113
§ 19 ... 12
§ 19(b) ... 187, 189
§ 19(b)–(c) ... 12
§ 19(c) ... 15, 187, 189
§ 19(d) ... 187, 190
§ 19(h) ... 187, 190
§ 20(a) ... 119
§ 20(e) ... 118
§ 20A ... 137
§ 20A(b)(1) ... 138
§ 20A(b)(2) ... 138
§ 21 ... 114
§ 21(d) ... 179
§ 21A ... 137
§ 21B ... 101
§ 21D(a)(3)(A) ... 141
§ 21D(a)(3)(B) ... 141
§ 21D(a)(3)(B)(iii) ... 142
§ 21D(a)(3)(B)(vi) ... 142
§ 21D(a)(4) ... 142
§ 21D(a)(5)–(7) ... 144
§ 21D(b)(2)(A) ... 128
§ 21D(b)(3) ... 143
§ 21D(b)(3)(A) ... 128
§ 21D(b)(3)(B) ... 129
§ 21D(c) ... 144
§ 21D(d) ... 141
§ 21D(e) ... 132, 144
§ 21D(f) ... 138, 144
§ 21E ... 120, 128
§ 21E(a) ... 121
§ 21E(b) ... 121
§ 21E(c)(2) ... 122
§ 21E(i)(1) ... 121
§ 25 ... 115
§ 27 ... 114, 139
§ 27(b) ... 207, 234
§ 28(f) ... 212
§ 32(a) ... 178, 179

Table of Securities Act Rules

Rule 134 ... 32, 36
Rule 135 ... 28, 31
Rule 137 ... 29
Rules 137–139 ... 29
Rule 137(b) ... 30
Rule 138(a)(1)(i) ... 30
Rule 138(a)(1)(ii) ... 30
Rule 139(a)(1) ... 30
Rule 139(a)(2) ... 30
Rule 141 ... 42
Rule 142 ... 42
Rule 144 ... 20, 42, 45, 88, 89, 218, 228, 230
Rule 144(a)(1) ... 88
Rule 144(a)(3) ... 88
Rule 144(b)(1)(i) ... 88
Rule 144A ... 29, 42, 89, 90, 204, 211
Rule 144A(a)(1)(i) ... 29
Rule 144A(a)(1)(ii) ... 29
Rule 144B(c)(2) ... 29
Rule 147 ... 77, 78, 79, 80, 81, 218, 230
Rule 147(c)(1) ... 78
Rule 147(c)(2) ... 78
Rule 147(d) ... 77, 80
Rule 147(e) ... 79
Rule 147(f) ... 79
Rule 147(f)(1)(iii) ... 77
Rule 147(f)(3) ... 77, 78
Rule 147A ... 79, 80, 81, 218, 230
Rule 147A(c)(1) ... 80
Rule 147A(c)(2) ... 81
Rule 147A(e) ... 81
Rule 147A(f) ... 81
Rule 147A(f)(1)(iii) ... 80
Rule 147A(f)(3) ... 80
Rule 152(a)(1) ... 86
Rule 152(a)(2) ... 86
Rule 152(b)(1) ... 85
Rule 152(b)(2) ... 86
Rule 152(b)(4) ... 85, 86
Rule 163 ... 27, 28, 226
Rule 163(b)(1) ... 27, 226
Rule 163A ... 27, 226
Rule 163B ... 29, 33
Rule 163B(b)(1) ... 28
Rule 164 ... 33, 36
Rule 164B(c) ... 29
Rule 168 ... 27, 28
Rule 168(b)(1) ... 27
Rule 168(b)(2) ... 27
Rule 168(c) ... 27
Rule 169 ... 28
Rule 169(b) ... 28
Rule 172 ... 36, 37
Rule 174(d) ... 38
Rule 405 ... 25, 34, 41, 88
Rule 408 ... 53
Rule 413(a) ... 63
Rule 413(b) ... 63
Rule 415 ... 62, 63
Rule 415(a)(5) ... 63
Rule 415(a)(6) ... 63
Rule 421(b) ... 57
Rule 430(a) ... 36
Rule 430A ... 35
Rule 430B ... 63
Rule 430B(a) ... 63
Rule 430B(d) ... 64
Rule 431 ... 33
Rule 433 ... 33, 36
Rule 433(b)(1) ... 34
Rule 433(b)(2) ... 34
Rule 433(c)(1)(i) ... 34
Rule 433(c)(2) ... 34
Rule 433(d)–(f) ... 34
Rule 433(d)(1) ... 34
Rule 433(d)(8)(i) ... 34
Rule 433(d)(8)(ii) ... 34
Rule 433(f)(1) ... 34
Rule 456(b) ... 63
Rule 460(b)(1) ... 35
Rule 461(c) ... 103
Rule 462(e) ... 63
Rule 477 ... 61
Rule 501 ... 70
Rule 501(a) ... 29, 68
Rule 501(a)(1) ... 29, 68
Rule 501(a)(2) ... 68
Rule 501(a)(3) ... 68
Rule 501(a)(4) ... 68
Rule 501(a)(5) ... 68
Rule 501(a)(6) ... 68
Rule 501(a)(7) ... 29, 68
Rule 501(a)(8) ... 29, 68
Rule 501(a)(9) ... 69
Rule 501(a)(10) ... 69
Rule 501(a)(11) ... 69
Rule 501(e)(1)(iv) ... 68
Rule 502(b) ... 69
Rule 502(b)(2) ... 69
Rule 502(b)(2)(v) ... 69
Rule 502(c) ... 70
Rule 502(d) ... 71
Rule 503 ... 71, 72, 74
Rule 504 ... 67, 73, 74, 75
Rule 504(a) ... 74
Rule 504(b)(1) ... 74, 75
Rule 504(b)(2) ... 74
Rule 506(b) ... 66, 70, 71, 87, 211
Rule 506(b)(2)(i) ... 68
Rule 506(b)(2)(ii) ... 69
Rule 506(c) ... 67, 71, 72, 73, 211, 218, 229, 230
Rule 506(c)(2)(ii) ... 72

Rule 506(d) 70
Rule 507..71, 73, 74
Rule 508..71, 73, 75

Table of Securities Exchange Act Rules

Rule 10b–5 .... 12, 20, 49, 50, 90, 107, 113, 115, 116, 117, 118, 119, 120, 122, 123, 124, 126, 127, 129, 131, 132, 133, 134, 135, 136, 138, 139, 140, 144, 145, 153, 155, 156, 169, 173, 174, 175, 178, 190, 194, 196, 197, 198, 201, 207, 212, 219, 220, 221, 222, 223, 231, 232, 233, 234, 239
Rule 10b–6 195
Rule 10b5–1(c)(1) 135
Rule 10b5–1(c)(2) 135
Rule 10b5–2 133
Rule 12g–6 108
Rule 12g3–2 206
Rule 12g3–2(b) 206
Rule 13d–1 112
Rule 13f–1 112
Rule 14a–1 160
Rule 14a–1(*l*) 158
Rule 14a–1(*l*)(1)(iii)(A) 158, 169
Rule 14a–1(*l*)(2)(iv) 159
Rule 14a–2(a)(1)(iii) 168
Rule 14a–2(b)(1) 161, 162
Rule 14a–2(b)(2) 161
Rule 14a–2(b)(3) 162, 169
Rule 14a–2(b)(9) 162, 169
Rule 14a–3 .... 159, 160
Rules 14a–3—14a–6 .... 158, 169
Rule 14a–3(a) 160
Rule 14a–3(f) 161
Rule 14a–4(f) 161
Rule 14a–6 162
Rule 14a–6(a) 162, 163
Rule 14a–8 .... 158, 162, 164, 169
Rule 14a–8(a) 164
Rule 14a–8(b) 164
Rule 14a–8(c) 164
Rule 14a–8(i) 165
Rule 14a–8(i)(7) 167
Rule 14a–8(j) 165
Rule 14a–9 ..... 158, 159, 160, 163, 166, 169, 170, 171, 173, 232
Rule 14a–9(a) 171
Rules 14a–10 through 14a–14 169
Rule 14a–11 .... 162, 169
Rule 14a–12 162
Rule 14a–13 168
Rule 14b–1 168
Rule 14b–2 168
Rule 14e–2 152
Rule 15c1–2 .... 194, 201
Rules 15c1–2—15c1–9 195
Rule 15c1–8 198
Rule 15g–2 191
Rule 15g–3 191
Rule 15g–4 191
Rule 15g–5 191
Rule 15g–6 191
Rule 15g–9 191
Rule 15g–9(a)(2)(ii) 191
Rule 16a–1(a)(1) 147
Rule 16a–1(a)(2) 148
Rule 16a–1(a), note 148
Rule 16a–1(f) 146
Rule 16a–2(a) 147
Rule 16a–4(a) 150
Rule 16b–3(a) 152
Rule 16b–3(d) 152
Rule 16b–3(e) 152
Rule 16b–5 152
Rule 19c–1 188
Rule 19c–3 188

Index

ACCELERATION
Amendments and, 58
Effective date and, XVII, 35, 58–60
Preliminary prospectus delivery required, XII, 35
S.E.C. policy, XXVI, 35, 59, 102

ACCOUNTANTS
Liability under SA, XL, LIV
SA section 11, 94–100
Liability under SEA, XL, LIV
Insider trading, 132
SEA section 10(b), 118
SEA section 14, 172
Public Company Accounting Oversight Board, VIII, 15–16
Role, XVI
SOXA provisions, 12, 113, 181

ACCREDITED INVESTORS
See also Issuer Exemptions
Defined, 29, 68–69

AFFILIATES
See also Control Persons
See also Resale Exemptions
Defined, 88

AIDERS AND ABETTORS
See also Control Persons
Liability, XXXVIII–XLI, 118–119, 175

AMERICAN DEPOSITARY RECEIPTS, 47, 205

ANNUAL REPORT
Form 10-K, LIII, 108–109, 123
Regulation CF, 83–84, 108
Shareholders, XXXIV, LIII, 159–160

ATTORNEYS
See Lawyer

BANKRUPTCY
Code, 13
Exempt securities, XIX, 65
Ineligible issuer, 24

BANKS
See also Underwriters
Glass-Steagall Act, 6

"BLANK CHECK" OFFERINGS
Definition, XIX
Ineligible issuer, 24

BLOCK TRANSACTIONS, 188

BROKER-DEALERS
See also FINRA
Defined, 6
Liability, XLV, 194–195
Pre-filing period, 29–30
Proxy contests, 168–169
Registration, XLIV, XLVI–XLIX, 12, 15, 110–111, 185–191, 200–201, 210, 212
Regulation BI, 201–202
Regulation FD, 136
Underwriter, 41–42

CLASS ACTIONS
See also Private Securities Litigation Reform Act of 1995
See also Securities Litigation Uniform Standards Act of 1988
Certification, 129–131, 139–140, 172–173
Lead Plaintiffs, 141–142

COMMISSIONS
S.E.C. and FINRA policy, XVIII, XLVII
Usual and customary, 43

COMMODITIES FUTURES TRADING COMMISSION, 7–8

CONTRIBUTION
See also Indemnification
SA generally, 102
SA section 11, XXIV, 100
SEA section 10(b), XXXI, 138

CONTROL PERSONS
See also Affiliates
See also Resale Exemptions
Definition of underwriter, XIV, XX–XXI, 39–45, 86–89
Indemnification, XXVI, 102
Liability, XXII, XXIV, XXXIX, LIV, 91, 119

CRIMINAL LIABILITY, IX, XXII, XXV, XXXI, XXXIII, XLII–XLIII, 10, 23, 102, 109–110, 112, 119, 137–138, 178–182, 206

DAMAGES
See also Contribution
Capped in SEA actions, XLI, 143–144
Insider Trading, XXX–XXXI
SA section 11, XXI, XXIII–XXIV, 99
SA section 12(a)(1), XXI, XXIV, 92
SA section 12(a)(2), XXI, XXV, 94
SEA section 10(b), XXX–XXXI, 113, 132, 138
SEA section 14(e), XXXIII, 153–156
SEA section 16, XXXVIII, 113
SEA section 18, 113

DEALERS
See Broker-Dealers

DEFENSES
SA section 11, XXIII, 96–99
SA section 12(a)(1), XXIV–XXV, 92
SA section 12(a)(2), XXV, 94
SA section 15, XXXIX
SEA rule 10b5-1, 135
SEA section 10(b), XXXI, 138–139
SEA section 16, XXXVIII, 151
SEA section 20 XXXIX

DIRECTORS
See also Control Persons
Accredited investors, 68
Affiliates, 88
Bad actors, 70
Election, XXXIV, LIII, 160–163, 167
Indemnification under SA, XXVI, 102–103
Insider trading, XXX, 132
SA section 11 liability, XXII, XL, 95, 97–98, 100, 114, 174
SEA section 14 liability, 172
SEA section 16 liability, XXXVI–XXXVII, 145–152
SEA section 16 reporting, XXVII, 11, 112

DODD-FRANK WALL STREET REFORM AND CONSUMER PROTECTION ACT OF 2010, XLVII, 8, 12, 68, 101, 207

EFFICIENT CAPITAL MARKET HYPOTHESIS, 58

ERISA, 50

EXPERTS
SA section 11 liability, 99

FAMILY RESEMBLANCE TEST, 46–47

FEDERAL DEPOSIT INSURANCE CORPORATION, 6, 50, 113

FEDERAL RESERVE BOARD, 6, 113

FINANCIAL INDUSTRY REGULATORY AUTHORITY
See FINRA

FINRA
Broker-dealers, regulation of, XLIV, XLVI, 189–190
Civil liability for rule violations, 202
Clearance of underwriting commissions, XVIII, 61
Generally, VIII, 15, 189, 201
Hot issues, 198
Markups policy, XLVII, 190
Registration requirement, 15, 111

FOREIGN CORRUPT PRACTICES ACT
Bribery, 206
Integrity of accounting, XXVII, 109–110, 206

FORMS
8-K, LIII, 108
10, 108
10-K, LIII, 108–109
10-KSB, LIII
10-Q, LIII, 108
10-QSB, LIII
13F, 112
20-F, 206
C, 83–84
D, 71–72, 74
F-1–F-4, 205
S-1, XVI, 53, 108–109, 205
S-2, 205
S-3, X, XVI, XIX, 24, 53, 62–63, 205
S-4, 205
S-8, XVI
SB-1, XVI
SB-2, XVI

FRAUD-ON-THE-MARKET PRESUMPTION, 129–130

GENERALLY ACCEPTED ACCOUNTING PRINCIPLES, 205

GLASS-STEAGALL ACT, 6

HOT ISSUE, XLVI, 197–198

INDEMNIFICATION, XXVI, 102–103
See also Contribution

INITIAL PUBLIC OFFERING, XIII, 38, 53, 59, 93, 96, 120–121, 195, 198

INSIDER TRADING AND SECURITIES FRAUD ENFORCEMENT ACT OF 1988, XXX, 137–138

INSIDER TRADING SANCTIONS ACT, XXX, 137

INTEGRATION
Disclosure, VII–VIII, XXVII, 13–14, 109
Offerings, 84–86

INVESTMENT ADVISOR, 13, 29, 69, 136, 201

INVESTMENT ADVISORS ACT, 13, 201

INVESTMENT COMPANY ACT OF 1940, XLVIII, 13, 69, 163, 211

ISSUER EXEMPTIONS
Integration, 84–86
SA Section 3(a)(11), 75–77
SA Section 4(a)(2), 65–67
Regulation CF, 81–84
Regulation D, 67–75
Rule 147, 77–79
Rule 147A, 79–81

JOBS ACT
See Jumpstart our Business Startups Act of 2012

JUMPSTART OUR BUSINESS STARTUPS ACT OF 2012, X, 25, 71, 81, 90

JURISDICTION
See also Multinational Transactions
SA, 14, 92, 94, 100
SEA, XXVIII, XXXIII, XXXVIII, 114, 116, 139

MANAGEMENT'S DISCUSSION AND ANALYSIS, XVII, 55–56, 97, 120

MISAPPROPRIATION THEORY, 133, 182

MULTINATIONAL TRANSACTIONS
Foreign Corrupt Practices Act, XXVII, 109–110, 206
International securities fraud, XLVII, 207
Registration under SA, 204–206
SEA regulation, XLVII, 206

NATIONAL SECURITIES MARKETS IMPROVEMENT ACT, 210–212

NO-ACTION LETTERS, 9

OFFICERS
See also Control Persons
Accredited investors, 68
Affiliates, 88
Bad actors, 70
Executive compensation, 164
Indemnification under SA, XXVI, 102–103
Insider trading, XXX, 132
SA section 11 liability, XXII, XL, 95, 97–98, 100, 114, 174
SEA section 14 liability, 172
SEA section 16 liability, XXXVI–XXXVII, 145–152
SEA section 16 reporting, XXVII, 11, 112

PRIVATE SECURITIES LITIGATION REFORM ACT OF 1995
Contribution, right of, 144
Damages capped in SEA actions, 132
Discovery, stay of, 129, 143
Generally, XLI–XLII, 140–144
Joint and several liability limited, 138
Pleading scienter, XXXI, 128–129
Safe harbor for forward-looking statements, XVII, 93, 96, 120–122, 128

PUBLIC COMPANY ACCOUNTING OVERSIGHT BOARD, VIII, 15–16, 109

PUBLIC UTILITY HOLDING ACT OF 1935, 13

QIB
See Qualified Institutional Buyers

QLCC
See Qualified Legal Compliance Committees

QUALIFIED INSTITUTIONAL BUYERS, XXI, 29, 89, 204, 211

QUALIFIED LEGAL COMPLIANCE COMMITTEES ("QLCC"), 177–178

REGULATION
14A, 158–159
AC, XLVI, 199–200
ATS, 186
BI, XLVII, 201–202
C, 56
CF, 81–84, 108, 211
D, 20, 67–75, 88, 89, 211
FD, XXX, 136–137
S, 204
SHO, 193
S-K, VIII, 13–14, 33, 53–54, 164
S-X, 53–54, 109, 205
M, XLVI, 193–197

RESALE EXEMPTIONS
4(a)(1½), 87
Dealers, 43–45
Rule 144, 87–89
Rule 144A, 89
SA 4(a)(7), 89
Underwriters, 38–43

SARBANES-OXLEY ACT OF 2002 ("SOXA")
Culpability standards for SOXA crimes, XLII–XLIII, 179–181
Enhancement of penalties, 182
Generally, VII, 12
Integrity of accounting, XXVII, 15–16, 110
Lawyers, XXVIII, XL–XLI, 174–177
Public Company Accounting Oversight Board, 15–16
Secondary liability for aiders and abettors, XXXIX
Securities analysts, XXVIII, XLVI, 199–200
Statute of limitations for Rule 10b-5, 138–139
Up-the-ladder reporting, XLI, 175–177

SCHEDULE
13D, 112, 152
14A, 160, 163–164, 168
14C, 160
14D, 152
15G, 191
A, 53
B, 205
TO, XXXII–XXXIII, 152

SECURITIES ENFORCEMENT REMEDIES AND PENNY STOCK REFORM ACT, XLIV

SECURITIES INVESTOR PROTECTION ACT OF 1970, 13

SECURITIES LITIGATION UNIFORM STANDARDS ACT OF 1998, XLII, XLVIII, 126, 141, 143, 210–212

"SOXA"
See Sarbanes-Oxley Act of 2002 ("SOXA")

TRUST INDENTURE ACT OF 1939, 13

UNDERWRITERS
Agreements with issuers, IX, 21–22, 52
Commissions, XVIII, XLVII
Definition of under SA, XIII–XIV, 38–43
Disclosure required by SA, 108
Distribution process, 20–22
Indemnification, XXVI, 102–103
Post-effective period, XII–XIII, 36–38
Pre-filing period, X–XI, 25–31
Refusal to proceed, 61
Regulation M, 195–198
Resale exemption, 86–90
SA section 11 liability, XXII, XXXVIII, XL, 94–100
SA section 12(a)(2) liability, 92–94
SEA liability, XL
Statutory underwriters and resales, XX–XXI
Waiting period, XI–XII, 31–36

UNIFORM SECURITIES ACT, XLVIII, 210, 212

WILLIAMS ACT, XXXII, 152, 154